A MILTON ENCYCLOPEDIA

A MILTON ENCYCLOPEDIA

VOLUME 6 O–Po

Edited by

William B. Hunter, Jr., *General Editor*

John T. Shawcross *and* John M. Steadman, *Co-Editors*

Purvis E. Boyette and Leonard Nathanson,
Associate Editors

Lewisburg
Bucknell University Press
London: Associated University Presses

Associated University Presses, Inc.
Cranbury, New Jersey 08512

Associated University Presses Ltd.
Magdalen House
136–148 Tooley Street
London SE1 2TT, England

A Milton encyclopedia.
Includes bibliographical references.
1. Milton, John, 1608–1674—Dictionaries, indexes, etc.
I. Hunter, William Bridges, 1915–
PR3580.M5   821'.4   75–21896
ISBN 0–8387–1839–6

PRINTED IN THE UNITED STATES OF AMERICA

SYSTEM OF REFERENCES

Organization of the material in this Encyclopedia is alphabetical with cross-referencing achieved in two ways. First, a subject may appear as an entry in the main alphabet, with citation of another entry under which that subject is treated. Second, subjects mentioned in an entry that are also discussed in other entries are marked with asterisks, with the exception of certain ones appearing too frequently for such treatment to be practical: the titles of all of Milton's works, each of which has a separate entry; the various named characters who appear in the works; and the names of Milton and his family, including his wife Mary Powell and her family, and his sister Anne Phillips and her family.

Titles of articles in serials have been removed, as have the places of publication of modern books. The titles of Milton's various works have been uniformly abbreviated in forms to be found in the front matter, as have references to the major modern editions and biographical works. All quotations of his writing are taken, unless otherwise indicated, from the complete edition published by the Columbia University Press (1931–1938).

SHORT FORMS USED
IN THIS ENCYCLOPEDIA

AdP	Ad Patrem
Animad	Animadversions upon the Remonstrant's Defense
Apol	An Apology
Arc	Arcades
Areop	Areopagitica
BrM	Bridgewater Manuscript
BN	Brief Notes upon a Late Sermon
Brit	The History of Britain
Bucer	The Judgement of Martin Bucer
CarEl	Carmina Elegiaca
Carrier 1, 2	On the University Carrier; Another on the Same
CB	Commonplace Book
CharLP	Character of the Long Parliament
Circum	Upon the Circumcision
CD	De Doctrina Christiana
CM	*The Works of John Milton* (New York : Columbia University Press, 1931–1938). 18 vols. The so-called Columbia Milton.
Colas	Colasterion
CivP	A Treatise of Civil Power
DDD	The Doctrine and Discipline of Divorce
1Def	Pro Populo Anglicano Defensio
2Def	Defensio Secunda
3Def	Pro Se Defensio
Educ	Of Education
Eff	In Effigiei ejus Sculptorem
Eikon	Eikonoklastes
El	Elegia
EpDam	Epitaphium Damonis
Epistol	Epistolarum Familiarium
EpWin	Epitaph on the Marchioness of Winchester
FInf	On the Death of a Fair Infant

French, *Life Records*	J. Milton French. *The Life Records of John Milton* (New Brunswick, N.J.: Rutgers University Press, 1949–1958). 5 vols.
Hire	Considerations Touching the Likeliest Means to Remove Hirelings out of the Church
Hor	The Fifth Ode of Horace
Idea	De Idea Platonica
IlP	Il Penseroso
L'Al	L'Allegro
Literae	Literae Pseudo-Senatûs Anglicani Cromwellii
Lyc	Lycidas
Logic	Artis Logicae
Mask	A Mask (Comus)
Masson, *Life*	David Masson. *The Life of John Milton* (London, 1859–1880). 6 vols. plus Index.
May	Song : On May Morning
Mosc	A Brief History of Moscovia
Nat	On the Morning of Christ's Nativity
Naturam	Naturam non pati senium
NewF	On the New Forcers of Conscience
Parker, *Milton*	William Riley Parker. *Milton: A Biography* (Oxford: Clarendon Press, 1968). 2 vols.
Peace	Articles of Peace
PL	Paradise Lost
PR	Paradise Regained
PrelE	Of Prelatical Episcopacy
PresM	The Present Means
Prol	Prolusion
Ps	Psalm
QNov	In Quintum Novembris
RCG	Reason of Church Government
Ref	Of Reformation
Rous	Ad Ioannem Rousium
SA	Samson Agonistes
Shak	On Shakespeare
SolMus	At a Solemn Music
Sonn	Sonnet
StateP	State Papers
Tenure	The Tenure of Kings and Magistrates
Tetra	Tetrachordon
Time	Of Time
TM	Trinity Manuscript
TR	Of True Religion
Vac	At a Vacation Exercise
Variorum *Commentary*	*A Variorum Commentary on the Poems of John Milton*. 3 vols. to date (New York: Columbia University Press, 1970–).
Way	The Ready and Easy Way to Establish a Free Commonwealth
Yale *Prose*	*Complete Prose Works of John Milton*. 6 vols. to date. (New Haven, Conn.: Yale University Press, 1953–).

A MILTON ENCYCLOPEDIA

OATES, TITUS: *see* CATHOLICISM, MILTON'S ALLEGED ROMAN.

OBEDIENCE. In *CD* Milton defines obedience as "that virtue whereby we propose to ourselves the will of God as the paramount rule of our conduct, and serve him alone" (17 : 69). Hence obedience is not the mere outward compliance with an arbitrary rule, but the natural fulfillment of love* and in a sense identical with it (14 : 25; 17 : 19, 51). It follows that obedience is necessary for salvation (14 : 107–9, 153). In the special case of Adam, obedience was the sole means of testing his fidelity (15 : 113–15). The sin* common to all men is that which Adam and Eve, and in them all their posterity, committed in "casting off their obedience to God" and tasting the fruit of the forbidden tree; all sin was included in this one act (15 : 181–83).)

The theme of obedience in *PL* appears primarily in conjunction with Adam and Eve. The Father remarks to the Son that man will hearken to the "glozing lyes" of Satan and will "easily transgress the sole Command, / Sole pledge of his obedience : So will fall / Hee and his faithless Progenie" (3. 93–96). The first words of Adam to Eve include a statement that the prohibition of the fruit of one tree is "the only sign of our obedience" that God has imposed, adding that this prohibition is an easy one (4. 419–35). Raphael, immediately after his arrival in Eden, informs the pair that their happiness will continue "if ye be found obedient" (5. 501), and at Adam's request he elaborates upon the meaning of these words (5. 520–43). After finishing his account of the rebellion in heaven,

Raphael reveals the reason for giving this narrative : to warn Adam that Satan is now plotting on "how he may seduce / Thee also from obedience" (6. 901–2). Adam in turn gives an account of his awakening to consciousness; he quotes the words of the Father that the prohibition of the fruit is "the Pledge of thy Obedience and thy Faith" (8. 325), a condition that Adam accepts. Raphael's final words as he is about to depart consist of an admonition to be strong, live happy, and love, "but first of all / Him whom to love is to obey, and keep / His great command" (8. 633–35). And as *PL* draws to an end, Adam, now conscious of the disastrous consequences of his sin, concludes that "to obey is best" (12. 561).

PR opens with a link between the two works that emphasizes the theme of obedience. Milton explains that he, who once sang of the happy Garden "by one mans disobedience* lost," now sings of a Paradise recovered "to all mankind, / By one mans firm obedience fully tri'd / Through all temptation" (1. 1/5). Like the apostle Paul (Rom. 5 : 19). Milton explicitly compares the actions of Adam and Christ and emphasizes the Reformed concept of obedience. According to Calvin*, Christ acquired righteousness for fallen mankind "by the whole course of his obedience," which began with the incarnation itself (*Institutes of Christian Religion* 2. 16. 5). Christ's active obedience of the laws of God as they had been revealed in the Old Testament led to his passive obedience on the Cross. In *CD*, Milton says that Christ's satisfaction is "the complete reparation," which he made "by the fulfillment of the law [that is, by active obedience], and payment of the required price for all mankind [by passive obedience]" (15 : 315–17). Christ's (twofold) obedience is, in turn, imputed to mankind through faith (*PL* 12. 390–410). [RF]

OBSERVATIONS UPON THE ARTICLES OF PEACE.

In the Articles of Peace (signed January 17, 1649), James Butler*, Earl of Ormond and Charles I's general in Ireland, attempted to strengthen the Royalist cause by offering political independence to Ireland and religious freedom for Irish Catholics in exchange for military help against the Parliamentary forces. On February 15, 1649, the Scottish Presbyterians of Ulster, horrified by Charles's execution, issued *Representation of the Present Evils,* aligning themselves with Ormond. On March 9, 1649, Ormond wrote to Colonel Michael Jones, Parliamentary governor of Dublin, urging him to declare for Charles II, but Jones refused. The Council ordered Milton to write Observations upon the Articles of Peace, the Presbyterians of Ulster, and Ormond's letter; it was published with the three documents by Matthew Simmons* on or before May 16, 1649. The Council hoped to rally support against Ormond by playing on English fears of the Irish and Roman Catholicism. The *Observations* attacks the hypocritical Scotch-Irish Presbyterians, accuses Ormond of treason to both country and religion, condemns the treacherous Irish, praises Cromwell (whom Ormond insulted in his letter to Jones), and defends Parliament and its actions. Edward Phillips was the only early biographer to include the *Observations* in the list of Milton's works; it was reprinted in both the 1697 and the 1698 collections of prose. [WM]

OCHINO OF SIENA, BERNARDINO

(1487–1564), sometimes cited as a source or as a kindred spirit of Milton. As a youth Ochino had been a Franciscan, rising to General of the Observants. Then at the age of 41, disillusioned with the loose living in his order, he began a new life as a Capuchin, rising to Vicar-General within a dozen years. But once more disillusioned, at the age of 55, he went into exile at Geneva, where Calvin* welcomed him for his fame as an evangelical preacher. Ochino's tracts defending his change of faith now earned him wider reputation, so that when war broke out on the Continent in 1547, Archbishop Cranmer invited him to England, making him a prebendary of Canterbury and giving him leisure and encouragement to write. He was a pastor of the Strangers' Church when Queen Mary scattered that congregation into exile in 1553. Like many others before him, Ochino fled first to Switzerland and then went on to Poland, where he found honor among anti-Trinitarians for the rest of his long life.

Some of Ochino's writings reflect concerns that Milton would later write about also, and his "Tragedy or Dialogue of the Unjust Usurped Primacy of the Bishop of Rome" (1549) features Lucifer and Beelzebub in a dialogue foreshadowing Satan and Beelzebub in *PL*. Two dialogues on the Trinity* ironically defend trinitarian orthodoxy while furnishing arguments against it drawn from reason and Scripture; another argues that the purpose of atonement* was to make a new moral impression upon mankind by stirring up charity in men's hearts; and still another provides arguments for polygamy*. Because of these shared concerns, later writers like Louis Aubrey Wood and Richard Garnett see direct influences on Milton. Yet Milton's only reference to Ochino is in *CB* (18 : 158), a bibliographical note with no indication of his even having read the work. [PMZ]

ODE

comes from the Greek *ōidē* (song) from *aeidein* (to sing). In the fifteenth and sixteenth centuries, Renaissance humanists applied this classical term to poems that were invested with more dignity than was usually attached to *carmen,* the popular song and carol. Though definition of the ode is complicated by the great variations in its form and subject matter, critics agree that all odes share the following characteristics: they are lyrics of moderate length, formal and ceremonial; complex in structure and thought, dignified and serious. They are a form of panegyric, as are compositions such as the literary hymn and epithalamium.

The publicly celebrative odes of the Greek Pindar and the philosophical odes of the Roman Horace* were the chief models for the early Renaissance humanists of Italy and France. Pindar's odes that survive complete are the Songs of Victory, written to praise champions of national athletic games. These triumphal odes are the culmination of the elaborate heroic compositions of Stesichorus and Simonides. Only the words are now extant in what was originally a celebration that combined choric song (accompanied by a cithara or a flute), dance, and poetry.

Structurally, Pindar followed Stesichorus in developing rhythmical patterns of triads, in which a complex metrical stanza of irregular lines (strophe) was followed by a second corresponding one (antistrophe), and then by a concluding third (epode) that complemented the two. This pattern was repeated throughout each ode. The Pindaric ode typically starts with the poet's announcement of the occasion being celebrated and the name of the victor. The poet-priest invokes the muse* to help praise the glory and magnificence of the Greek race, exemplified by the hero of the celebrated event. The poet also introduces a myth that links the trials and accomplishments of the victor with those of demi-gods like Herakles, in order to give cosmic importance to the celebration. Pindar's odes are reminiscent of the epic* in such qualities as heightened diction and exalted verse, appeal to the muse for inspiration, formal public address, high seriousness, and a central myth that embodies the eternal meaning of the literal event.

Horace's *Carmina* were written to be read or recited, with the exception of the *Carmen Saeculare,* written by Augustus's command for the Secular Games and sung by a chorus of 27 boys and 27 girls. Horace's odes derived from the personal,

less formally complicated ode tradition of Alcaeus, Sappho, and Anacreon (to whom some sixty sweet, hedonistic poems, which we now believe to have been composed over a thousand year period—500 B.C. to A.D. 500—were attributed). The Horatian ode uses the same stanzaic form throughout. It usually begins with an address to the person who is the subject of the poem, and occasionally invokes the muse for inspiration. In the main body of the ode, a series of constrasting images and themes form a structural pattern. By means of these carefully balanced antitheses, the ode progresses toward a resolution at the close, and a vivid picture usually reinforces the central idea. The Horatian ode is finely chiseled and urbane. Its celebration of virtues, such as friendship, economy, and the simple life, has a dignified rational emphasis, as compared to the grand heroic quality of Pindar.

In addition to the odes of Pindar and Horace, the Renaissance ode also was indebited to Greek hymns, like those ascribed to Homer and the Alexandrian poet Callimachus, and to Psalms (particularly those of David), which were translated by Milton and his contemporaries.

Fifteenth and early sixteenth-century Italian poets, such as Filelfo (who wrote poems in Latin and Greek) and the early writers of the neo-Latin ode—Landino, Campano, Pontano, Marullo, and Flaminio—reintroduced the ode in Western literary culture. They wrote in classical meters, and they also experimented with new metrical and stanzaic arrangements. They imitated the heroic attitude of Pindar and the philosophical stance of Horace. They experimented with varieties of emotion and mood in the ode. And they expanded the subject matter of the ode to cover the multiple aspects of the social scene of Renaissance Italy.

In the early sixteenth century, in Italy, Trissino, Alamanni, and Minturno*, and, in France, the writers of the Pléiade wrote vernacular odes. Pierre de Ronsard, the Pléiade's most famous member, strongly influenced his contemporaries by publishing in 1550 an original collection of odes in imitation of Pindar, Anacreon, and Horace. Ronsard also contributed to the development of the vernacular ode in Italy by influencing writers like Chiabrera and his seventeenth-century followers, Barberini, Cebà, Rinuccini, and Testi. Ronsard's fame extended not only to his contemporaries in France and Italy, but also to Germany and to England as well.

Ronsard influenced the early English ode writer John Soowthern, who imitated Ronsard's Pindarics in the volume *Pandora: The Musyque of the Beautie of His Mistresse Diana* (1584). However, English poets soon turned to the classical Greek and Latin writers for their inspiration in order to acclaim contemporary events. Michael Drayton praised the Virginian expedition in the Horatian "To the Virginian Voyage." Ben Jonson* praised the virtues of a dear friend in "Ode on the Death of Sir H. Morison," in which he used "Turne," "Counter-turne," and "Stand" to denote the Pindaric divisions of his four triads. Herrick used an Anacreontic theme to fit a Cavalier subject in "Corinna's going a-Maying." And Andrew Marvell* sublimely celebrated Cromwell's martial valor and dedicated sense of glory in the "Horatian Ode" (1650).

Milton wrote few odes, yet his *Nat* is considered by many to be "perhaps the finest in the English language" (Henry Hallam). Its twenty-seven eight-line stanzas, each building to the impressiveness and formality of a final Alexandrine, is said to have made the English ode spring "into full-blown life." *Nat* is of Pindaric exaltation. Its subject matter is Pindaric (triumphal celebration), as well as biblical, and its form is Milton's own variation of the Horatian (a regular series of stanzas). *Nat,* like the classical ode, is a sublime celebration of the magnificent potential of man, amplified in the poem through the eternal glory of Christ. Like Pindar, Milton speaks as poet-priest, triumphantly extolling the birth of Christ. The poem marks a high point in the development of the English ode and indicates Milton's early and successful efforts (described in

RCG) in the tradition of the "magnifick Odes and Hymns wherein Pindarus and Callimachus are in most things worthy."

Milton's translation of the ode to Pyrrha—a celebration of a "joyless victory"—is a Horatian experiment. This translation of the fifth ode of Horace suggests the influence of classical rhythms on Milton's style* and has been cited by critics as a means of understanding Milton's imitation of classical prosody in *PL,* the choral odes of *SA,* and the later sonnets. The flow of the lines running continuously onward, the pauses that occur in different parts of each line, the juxtaposition of words and phrases so that one word colors the meaning of another without being syntactically related to it, the deep melancholy tone of lines (such as "and Seas / Rough with black winds and storms")—these are the elements that indicate the richness of Milton's classical learning. Milton's headnote calls attention to his experimentation: "Quis multa gracilis te puer in Rosa, *Rendred almost word for word without Rhyme according to the Latin Measure, as near as the Language will permit.*" The translation is an example of "prosodical marvels," whether scanned in terms of syllabic English verse or in terms of classical quantitative rhythms. In the eighteenth century, Milton's rendition became a model for poetic imitation: "From 1700 to 1837 no fewer than eighty-three poems, and probably many more, were written in Milton's Horatian stanza, which thus had a vogue almost as great, in proportion to the length and importance of the poem, as any of his other verse-forms enjoyed" (Havens).

Milton's Latin ode "Ad Joannem Rousium" (1647) is a Pindaric experiment. In it Milton combines stateliness and wit to praise his lost volume of poetry (1645 edition), which Rouse* asked to be replaced in the Bodleian Library. In the tradition of classical odes, "Ad Joannem Rousium" celebrates the most worthwhile in man—his poetic production, which will outlive envy in "the blest abodes that kindly Hermes and the skilful guardianship of Rouse will vouchsafe." The most worthy in man is also celebrated in an acclamation of the aesthetic sense that draws Rouse toward the poetry. Milton divides the ode into three strophes and three antistrophes (not bound by matching stanzaic patterns) and finally one epode at the close. The divisions, he maintains, are "with a view rather to convenience in reading than to conformity with the ancient rules of versification." Milton calls the verse "monostrophic," not in the traditional sense of "consisting of repetitions of one and the same strophic arrangement" (OED), but rather in the Greek sense of apolelymenon, being composed of individual strophes, "in part free," that is, "not bound by strict divisions into the elaborate stanzaic patterns of the strophe, antistrophe and epode" (Hughes). (Milton uses the same terms to describe the choral odes of SA.) The Latin ode shows complexity and variety as it works within different classical systems without being bound by them, a tribute to Milton's appreciation of the richness of classical verse. John Shawcross scans and comments on the complex variations in the first six lines:

> The ode is a dactylic lyric. Similar to Horace, II, 14, 3–4, is line 1: alcaic ennea-syllable (iamb + penthemimer) + dactyl; and line 2: hemiepes (3 dactyls). Line 3 consists of 1 hemiepes + 2 dactyls; line 4, of 2 dactyls. Line 5 may be a third pæon + 1 trochee, or 3 trochees (with the first quantity defective). Line 6 is 1 dactyl + a hipponactean.

Milton used irregular verse in his English odes Time and SolMus in order to achieve, in his native language, the fullness and freedom characteristic of apolelymenon verse in classical poetry. The prosody* of Milton's English odes is an early example of the seventeenth-century trend that Abraham Cowley's Pindarique Odes (1656) popularized. Irregular verse became a fashionable way of imitating Pindar, a "libertine" method of emulating the "stile and manner of the odes" without reducing the verses "into regular feet and measures" of classical

systems (Cowley). Although such openness of form often led to what Samuel Johnson* termed "lax and lawless versification" that "flattered the laziness of the idle," it also helped develop flexibility and variation in the ode and became a touchstone for the freedom in form and subject matter that characterized the ode in England from the latter part of the seventeenth century through the middle of the nineteenth. [EBS]

OF EDUCATION is written in the form of a letter addressed to Samuel Hartlib*, an acquaintance of Milton, an ardent advocate of the educational theories of the prominent Bohemian scholar, John Amos Comenius*, and in the early 1640s a solicitor from Milton, among others, of tracts proposing educational reform in England. Milton's letter to Hartlib was his first work registered and licensed for printing. It appeared in print in June 1644, unacknowledged by its author. Some thirty years later, Milton included the tract, virtually unchanged, in Poems, etc. upon Several Occasions with a Small Tractate of Education to Mr. Hartlib (1673).

Milton refers in the tract to conversations about education with Hartlib that apparently led to the request that Milton put in writing some of his observations of educational practice and some ideas for reform. Ernest Sirluck argues convincingly (Yale Prose 2:208–12) that Hartlib, in all probability, found Milton's opinions, as expressed in the tract, less compatible with his own Comenian notions of universal, state-supported, and heavily vocational education than he had anticipated. He failed to publish the tractate and thus Milton very likely arranged himself for its original publication.

Milton's tract on education has two thrusts: first, it responds directly to the request of Hartlib that he "set down in writing . . . that voluntary Idea, which hath long in silence presented it self to me, of a better Education, in extent and comprehension far more large, and yet of time far shorter, and of attainment far more certain, than hath been yet in practice"; second, it denounces the abuses and failures Milton saw in current educational practice. As both critic and reformer, he thus had the opportunity to employ a wide range of style and tone and to incorporate into his short essay a variety of critical observations and a specific program of education.

By the time he published *Educ,* he had for four years been teaching a small number of students, among them his nephews, John and Edward Phillips. Edward Phillips, many years later, indicated that Milton followed in his own teaching a program similar to that described in the tract. Some of Milton's most compelling arguments reveal an author not only familiar with current controversy over education and with the long tradition of humanistic educational theory, but also personally experienced in the art of teaching. Milton repeatedly condemns, for example, the introduction to students of materials wholly inappropriate to their interests and abilities—a notoriously common practice in the education of his own age as of this one. He advocates thoughtful attention to ways of engaging students' interests and attention, considering them as something more than receptacles of information. He denounces the wasteful and painful process of learning foreign languages as an end in itself. His tract, moreover, is punctuated with marks of flexibility within a discipline that initially appears rigid.

Milton's theories show affinities with both classic and Renaissance pedagogical ideas. He speaks confidently and proudly of the similarities of his program to "those ancient and famous Schools of Pythagoras, Plato, Isocrates, Aristotle and such others. . . ." He shares with the Comenians emphases on the instrumental value of languages, the importance of progressing from simple and concrete matters toward the complex and theoretical, and the need to rid education of useless knowledge destructive of the human desire to learn. No less influential is Milton's personal experience of education : his fine training

at St. Paul's*, his mixed experiences at the tradition-bound Cambridge of the late 1620s and early 1630s, and, perhaps equally significant, his vocation of teaching in London from 1639 through the time he wrote his tract.

The tract itself begins with a rather long, formal address to Hartlib. Before he addresses himself to educational reform, Milton indicates something of his method in the tract. He will be brief, for the need for reform is great and, by implication, time is limited both for instituting reform and for the otherwise preoccupied author. He will not pause to document his observations on the topic with citations from even such authorities as Comenius : ". . . to search what many modern *Janua's* and *Didactics* more than ever I shall read, have projected, my inclination leads me not."

Prefacing his description of the nature and program of the ideal academy and separated by a lively attack on contemporary educational practices and products are Milton's two eloquent definitions of education. The first is based on religious principles, the second on civic ideals. Together they comprise the assumptions of that Christian humanism* basic not only to Milton's educational philosophy, but to virtually all his major writings. "The end of Learning," he writes,

> is to repair the ruines of our first Parents by regaining to know God aright, and out of that knowledge to love him, to imitate him, to be like him, as we may the nearest by possessing our souls of true Vertue, which being united to the heavenly grace of faith makes up the highest perfection.

From the point of view of civic virtue he defines "a compleat and generous Education" as

> that which fits a man to perform justly, skilfully, and magnanimously all the offices both private and public of Peace and War.

There is nothing innovative or original in either of these statements. And few of Milton's contemporaries would have objected to anything in them, with the exception of the policy that would limit admission (women are not among Milton's projected students nor, for that matter, are most men) to "our noble and our gentle Youth." Yet combined, the statements are lucid syntheses of the generating principles of Milton's system and of much of the best and sagest writing of Renaissance England. Milton would educate men equally prepared to excel as citizens in this world and as exemplary Christians.

The academy that he now describes combines secondary and university education. Students enter at age twelve and graduate at twenty-one. Technical and professional schools are entirely separated from Milton's academy of "general studies." Vacations are minimal. The curriculum, a description of which constitutes the better part of the tract, appears at first glance formidable. Milton presents it chronologically. His twelve-year-old commences with introductory Latin and concludes his education with study and practice of the "organic arts" of logic*, rhetoric*, and poetics*. Although time allotted for any one discipline is not defined at all and although several "courses" such as language* and religion* clearly continue through all stages of the program, one can construct the following units of study, albeit loosely:

I. Mastery of the tools essential for advanced learning
   A. Latin: grammar, pronunciation, and reading
   B. arithmetic and geometry
   C. religion
II. Theoretical and applied studies of the physical world
   A. agriculture
   B. geography and astronomy
   C. natural philosophy
      1. general studies
      2. geology
      3. botany
      4. zoology
      5. anatomy
   D. trigonometry (leading to more explicit subjects such as fortification, architecture, mechanics, navigation)
   E. medicine
   F. poetry (selected for its application to

the preceding subjects)
   G. Greek
III. Ethics
   A. morality
   B. economics
   C. Greek, Latin, and Italian comedies and "domestic tragedy"
   D. Italian
IV. Politics
   A. political history
   B. law
   C. church history and theology
   D. classical history, heroic poetry, Greek tragedy, classical oratory
   E. Hebrew (and its principal dialects)
V. Organic Arts
   A. logic
   B. rhetoric
   C. poetics
   D. composition (in the highest sense of public oratory and preaching; if not composition, then comprehension at the highest level of poetry, tragic and epic).

Milton concludes his outline of "studies" with emphasis on the methodical nature of the program and on the pedagogical importance of frequent review and even return to earlier stages of the curriculum as well as steady progression through it.

At the end of the tract, he notes that his program is not "a Bow for every man to shoot in that counts himself a Teacher, but will require sinews almost equal to those which *Homer* gave *Ulysses*." Most modern students, upon first viewing the tract, will applaud that caution. Yet given the character of Milton's academy as a preparatory ground for leaders of a Christian nation; given the assumption that his students will be drawn at age twelve from the aristocratic ranks of "our gentle and our noble Youth" (and likewise, it seems, from the ranks of young men of extraordinary virtue and talent); and given also the striking changes over the past three centuries in educational theory and practice, one dare not ignore Douglas Bush's more recent caution: "Renaissance humanists did not believe in adjustment to life through prolonging infancy" (*John Milton* [1976], p. 93). Milton's curriculum constitutes a great challenge, yet its presentation reveals coherence, method, and, no less important, a synthesis of thoughtful reading and practical experience.

Embodied in the program are the religious and civic goals Milton states at the beginning of the tract. Equally informing is another principle, widely held by Comenian theorists, among others, yet often ignored in practice. "But because our understanding cannot in this body found it self but on sensible things," he argues,

> nor arrive so clearly to the knowledge of God and things invisible, as by the orderly conning over the visible and inferior creature, the same method is necessarily to be follow'd in all discreet teaching.

The conviction that learning must progress from concrete to abstract or from "sensible" to intellective and creative experience does, in fact, govern the curriculum of Milton's academy. While the first stage of studies provides for the acquisition of instruments of further learning, the remainder, as B. Rajan notes (*Review of English Studies* 21 (1945): 291–93) "is clearly based on prevalent interpretations of the Great Chain." A student moves from the study of matter to plants, living creatures, and then man. And man himself is studied by the orderly investigation first of the individual, then the individual in society, the individual as a citizen of a nation, and finally as a creation of God. Only at the end of this educational chain is Milton's student sufficiently mature, knowledgeable, and insightful to be himself a creator and interpreter of the highest forms of human discourse. Milton constructs his curriculum, then, on the basis not only of a popular educational theory, but also of a traditional religious metaphor, to which he is deeply, personally committed.

Also worth noting is the conviction regarding the importance of practical knowledge and personal experience as supplemental to the gaining of "academic" knowledge. In order to grasp the value of grammatical rules of Latin, a student listens to the reading (in Latin) of "some easie and delightful Book of Education."

Likewise, in order to validate or substantiate studies of natural philosophy and mathematics,

> what hinders, but that they may procure, as oft as shall be needful, the helpful experiences of Hunters, Fowlers, Fishermen, Shepherds, Gardeners, Apothecaries; and in the other sciences, Architects, Engineers, Mariners, Anatomists.

An abundance of nonacademic visiting lecturers will provide Milton's young philosophers with the most wholesome kind of practical knowledge. And in his discussion of "exercises" emphasis falls again on immediate personal experience. Milton advocates observation of nature "In those vernal seasons of the year, when the air is calm and pleasant"; he urges visiting of towns, harbors, and trading centers. In order "to learn there also what they can in the practical knowledge of sailing and of Sea-fight," he would take his students to sea. Finally, he approves travel abroad for his young graduates, "not to learn Principles but to enlarge Experience, and make wise observation." Thus, the education Milton proposes clearly blends the experience of books and teachers with direct and wide-ranging participation in the activities of nature and man.

The remainder of the tract recommends "Exercise" and "Diet," both of which, we may assume, Milton sees as crucial for the nurturing of the whole man. Noting first the academic excellence of those ancient Greek institutions which have served partially as models for his curriculum, and then, by contrast, noting the military excellence bred in Spartan schools, Milton, writing of course during wartime, insists that his own academy "shall be equally good for Peace and War." He requires daily exercise for one and a half hours late in the morning with "due rest afterwards." Mastery of swordsmanship, a skill he himself practiced until he became blind*, must be acquired for its self-evident military value. But Milton expands upon the skill. It will keep his students "healthy, nimble, strong, and well in breath"; it will make them "grow large and tall"; and, no less important, it will nurture self-confidence and even courage. Wrestling, which he notes as a peculiarly English exercise, likewise encourages a strong body, whatever its military value. Late each afternoon, Milton's students are called out for military drill, "first on foot, then as their age permits, on Horseback, to all the Art of Cavalry. . . ." The purpose of such training is, of course, to develop men who will be ready, when called upon by their nation, to act as experienced, responsible, and successful military commanders. The ensuing derogation of military leaders may be assumed to reflect Milton's contempt for some in command of English forces at the time of writing.

The travels of students to make personal observations and gain practical knowledge of worldly affairs also fall, as mentioned above, among recommended exercises. And so also does music*, a part of traditional learning ignored in many proposals for reform. Not surprising to one familiar with Milton's writings, the topic of music is embodied in some of the tract's most eloquent prose. As for its use, Milton would have his students listen to, and participate in, music after hard exercise and after meals as a means, respectively, of "recreating and composing their travail'd spirits with the solemn and divine harmonies of Musick" and of assisting "Nature in her first concoction."

And as for "Diet," Milton says only that it should be served "on campus" and that it should be "plain, healthful, and moderate." That he dwells on the significance of exercise and that he mentions diet at all signify, once again, a distinguishing feature of the proposal—its consideration not only of academic and moral virtues, but of all aspects of man at his potential finest.

Milton's brief tractate has obvious and long-acknowledged value as the coherent statement of his beliefs about the nature and practice of education. At the same time, it illustrates more concisely and perhaps with clarity and comprehensiveness equal to any of his prose writings, the gifts of a poet writing, as he would have it, with his left hand. The stylistic range of the tract incorporates formal, elegant prose; argument closely woven yet lucid; rough, witty satire; and eloquent description charged with something sensuous and passionate, if not exactly "simple" in every sense. The most dominating and impressive characteristics of Milton as a prose writer may be discovered here, though not, for example, with the sustained power and eloquence of *Areop* nor the contempt, anger, and righteousness of *2Def*. Yet general characteristics, such as the remarkably long sentences, syntactical complexity, wide range of diction, incorporation of classical and biblical allusion, intensity of tone, studied rhythm, extended figures—all may be savored in the space of a very few pages.

In many ways, Milton's *Educ* remains a convincing and pertinent educational document, historically interesting in its assumptions about learning and still incisive in its condemnation of shortsighted, tradition-bound teaching. So long as secondary schools, colleges, and universities continue to graduate students miserably lacking in humane values, addicted to verbal affectation, and generally both unresponsive to, and disrespectful of, the process of learning itself, Milton will continue to speak valuably of education. And so long as educators care to consider, in the lively, powerful prose of a poet, the pedagogical values of combining intelligently in the process of teaching the practical with the theoretical, the traditional with the innovative, the sensible with the abstract; and so long as they care to test the virtues of an educational process rooted initially in concrete matters and working only gradually toward the goal of intellectual and creative excellence, so long will Milton's letter reach an audience more fit and perhaps less parochial than Samuel Hartlib. [RHS]

OF PRELATICAL EPISCOPACY. In answer to Joseph Hall's* *Episcopacie by Divine Right Asserted* (February 1640), the anonymous *A Compendious Discourse*

(ca. May 31, 1641), and James Ussher's*
*The Judgement of Doctor Rainoldes
touching the Originall of Episcopacy* (May
1641), which is referred to on the title
page, Milton produced his second anti-
prelatical tract in June or July of 1641.
The printers* were Richard Oulton and
Gregory Dexter, and the publisher* was
again Thomas Underhill. A short pam-
phlet of only twenty-four pages, *PrelE* is
given over to trying to persuade a general
audience that presbyters and bishops are
equals and thus that an episcopal hier-
archy is unreasonable. He argued through
a rejection of patristic authority in favor
of Scripture, through an alignment of
patristic authority with the sources of
papal hierarchy, and through the con-
tention that Ussher's pleas for episcopacy
lacked common sense. Partially this is
achieved by satire and scorn of his op-
ponent's view and partially by under-
cutting the supposedly venerable position
of Leontius, Bishop of Magnesia (in Asia),
an obscure bishop who spoke at the
Robber Council of Ephesus (449) and who
was quoted by various patristic writers
and in turn by the author of *A Com-
pendious Discourse* and Ussher to give the
weight of age-old authority. At times,
though, Milton argues by using material
out of context or not objectively repre-
senting opposing positions. Although there
is an appeal to reason to further his
argument, the primary appeal is to
emotion and ridicule. The work seems not
to have stirred any direct reaction or
particularly to have influenced anyone to
turn against the bishops. Only in Robert
Greville*, Lord Brooke's *A Discourse
Opening the Nature of that Episcopacie*
(ca. November 1641) may we have
evidence of influence through purported
paraphrases. [JTS]

OF REFORMATION. Published anon-
ymously in the spring of 1641 (perhaps
in May), *Ref* represents the first of
Milton's five extended sallies into the
prelatical disputes that had been raging
for some time. Already, during the course
of the Long Parliament, convened in 1641,

England had witnessed a proliferation of
prose tracts defending, on the one hand,
the cause of reformation and, on the
other, the cause of episcopacy. If Milton
had already aided the Smectymnuan*
cause by way of *A Postscript* to their
Answer, he was able to apply his earlier
attempts at polemic to this new venture.
Through it, he found the means to redress
what he felt were the prevailing corrup-
tions hindering the course of reformation
in England : among others, the exiling of
dissenting Englishmen, the persecutions
enacted by the ecclesiastical courts, the
imposition of high church ceremonies, the
enforced tithing of the people, the use of
Romish vestments, the railing in of the
altar, the voting of the bishops in the
House of Lords, and the power of epis-
copacy in matters of state. The way
Milton dealt with these and similar cor-
ruptions will become clear if we attend to
the form and content of his first anti-
prelatical tract.

Written in the form of an epistle to
a friend, *Ref* is divided into two books.
The first book begins by expressing Mil-
ton's dismay over the corruption and
degeneration undergone by the apostolic
church. Having graphically described the
depravities resulting from its concern
with the material, Milton celebrates the
glorious reformation that purged the
church of those depravities. He next
attempts to suggest why England should
presently lag behind the rest of Protestant
Europe. The reason may be found in
causes both past and present. The past
causes, as Milton's historical account
makes clear, arise out of the episcopal
corruptions during the reigns of Henry
VIII, Edward VI, and Elizabeth. The
present causes arise out of the misconcep-
tions of antiquarians, libertines, and
politicians. To refute the antiquarians,
those who defend episcopacy through the
example of the primitive church, Milton
resorts to the Fathers themselves in order
to point up the fundamental distinction
between the primitive and modern bishop.
Furthermore, he proves that those ancient
times and their writers were not so pure

as might be expected. Next, he argues against the worshipers of antiquity by showing that the most respected Fathers advised using Scripture, rather than their own works, as the ultimate authority. Finally, at the end of the first book, he refers briefly to the libertines as those who object to the Presbyterian* system because they are licentious and incapable of living under the discipline of Presbyterianism. Judging by the unequal amount of space Milton devotes to antiquarians and libertines respectively in the first book, it would appear that more immediate concerns took precedence over proportion in this particular instance. Indeed, when at last he turns to the politicians in the second book, we have to be reminded that they constitute the third category of present causes hindering the course of reformation in England.

In his argument against the politicians, Milton first attempts to undermine what he feels to be their two basic positions: that church government and civil government must correspond in form and that episcopacy is the only form of church government that the civil government may depend upon. As an alternative to the episcopal form of government, Milton proposes the Presbyterian system and points out its advantages both to church and state. Then he refutes four current objections to that system: first, that its institution would be too extreme and sudden; second, that it does not have the support of antiquity; third, that a greater inconvenience would arise in connection with the corruption of any other discipline than episcopacy; fourth, that Presbyterianism is alien to common law and will endanger the king. After responding to these objections, Milton exhorts his countrymen to reject episcopacy and adopt Presbyterianism. Finally, he concludes his argument with an impassioned prayer for the fulfillment of reformation in England and a curse upon those who would impede its course.

If such an overview indicates something of the form, and, by implication, the content, of Milton's tract, one must also take note of its tone, which is uncompromising in its use of invective. As objects of reproach, the prelates become "obscene," "canary-sucking" (3 : 19) figures "belching the soure Crudities of yesterdayes *Poperie*" (3 : 13) and stumbling forward into the "new-vomited Paganisme of sensuall Idolatry" (3 : 2). Because of the disgust they engender, they give "a Vomit to God himselfe" (3 : 12). In the second book, they are depicted as "a huge and monstrous Wen" growing out of the Head "by a narrower excrescency" (3 : 48). Having been concluded that the Wen is nothing but "a bottle of vitious and harden'd excrements" (3 : 48), it is decided that, in order to preserve the health of the body politic, the Wen must be cut away from the Head. The allusion to the Wen and the bodily Members, as Milton freely adapts it from Livy* and others, is used to indicate the necessity of separating the corrupt episcopacy from the state. As such, it reflects Milton's agreement with the 1640 London Petition, which advocated the abolishment of episcopacy from the commonwealth "root and branch." Made evident in Milton's views regarding policy, that "root and branch" radicalism is likewise implicit in Milton's views regarding rhetoric*. If the prelates are to be expunged "root and branch," they are to be castigated "root and branch" as well. Support for that castigation may be found partly in such classical rhetoricians as Aristotle*, Cicero*, and Quintilian*, who counsel the use of pathetic proof (*affectus*) as an integral part of one's argument. Moreover, Milton's uncompromising approach may similarly be found among contemporary tract writers like John Bastwick, William Prynne*, and Henry Burton. But the most compelling support for his practices resides in the fact that, for Milton, God himself resorts, when necessary, to vehement language. Appropriately, Christ, "speaking of unsavory traditions, scruples not to name the Dunghill and the Jakes" (3 : 308). In this respect, *Ref* becomes one of the first extended expressions of Milton's polemical practices. His tract is important not only for the views it articulates but for the way it articulates them. [ML]

OF TRUE RELIGION, HERESY, SCHISM, TOLERATION, AND WHAT BEST MEANS MAY BE USED AGAINST THE GROWTH OF POPERY

(1673), Milton's last pamphlet. On March 15 Charles II* proclaimed a Declaration of Indulgence, which suspended the laws against recusants and dissenters. Although apparently a move toward toleration, the Declaration was widely suspected to be an attempt to establish Popery in England. Before the end of the month Parliament succeeded in having it canceled and in its place passed a Test Act, which required that all civil and military personnel take the Anglican sacraments. Milton's response to this popular movement is TR, one of his shortest and clearest prose statements, its purpose the support of toleration* of nonconformity but not of Popery. The treatise is especially interesting in its acceptance of various Christian sects that Milton would permit as containing perhaps "errors" without being heretical: Lutherans*, Calvinists*, Anabaptists*, Arians*, Socinians*, and Arminians*. Observing that Protestants sometimes persecute one another "upon every slight pretence," he argues that true Protestantism should permit all manner of dissent —but not heresy, which should not be permitted at all. For him, "Popery is the only, or the greatest, heresy . . . , the worst of superstitions." Free speech does not reach so far as to permit its doctrines to be published—the same restriction that appears in Areop. In conclusion, Milton recommends that the "last means to avoid Popery is to amend our lives." The tract is simple in its arguments and unadorned with rhetoric*. Readers who are accustomed to the excitement of Areop or Tenure or who expect to find the unlimited tolerance in it of a Roger Williams* read it with disappointment. It seems to have aroused no contemporary comment whatsoever and has since received relatively little. [NH]

OLDENBURG, HENRY (1615?–1677?), natural philosopher, secretary to the Royal Society, diplomat, translator, and tutor. A native of Bremen, he took his degree there in 1639 and resided in London from 1640 to 1648. After continental travel, he returned to England in 1652 as agent for Bremen to the Cromwell government. Not long after that, perhaps in the spring of 1654, he made the acquaintance of Milton. Writing on July 6, 1654, to Oldenburg (the first of several exchanges between the two), Milton acknowledged an earlier letter from Oldenburg, complimented him on the idomatic fluency of his English, and remarked upon Oldenburg's newly expressed suspicions that Alexander More* may not have been the author of Clamor. Later Milton may have recommended Oldenburg as tutor for his former pupil, Richard Jones, for in 1656 Oldenburg accepted such a post. That year he and his charge were at Oxford, where Oldenburg was actually enrolled as a student. The relationship with Jones brought about additional correspondence with the poet. Oldenburg felt obliged to write to Milton in May or June 1656 to tell him of the advantages offered by Oxford and the Bodleian, but Milton, in his reply of June 25, expressed a predictable skepticism about Oxford's values. A later letter from Oldenburg speculated about the date of Christmas (December 28, 1656), and when he and Jones embarked upon a continental tour, he became one of Milton's several sources for foreign political news. From Saumir on June 27, 1657, he reported confirmation of the appointment of More to the post of minister at Charenton. On August 1 Milton answered, thanking Oldenburg for distributing the copies of 3Def he had given him. Another letter, from Paris on December 2, 1659, mentioned news of Cardinal Mazarin, Salmasius*, and, again, More (Milton answered on December 20). Once Oldenburg returned to England in 1660, however, the correspondence between the two seems to have ceased.

Oldenburg is perhaps best remembered as secretary to the Royal Society. He went originally to Oxford to meet those who formed the "Invisible College," and after having been elected to their group in 1660, he was named secretary in 1663. Responsible for a voluminous body of correspondence, he performed the duties of secretary in an exemplary manner. Perhaps such correspondence led to his imprisonment in the Tower for a few months in 1667, but he was soon released. He continued his work as a prolific translator of scientific documents throughout the remainder of his life. Oldenburg married twice. His first wife died in 1666, and his second was Dora Katharine, daughter of another of Milton's acquaintance, John Dury*. [JGT]

OLIVER CROMWELL'S LETTERS TO FOREIGN PRINCES AND STATES: see LITERAE PSEUDO-SENATUS ANGLICANI, CROMWELLII.

ON SHAKESPEARE. Milton's first published English poem, entitled *An Epitaph on the admirable Dramaticke Poet, W. Shakespeare,* appeared anonymously among the commendatory verses prefixed to the Second Folio of Shakespeare's* plays, 1632, sig. A5ʳ. There are three states of printing of this Folio page, but the textual variation between them is slight. The poem was published also in Shakespeare's *Poems,* 1640, sig. K8, with the initials "I. M."; however, it was printed anonymously in the Third Folio (1663–64) and in the Fourth Folio (1685). Entitled *On Shakespeare* and dated 1630, presumably by its author, the poem was published in the 1645 and 1673 editions of Milton's *Poems* with slight variation from its versions in the Folios and in Shakespeare's *Poems.*

Shak was written while Milton was a student at Christ's College*, Cambridge, but the circumstances of its composition and of its publication with the Second Folio are uncertain. Because Milton was then unknown as a poet, it seems unlikely that the publishers of the Second Folio would have invited him to write the epitaph; nor is it likely that he volunteered

the verses if they were unsolicited. Perhaps Henry Lawes*, who composed the music for the songs in *Mask* and assisted Milton in gaining recognition, was the intermediary between the young poet and publishers of the Second Folio. Lawes would have made his connection with the Second Folio through his patron, William Herbert, Third Earl of Pembroke, to whom the First and Second Folios were dedicated.

Shak, a sixteen-line epigram in heroic couplets, resembles other epitaphs on Shakespeare that were published in the First and Second Folios; and it embodies the dominant theme, which was commonplace in Elizabethan literature, that an author achieves immortality through his work. Milton states in lines 9–16, for example, that Shakespeare's readers are his monuments. Other epitaphs on Shakespeare likewise develop this theme of immortality, though their treatment of it differs somewhat from Milton's. For example, the epitaphs by Ben Jonson* and Leonard Digges, both of which were published in the First and Second Folios, state that Shakespeare's work, not every reader, is his monument and that he continues to live so long as he is read. *Shak* also alludes to the prevalent critical opinion, reflected in other commendatory verses, that Shakespeare was primarily a natural and spontaneous poet whose "easie numbers" contrasted with the laborious composition or "slow-endeavouring art" of others. This view is iterated in *L'Al* (133–34) in which Shakespeare is described as "fancies childe" producing "his native Wood-notes wilde."

Though numerous verbal and imagistic parallels have been adduced between *Shak* and other Elizabethan epitaphs and between *Shak* and Elizabethan literature generally, Milton's indebtedness to specific works cannot be determined. For instance, Milton's image that a reader becomes a marble monument seems to echo a similar conceit developed in William Browne's elegy on the Countess of Pembroke (1629). But other parallels for this same image may be cited not only from epitaphs but also from Elizabethan plays, including Massinger's *The Fatal Dowry* (2.1) and Tomkis's *Albumazar* (1.4.3–4). Another poem sometimes mentioned as a possible influence on *Shak* is *An Epitaph on Sir Edward Standly,* which was ascribed to Shakespeare. The image of "sky-aspiring Piramides" in this poem may be echoed in "Star-ypointing *Pyramid*" (line 4) in *Shak.* But this image is rather common in Elizabethan literature, so that specific influence on Milton cannot be acknowledged. Thus *Shak* is a conventional poem suggesting Milton's knowledge of epitaph literature and reflecting perhaps his awareness of other epitaphs on Shakespeare. [ACL]

ON THE DEATH OF A FAIR INFANT DYING OF A COUGH.

Milton's earliest original poem in English appears only in the second edition (1673) of the minor poems. The reason for its omission from the 1645 *Poems* is uncertain. The two most frequent conjectures are its family association and its youthful composition. The occasion for this elegy, according to Edward Phillips, was the death of Milton's niece. Anne, the first daughter of Milton's sister Anne and Edward Phillips, was baptized on January 12, 1626, and buried on January 22, 1628. Line 76 implies the expected birth of another child, and Milton's niece Elizabeth was baptized on April 9, 1628. The date of composition, which according to these facts should be January–April 1628, has been questioned because a headnote in 1673 states, "Anno aetatis 17" ("at the age of seventeen"). Milton was seventeen between December 1625 and December 1626, but no daughter of the Phillipses died during this period. There is no certainty as to whether the error was committed by the printer (or scribe supplying copy), who may have misread "19" as "17," or by Milton himself in dating the poem. (See J. H. Hanford, *Review of English Studies* 9 [1933]: 312–15; W. R. Parker, *Times Literary Supplement,* December 17, 1938, p. 802; Harris Fletcher, *The Intellectual Develop-*

ment of John Milton [1962], 2 : 455–56.

The elegiac tradition to which *FInf* belongs is most impressively represented in the earlier seventeenth century by Donne's *Anniversaries.* Its lamentation and consolation focus on transforming the subject into a meditative symbol of the power of heavenly virtue as it enters into the world for the benefit of fallen nature and mankind. Don Cameron Allen has pointed out the pagan and Christian background of this tradition and has applied it to *FInf* (*The Harmonious Vision* [1954], pp. 41–52). Greek and Latin writers offered as consolatory topics the inescapability of death as a debt all men must pay to nature and the release death gives from the troubles and pains of life. Allen has shown how this rhetorical tradition was adapted to Christian use in the funeral orations of Gregory Nazianzen and Jerome*. The distinction, however great, of a man's earthly career is subordinated to the soul's joy in a higher life, and the theme of Christian elegy is that "the pagan dies out of his glory, the Christian into his." *FInf* provides the first example of what was to be an almost constant feature of Milton's entire poetic production from *Nat* to *SA* : the employment of classical form and conventions to convey Christian ideas and meaning.

The death of the infant—a private event not lending itself to the rhetorical topics of the funeral oration—is at once accounted for by a "cause," as convention requires, and is magnified in significance through the use of classical story and symbol. The initial lamentation is expressed in terms that elevate the infant to the level of the mythical figures whose fate of too early death she shares. Through simile she is mythologized and transformed into a figure capable of supporting meanings of crucial import to the universe —meanings comparable to those assigned by Donne to Elizabeth Drury in the *Anniversaries.* The symbolic transformation that the poem works upon the infant makes it possible for grief to give way to a consolation that is enlarged into a triumphant acceptance of the specifically

Christian, as opposed to the natural, attitude toward death.

This progression provides the structural development of the elegy, which has been analyzed by Hugh Maclean (*ELH: A Journal of English Literary History* 24 [1957] : 296–305) into a threefold movement. The ten stanzas constituting the body of the poem (that is, all but the final eleventh stanza, addressed to the infant's mother) may be partitioned into three groups of three, three, and four stanzas respectively. The poem opens by addressing the infant in terms of a familiar symbol for those who have died young :

O fairest flower no sooner blown but blasted,
Soft silken Primrose fading timesslie . . .

Todd pointed out the echo in these lines of the tenth sonnet in *The Passionate Pilgrim* :

Sweet rose, fair flower, untimely plucked,
    soon vaded,
Plucked in the bud, and vaded in the spring!

The primrose, sprung from the blood of the young Adonis, was the common emblem in epitaphic art for those who died young. Milton extends the significance by mythologizing the death of the infant as an unwitting destruction by a god enamored of her beauty. The physical circumstances are absorbed into the elegy's pattern of meaning by personifying Winter as elderly and childless. In jealousy of Aquilo (the north wind)—who, according to Ovid*, took the Athenian princess Orithyia as his wife—Winter "descended from his Snow-soft chaire, / But all unawares with his cold-kind embrace / Unhous'd thy Virgin Soul from her fair biding place."

The cause of the infant's death, as lamented in stanzas I–III, is an unconscious blunder on the part of nature. In IV, the tissue of mythological association, again by connecting a "dearly-loved mate" slain by an "unweeting hand," dignifies the fate of the infant by equating it circumstantially to that of Hyacinth, killed by Apollo. The denial of death's power asserted in stanza V marks a more decisive division in the elegy than does stanza IV, which in its allusion to Hyacinth, and differentiation of the infant's fate from his, only makes conclusive the futility of seeeking recompense in some natural transformation, which, after all, has already made dry the blossom-infant. The announcement of faith in a better life that denies the final reality of "earths dark wombe" allows the speaker to address the infant as "Soul most surely blest" in stanza VI and to ask quite different questions from anything that could be posed within the mythologizing terms of I–IV.

Stanzas V and VI function transitionally as a pivot between the inadequate, frustrating pagan view of death climaxed in IV with the infant *not* changed into a flower and the assurance of Christian consolation that the elegy finally reaches. The questions the speaker asks to have "resolved" in VI—whether the infant's soul now resides in a Christian or a classical heaven, whether the infant was mortal or divine, and why she took flight so soon from the world—are the substance of stanzas VII–X. Typologically, the infant prefigures a type of Christ in preparation for the explicitly redemptive role ("To stand 'twixt us and our deserved smart") attributed to her in stanza X, which turns to the last question posed in VI—why has the infant left the world so soon?—by first deepening the sense of loss suffered at her departure : "thy heav'n-lov'd innocence" is needed "To turn Swift-rushing black perdition hence." And in the power "To stand 'twixt us and our deserved smart," Milton elevates the infant in effect to a redeemer who can intercede for sinful man with God.

Stanza XI declines from the extravagant heights of rhetoric and symbol scaled in VII–X to the simpler plane of assuaging the grief of the infant's mother. The Christian consolation offered here is related, of course, to the exercise in faith that the main body of the poem has pursued, but transposed to a lower key and to a human level. There is less of an abrupt shift of thematic focus than has often been thought by critics. For parallel to the earthward and heavenword movements running through the allegorical texture of the poem, the mother is told finally that if the child lent by God is "render[ed] him with patience," another child will be sent down to her: "This if thou do he will an off-spring give, / That till the worlds last-end shall make thy name to life."

The thematic design of *FInf* is clear enough: through a complex fabric of mythological* simile, moral allegory*, and Christian symbolism, the infant progresses from a fading flower to a Christian saint with the power to "drive away the slaughtering pestilence" (itself a sign of the world's disease and man's fallen condition) that carried off the infant. Reading the elegy against its religious and literary background enables us to perceive important relations between Milton's poetic method and his intended patterns of meaning. However, this historical illumination does not amount to a demonstration of the poem's artistic success. The critical question remains whether the thematic burden of *FInf* finds appropriate and convincing expression in the poem itself, a question each reader must finally answer for himself.

Stylistically, Milton's earliest original attempt at English poetry indicates his allegiance to what in the 1620s counted as conservative Elizabethan models. The elaborate schemes of alliteration and assonance, the archaisms, the dying fall of the feminine endings in the opening lines, the strong congruency of syntactic junctures with the verse—all enhance the effect of decorative sweetness and fluidity of texture characteristic of Elizabethan verse in general and of Spenser* and his followers in particular. The eleven stanzas of *FInf* are rime royal with an alexandrine substituted in the final line (a_5, b_5, a_5, b_5, b_5, c_5, c_6). The final alexandrine is a key device of the Spenserian stanza, and Milton's form can also be viewed as an adaptation of the nine-line Spenserian stanza, with the sixth and seventh lines

omitted. The stanza of *FInf* was employed by Spenser's follower Phineas Fletcher* in an elegy on Sir John Irby, titled *Elisa*, not published until 1633. Milton used the form later in the four-stanza induction to the Hymn of *Nat* and in the prelude to the unfinished fragment *Passion*. [LN]

ON THE MORNING OF CHRIST'S NATIVITY. Milton gave first place to *Nat* in the 1645 and 1673 editions of his poems. The phrase "Compos'd 1629" follows the title in the 1645 edition but is omitted in 1673. The 1645 edition has no Table of Contents; the 1673 edition places "The Hymn" separately in the Table of Contents. There is no manuscript for *Nat* and the variants between the earlier and later edition (with the exception of the clarification that changes "Truth, and justice . . . / Th'enameld Arras of the Rainbow wearing, / And Mercy set between" (XV) to "Truth, and Justice . . . / Orb'd in a Rain-bow; and like glories wearing / Mercy will sit between") are of little consequence.

The proem to *Nat* and *El* 6 both state that the poem was written as a "gift on the birthday of Christ" and was begun in the early hours of Christmas Day, 1629, when the stars "in squadrons bright" still shone in the sky. Milton composed *Nat* at an important point in his life, shortly after he celebrated his twenty-first birthday on December 9, and came of age. *El* 6 indicates the seriousness with which the young poet took *Nat*. In the elegy, written to his friend Charles Diodati*, Milton speaks of the virtue needed by the epic poet. Unlike the writer of light elegiac poetry, inspired by love and the pleasures of wine and festivities, the writer of lofty verse (by implication the writer of *Nat* referred to in the elegy) must lead a disciplined life.

Nat strikes a new note in Milton's poetry and illustrates his belief in himself as a poet-prophet, inspired by God and committed to writing serious poetry. *Nat* signals the poet's turn to devotional poetry: serious, elevated verse befitting his coming of age poetically. Indeed, in

1629 Milton had not yet been "church-outed" by the prelates. Still studying for the ministry, he viewed poetry as a form of ministry and emphasized the close relationship between the art of poetry and the art of pulpit oratory. Stanzas IX through XIV of *Nat,* which describe the angelic choir and the harmony of the angels, are, as Thomas Stroup observes, Milton's means of singing the joyous canticle *Gloria in excelsis.* Milton creates his own liturgy by drawing upon the words of the Herald Angels (Luke 2 : 14) or the elaboration of their pronouncements at the end of the Communion Service in Elizabeth's *Book of Common Prayer.* (See Thomas Stroup, *Religious Rite and Ceremony in Milton's Poetry* [1968], pp. 6–14.)

Nat, together with *Passion* and *Circum* may have been part of a plan to write elevated verses in commemoration of the events in the life of Christ and the Church calendar. All three are examples of the occasional verse that characterizes most of Milton's poetry prior to *PL.*

Nat, together with *Passion* and *Circum,* Jonson*, owes much to the classical tradition of Pindar and his followers, Anacreon and Horace*, as well as to the Psalms of David, and the ode tradition in both Renaissance Italy (established by Trissino, Alamanni, Minturno*, and Tasso*) and France (as exemplified by Ronsard and the Pléiade). Milton's comments in *RCG* show that he studied Pindar and had planned to write "magnifick Odes and Hymns wherein Pindarus and Callimachus [the Alexandrian poet] are in most things worthy." *Nat* follows the ode tradition because it is formal and public (not personal); it celebrates an occasion, and it relates the occasion to its cosmic meaning. The proem introduces the specific event—the birth of Christ—and establishes its larger Christian significance. Milton, like Pindar, speaks as poet-priest (invoking the Heavenly muse*) and, like Pindar, returns to the opening scene (the manger at the close of the poem), to reinforce the momentous significance of the event.

Milton broadens the event's significance through a series of emotionally evocative pictures associated with the Nativity : the Pre-Fall existence, when Christ, "at Heav'ns high Councel-Table," volunteers to forsake "the Courts of everlasting Day"; the Fall of man and its "deadly forfeit"; and the everlasting future when man's redemption will be achieved. Topographically, the poem soars to heaven, with its magnificent angelic harmony, returns to earth, darkened by pagan deities and their false religion, descends to hell, the "infernal Jail" toward which the routed gods are fleeing, and back to earth where Christ is attended by angels. This use of suggestive detail recalls Pindar's method of glorifying a hero. Carol Maddison (*Apollo and the Nine,* pp. 318–30) notes of the Pindaric ode: "The myth assimilated the hero to the demi-gods, it idealized the present and transfigured the real, it made the temporal event timeless."

Pindar's extant lyrics are triumphal odes, which celebrate athletic victories. Milton appears to adapt this tradition to his depiction of the victory of Christ, who "Can in his swadling bands control the damned crew" of pagan gods. The emphasis in *Nat* is not on the peaceful Babe lying in His cradle, but on the transformation brought to this world by the enthroned Christ, surrounded by "Bright-harnest Angels," who "sit in order serviceable." An analogue for the Infant's performing prodigious feats is found in Pindar's first Nemean ode, in which the young Hercules strangles huge serpents.

Together with the tradition of Pindar, Anacreon, and Horace, psalmody (especially the Psalms of David) influenced the English ode. Like many other Renaissance poets (Sir Philip Sidney*, George Wither, George Sandys), Milton translated Psalms. In the Renaissance the word *Psalm* was often interchanged with *Song,* which was further interchanged with the term *Ode.* The fact that Milton calls *Nat* both a "humble ode" and a "Hymn" indicates his awareness of the close connection between these forms and implies that he is reaching toward the inspired mood of David's Psalms. In *Nat* a joyful, reverent tone prevails, a tone that is later echoed in the morning hymn of praise in *PL* 5. 153–208.

It is difficult to ascertain direct sources for *Nat,* a poem steeped in pagan and Christian tradition. James Holly Hanford notes the poem's similarity to Virgil's* fourth eclogue, which describes the Golden Age that will follow the birth of a son to Pollio. Milton's belief that the oracles ceased at the birth of Christ can be traced to chapter 17 of Plutarch's* "Of the Oracles that have ceased to give Answere" (a treatise commonly interpreted in Christian terms and quoted by Spenser* in the *Shepheardes Calendar*: May, 1. 54), to Prudentius's fourth-century *Apotheosis,* to Tasso's *Rime Sacre* (which describes the overthrow of pagan deities in Greece and Egypt), and to Giles Fletcher's* "Christ's Victory in Heaven" :

The angells caroll'd lowd their song of peace;
The cursed oracles wear strucken dumb; . . .
(st. 82)

Nat also resembles Prudentius's Nativity hymn "Kalends Ianuarius," Tasso's "Canzone sopra la Coppella del Presepio," and early sixteenth-century works by Mantuan and Sannazaro.

The presentation of the angels as stars derives from passages in Revelation (9:1, 2; 12:4), 1 Kings (22:19), and Judges (5:20). The connection between the angelic song of praise and the music of the spheres has its source in Job (38:7). The subject of the music of the spheres* (also developed in his *Prol* 2) goes back both to Plato* (*Republic* 10.617[B]), where, in the vision of Er, music is produced by the sirens "aloft upon each of the circles," and to Cicero* (*De republica* 6. 17, 18), who speaks of nine spheres.

In Renaissance England, the Nativity tradition was drawn upon by many poets prior to the publication of Milton's poem: Edmund Spenser ("Hymn of Heavenly Love"), Robert Southwell ("The Sequence on the Virgin Mary and Christ"), John Donne ("Nativity" in *La Corona*), Giles Fletcher ("Christ's Victory and Triumph"), Ben Jonson* ("A Hymn on the Nativity of my Saviour"), William Drummond ("Hymn upon the Nativity"), Sir John Beaumont ("An Ode of the Blessed Trinity"), and George Herbert ("Christmas"). The subject also appears in other seventeenth-century poems by Richard Crashaw ("On the Holy Nativity"), Henry Vaughan ("Christ's Nativity"), Robert Herrick ("An Ode of the Birth of Our Saviour"), and Thomas Traherne ("On Christmas Day"). Milton differs from his contemporaries by not concentrating on the manger scene with the shepherds and peaceful animals and by not dwelling extensively on Mary's motherhood. Instead, Milton symbolically amplifies the idea of Mary's purity by referring to her emphatically in the opening and concluding stanzas and by indirectly contrasting her truly immaculate state with Nature's attempted disguise of "innocent Snow," the "Saintly Veil of Maiden white."

Nothing was said about *Nat* by Milton's contemporaries. A century later, Samuel Johnson* chose to ignore *Nat* in his discussion of Milton in *The Lives of the Poets,* and Thomas Warton*, in *Poems upon Several Occasions* (1785), cursorily dismissed all but one or two stanzas of the poem for consisting of "a string of affected conceits, which early youth, and the fashion of the times, can only excuse." Nineteenth-century critics praised the Ode as being "perhaps the finest in the English language (Henry Hallam), as being "nearly all beauty" (Thomas Keightley), a "magnificent Ode" (David Masson*). But it was not until the twentieth century, following A. S. Cook's scholarly "Notes on Milton's Nativity Ode" (1909), that extensive explication of the poem's thematic and structural patterns began. For the most part, modern critics view *Nat* as "the first of Milton's inspired poems" (Barker), his "Messianic eclogue" (Hanford*), his "most perfect early work" (D. C. Allen*).

Modern critics have focused on different themes in *Nat*: the "moral significance of Christ, who serves as a symbol of ethical and religious truth" (Hanford); the unity of religious and aesthetic experience, which is achieved only by those who have spotless hearts and which corresponds "in general to the effects of the Puritan conversion" (Barker); the austere movement toward Puritan victory, in which "harshness wars with, and in the end overcomes . . . peace and mercy" (T. K. Meier); the joyful acceptance of "the order of grace and its supremacy over nature itself . . . symbolized by the triumphant images of light, form, and harmony" (Woodhouse*); "the effect of the Nativity, the routing of the heathen gods by Christ," which can be considered the "intellectual core" of the poem (Woodhouse); the profound celebration of peace, so integral to the Incarnation (Tuve); the harmony of the universe achieved by a series of balances leading to "timelessness," "Nature as immutable and untarnished," and the "harmony of God" (Allen); the interlocking of past, present, and future time, "the simultaneity of all moments under the aspect of eternity" (Lowry Nelson).

Structurally, the poem is divided into three movements. Apart from the four introductory stanzas, as Barker states, "the first eight stanzas . . . describe the setting of the Nativity, the next nine the angelic choir, the next nine the flight of the heathen gods. The . . . last stanza presents the scene in the stable." The three movements are held in relation to each other by various threads : imagery of "light and discord" counterbalance one another (Barker); patterns of heavenly light and harmony reinforce Milton's theme of peace, "God's reconciling of all things in earth and heaven to Himself" (Tuve); and "an undercurrent of music" prevails throughout (Spaeth). The first movement is hushed : the night is "peacefull," the winds whisper, and "Birds of Calm sit brooding on the charmed wave" at the birth of the Savior; the second movement details the orchestral harmony of angelic song; the third movement reverberates with the discordant sounds of the fleeing pagan deities.

Milton, as Nelson observes, uses time as a structural device in *Nat* to move toward the timelessness of the everlasting future. The proem shows two time planes: before dawn, December 25, 1629, when "all the spangled host" are still in the sky and Milton is writing the ode; and the actual birth of Christ, indicated by the past tense : "Our great redemption from above *did bring* "(emphasis added). Milton puts himself into the poem and moves back in time to present the ode as a birthday gift to Christ. The timelessness of *Nat* attests to Christ's power as well as to the inspiration His love exerts on the birth of the poet's "humble ode." In stanzas III and IV of the proem the past and present merge as the narrator tells us that he aims to lay his poem at the "blessed feet" of the "Infant God" *before* the "Star-led Wisards" arrive to welcome Him with their splendid gifts. Milton continues this alternation of tenses in the "Hymn" :

It *was* the Winter wilde,
While the Heav'n-born-childe,
All meanly wrapt in the rude manger *lies*; . . .
        (st. I [emphasis added])

Stanzas XII–XV bridge past, present, and future : the Creation, the golden age, the Nativity, and the Second Coming. Then, once the "Hymn" arrives at its final point in Divine history—the Last Judgment—the narrator stops alternating tenses and uses a heightened present tense to depict the fusion of time : "But now begins" intensifies the future bliss, which starts at the Nativity.

The narrator throughout *Nat* incorporates details from the broader context of Christian history to give meaning to the temporal event. Christ's birth is an event that occurs in a specific "Month" on a "happy morn," as well as an event that extends back to preexistent time and forward to the infinite future. The occasion heralds the birth of "Heav'ns eternal King," who was "wont at Heav'ns high Councel Table, / To sit the midst of trinal Unity" in "the Courts of everlasting Day."

In our world, Jesus acts in time to release us from our "deadly forfeit"; in eternity, He will "work us a perpetual peace." Once Judgment Day arrives, the boundaries of space and time will be obliterated.

In the opening stanzas of the proem Milton provides factual information and establishes a narrative frame that guides the reader toward the eternal future, when redeemed man will live in "bliss / Full and perfet" (st. XVIII):

This is the Month, and this the happy morn
Wherein the Son of Heav'ns eternal King,
Of wedded Maid, and Virgin Mother born,
Our great Redemption from above did
    bring; . . .

The subject (redemption) and occasion (the Nativity) are introduced, and the speaker focuses on key words: *wedded Maid* and *Virgin Mother*. What should normally read "Virgin Maid" and "wedded Mother," the narrator changes by crossing the adjectives (*chiasmus*). He thereby stresses the paradoxical nature of the event and thus implies the mystery of the Incarnation*; the *chiasmus,* or X, achieved is a sign of Christ. He brings in the details of Christian history as a framing story (noted by Frank Kastor) with which to interpret the event: "That he our deadly forfeit should releasee, / And with his Father work us a perpetual peace." The "deadly forfeit" that man must pay for Adam and Eve's "First Disobedience" suggests man's Edenic perfection, the Fall, man's atonement, and his future salvation in Heaven, where peace will reign in a "Recover'd Paradise" (*PR* 1. 3).

The narrator also provides important information about himself; he is inspired by the "Heav'nly Muse" to speak in a "sacred vein" and to join the "Angel Quire / From out his secret Altar toucht with hallow'd fire." He, like the narrator of *PL* and *PR,* is speaking of the heroic achievement of Christ. He continues, in the proem, to prepare the reader for Christ's birth by contrasting the "Light," "far-beaming blaze," the "Courts of everlasting Day" with the fallen world that is to be changed by the Nativity.

Stanzas I–VIII, which describe the setting of the Nativity, begin with pagan Nature's reaction to the birth. She is the first worldly representative to be subdued by Christ. The narrator reinforces her submission by reducing light and sound and motion to a minimum. Nature doffs "her gaudy trim" and covers her face with a "Saintly Veil of Maiden white." Nature reaches toward the immaculate purity that is in contrast to her post-Fall state, where war and hate prevail. Milton repeats the word *peace,* as there is a suspension of all postlapsarian activities: the "Battels sound" of war, the trumpets, and the Kings' pronouncements. "The Winds with wonder whist, / Smoothly the waters kist"; the Ocean forgets to rave, and "Birds of Calm sit brooding on the charmed wave." Intensifying the scene, the stars "Stand fixt," their "glimmering Orbs" dimly lighting the morning, and the "inferiour" sun is ashamed to rise, for he sees "a greater Sun appear." Time is suspended while stars and sun halt their customary functions and Nature prepares to meet her master.

In stanza VIII the Shepherds, unlike Nature, are unconscious of the meaning of the Nativity. These innocent folk sit "chatting in a rustick row," their "silly" (naive and innocent) thoughts on "Perhaps their loves, or else their sheep." They are unaware that Christ, "the mighty Pan / Was kindly [gently and with kinship] come to live with them." On these simple folk the music of the spheres bursts. The new music astonishes them to such an extent that it takes "their souls in blissful rapture." Now man, too, is subdued by the great event.

In stanzas IX–XV light, sound, and motion intensify in order to portray the eternal, cosmic music of the spheres. "A Globe of circular light" illuminates the "glittering ranks" of angels, who sing as harmoniously as they did at the creation of the world. Through light imagery the narrator conveys the effect of the harmony on man: "Time will run back, and fetch the age of gold"; Truth and Justice,

"Orb'd in a Rain-bow," will "return to men" and Mercy, "Thron'd in Celestial sheen," is "set between" them. (The 1673 edition makes "And Mercy set between" more emphatic by using the active voice: "Mercy will sit between." It also specifically garbs Mercy in the "like glories" of Truth and Justice, who are "Orb'd in a Rain-bow").

The music of the spheres is reminiscent of the harmony that existed at the creation of the world (Job 38 : 7) when order was brought out of chaos by the Logos :

Such Music (as 'tis said)
Before was never made,
    But when of old the sons of morning sung,
While the Creator great
His constellations set, . . .

(st. XII)

The ordered beauty of musical concord reflects God's "well-ballanc't" master plan. Angelic reverberations resound in this central movement of the poem. Cherubim and Seraphim are heard singing "in loud and solemn quire." The "Crystall sphears," representing the ordered universe, "Ring out" their "silver chime" and "Move in melodious time," together with the "Base of Heav'ns deep Organ." The "ninefold harmony" of the spheres makes "full consort to th' Angelike symphony."

The heavenly orchestra brings about a sense of transport, bridging distinctions between past, present, and future. The narrator ponders the Golden Age, the Nativity, and the Second Coming. But then he abruptly turns to the Crucifixion and to the pain and woe of fallen man, accentuated by dissonant images of sight and sound : "bitter cross," "wakeful trump of doom," with its "horrid clang," "smouldring clouds," and "dreadful Judge." The narrator moves from the "bitter cross" back to the Fall of man, then to God's giving Moses the Ten Commandments, and finally to Last Judgment. "But now begins" heralds the alteration of the fallen world, which "from this happy day" has the promise of future perfection : "And then at last our bliss /

Full and perfet is" (st. XVIII). Bliss is not yet achieved, but it is anticipated, particularly in the fleeing of the pagan deities at the birth of Christ.

The last movement (st. XVIII–XXVI) foreshadows the pagan gods' final departure to Hell at the Second Coming. The narrator selects gloomy images of sight and sound to convey the discord of the false gods and also to anticipate the turmoil of the "infernal Jail," which will ultimately house them. Grotesque forms and harsh sounds depict the false gods and their rout. Satan, the "old Dragon," now powerlessly "Swindges the scaly Horrour of his foulded tail." There is a "hollow shreik," a "drear and dying sound," a "voice of weeping," "loud lament," "sighing," "lowings loud." The followers no longer can summon their gods : "In vain with Cymbals ring" and "In vain with Timbrel'd Anthems dark" they appeal to the deities, but their reign is over; the "hideous hum" of their rites has ended. The "Lars and Lemures moan with midnight plaint." "Peor, and Baalim, / Forsake their Temples dim," as do Dagon, "that twice batter'd god of *Palestine*," and "sullen *Moloch*," the "grisly King." This catalogue of false gods, with impressive sounding names, undergoes extensive development in *PL* 1. 376–522. So, too, the dismal scene, with its images of darkness and smoldering fire, anticipates the fire, wind, "stench and smoke," and "mournful gloom" of Milton's Hell.

In stanza XX of this last section a sense of regret accompanies the banishment of the classical gods who haunt the "lonely mountains" and the "resounding shore" :

The lonely mountains o're,
And the resounding shore,
    A voice of weeping heard, and loud
        lament;
From haunted spring, and dale
Edg'd with poplar pale,
    The parting Genius is with sighing sent,
With flowre-inwov'n tresses torn
The Nimphs in twilight shade of tangled
    thickets mourn.

(st. XX)

Does the handling of the pagan "Nimphs in twilight shade of tangled thickets" and the "parting Genius [who] is with sighing sent" conflict with the point of view of the poem as a whole? Most critics say there is little conflict, as they attempt to explain the sense of regret for the loss of the classical deities in Milton's Christian poem. W. R. Parker* says that Milton's childhood readings made him treat these pagan figures with fondness. Woodhouse observes that the poet banishes the deities (divinities in which he had rejoiced in *El* 5) because he is ready to accept "the order of grace and its supremacy over nature itself." Barker views the poem as "transcending the conflict between the two traditions" (pagan and Christian), as it develops a harmony symbolized by the music of the spheres. Brooks and Hardy believe that "the tone of the poem is too simple to admit of such tensions." The "aesthetic distance," the sense of "detachment," achieved by the "cosmic sweep of the Hymn" prevents a "contradiction between . . . regret [for the loss of the classical figures] and the greater joy caused by Christ's birth." Differing with these critics, Lawrence Hyman emphasizes that we do feel "a genuine regret" as the divinities depart and that this regret fits the pattern of the poem as a whole. The poem's ultimate harmony does "not erase the immediate sensation of darkness or of helplessness or of pain." This position is underscored by the fact that the "bitter grief which we feel at the Crucifixion is part of the joy that we feel at the eventual triumph over death. The ecstasy of the Christian is made up of both the pain and the triumph."

It is also possible that the gentle handling of the pagan nymphs and Genius of the shore is Milton's decorous means of softening the harsh clang and moaning accompanying the retreat of the fallen Osiris, "sullen Moloch," and Dagon, "that twice batter'd god of Palestine." By this method, the pagan deities and their enchantment of evil are dispelled by Christ as smoothly as the shadows of the night are by the physical sun:

> . . . the yellow-skirted Fayes,
> Fly after the Night-steeds, leaving their
> Moon-lov'd maze.

The harshness of Christ's battle is thus ameliorated, allowing for a renewed emphasis on mercy, peace, and joy, which are traditionally associated with the Nativity.

In stanza XXVI, Milton uses the image of the sun's rising from bed to imply a similarity between the beginning of its day and the beginning of Christ's ministry as he lies in his cradle. This conceit, though clumsy, recalls the earlier section of the poem in which the sun, like the other temporal aspects of our world, is placed in submission and withholds "his wonted speed" at the birth of a greater Son. This image thus recaptures the mood of the earlier stanzas and prepares us for the conclusion, in which the stable is illuminated by the "Handmaid Lamp" of "heav'ns youngest teemed Star," which had guided the Wise Men. The star symbolizes the light Christ brings to the pagan world and the light of wisdom which shines within the Savior.

In the last stanza the star, at evening, is above the stable, where "Bright-harnest Angels ["helmed cherubim" and "sworded Seraphim"] sit in order serviceable," ceremoniously waiting on the Lord. Thus, at the close of the poem heavenly light and order return, and the pagan deities are now as submissive to Christ as are the sun, Nature, and man. The "rude manger" has been transfigured to a "Courtly Stable," where Christ is surrounded by a mighty army of angels who wait upon him and "at his bidding speed" (*Sonn* 19). They attend the cradle of the "Son of Heav'ns eternal King" (st. I). The splendor and glory at the close thus anticipates the Eternal Day, the Second Coming when Christ will once again be in the "Courts of everlasting Day," "midst of Trinal Unity."

In *Nat* Milton adapted and varied several literary traditions to create a form that is apparently his own invention. The stanzaic pattern of the proem is very close to rhyme royal, suggesting the lofty style of Chaucer* (first appearing in "Complaint unto Pity"), Spenser* ("The Ruines of Time" and "Fowre Hymnes"), and Shakespeare* ("The Rape of Lucrece"). Instead of a final iambic pentameter line, Milton concludes each stanza with an alexandrine. It is the same form that he used in *FInf*. But the "Hymn" proper has a unique eight-line stanza, radically different from the seven-line proem. As Røstvig (*The Hidden Sense*, pp. 54–58) and Butler (*Number Symbolism*, pp. 140–43) have noted, this difference suggests a movement from the worldly and transitory to the eternal. The number *8* in Christian numerology* signifies the beginning of life with Christ and the end of mundane concerns. The number *7* marks the close of man's earthly pilgrimage. The seven-line stanza is thus appropriate for the proem to *Nat* and for the verses on the death of Milton's infant niece.

The "Hymn" has twenty-seven eight-line stanzas. It is a tour de force, metrically speaking, because four different kinds of lines are employed : $a_6\ a_6\ b_{10}\ c_6\ c_6\ b_{10}\ d_8\ d_{12}$. Lines with three metrical feet alternate with five-foot lines, heralding, once again, the arrival of Christ. These first six lines, of alternating three-foot and five-foot combinations, are a construction that was common in fourteenth-century lyrics and in Elizabethan song and carol (in, for example, the canzonets and madrigals of Thomas Morley). By adding a final alexandrine, Milton achieves a stately sublimity for his "humble ode" (Martz). He also develops this effect by using strong monosyllables at the end of the first two lines in each stanza (except for "around," "amaze," and "Baalim").

The stately tone is also amplified by the roll call of the exotic, sonorous names of pagan deities whose powers have ceased at the Incarnation : Peor, Baalim, Ashtaroth, Hammon, Thamuz, Moloch, Isis, Orus, Anubis, Osiris. These names and the baroque* description of the false gods contribute to the impressiveness and formality that we associate with odes.

Resounding names, and the baroque description accompanying them, are part of the combination of the simple and the complicated, so characteristic of the "humble ode." The alternate levels of complexity underline Milton's method of describing both the Christ-child's lying in a "rude manger" and the sublime subject of man's restoration. The blending of the unsophisticated and the intricate is apparent in the use of two traditions : the ballad tradition (observable in the first six lines of each stanza) and the literary tradition (observable in the alexandrine that concludes each stanza). A homely picture of "The Shepherds on the Lawn," who "Sate simply chatting in a rustick row" (VIII) accompanies the baroque details of Last Judgment, where "The wakeful trump of doom must thunder through the deep." The mixture of elaborate Elizabethan conceits with the plain descriptions that precede or follow them further demonstrates the poet's method. Nature is compared to a maiden covered with snow (II) and the sun to a man in bed who "Pillows his chin upon the Orient wave" (XXVI). The first conceit follows the image of the "rude manger" (I) and the second precedes the simple picture of the Virgin putting "her Babe to rest" (XXVII). E. M. W. Tillyard* points to the "unique charm," the "clean exuberance" that these combinations provide:

A fifteenth-century Italian picture of the Nativity gives the simplest comparison. Here the absurdities—the rickety shelter, the far from new-born physique of the child, the cows peering with imbecile faces over a broken wall, and the rest—unite with the simple brilliant colouring to create a most captivating sense of youthfulness and simplicity. The essence of the poem is not stateliness excusing conceit, but homeliness, quaintness, tenderness, extravagance, and sublimity, harmonised by a pervading youthful candour and ordered by a commanding architectonic grasp.

The poem moves, as Parker observes, from "strikingly simple" pictures to "crowded, almost baroque panels"; the different styles reflect the opposing elements within *Nat* : Christ and the pagan gods; peace and discord; harmony and chaos; Heaven and Hell. For some critics (e.g., Sypher and Hyman) the thematic clash remains unresolved. For others (e.g., Allen, Tillyard, and Barker) *Nat* builds toward a joyous acceptance of God's grace. *Nat* thus becomes almost unique in Milton's poetry because of its sheer joyousness, its enthusiasm and happiness, similar in tone to the hymn of praise in *PL* 5. 154–208, and to the Psalms of David. [EBS]

ON THE NEW FORCERS OF CONSCIENCE UNDER THE LONG PARLIAMENT.

Perhaps composed in the early months of 1647, *On the New Forcers of Conscience* appears in *TM* and in the 1673 edition of the poems. Although Milton's sonnet, written in the hand of an amanuensis (John Phillips), stands without number after the sonnet to Vane in the manuscript, there is some difficulty in determining where Milton originally intended *NewF* sonnet to be placed. Two notes, one by Milton and one by the scribe, both indicate that it should stand between the *Tetra* sonnet and the sonnet to Fairfax, a placement with possible chronological significance. In the 1673 edition of the poems, on the other hand, *NewF* is not only excluded from the sonnet sequence but separated from it by the translation from Horace and *Vac*. Such changes surely indicate that the problem of determining proper placement is at times vexed.

Based upon the various topical allusions, the precise occasion of the sonnet is similarly difficult to define. For example, the reference to "shallow *Edwards* and Scotch what d'ye call" (12), denoting Thomas Edwards, on the one hand, and probably Robert Baillie, on the other, suggests one possibility. Because of Milton's ideas concerning divorce*, both men had attacked him in their respective tracts, Baillie in *Dissuasive from the Errours of the Times* (1645), and Edwards in *Gangraena* (1646). On the other hand, Milton's statement about the adjuring of

the "Civill Sword / To force our Consciences that Christ set free" (5–6) might allude to the Presbyterian* movement during the last months of 1646 and the early months of 1647 to demand immediate legislation for the repression of heresy and error. Despite the specific references in date and occasion suggested by these allusions, they do concur in providing a way to understand those underlying forces which prompted Milton to write his sonnet in the first place. The poem has been dated on such evidence from 1645 through 1647.

Having supported the Presbyterian form of church government in his anti-prelatical tracts (1641–42), Milton grew disenchanted with what he considered to be the Presbyterian intolerance of any ideas that might differ from their own. (The Presbyterian reaction to Milton's ideas concerning divorce is a case in point.) Appropriately, Milton directed his sympathies toward the more tolerant Parliamentary minority, the Independents*. With them, he was critical of the power the Presbyterians were gaining in the Assembly of Divines, or the Westminster Assembly* (1643–1649), commissioned by Parliament to deliberate on matters of church discipline and ceremony now that episcopacy had been formally abolished (1643) and the Anglican *Book of Common Prayer* renounced (1645). What resulted, particularly during the years 1644–1646, were the manifold contentions between the Independents and the Presbyterians, contentions signaled by a flood of pamphlets and treatises on both sides.

With the fervor of these pamphlets, Milton's sonnet succinctly expresses the Independent argument against the Presbyterians by emphasizing what it feels to be the two fundamental evils of the Presbyterian party : "force" and "hire." The precise character of those evils Milton was later to delineate in such tracts as *CivP* : "Two things there be which have bin ever found working much mischief to the church of God, and the advancement of truth; force on the one side restraining, and hire on the other side corrupting the teachers thereof. Few ages have bin since the ascension of our Saviour, wherein the one of these two, or both together have not prevaild . . ." (6 : 4). In *NewF*, "force" takes the form of the "Civill Sword" compelling our free consciences, and "hire" takes the form of the Presbyterian movement to return to the corruptions of episcopal pluralism, or the holding of multiple posts.

Corresponding with these criticisms are Milton's attacks on the desire of the Presbyterians to substitute their synodical hierarchy or "classis" for the episcopal form of church government and the Scottish support of the English Presbyterians with such men as Adam Stuart and Samuel Rutherford, both Scottish members of the Westminster Assembly*. In contrast with the Scottish supporters, Milton invokes the Independents (such as Thomas Goodwin, Philip Nye, Jeremiah Burroughs, Sidrach Simpson, and William Bridge), "Men whose Life, Learning, Faith and pure intent / Would have been held in high esteem with *Paul*" (9–10). These men, branded heretics by the Scotch, will uncover the Presbyterian deceptions, their "plots and packing wors then" those perpetrated by the Catholics at the Council of Trent* (13–14).

As a result, Milton has faith that the Parliament will rectify the evils of the Presbyterians by "clip[ping]" their "Phylacteries" though "bauk[ing]" their "Ears" (17). The allusion to the phylacteries recalls Christ's charge that the Pharisees were displaying these insignia of devotion only in order to impress others (Matt. 23 : 5). Thus, Milton warns that the Presbyterians will suffer the removal of their hypocritical claims to piety, even though their ears are spared. In effect, the allusion threatens them, according to Mosaic law, with being rendered incapable of priesthood of any kind. (Significantly, lurking behind the reference to the severing of ears is the *TM* version of the line, which alludes to the fact that William Prynne* had been shorn of his ears in 1637.) This castigation of Pres-

byterian hypocrisy culminates in the final line of the sonnet : *"New Presbyter* is but *Old Priest* writ Large" (20). The etymological identification of *priest* and *presbyter,* both deriving from the Greek *presbyteros,* completes a series of exposés that have shown the Presbyterians to be nothing more in their practices (and now in their very name) than another version of prelatical, popish, and pharisaical hypocrisy. Thereby, Milton has been able, in the final portion of his sonnet, to "find out all [their] tricks" (13).

What has aided him in his exposé is his use of the uncommon Italian form *sonetto caudato,* containing a stinging tail or *coda* to be used something like a whip. In *NewF* the device is appended to the body of what would otherwise be a conventional Petrarchan sonnet (abbaabbac-dedec). As appended, the tail takes the form of two tercets, each consisting of a trimeter followed by a pentameter couplet (cfffgg). In that form, it becomes a very effective way of giving expression to Milton's satiric purposes. [ML]

ON THE UNIVERSITY CARRIER.

This eighteen-line poem appeared in both the 1645 and 1673 editions of Milton's works and in a jestbook, *Wit Restor'd,* published in 1658. Early copies of it may also be found in non-Miltonic manuscripts now located in the Bodleian and Folger libraries. It is one of two, possibly three, poems that Milton wrote on Thomas Hobson, who died January 1, 1631, at the age of eighty-six. *See* ANOTHER ON THE SAME.

In Cambridge, Hobson's longevity and picturesque ways had made him something of an institution. As the owner of a livery stable, he had been noted for always allowing his customers to "choose" the horse nearest the door, thus giving rise to the expression, "Hobson's choice," which means no choice at all. For over sixty-five years, too, he had driven a weekly coach between Cambridge and the Bull Tavern, London. Unfortunately, he had been forced to discontinue his trips in 1630 because of plague in Cambridge, and it may have been that the enforced idleness hastened his demise.

Such at least was the verdict of the students—Milton among them—who greeted his death with an outpouring of light verse. Milton's poem, which is written in rhyming couplets of iambic pentameter, opens with phrases that liken Death to an interruption of Hobson's long journey : it is as if Hobson had been "stuck in a slough, and overthrown." Lines 5–10 observe that Death would never have caught up with him at all had he not been forced to stay at home for a while. In the concluding lines, that home becomes the last inn at which Hobson stops and Death, the kindly chamberlain or attendant who shows Hobson to the room where he must spend the night, pulls off his boots, and t kes away the light.

Milton's touch is gentle, his humor not at all unkind. By joining in an activity that was currently very popular at Cambridge, he clearly hoped to produce work that would appeal to his contemporaries; and it is gratifying to think that he succeeded. Indeed, given the context of Milton's career, *Carrier* may be most useful as a corrective to the view that his soul *always* "was like a Star, and dwelt apart." Because of its relative simplicity, *Carrier* has not been accorded detailed critical analysis. The substantial commentary it has occasioned reflects rather difficulties that have occurred in establishing the text, in determining Milton's possible authorship of a third Hobson poem, and in presenting and analyzing the large family of Hobson poems. *See* BANQUET OF JESTS. [ERG]

ON TIME. This poem appeared in both the 1645 and 1673 editions of Milton's poems. It also appears in *TM,* although it is only transcribed there and not, like *SolMus,* actually composed there. Its resemblances to *SolMus* suggest that the two poems were composed during the same period. Any attempt to date *Time* therefore depends upon the period when Milton began using *TM,* a matter ad-

mittedly conjectural, with estimates ranging from the early 1630s to 1637.

In *TM,* Milton originally entitled his poem, "[to be] set on a clock case," then later scratched through these words and wrote above them its present title, "On Time." The poem is a madrigal, a loose Italian form that Milton freely employed in English. The madrigal, F. T. Prince observes, had been much used by sixteenth-century Italian writers to reproduce the Greek epigram, a genre that originally consisted of poetry suitable for inscription. Milton's own poem, like *SolMus,* though longer and more ambitious than most poems of this type, nevertheless retains the essential features of "a triumphant epigrammatic close" and of "wit-writing" (*The Italian Element in Milton's Verse* [1954], p. 64). In addition to the sixteenth-century Italian writers, some scholars (Parker, Hughes, Le Comte, for example) have seen a knowledge of the Beatific Vision in Dante's* *Paradiso* reflected in the reference of line 18 to God's "happy-making sight."

The poem divides into two sentences that present an opposition between time* and eternity*. In the first sentence (1–8), time and that which it can consume are denigrated. In the second (9–22), Milton turns to the happiness that souls in heaven will enjoy for eternity when time comes to an end. O. B. Hardison, Jr., has argued that lines 11–12—

Then long Eternity shall greet our bliss
With an individual kiss—

show an awareness of Aristotle*, particularly as he was interpreted by the moslem philosopher Averroes (1126–98) and his medieval and Renaissance disciples. Taking their point of departure from a passage in Aristotle's *De Anima,* they had argued against personal immortality. According to Hardison, however, *Time* upholds the orthodox Christian position that each soul survives as a separate entity. The lines above then might be paraphrased for clarity as saying that Eternity will greet each soul "individually with a kiss" (*Texas Studies in Language and Literature* 3 [1961–62]: 107–22).

Time is written in a basically iambic meter with line lengths varying from six to twelve syllables. The first sentence uses alternate rhyme (abab) in the first four lines, then switches to enclosed rhyme (cddc). Thereafter, succeeding lines rhyme with each other, except for the last four, which again use enclosed rhyme. Though based on an Italian form, the poem reveals Milton's growing sense of freedom in rendering such a form into English. This is particularly obvious if we compare *Time* with his very careful imitation of the *canzone* in *Circum*. Probably growing out of Milton's well-controlled variations within the form is the syntactical complexity of the second sentence. It is noteworthy in that it helps to create dramatic intensity in the work and also in that it foreshadows his later use of syntax as a structural element in his poetry. [ERG]

ONSLOW PORTRAIT: *see* PORTRAITS.

ORDER BOOKS OF THE COUNCIL OF STATE, those volumes in which the Interregnum government entered regulations and authoritative directions of appointment, commission, salary, etcetera. A number of entries cite Milton, others concern matters directly connected with him or his works, and still others may refer to him without specific citations. Those entries that do record official notices mentioning Milton include such items as his appointment as Secretary for Foreign Tongues* (March 15, 1649), the order to answer Salmasius* (January 8, 1650), orders to translate state papers, matters regarding his residence* in Whitehall (June 11, 1651), and a reduction of salary but lifetime payment (April 17, 1655). The order in SP Dom 25/6 (unpaged) is in Milton's holograph: "30° : Apr : 1650: . . . That Mr Chambers in ye gatehouse be released upon his own engagement, & twenty nobles givn him for his releif" (French, *Life Records*, 2 : 307, with correction). The Order Books are now in

the Public Record Office; those in which Milton's name appears most frequently are catalogued SP Dom 25/62, 25/63, 25/64, 25/65, 25/66, but a few such entries also occur in SP Dom 18/6 ("Warrant Books"), 25/5 ("Foule Book of Orders"), 25/6, 25/8, 25/15, 25/17, 25/34, 25/35, 25/36, 25/41, 25/55, 25/70, 25/72, 25/75, 25/105 ("Warrants for Money"), and 25/107 ("Warrants for Money"). Entries that refer to Milton directly are printed in French, *Life Records*, as follows: 2 : 234, 236, 238, 239, 239–40, 240, 245, 250, 251, 254–55, 256, 256–57, 257, 268–69 (2), 269, 273, 274, 286 (3), 291–92, 292–93, 293, 295, 299, 300, 304, 304–5, 307 (3), 307–8, 314 (3), 315, 317, 321, 334–35, 349 (3), 3 : 6, 13, 13–14, 20, 30, 31, 33–34, 42, 43–44, 51, 94–95, 115, 130, 133, 156 (2), 157–58, 160, 167–68, 205, 207–8, 208, 211, 213, 214, 231, 231–32, 258, 278, 283, 327, 335–36, 347, 355, 356; 4 : 22–23, 280–81. (See also vol. 5 for additional comments on these entries.) [JTS]

ORIGEN (ca. A.D. 185–254), perhaps the most influential of the early Christian Fathers. He was born of Christian parents in Alexandria. His father, Leonidas, sometimes said to have been a bishop, was probably a teacher of literature. In Alexandria, the second city of the Roman Empire, exceeding Rome herself in culture, in freedom, in religious and philosophical teaching, and in its famous library, Origen was schooled under Pantaenus, Clement of Alexandria*, and Ammonius Saccas. By the latter he may have been taught that creation was *ex deo*, that body and soul are indivisible, and that evil is the result of choices made by free agents. Plotinus*, the father of Neoplatonism*, was Origen's fellow student under Ammonius. Origen was educated in the classics and in Greek science; he very early became noted as a theological scholar. At eighteen he headed the famous catechetical school in Alexandria. In an excess of zeal at about this time he castrated himself, an act that he later regretted.

He was the author of an extraordinary number of books, most of which are now lost; but still extant are almost two hundred homilies, a few commentaries, short pieces, and letters, and two long and very important works, the *De Principiis* and the *Contra Celsus,* from which much of Origen's thought can be seen to have been influential in the shaping of Church doctrine. His knowledge of the Bible was encyclopedic. In 231 he founded a school as Caesarea that was attended by his pupil and biographer Gregory the Wonder Worker. Tortured during the persecution of Decius (249–51), he died soon afterward.

As exemplars of the climate of opinion largely held by the Christian community prior to the Council of Nicaea in 325, Origen's works are unequaled. They are known to us largely in Latin translations by Rufinus, who, through no fault of his own, became embroiled in a bitter quarrel with St. Jerome*. Jerome's vindictiveness toward Rufinus eventually led to Origen's works being anathematized by the Church. In spite of this, his writings have strongly influenced the foremost theologians of succeeding ages.

Origen's beliefs and Milton's are frequently congruent. Among the most significant correspondences may be found the following : 1) The Bible is the word of God accommodated to the limited intelligence of mankind. Each individual must find his own salvation in it—the more gifted probing more deeply into its doctrinal complexities, but all men, by the aid of the Holy Spirit in them, able to achieve salvation. 2) God the Father* is by His nature invisible, inaudible, and incomprehensible. His omnipotence is limited only in that He does not exercise His power in contradictions. Creation* is *ex deo,* not *ex nihilo.* God's foreknowledge does not cause events. At the end of time God will be all in all. 3) The Son* is a lesser deity, the agent of the Father in all things, including the creation of the cosmos. His generation is both literal and metaphorical, and his place is achieved through merit*. As Christ upon earth he is *theanthropos,* both God and man. 4) Heaven* and Hell* are real places and also states of mind. 5) Evil* is the result of wrong choices by free agents. Untested virtue is without value. 6) Origen and Milton are subordinationists, millenarians*, mortalists*, and pantheistic materialists. [HFR]

ORIGINAL SIN. The doctrine of original sin is the belief that depravity or a tendency to evil* is innate in mankind, transmitted from Adam to the race in consequence of his sin. The term does not occur in the Bible, and the doctrine was not systematically developed in the Old Testament, although Psalm 51 : 5 speaks of sin as inherent from birth. The doctrine was more fully developed in uncanonical Jewish literature, such as Wisdom 12 : 10–11, Ecclesiasticus 25 : 24, and 2 Esdras 7 : 46–48. Romans 5 : 12–21 connects human sin with Adam, but leaves the "how" sufficiently vague to accommodate all theories. Tertullian* was the first to intimate original sin founded on the idea of the soul as matter, transmitted from parent to offspring; but it remained for Augustine* to give the doctrine systematic development. Augustine misconstrued the Greek phrase meaning *"because* all have sinned" (Rom. 5 : 12) into *"in whom* all have sinned," and the whole Western Christian doctrine of original sin was constructed squarely on this error.

Milton defines original sin as *"nature corrupted"* (11 : 271), "an innate propensity to sin" (15 : 193), or "that evil concupiscence, the law of sin . . . naturally bred in us" (15 : 195). If by original sin Augustine meant sin passed on to each man in his origin or generation, Milton finds the term too limited, for Adam was afflicted by evil concupiscence after his fall, yet obviously no sin was transmitted by his origin (15 : 195). Furthermore, Milton repudiates the idea that original sin is "specially guiltiness," for Adam and Eve had no original sin, yet were guilty as soon as they fell; and guiltiness is removed from the regenerate, yet original or indwelling sin is not altogether removed (15 : 197). He also denies the concept that original sin may be equated with "loss of original righteousness, and the corruption of the whole mind," for these are consequences of sin rather than sin itself (15 : 197–99).

From the fact that Genesis 3 : 16 passes judgment on the race, and that 1 Corinthians 15 : 22 says that "in Adam all die," Milton reasons that "undoubtedly . . . all sinned in Adam. For Adam being the common parent and head of all, it follows that . . . he either stood or fell for the whole human race" (15 : 183; cf. *PL* 3. 95–96, 209, 280; 8. 637–38;· 10. 817–18, 822–28; 11. 106–8, 423–26; 12 285–86, 398–400). He therefore argues that the rational soul is propagated from father to son in natural order, as opposed to the doctrine that each soul is individually and directly created by God (15 : 45–51). Christ alone was exempt from the contagion of original sin, because He was "born by supernatural generation" (15 : 197; cf. 15 : 281). [VRM]

ORMOND(E), JAMES BUTLER, EARL OF. A Royalist who commanded Charles I's troops in Ireland, Ormond (1610–1688) signed the Articles of Peace, promising political independence for Ireland and religious freedom for Irish Roman Catholics, in order to secure Irish help against Parliament's forces. Parliament decided to publish these Articles to arouse English anger against Ormond, along with Ormond's letter to the Parliament-appointed governor of Dublin, Colonel Jones, who refused to join Ormond. To these Articles Milton appended *Observations upon the Articles of Peace with the Irish Rebels, on the letter of Ormond to Col. Jones, and the representation of the Presbytery at Belfast*. Milton treats the Articles as treasonable, and calls Ormond the "Ringleader" of the Irish rebels in a "horrible Conspiracy." [WM]

OROSIUS, PAULUS (fl. 415). Christian apologist, student of Augustine*, and historian, his *Adversus Paganos* is said to be the first attempt to write the history of the world as a history of God guiding humanity. Renaissance editions of Orosius were published in 1510, 1524, and 1526, one of which Milton used as a source for *Brit.* [WM]

ORPHEUS AND MILTON. Son of Calliope (the Muse of epic poetry) and Oeagrus (a Thracian river-god) or Apollo, Orpheus as a poet of cosmogonical hymns and a reforming priest-prophet of the Dionysiac (Bacchic) religion is remembered for the magical power of his music that charmed all nature (Aeschylus *Agam.* 1629f.). He participated in the expedition of the Argonauts in which this virtue pacified the squabbling participants, launched the *Argo,* and mesmerized the dragon at Colchis (Pindar *Pythian* 4; Apollonius Rhodius *Argonautica* 1. 494ff.; the anonymous 4th-c. A.D. Orphic *Argonautica* 245ff., 991ff. See W. K. C. Guthrie, *Orpheus and Greek Religion,* 2d rev. ed. [1952], p. 28). By his music he entered Hades and won from Pluto permission to bring back to life his wife Eurydice, who, while fleeing from Aristaeus (Virgil *Georgics* 4. 453), had been killed by a serpent. But violating Pluto's injunction not to look backward at her before reaching the upperworld, he lost her again (Ovid, *Met* 10. 1–77). By music he mourned for her a long time, attracting men, beasts, trees, and rocks alike. Either because of his ascetic devotion to Eurydice or because of his love for young boys (Ovid *Met* 10. 48), he rejected the love of some Thracian women, the bacchantes, who, in a jealous frenzy, tore his body to pieces and cast his head and lyre into the river Hebrus. Enshrined by the islanders of Lesbos, the head uttered oracles until silenced by Apollo; Orpheus's lyre was transformed by the Muses into the constellation Lyra (Philostratus *Life of Apollonius of Tyana* 4. 14; Pseudo-Eratosthenes *Casasterismi* 3. 28–29. See J. B. Friedman, *Orpheus in the Middle Ages* [1970], pp. 1–12).

Because of his thorough and wide-ranging command of classical, Christian, and Renaissance learning, Milton's knowledge of Orpheus cannot be confined to specific references in his work to the legendary poet-musician. Nevertheless, they do reflect his abiding interest in and his fondness of using the Myth. His familiarity with Orpheus's part in the Argonautic expedition, for instance, may be inferred from his marginal note to *Pythian* 4 on p. 357 of his 1620 Saumur edition of Pindar (18 : 294). Considering Orpheus to be the author of *Lithica* (a late antique poem on magical qualities of stones ascribed to him) and of the hymns (which are really the works of Neoplatonic* writers of the late hellenistic and early Christian periods), Milton shows his acquaintance in *Educ* (4 : 284), *1Def* (7 : 166), *Prol* 1 (quoting five lines dircetly from the Orphic *Hymn to Aurora* 12: 140), and possibly in *PL* 3. 17 (referring to the Orphic *Hymn to Night,* but see C. G. Osgood, *Classical Mythology of Milton's Poems* [1900], p. 66). Through specific references to Orpheus's heroic adventures, Milton also reveals his idea of the power of music*, his aspiration of becoming like Orpheus a vatic poet, and his treatment of pagan myths.

Milton's lifelong interest in music is well-known. His minor poems are especially full of music imagery, and Orpheus's magical power through his harp and song is frequently cited to illustrate the affective force of music. In both *L'Al* (144ff.) and *IlP* (105ff.) the poet reiterates the power over Pluto of Orpheus's music, which "Drew Iron tears down" the underworld king's cheek and won his permission to let Eurydice go. "Ignorance," in *Prol* 7, rejected by humans who incline by nature toward "Knowledge," finds no fellowship either among beasts, trees, or stones because they all are capable of being attracted by "the elegant music of Orpheus" (12 : 282). Powers of music and learning are once more compared in *Educ,* where Milton's new program is likened to "melodious sounds on every side that the harp of Orpheus was not more charming" (4 : 280). Of greater significance in revealing Milton's knowl-

edge of Renaissance musical theories is the distinction drawn between instrumental music and song, the latter being identified with poetry (G. L. Finney, *Musical Backgrounds for English Literature* [n.d.], p. 133). Their bantering tone notwithstanding, the passages from *Prol* 6 and *AdP* confirm a serious belief in the superiority of poetry to music. In the former Milton exalts the power of his words over the sweet music out of the harps of both Orpheus and Amphion (12 : 210). In the address to his father defending his choice of a poetic career, Milton argues convincingly : "What pleasure will there be in music well attuned if it is empty of voice, empty of words and of their meanings, and of numbers that talk? Such strains befit the woodland choirs, not Orpheus, who by his songs held fast the streams, and added ears to the oaks by his songs, not by his lyre, and by his singing compelled to tears the shades that were done with life: it is from his *song* that he has these praises" (50ff.). Although he goes on to emphasize the traditional affinity between poetry and music so as to persuade his father, who was a competent musician, to accept his choice of a poet's career, Milton's exaltation of poetry here goes far to reflect his perennial aspiration of becoming a poet, a vatic poet like Orpheus.

That Orpheus is regarded in the Renaissance as the prototype of a poet-prophet can be seen from the writings of Walter Ralegh*, Michael Drayton, Francis Bacon*, Joshua Sylvester*, George Sandys, and Henry Reynolds (Caroline W. Mayerson, *Publications of the Modern Language Association* 64 [1949] : 192ff.). As a vatic poet Orpheus not only teaches men through his theogony and cosmogony but also civilizes society by curbing the barbarous instinct of nature (e.g., cannibalism) and by inventing the arts of farming and writing. Milton finds in the simple mode of living the secrets of the prophetic power of Tiresias, Calchas, Linus, and Orpheus, the last who so lived "in lonely grots, after he had tamed the wild beasts" (*El* 6, 70). In the same verse epistle to Diodati*, he vows to emulate the life of a vatic poet : ". . . let him live a simple, frugal life . . . let herbs offer him food that works no harm, let pellucid water stand near him, in a tiny cup of beechen wood, and let him drink only sober draughts from a pure spring" and to be ". . . free of crime, pure and chaste, and a character unyielding, and a name without taint . . . resplendent with holy vestments and with lustral waters, . . . minded to go forth to face the angry gods." But it is Orpheus the reforming prophet of the Dionysiac cult that perhaps arouses the greatest sympathy from Milton, who devoted a portion of his life to advocating true reformation of his country's religion. For Orpheus's death is due not simply to his ascetic life after losing Eurydice, but also, according to one version, to his "apostasy" in the eyes of the bacchantes, worshipers of the Dionysiac cult. It is the calming, rational, and civilizing influence of the ascetic Orpheus, leading men away from the bacchic orgy, that led Dionysos to order the barbaric execution (Guthrie, pp. 54–55). This is why Orpheus's death meant so much to Milton. In *Lyc* the death of Edward King* who stands for both Orpheus and Milton's alter ego, has shaken the young poet's confidence in his newly chosen career :

What could the Muse her self that *Orpheus* bore, . . .
When by the rout that made the hideous roar,
His goary visage down the stream was sent,
Down the swift *Hebrus* to the *Lesbian* shore?
(58, 61–63)

"What boots it with uncessant care," he wonders seriously, "To tend the homely slighted Shepherd's trade?" That he entertains a genuine fear of meeting the same fate as Orpheus can be seen from Book 7 of *PL* (32ff.), where he invokes the heavenly Muse* Urania* not to fail to protect him and to drive off

. . . the barbarous dissonance
Of *Bacchus* and his revellers, the Race

Of that wilde Rout that tore the *Thracian* Bard.

The personal identification with Orpheus gains significance when the autobiographical details that precede the invocation —"On evil days though fall'n, and evil tongues; / In darkness, and with dangers compast round"—are remembered.

In Milton's allusions to Orpheus, Douglas Bush has found "a summary of his artistic and spiritual evolution" (*Mythology and the Renaissance Tradition,* rev. ed. [1963], p. 296). The poet's attitude toward, and his treatment of, pagan myths underwent a change that is mirrored in such references. From the "unclouded lyricism" in *L'Al,* to the "disenchanted questioning" of *Lyc,* to the apparent denigration in *PL,* where Calliope is labeled "an empty dream" (7. 39), Milton moves from treating myths as pure adornment, to Christian allegorization*, to fables or fictions. Such an evolution is particularly meaningful when it is viewed in light of the spirit of the age. From the start Milton's age was unfriendly toward classical mythology* and became more and more hostile as the century wore on. The value of allegorizing classical myths, maintained by early Christian apologists and Renaissance mythographers, was denounced by Prynne* and Cowley* (Bush, pp. 258f.), attacked by Bishop Sprat, Hobbes*, and Spinoza, and finally discarded by Trapp, Addison*, and Johnson* in the next century (D. C. Allen, *Mysteriously Meant* [1970], pp. 300–11). Moreover, in the last third of the seventeenth century, the Restoration vogue of travestying and burlesquing Virgil* and Ovid* and the rising tide of skeptical rationalism and mechanical deism hastened the end of regarding classical myths as conveyors of ontological and moral truths. Viewed in this light, Milton may truly be considered as the last Christian humanist who, whenever appropriate, turned all things classical and pagan to Christian ends. Although Milton certainly knew the allegorical and moralizing traditions, he seldom relied on them except occasionally to emphasize a Christian position. For instance, the tradition identifying Orpheus with Christ (which was firmly established in the late classical and early Christian periods, Friedman, pp. 38–85) is neither implicit in nor central to *Lyc* (but see Mayerson, p. 192); it is at best inferential when Christ is referred to in "Through the dear might of him that walk'd the waves" (173). True to his Christian humanism, Milton, when expounding on Christian themes, always treats pagan deities as "poor seconds, and the lessons to be drawn from their myths . . . as worthless as all second-rate things" (Allen, p. 299). In dealing with other themes, his treatment of pagan myths, like those of Orpheus, remains largely metaphorical, intensifying his thought or image through comparison and contrast. Thus, although Milton's allusions to Orpheus may not reflect so clear-cut and progressive an evolution of his attitude toward pagan myths as has been made out, they do reveal much of Milton the man and the poet. [MT]

ORTELIUS, ABRAHAM (1527–1598), a Flemish geographer of German extraction and one of the best-known cartographers of his day. Though his chief work, *Theatrum Orbis Terrarum* (1570), was faulty by modern standards, it was widely accepted as authoritative. Clearly Ortelius was one of Milton's favorites. A reference in *Animad* (3:138), where Milton is poking fun at Bishop Hall's* fanciful *Mundus Alter et Idem,* proves Milton's faith in the geographer. You will never, Milton says, find any of the silly countries that the Bishop mentions in a reputable geography* like Ortelius's.

Though commentators (notably A. W. Verity*) have been inclined to see Ortelius behind passages in *PL* where other geographers such as Peter Heylyn* are more apt to be, the poet looked upon him with respect. Perhaps it was because Ortelius brought so much classical and biblical lore up to date. For example, in Book XI where Michael is unfolding to Adam the future history of the world, the angel

speaks (400) of "*Sofala* thought *Ophir.*" Under *Sofala* Heylyn (*Cosmographie,* 4:75) writes: "This Country for its abundance of *Gold* and *Ivory* is by some thought to be that land of *Ophir,* to which Solomon sent." Then Heylyn goes on to give credit: "Of this opinion *Ortelius* in his *Thesaurus* was the first Author." Similarly in *PL* 4.268–72, Milton compares the Garden of Eden with other ideal gardens:

> Not that faire field
> Of *Enna,* where *Proserpin* gathering flours
> Herself a fairer Floure by gloomie *Dis*
> Was gathered, which cost *Ceres* all that pain
> To seek her though the world.

The poet's mind was of course on the classical origin, but he may well have been reminded by Ortelius's retelling of the story. Even the geographer's rather detailed following of Odysseus's wanderings may have had its bearing on Milton's reproduction of the material. [RRC]

OSGOOD, CHARLES GROSVENOR (1871–1964), scholar who, after earning his doctorate at Yale University, was called to Princeton by Woodrow Wilson as one of its original preceptors in 1905 and who remained there until his retirement. A student of the classics and of the Italian Renaissance, he is best known for his long-term commitment to the Spenser Variorum, which he brought to completion with the two volumes of the minor poems. Earlier, unassisted by a computer, he had compiled the huge *Spenser Concordance.* In Milton studies, he published his dissertation, *Classical Mythology of Milton's English Poems* (1900), an alphabetical listing of its subject by name, preceded by an informative introduction. It remains the standard treatment although at that early date the significance of Renaissance mythographers like Conti had not yet been appreciated. His other Milton publications are minor, often explaining mythological* allusions. [WBH]

OULTON, RICHARD: *see* PRINTERS.

OVERTON, ROBERT (1609?–1667), Major-General of the Army. A soldier with Sir Thomas Fairfax* in the early years of the Civil Wars, Overton defended Hull and fought at Marston Moor. A colonel, he was appointed deputy in August 1645 to Fairfax, who was named governor of Pontefract. About July 1647 Fairfax was finally able to obtain a regular army command for Overton, that of the late Colonel Herbert's foot regiment and also the governorship of Hull. A year later the mayor and corporation of Hull petitioned for his removal, but Fairfax and some of the townspeople backed him up. He held Hull in the second Civil War while his regiment fought under Cromwell in Wales. He took no part in the trial of the king or the establishment of the new government, which he opposed on several points. He was with Cromwell* in the invasion of Scotland in 1650, becoming governor of Edinburgh in September. He helped complete the defeat of Scotland through the invasion of Fife in July 1651 and of the Orkneys in nearly 1652. He was appointed commander of the English forces in the west when General Monck* returned to England. Returning to England himself in 1653 and resuming his governorship of Hull, Overton, a Fifth Monarchy man, was pleased with Cromwell's dissolution of Parliament but dissatisfied with Cromwell's assumption of the Protectorate, which he considered a step toward self-aggrandizement. (The implications in Milton's *Sonn* 16 and Marvell's* "Horatian Ode" concerning Cromwell's bid for power are not dissimilar.) Overton made his feelings known to Cromwell and promised to give up his command when he could no longer serve the Protectorate. He returned to Scotland in September 1654 but was imprisoned in December on the charge of intending insurrection against the government. Various partisan groups that had developed tried to woo his help in overthrowing the government, but apparently he was innocent of the charges that kept him prisoner until 1659, first in the Tower and then on the isle of Jersey. In February 1659 his sister petitioned Richard Cromwell's Parliament, which in March voted Overton's immediate release. After the restoration of the Long Parliament, Overton was restored to his commands and appointed one of seven commissioners to govern the army. He resisted joining forces with Monck but finally was forced to give up his command peacefully. As a leader of the Fifth Monarchy men, he was again arrested after the Restoration, spending most of his remaining years in prison.

Much has been made of Milton's statement concerning Overton in *2Def*: "you Overton, who have been connected with me for these many years in a more than brotherly union, by similitude of studies, and by the sweetness of your manners: in that memorable battle of Marston Moor, when our left wing was routed, the chief officers looking back in their flight beheld you keeping your ground with your infantry, and repelling the attacks of the enemy, amid heaps of slain on both sides and afterwards, in the war in Scotland, no sooner were the shores of Fife occupied, under the auspices of Cromwell, with your troops, and the way opened beyond Sterling, than both the western and northern Scots acknowledged you for the humanest of enemies, and the farthest Orcades for their civilizing conqueror" (8 : 233, 235). The statement certainly says that Milton and Overton had been friends for a number of years, perhaps from college days when Overton matriculated at St. John's, Cambridge, in early 1627. Parker* even suggests that Overton's son John had been a student of Milton's. In this section of *2Def* Milton seems to be urging Cromwell to consider the men named as possible members of the Council of State*, a daring proposal in Overton's case. The only other known connection between the two is the reference in Andrew Marvell's letter to Milton, dated June 2, 1654, asking about "what becomes of Colonel Overton's business." The date implies that Overton's opposition to Cromwell was well-known—he had published his approval of the dissolution of Parliament in *More Hearts and Hands appearing for the work . . . being two Letters . . . from Colonel Robert Overton, Governor of Hull . . . and the Officers of the said Garrison* in 1653—and that he was generally out of favor. His arrest some few months later was not, probably, surprising. One other fact should be noted. Marvell came from Hull and had been tutor to Fairfax's daughter; it is possible that Milton, Overton, Fairfax, and Marvell's relatives were mutually acquainted, and Overton may be the link between Marvell and Fairfax, and Marvell and Milton. [JTS]

OVID, MILTON AND. Like every educated man of his day, Milton must have first experienced literature through the reading of Ovid, either with his tutor Thomas Young* or at St. Paul's School*. This educational heritage from the Middle Ages persisted long into the seventeenth century. There were several reasons for such continuing popularity of a pagan writer : his Latin is simple and clear, the mythology* of the *Metamorphoses* then as today was considered good intellectual fare for young people, and from the fourteenth century it had been "moralized" to show what were supposedly its Christian elements. Thus Ovid's influence upon European culture via the grammar school curriculum is almost incalculable. In 1498 the full scholarly apparatus of Raphael Regius was printed, to be followed with further annotations by others. In 1565 Arthur Golding's enormously popular English translation began to appear, and in 1632 George Sandys published another, a fully allegorized or Christian version. It is not surprising to find Milton's early Latin poems dominated, like Shakespeare's early comedies, by this omnipresent writer.

The Latin elegies are especially imbued, Milton virtually having Ovid "by heart" as E. K. Rand observed (*Studies in Philology* 19 [1922] : 111). As they read him in the lower grades, students were required to write imitations, receiving their introduction to literature from his models. Thus it is not surprising to find his mark everywhere in Milton's own school poetry. Davis P. Harding, *Milton and the Renaissance Ovid* (1946), pp. 44ff., distributes his imitations into five categories : 1) repetition of Ovidian epithets, such as *doctissimus* applied to Socrates; 2) application of an epithet to a word similar to but not identical with Ovid's (Ovid's ocean, *refluum mare,* becomes Milton's Thames, *reflua . . . unda*); 3) adaptation of longer Ovidian phrases to new context; 4) combination of two Ovidian phrases into a single new one; and 5) the wealth of mythological allusions, for which *Met* was most famous, a source drawn upon by all contemporary poets except the metaphysicals. A long list of verbal parallels appears in Mary Brill's dissertation, *Milton and Ovid* (Cornell University, 1935). Harding believes, however, that at about his twenty-first birthday Milton committed himself to a career as a Christian poet and thereafter "the influence of Ovid [upon him] is greatly reduced" (p. 55). Writing mostly thereafter in English, Milton turned to other resources.

Of the minor English poems, only *Mask* seems to echo Ovid, especially in the relationships of Comus with the Circe story. Besides the Homeric account it would have been even more widely known in Ovid's redaction, *Met* 14; editors since Warton* have argued for his importance rather than Homer's*.

Although neither *PR* nor *SA* reveals any significant indebtedness to Ovid's writing, *PL* owes a great deal to *Met* 1. In this opening book the Roman describes the creation in details that for centuries had been viewed as derivative from the account in Genesis. Owing to this fact, Ovidian details might be freely introduced into the Christian hexameral* tradition Similarities are accordingly especially evident in Milton's account of creation (*PL* 7), of the Garden of Eden (4), and of Noah's Flood (11), which is much like that associated with Ovid's Deucalion. For instance, Milton's conclusion, "And Earth self balanc't on her Centre hung" (7. 242) echoes Ovid's "Nec circumfuso pendebat in aere tellus / Ponderibus librata suis" (*Met* 1. 12f.). The world, "Built on circumfluous Waters calme, in wide / Crystallin Ocean" (7. 270–71), translates partly "circumfluus humor / Ultima possedit, solidumque coercuit orbem" of *Met* 1. 30–31. In a similar way Ovid later details the Golden Age (*Met* 1. 88ff.) suggesting the biblical Paradise and Milton's, though details may be so generally available as to make specific ascription a difficulty. Obvious throughout the poem is Milton's employment of Ovidian mythology for comparison or ornament, like those to Typhon (*PL* 1. 199; *Met* 5. 346ff.) or to the battle of the giants (*PL* 1. 576f.; *Met* 10. 151). Annotators have detected hundreds of such allusions, though Milton seems not to have followed the common contemporary practice of allegorizing* any of them. Harding suggests only one example of an allegorizing interpretation: the similarity of Sin's hell hounds (*PL* 2. 654 to Scylla's (*Met* 14). It seems a fact that Ovid's total influence on Milton's epic is even more pervasive than Virgil's*. Certainly it has had more scholarly attention. [WBH]

OXFORD UNIVERSITY, MILTON'S CONNECTION WITH.

According to Anthony Wood*, Milton was incorporated Master of Arts of Oxford University in 1635 as a graduate of Cambridge, a common reciprocal procedure between the two universities upon application of the graduate. Wood wrote, "This Year was incorporated Master of Arts *John Milton*, not that it appears so in the Register, for the Reason I have told you in the Incorporations 1629, but from his own mouth to my friend, who was well acquainted with, and had from him, and from his Relations after his death, most of this account of his life and writings following" (*Athenae Oxonienses*, 1 [1691], "Fasti," col. 880). The reason given for the lack of evidence of incorporation in the records is that John French, "public Scribe or Registrary of the University," was careless about such details and entered

no incorporations of Cantabrigians during his term of service. Wood's friend is presumably John Aubrey*, except that Aubrey did not know Milton personally. Milton, who was residing in Horton* in 1635, about thirty-six miles from Oxford, may have desired the incorporation, known as an *ad eundam* degree, in order to use the Bodleian Library. For a skeptical view of Wood's testimony, see William R. Parker, *Papers of the Bibliographical Society of America,* 52 (1958) : 1–22; for a defense, see J. Milton French, *Publications of the Modern Language Association of America* 75 (1960) : 22–30. [JTS]

PACKER, MR.: *see* AMANUENSES.

PAGET, NATHAN (1615–1679), physician and friend of Milton. He took his M.A. at Edinburgh in 1638 and his M.D. at Leyden in 1639. He was admitted an extra licentiate of the College of Physicians of London in 1640, incorporated M.D. at Cambridge in 1642, and elected a fellow of the College of Physicians on November 4, 1646. In 1649 Paget was nominated physician to the Tower.

It is not known exactly when Dr. Paget became acquainted with John Milton; however, he was a regular visitor at Milton's house in Jewin Street, a frequent companion of the poet's brief walking excursions, and, very probably, Milton's personal physician after the Restoration. He resided in the parish of St. Stephen, Coleman Street, and was a familiar, learned acquaintance of Milton's, according to Aubrey*, and an old friend by 1663, according to Phillips. He figures specifically in Milton's biography in two ways that we know of : he made arrangements for Thomas Ellwood* to study and work with Milton and introduced Elizabeth Minshull to Milton. Through Isaac Penington*, son of the Lord Mayor of London and member of the Council of State executed in 1660, Paget learned of Ellwood, who with the younger Penington was important in the rise of the Society of Friends. In March or April

1662 Ellwood came to Milton's home to begin reading Latin with him and apparently to discharge various scribal tasks. Second, sometime before February 1663 Paget "recommended" Elizabeth to Milton as his third wife. She was Paget's second cousin, that is, the daughter of Paget's cousin Randall Minshull, who was the son of his mother's sister.

After Milton's death, Dr. Paget visited Mrs. Milton often at her home in Artillery Walk, Bunhill. When he died, in January 1679, he left Mrs. Milton a bequest of twenty pounds. His library, which contained many of Milton's works, was sold at auction on October 24, 1681. [JLG]

PAGITT, EPHRAIM: *see* ANTAGONISTS.

PAINE, THOMAS: *see* PRINTERS.

PALMER, HERBERT: *see* ANTAGONISTS.

PALUDANUS, L.: *see* TRANSLATIONS OF MILTON'S WORKS.

PAMELA'S PRAYER: *see* EIKON BASILIKE.

PANDAEMONIUM, an assembly or abode of all the devils. The term is used in *PL* 1. 756, and 10. 424, and was coined from *pan* (all), *daemon* (demon, evil spirit) and *ium* (assembly). The opposite is "pantheon," the palace of the gods. The OED lists no entry earlier than Milton's in 1667, but Henry More, in *Psychozoia*, 1. 3. 12, uses "Pandaemoniothen," meaning all from the devils, or the dominion of the devils, and "Pantheothen," all from God, or the dominion of the gods. Rebecca W. Smith (*Modern Philology* 29 [1931]: 187–98), argues that the description of Pandaemonium, the capitol of Hell, is based on St. Peter's in Rome. [WM]

PAPERS, STATE, those documents, primarily letters, which Milton produced in his capacity as Secretary for Foreign Tongues* to the Council of State*. Among Milton's duties as Secretary was the translating of letters or similar documents from foreign powers to the Cromwellian government, preparing answers to such letters, and otherwise processing correspondence with these having official business with government. Subjects of the state papers range from introductions of envoys to information about the English government, to complaints against a state's action toward merchant ships or English residents of another country, to negotiations for peace or similar settlements, and the like. Milton was appointed Secretary on March 15, 1649, and continued in that office, although at times with reduced activity, through at least October 22, 1659. The earliest state paper is dated April 2, 1649, and the latest, May 15, 1659. Generally Milton wrote in Latin and translated from Latin, although some few letters accepted as his were written in English and some translations were from Dutch, Spanish, German, and French. State papers usually resulted from action by a committee of the Council of State, a written draft (sometimes in English, sometimes one in English and one in Latin) being produced by the chairman of the committee or his delegate. Once the draft was approved by the Committee, it went to the Council of State, Parliament, or the Protector for approval or revisions. Next a secretary (that is, Milton for those letters which were sent to him) turned the English draft into Latin or refined the Latin draft. ometimes, however, Milton worked directly with the committee in charge or was specifically ordered to compose a letter on his own. (Such orders often appear in the Order Books of the Council of State.) The state papers that we can assign to Milton show differences from others that exist and that seem to have no connection with him in their rhetoric, style, or execution of ideas. It should be remembered, also, that Milton was not the only secretary employed in this capacity and that there is no evidence of his supervising others. The state papers are significant for their biographical information about diplomatic life during the Interregnum, and for the stylistic features that set them apart from non-Miltonic documents.

It is assumed that the publication of 137 state papers in 1676 (one is a duplicate) came from a manuscript derived from Milton's own copies of those papers which he had written. But original letters sent and such contemporary copies as have been discovered indicate that *Literae Pseudo-Senatûs Anglicani, Cromwellii, Reliquorumque Perduellium nomine ac jussu conscriptae a Joanne Miltano* contains a number of variants and even errors (as in dates) in the versions printed; and two important manuscript collections of the state papers make clear that *Literae* is not complete. We can, however, accept these 1676 state papers as authentic, wherever their texts come from. A manuscript prepared by Milton's last amanuensis, Daniel Skinner*, omits thirteen papers included in the 1676 edition and gives fourteen not found there (see SKINNER MS). A manuscript now in the Columbia University Library omits three letters found in the 1676 collection but gives twenty additions, ten of which also appear in the Skinner MS (see COLUMBIA, MS, THE). And Milton's nephew Edward Phillips translated *Literae* into English in 1694, omitting three items. Skinner and Phillips each omit one of the duplicate letters (*Literae*, pp. 22 or 27); Phillips includes both of the additional omissions in Columbia, and Skinner gives one of those; and both Skinner and Columbia include the other two omissions in Phillips. Thus all the 1676 letters are authentic, and the authenticity of the ten letters found in both the Skinner and Columbia MSS seems assured by that fact. The four additional letters in the Skinner MS are also accepted as Milton's because of the apparent provenance of their texts; other versions of each are known in original or contemporary or printed copies. Whether the additional ten letters found in the Columbia MS should be added to the canon is uncertain, although they usually are. They are all in English and four of them are translations of letters from Spain or Denmark; two of these appear in John Thurloe's* *A Collection of State Papers* (1742).

Some of the state papers had appeared prior to publication of the 1676 collection; for example, one letter is printed in *Literae Ab Olivario Protectore Angliae &c.* (1656); one in *Apographum Literarum Serenissimi Protectoris Oliverii Cromwelli* (1656), and the same one in *Verax Prodromum in Delirium* (1656?); and eight in Samuel Morland's* *The History of the Evangelical Churches of the Valleys of Piemont* (1658), as well as one included in the Skinner MS. Letters discovered in various repositories, being originals or contemporary copies of those published in *Literae,* number eighty (including multiples of the same letter) and eleven (including multiples of the same letter) of the fourteen additional Skinner items. Of the 152 letters noted above, originals or copies have been discovered for 63 individual letters. Further original or manuscript state papers have been suggested as Milton's, but these are questionable except for two letters to Hamburg, dated August 2, 1649; translations of two letters from Princess Sophie* to Prince Rupert* and to Prince Maurice, dated after April 13, 1649; and the Safeguard for Henry Oldenburg*, dated February 17, 1652. The two letters to Hamburg are in Henry Martin's hand, with corrections by Milton; the two translations are in the hand of Milton's nephew, John Phillips, with corrections by Milton in one of them; and the Safeguard was published by J. J. Winkelmann in *Oldenburgische Friedens und der benachbarten Oerter Kriegs-Handlungen* (1671), pp. 390–91, and in Thurloe's *State Papers*, 5 : 192. A treaty between Sweden and England, dated April 1656, has been assigned to Milton on the basis of the testimony of Bulstrode Whitelocke* in *Memorials of English Affairs* (1682), p. 633; but that statement says only that Milton was called on to put "a few Articles into *Latine.*" The account of Samuel Pufendorf in *De Regus a Carolo Gustavo* (1696), seems to corroborate this; see his version and remarks on pp. 221–22 and appendix, pp. 3–10. He dated the treaty July 17, 1656. An outline of the treaty is given by Thurloe

(4 : 486), and is printed in full in three different collections of treatises in the eighteenth century. The question of *Scriptum Parlamenti* and *Scriptum Domini Protectoris* is taken up under attributions*.

In his edition of the state papers in the Yale *Prose* 5 (1971), J. Max Patrick prints for the first time one of the letters to Hamburg, dated April 2, 1649, and a final version of a letter to Mazarin, dated May 20, 1658 (previously and erroneously cited by others); prints or notes some new versions of previously known papers; notes a number of nonextant documents that Milton may have produced; and prints versions of papers from which Milton translated, his translations being lost. Of particular importance are the papers, both English and Latin, found in the Nalson papers in the Bodleian Library. These are copies or original drafts of state papers. John Nalson, Rector of Doddington and Canon of Ely, acquired the papers sometime before 1682.

Yet a number of questions surround the state papers, such as dates and recipients. Patrick has been able to alter or affirm certain dates as given by French in *Life Records*. However, none of the previous work on the state papers, including Wilbur C. Abbott's in *The Writings and Speeches of Oliver Cromwell* (1947), four volumes, has explored all of the materials available, such as Gregorio Leti's printing of forty-nine letters in the second volume of *Historia, e Memorie recondite sopra alla vita di Oliviero Cromvele* (1692) or Johan Christion Lünig's printing of 115 letters in *Literae Procerum Europae* (1712), three volumes. These two collections do not derive from the 1676 edition or cognates of the Skinner and Columbia MSS. A full-scale study of all pertinent material and a careful stylistic analysis of Milton's contribution of the state papers should be helpful in determining texts and canon more reliably. [JTS]

PARADISE. "Standing on earth, not rapt above the Pole," Milton embodies the myth of Paradise concretely in an Assyrian pleasure garden, elevated high and difficult to reach. For details of terrain and location he used such sources as Ortelius's* *Theatrum*, Camden's* *Britannia*, and Fuller's* *A Pisgah-Sight of Palestine*. (See G. W. Whiting, *Milton's Literary Milieu* [1939], pp. 101, 115). Yet in his account of the destruction of Paradise in the Flood, Milton makes it clear that no sanctity attaches to place as such. Rather, he treats Paradise as a true myth, literal and historical, which may be approached only by what is given in the Bible or by the shadowy types of classical mythology.

It is not entirely true to assert (as C. S. Lewis does in *A Preface to Paradise Lost* [1942], p. 47) that Milton never really *describes*, but rather *evokes* in terms of Jungian memory; for Milton brilliantly amplifies such details from Genesis as the four rivers in a style eminently "answerable" to his theme. For a parallel he also turns to the garden in the Song of Solomon

> not Mystic, where the Sapient King
> Held dalliance with his faire *Egyptian* Spouse.
> (*PL* 9. 442–43)

Yet his most poignant ironic allusions are classical, and their indirection both suggests the beauty of Paradise and foreshadows the Fall. His technique is frequently to tell us what Paradise is not, or what it surpasses :

> *Hesperian* Fables true,
> If true, here only,
> (*PL* 4. 250–51)

for example, and

> Not that faire field
> Of *Enna*, where *Proserpin* gathering flours
> Her self a fairer Floure by gloomie *Dis*
> Was gatherd.
> (*PL* 4. 268–71)

Milton's artistic problem in describing Paradise was to make it not a mere pastoral idyll, but a setting that corresponded both to Heaven and to the state of innocence in man. Milton balances the sense of a constant and orderly world, a place without seasonal change but with the profusion of spring and autumn alike, with a sense of the variety and plentitude of nature. Because man was created relatively perfect, but capable of progressing, Adam and Eve creatively work to give form to the garden and to their own lives. Milton avoids artifice on the one hand ("not nice Art," *PL* 4. 241) and monotonous idleness on the other; for Adam finds that such work "declares his Dignitie" (*PL* 4. 619), and Eve expresses her domestic art in her choice and arrangement of the fruits and nuts to be served to Adam and Raphael and in her tending of the roses. As in other Renaissance visions of a pastoral Golden Age, such as Spenser's* in the *Faerie Queene,* the simplicity of innocence manifests man's original harmonious relationship to God, his fellow man, and external nature*. Such passages as Eve's love poem to Adam (*PL* 4. 639–56) and Adam's morning prayer (*PL* 5. 153–208) reflect this rapport.

When the Fall causes external nature to reflect the sinfulness of man, this rapport is destroyed. Alienated from God, from each other, and from the creatures, Adam and Eve repent, and are forgiven, but may no longer inhabit Paradise because the correspondence has been destroyed. Yet all is not lost : that virtue of which Paradise was but the external symbol may be regained, and Adam and Eve depart with a promise of "A paradise within thee, happier farr" (*PL* 12. 587). [AG]

"PARADISE OF FOOLS."

Of the apparent digression called "the Paradise of Fools" (*PL* 3. 431–99) or "the Limbo of Vanities," A. W. Verity in 1910 said that "the almost burlesque satire . . . seems scarce in keeping with the dignity of an epic." And Merritt Y. Hughes notes here that Milton "wrote an invective of the Roman Church as unexpected as his attack upon the venal clergy in *Lycidas.*" Bold in its almost scabrous humor, the passage follows the tradition of Sebastian Brandt's *Das Narrenschiff,* translated into

English by Alexander Barclay in 1509 as *The Ship of Fools.* Parallels have been found to *Orlando Furioso* (cf. line 459) and to Burton's* *Anatomy of Melancholy* (3. iv). Some scholars trace its source to the myth of Er in Plato's* *Republic* (10. 614), or to the description in the *Phaedo* of souls who because they fail to nurture themselves on reason will eventually "be scattered and blown away by the winds." But neither speculations upon its literary source nor biographical assumptions of Milton's antiprelatical stance can fully explain the passage.

One should concentrate, rather, on its juncture in Milton's plot, on the vulture simile that introduces it, and on the theological, ethical, and aesthetic links with the whole of *PL.* It coincides with Satan's reaching a midpoint in his journey. High on the top of our solar universe, buffeted by the tempests of Chaos*, he pauses to contemplate his mission. Stretching above him the chain reaches the ramparts of Heaven, once his home. Satan with angelic eye "Looks down with wonder at the sudden view / Of all this World at once" (3. 542). He cannot ascend. He might return to Hell and report failure to his peers. But impelled by envy and pride, the inner sin, and vanity, its outward show, he glides swiftly toward his goal.

Though Satan is alone now, he will not be alone once he has completed his nefarious scheme. "When Sin with vanity has filld the works of men" (446–47), he will populate this very place, thus cursed by his visit, with assorted souls awaiting their "final dissolution." Milton puns on "dissolvd on Earth" (457) and "till final dissolution" (458) in this Limbo—the first use in the ordinary sense, and the second in the sense of the "solution" of a question (OED, #10). To Milton no human souls can disappear into nothingness (*PL* 3. 287–88). A few, the merely vain perhaps, may eventually rise to Heaven; but others, unrepentant in their pride, will take the wider way. For to the blustery place where Satan is just now wandering alone, Sin and Death will anchor the nearer end of the causeway they build from Hell (10. 314–18). The future crowd, including idiots, embryos, a pair of famous suicides, Babel-builders, friars, and priests, will have journeyed oppositely from Earth up to this windswept plain.

The simile of the vulture (431) controls Milton's passage with remarkable homology. Both the vulture and winged Satan are bent on their innocent prey. The vulture starts his journey in Imaus, the "snowy ridges" of Tartary, pauses on a windswept plateau in China, on his way to India's fertile ground. Satan has recently come out of that part of Hell which is "a frozen continent" of "deep snow and ice" (2. 587–91), and pauses on the top of the universe on his way to another valley between two sacred rivers. Emblematically the ill-omened vulture is a hermaphroditic female that fertilizes its eggs by sitting on a high crag and allowing strong winds to blow on its tail, even as Satan on this windy headland makes the final and irrevocable decision to hatch his plot. A picture of a vulture fertilizing its egg by wind can be seen in J. P. Valerianus, *Hieroglyphica* (1678), p. 217; the process is described in *The Hieroglyphica of Horapollo Nilous,* translated by A. T. Cory (1840), p. 23; Sir Thomas Browne corrects the vulgar error in *Pseud. Epid.* (1646), Book 5, chapter 20.

Two sets of images emerge from the grotesquerie of the Limbo passage. A low-key set of images suggests miscegenation. embryonic and gigantesque births. These souls are the "fruit" of misalliance, "abortive, monstrous, or unkindly mixt" (456), that is, unnatural or not according to "kind." Thus the passage echoes the birth of Sin and Death, whom Satan on his way to this spot has just met at the gates of Hell—Milton's horrendous myth for the involution and unnaturalness of evil.

The more obvious images are of hypocrisy, disguise, vanity, and being tossed by winds. To bring sin into our world Satan stoops to guile, pretense, and a series of disguises; he "was the first / That practisd falshood under saintly shew" (4. 121–22). After hinting in the simile that the Chinese disguise their wagons as boats, Milton dresses some people in his Limbo in religious habits that billow in the wind like sails. The poor souls "here find / Fit retribution, emptie as thir deeds" (454), as they—with bits of paper and cloth, cowls, indulgences, and vain ideas—are blown sideways back and forth across the world's posterior (494).

The "Paradise of Fools," then, is not an extraneous bit of anti-Roman invective. Technically, its future history, in what may be called the opposite of the movie flashback, anticipates the lectures that Michael gives Adam in the last two books. And its images of misconception and wind bind up much of the doctrine that Milton gives us in the poetic account of "Man's First Disobedience, and the Fruit/ Of that Forbidden Tree." Some of the sinners Michael shows Adam by turning history forward are

> . . . the product
> Of those ill mated Marriages thou saw'st;
> Where good with bad were matcht, who of themselves
> Abhor to joyn; and by imprudence mixt,
> Produce prodigious Births of bodie or mind.
> (11. 683–87)

In Book 3 the futuristic nightmare is over soon enough, and Milton returns us to his epic. These "fools" are not all great sinners. Some attempted to mate good ideas with bad; others fell victims to hypocrisy, as the Red Cross Knight was fooled by Archimago. Many of the children of our first parents unthinkingly strive while on earth to become more than they really are. [FLH]

PARADISE LOST. While in the nineteenth century some critics followed Blake* and Shelley*, the revolutionary crusaders, in glorifying Satan as Milton's real hero, the main tendency was to dismiss his religious theme and celebrate his grand style as the only salvation of *PL*. This tendency, exemplified even by the religiously and classically minded but strongly anti-Puritan Matthew Arnold*, was summed up in Sir Walter Raleigh's* remark that "The *Paradise Lost* is not the less an eternal monument because it is a monument to dead ideas" (*Milton* [1900], p. 88). In the earlier twentieth century such audible voices as Ezra Pound, T. S. Eliot*, and F. R. Leavis damned the style and the man as well; more systematically, A. J. A. Waldock* (*Paradise Lost and Its Critics* [1947]) applied to Milton's story the criteria appropriate to a realistic novel and also showed himself tone-deaf in regard to religious and moral values. Such uncritical criticism stimulated the flood of defensive and freshly expository studies which, since C. S. Lewis's* *A Preface to Paradise Lost* (1942), have continued to multiply. But earlier, about 1917, several American scholars, Edwin Greenlaw, J. H. Hanford*, and Allan Gilbert, had replaced the dichotomized Victorian image of the sublime stylist and repellent Puritan with the unified image of the Christian humanist of the Renaissance; and Denis Saurat* (*Milton: Man and Thinker* [1925]), with aberrations, and E. M. W. Tillyard* (*Milton,* [1930]), with fewer, developed that conception. During the last forty years dozens of books and countless articles have carried criticism to new levels by combining historical knowledge, sympathetic understanding of Milton's beliefs, ideas, and purposes, and sensitive aesthetic insight. It can safely be said that *PL* has come to be appreciated far more fully and intelligently than it ever was before. Although Leavis could assume that Milton had been finally dislodged from his bad eminence, so sophisticated a critic as Frank Kermode (who has not the vested interest of a "Miltonist") has prophesied that the time cannot be far off when *PL* "will be read once more as the most perfect achievement of English poetry, perhaps the richest and most intricately beautiful poem in the world (*Romantic Image* [1957], p. 165).

While an encyclopedia article, however limited in scope, must aim at orthodoxy, the many excellent modern critics have naturally not been a chorus of angelic unanimity on all points, so that many things said here, especially in the later sections, might be modified, and some perhaps denied, by others; and even the most orthodox ideas could be, and have been, much elaborated, refined, and illustrated. It has not been possible to give many bibliographical references or to give any of later date than 1970.

In the proem to Book 9 of *PL* Milton, repudiating the traditional heroic poem in favor of his own higher theme, spoke of himself as "long choosing, and beginning late." Both phrases are borne out by his personal history. Whereas Aristotle* had made tragedy the supreme poetic genre, Renaissance critical theory gave that place to the epic*, and Milton, like many ambitious poets of the sixteenth and seventeenth centuries, dreamed of doing for his country what Homer*, Virgil*, and the rest had done for theirs. In his second original English poem, *Vac* (1628), the Cambridge undergraduate, now nineteen, confided to his college audience his desire to write heroic poetry that would take in both the physical universe and "Kings and Queens and *Hero's* old." His first great poem, *Nat* (1629), was at once religious and of epic range; it embraced all time, from the Creation to the Judgment Day and Eternity. In the Latin *El 6*, addressed in the same Christmas season to his friend Diodati*, Milton contrasted the convivial maker of light verse with his implied ideal of the ascetic, priestlike poet of heroic themes. In the Latin *Mansus,* written in Italy in 1638–39, and, more explicitly, in *EpDam* (1639–40), the elegy on Diodati, Milton spoke of his plan for a heroic poem on King Arthur* and his knights. This early choice of a hero of primitive national history was in accord with classical precedents and with Renaissance theory and practice. But we hear no more of Arthur. Milton abandoned the subject, partly, perhaps, because the research done for his *Brit* convinced him that Arthur was only a figure of monkish legend, and, more largely, because that story was an inadequate vehicle for what he now wished to say.

About 1640–1642 Milton compiled a

list of nearly a hundred possible subjects for dramas drawn from early British history and from the Bible (if he made a similar list of epic subjects it has not survived). His inclination toward the dramatic form, probably stimulated by his Italian experience, and his choice of the Fall as his theme, are concretely illustrated by four early and increasingly full outlines for a dramatic treatment of that story. (These scenarios are conveniently accessible in J. H. Hanford's *A Milton Handbook*, 5th ed., revised by Hanford and J. G. Taaffe [1970], pp. 151–53; also in *CM*, 18 : 228ff.) The numerous personifications, Ignorance, Fear, Death, Faith, and the like, suggest—apart from the use of a classical Chorus—a medieval morality play, but were presumably suggested to Milton by Italian religious dramas, which were one late manifestation of the medieval allegorical* tradition. Moreover, Edward Phillips, Milton's nephew and biographer, told John Aubrey that, about fifteen or sixteen years before *PL* was thought of, he had seen a portion of Satan's apostrophe to the sun (*PL* 4. 32–41) written as the opening speech of a tragedy (*Early Lives of Milton*, ed. Helen Darbishire [1932], pp. 13, 72).

We do not know what led Milton to return to his original plan for an epic. Perhaps the Renaissance veneration for the heroic poem reasserted itself. We may surmise a stronger reason : that, as the full scope and import of the theme developed in his mind, he felt cramped by the dramatic form and wanted the large temporal, spatial, and interpretative freedom of epic narrative—though *PL* was to be notably dramatic in structure and method. The actual beginning was indeed "late." For nearly twenty years the Christian humanist* had put his religious and civic duty before his poetic vocation—and we may think that the poem eventually gained in depth and timeless relevance from that self-denying ordinance and from its author's prolonged immersion in public affairs. He had also expended intermittent labor on his *Brit* and his

huge Latin treatise, *CD,* which seems to have been finished by 1658–1660. Blindness*, which became complete early in 1652 or at the end of 1651, when Milton was only forty-three or forty-two and the great poem was still unwritten, was a blow that the devout Christian needed all his faith and courage to sustain.

John Aubrey* (*Early Lives,* p. 13) and much modern opinion place the actual beginning of composition in or about 1658; some scholars would put it two or three years earlier. One passage can certainly be dated after the Restoration, the passage in the invocation to Book 7 in which the poet speaks so movingly of his being "fall'n on evil dayes" and denounces "*Bacchus* and his revellers," who had destroyed the archetypal poet, Orpheus*. We have Milton's own testimony in the poem to his composing much at night, so that in the morning he would need to be "milked," dictating to a paid amanuensis* or to whoever happened to be handy, a relative or a caller. According to Phillips, Milton said that "his Vein never happily flow'd, but from the *Autumnal Equinoctial* to the *Vernal*, and that whatever he attempted [at other seasons] was never to his satisfaction, though he courted his fancy never so much; so that in all the years he was about this Poem, he may be said to have spent but half his time therein" (*Early Lives,* p. 73). We have no knowledge of how composition proceeded. It might have been in an approximately straight line from beginning to end —which Alastair Fowler calls "the common false assumption" (*Poems of John Milton,* ed. J. Carey and A. Fowler [1968], p. 422)—though we do not *know* that it is false; and a poem often praised for its powerful forward march might have gained some of its momentum from such an effort. The obvious alternative is that the poem was composed in scattered blocks that were gradually worked into a coherent whole. Or Milton might have used both methods, as impulse moved him. In any case there must have been much recasting and revision on both a large and a small scale: one of the wonders of the poem, apprehended only by degrees with continual rereading, is the infinity of not only massive but minute links—parallels and contrasts in idea, image, phrase, word, and rhythm—which bind the poem together and greatly enrich its resonance.

According to Aubrey (*Early Lives,* p. 13), *PL* was finished by about 1663. It certainly must have been by the summer of 1665, when Milton gave the manuscript to his young Quaker friend, Thomas Ellwood*, to read. It was not published until the late summer of 1667. Whatever other reasons may have contributed to delay, there was the general public disorder attending the Great Plague in London—during which Milton and his family lived in Chalfont St. Giles in Buckinghamshire (apparently from July 1665 till February 1666)—and the Great Fire of September 2–5, 1666. According to one early biographer, John Toland*, publication was held up for a while by the clerical licenser, who smelled treason in the simile of *PL* 1. 594–99, in which "fear of change / Perplexes Monarchs." The poem was entered in the Stationers' Register on August 20, 1667, and published soon afterwards. By the terms of his contract Milton received £5 in April 1667, and a second £5 in April 1669, when the first impression of 1,300 copies was sold out (French, *Life Records,* 4: 429–31); Milton's widow got £8 more in 1680, when the printer acquired full title to the book. Of this first edition there were six issues, dated 1667, 1668, and 1669, and Milton took advantage of these to insert the brief preface in defense of blank verse, a prose Argument for the whole poem, and Errata. In this original form the poem had ten books. In the second edition (1674), which included the commendatory poems of Samuel Barrow* and Andrew Marvell*, the seventh and tenth books were each divided into two and some new lines were provided as beginnings for what were now the eighth and twelfth books; the Argument was split into twelve parts placed at the head of the respective books; and some small revisions were made. The initial sale of

1,300 copies in about a year and a half seems pretty good for a religious epic by a notorious "rebel" in the aftermath of the Plague and the Fire and in the London and England of Charles II and Restoration comedy and satire; and subsequent editions indicate the poem's rising prestige. The famous Jacob Tonson* issued the fourth, fifth, and sixth editions of 1688, 1692, and 1695. That of 1688, which was illustrated, carried the names of over five hundred subscribers, a number of them persons of worldly or literary eminence. The poem's classical status may be said to have been established by the 1695 edition, which was very elaborately annotated by a schoolmaster, Patrick Hume*, in the manner hitherto reserved for the sacrosanct Greek and Roman authors. The first century of Miltonic scholarship has been fully described and assessed by Ants Oras, *Milton's Editors and Commentators from Patrick Hume to Henry John Todd (1695–1801)* [1931; rev. ed., 1967]). The critical value of such eighteenth-century commentators as Jonathan Richardson* and Thomas Newton* has been stressed by Christopher Ricks (*Milton's Grand Style* [1963]); and the eccentric operations of the great classical scholar, Richard Bentley*, in his edition of *PL* (1732), have been turned to critical account by William Empson (*Some Versions of Pastoral* [1935]) and by Ricks.

The second edition of 1674 is naturally the basic text for modern editions, although it has occasional errors that must be corrected from the first edition. The number of errors in both editions is surprisingly small when we consider the difficulties involved at two stages: first, the standardizing and correcting of the manuscript as written by various persons from Milton's dictation, often—as Edward Phillips said—with little regard for spelling and punctuation; and, second, a blind man's dependence upon other people's eyes and ears in the correcting of proofs. No manuscript of *PL* has survived except a fair copy of Book 1 that was used by the printer of the first edition; this manuscript, now in the Morgan Library in New York, was edited by Helen Darbishire* in 1931. The full printed texts of 1667 and 1674 have been reproduced in the second and third volumes of Harris F. Fletcher's facsimile edition of the complete poetical works (1943–1948); a facsimile of the 1667 edition has been issued by the Scolar Press (1968). Textual variations in the early editions are recorded in *CM* 2 : 487–540), in Fletcher's edition just cited, and in Darbishire's edition of the complete poems (1 [1952]).

One special question may be briefly noticed. In her editions of 1931 and 1952 Darbishire confidently argued that Milton had a system of spelling* that provided for forms he favored (e.g., preterites ending in *d*, past participles in *t*) and for distinguishing emphatic from unemphatic pronouns (e.g., *wee, we, mee, me, their, thir*); cf. B. A. Wright, *Milton's Poems* (1956), xxi, xxiv–xxviii. This theory, which raised doubts in many minds, was well battered by R. M. Adams (*Modern Philology* 52 [1954–55] : 84–91; *Ikon: John Milton and the Modern Critics* [1955]) and demolished by J. T. Shawcross (*Publications of the Modern Language Association* 78 [1963] : 501–10; also in his essay in *Language and Style in Milton,* ed. R. D. Emma and Shawcross [1968]), who showed, by comparison with Milton's holograph spellings, that his supposed idiosyncrasies must be attributed to amanuenses or compositors. The debate is summarized in Carey and Fowler, pages xi–xii.

The problem of punctuation has been fully and expertly studied by Mindele Treip (*Milton's Punctuation and Changing English Usage 1582–1676* [1970]). She finds "the strongest arguments for the poet's control . . . in the impression of a strong poetic sensibility operating in the punctuation of the poem, especially that of the Manuscript [of Book 1], and in the fact that the printer so largely retained this pointing or respected its general style when correcting, although it was unrepresentative of the period" (pp. 6–7). Treip shows that, in his later autograph sonnets and in *PL,* Milton inclined

(with his own refinements) to the older rhythmical and rhetorical principle of punctuation but made a partial compromise with the newer logical and grammatical method (pp. 68–69, etc.). Modern editors have recognized the general problem (e.g., Carey and Fowler, pp. x–xi, 427–28). For so subtle an artist as Milton, punctuation governs not only continuity and breaks in rhythm but the rate of speed, degrees of emphasis, shades of meaning, desired parallels and contrasts. Hence in modern editions that preserve the original punctuation, the sense may sometimes puzzle the reader (this Treip discounts); and modernized punctuation (which she outlaws), while clarifying the general sense, may blunt or destroy syntactical, rhythmical, and emotive relationships and nuances of meaning.

Milton's changing plans for an epic were touched upon above. The genre was so alluring to Renaissance ambition that the sixteenth, seventeenth, and even the eighteenth centuries were strewn with epics that would—as Richard Porson was to say of Southey's—be read when Homer and Virgil were forgotten. There were several basic assumptions. The material, as we have noted, should be drawn, like Homer's and Virgil's, from the early or legendary history of the poet's native land, and the action should be a subject of national magnitude. The heroic poet should be a universal scholar, should try to comprehend in his work the whole range of life and knowledge and thought. Hence the epic must be the product of ripe maturity; and Virgil's career provided a canonical model of progression —the *Eclogues, Georgics,* and *Aeneid.* Such a poem should especially fulfill poetry's double aim of teaching and delighting, should set before the reader examples of virtue to be followed and of weakness and vice to be shunned.

Thus Spenser*, in his letter to Sir Walter Ralegh attached to *The Faerie Queene,* summarized the didactic conception of the heroic poem, citing exemplars from Homer and Virgil to Ariosto* (whose moral teaching we may find scanty) and Tasso*. Ariosto and Tasso had dealt with the conflicts of Christians and Saracens. The eclectic and more didactic Spenser had treated Arthur and imaginary knights under the religious and moral headings of his six completed books (Holiness, Temperance, Chastity, Friendship, Justice, Courtesy), all embraced in his general effort "to fashion a gentleman or noble person in vertuous and gentle discipline." Milton spoke in *Areop* of "our sage and serious" Spenser as "a better teacher than *Scotus* or *Aquinas,"* citing in particular the temptations Guyon met in the Cave of Mammon and the Bower of Bliss. He gave much fuller general testimony in *RCG*. Addressing Presbyterian* readers of doubtful literary sensibility, and explaining—with a kind of sublime naiveté—why he felt compelled to set aside his poetic ambitions in order to champion the Puritan cause, Milton declared his fervent faith in the power of true poetry to nourish virtue and religion in a people (3:237–41). More specifically, along with Homer, Virgil, and Tasso, he spoke of the book of Job and the choice of some knight "before the conquest" as "the pattern of a Christian *Heroe."*

The classical doctrine of delightful teaching, revived by Renaissance humanists, received further impetus—as the names of Spenser, Milton, and Tasso remind us—from the Reformation and the Counter-Reformation. That impetus often included a revulsion against the paganism of the classics and a demand for biblical and Christian themes: examples range from Du Bartas's* immense and immensely popular heroic poem (noticed below and elsewhere in this work) to Cowley's* preface to his poems of 1656 and his unfinished epic on David. (See B. O. Kurth, *Milton and Christian Heroism: Biblical Epic Themes and Forms in Seventeenth-Century England* [1959]). Milton's early abandonment of the story of Arthur for the far greater theme of the Fall* involved a drastic break with heroic tradition. In the proem to Book 9, with explicit reference to the *Iliad, Odyssey,*

and *Aeneid,* he repudiated war*, "hitherto the onely Argument / Heroic deem'd" in favor of the sad but "more Heroic" theme of sin and woe and death and, in the end, the way of salvation opened to erring man. That goes well beyond delightful teaching. Milton's characters became almost all supernatural (God, the Son, good and evil angels); the only earthly ones, Adam and Eve, were not ordinary human beings in a human society; and the essential action was now inward, its stage the souls of Satan and the Son, Adam, and Eve.

Such radical changes involved a radical change in the poet's conception of his own role. In *RCG* Milton said—echoing Isaiah 1:5, which long before he had echoed in the prelude to *Nat*—that the poem he hoped to write would be

a work not to be rays'd from the heat of youth, or the vapours of wine, like that which flows at wast from the pen of some vulgar Amorist, or the trencher fury of a riming parasite, nor to be obtain'd by the invocation of Dame Memory and her Siren daughters, but by devout prayer to that eternall Spirit who can enrich with all utterance and knowledge, and sends out his Seraphim with the hallow'd fire of his Altar to touch and purify the lips of whom he pleases. (3:241)

Thus in the poem Milton repeatedly insists on the unique truth of Christian revelation and hence the superiority of his Christian theme. He will soar "Above th' *Aonian Mount"* (1. 15); he sings "With other notes then to th' *Orphean* Lyre" (3. 17); the Urania whose inspiration he implores is not the pagan Muse*, "an empty dreame," but the Heavenly Muse who conversed "with Eternal wisdom . . ./ . . . In presence of th'Almightie Father" (7. 1–39). Milton thinks of himself as in the line of inspired prophets, the medium or voice of divine illumination, which will raise and support his human and personal insufficiency. In *RCG* the humanist had gone on to say that "to this must be added industrious and select reading, steddy observation, insight into all seemly and generous arts and affaires. . . ."

Like earlier Christian humanists, Milton, while profoundly assured of the uniqueness of Christian revelation, revered the art and the moral wisdom of the great ancients, and it was wholly natural that, as artist, the most scholarly classicist among Renaissance poets should bypass the more or less unclassical changes wrought in the heroic poem by Ariosto, Tasso, and Spenser and should, as far as his subject allowed, revert to the authentic classical structure and method—as *SA* was modeled on Greek, not Elizabethan, tragedy. In the first full critique of *PL,* Addison's* eighteen papers in the *Spectator,* the poem was inevitably assessed in terms of the established set of epic conventions; Addison's contemporary, John Dennis*, was much more independent and perceptive in his comments. (For both, see *Milton: The Critical Heritage,* ed. J. T. Shawcross [1970]).

Obviously Milton's central source was the Bible, not merely for the stories of Creation and the Fall, which he so greatly expanded, but for the Hebrew history presented to Adam in Books 11 and 12 and for a multitude of allusions, images, and phrases. (The standard survey of such materials is James H. Sims's *The Bible in Milton's Epics* [1962].) No less obvious is the biblical foundation of the theological scheme centering on the Fall and on redemption through the Christ foretold by the prophets. In an age of assiduous reading of the Bible, Milton's complete and intimate possession of the text was shared by many people; not so many shared the systematized and sophisticated knowledge displayed throughout his large Latin treatise *CD.* This work—which he called "my best and richest possession"— cannot be called a "source," but (as Maurice Kelley showed in *This Great Argument* [1941]) it provides chapter and verse for most of the theological beliefs and ethical principles embodied in *PL.* The poem is not always in strict agreement with the treatise, and, in any case, the poetic and dramatic presentation of such beliefs and principles has for the most part a very different effect from that of expository prose. And epic latitude prescribed or allowed for large departures from theology proper : for example, Satan and his fellows received only a couple of pages in the *CD* (15 : 107–11), compounded of biblical citations that include sparse and vague allusions to their being cast into hell. Moreover, in the poem Milton played down his personal "heresies"* : for example, the doctrine of "mortalism"* (the death of the soul as well as the body until the general resurrection, which in the *CD* (15 : 215ff.) is formally endorsed, becomes in *PL* only a dramatic utterance put into the mouth of the despairing Adam (10. 782ff.). It would seem, from *CD* (e.g. 1, vii and x), that Milton, like most other educated people of his time (and indeed well into the nineteenth century), took the story of Adam and Eve as literal history, although he enlarged and reinterpreted it so freely.

Milton's fable brings in two related kinds of material (much of it discussed by Grant McColley, *Paradise Lost* [1940] and J. M. Evans, *Paradise Lost and the Genesis Tradition* [1968]). A great mass of biblical commentary, both Jewish and Christian, and many literary redactions had through the centuries enveloped the brief and simple stories of the Creation and the Fall with interpretive, speculative, and imaginative accretions. It is clear that Milton knew some part of these exegetical and imaginative materials, but we cannot tell how far his knowledge went. The story of the six days' work of Creation had become itself a poetic genre, the hexaemeral*, which might remain separate or—as in *PL* 7—be united with the story of the Fall. Both themes, and much else, were elaborated in the most famous predecessor of *PL,* Du Bartas's *La Sepmaine* (1578ff.), which was translated, with an exuberance both flamboyant and flat, by Josuah Sylvester as *The Divine Weekes and Workes* (1591–92ff.). Du Bartas's grandiose poem owed its European fame to its subject, the picturesque energy of the writing, and the combination of religious and cosmic orthodoxy with a reassuring air of scientific authority. The young Milton (like the young Dryden* later) was evidently attracted by Sylvester, and the elderly Milton may have sometimes echoed him : one line of *PL,* "Immutable, Immortal, Infinite" 3. 373), was apparently recalled from *D. W. W.* 1. 1. 56. But we may discount the large claims—made chiefly by G. C. Taylor—for a large debt. External probabilities and points of internal resemblance have led modern scholars to take two dramas as less unlikely than other "sources" to have come under Milton's eye. These are *Adamus Exul* (1601), an early work of the great jurist Hugo Grotius*, whom Milton met in Paris, and G. Andreini's* *L'Adamo* (1613), which he might have seen in Italy. (Both works are translated, with other analogues, in Watson Kirkconnell's *The Celestial Cycle* [1952].) Such parallels as there are, are succinctly summarized in Hanford's *Milton Handbook* (pp. 210–14; on Grotius and *PL,* see also J. M. Evans, pp. 207ff.).

For us, two generalities may be enough. First, while no poet would tamper with the central truths of Christian faith (although, as we saw, Milton unobtrusively admitted some "heresies" he found in the Bible), tradition fully endorsed both poetic expositions of doctrine and, as we also saw, imaginative embellishment of characters and events. Second, since the huge body of exegetical and imaginative material was common property, it is mostly vain, and certainly tedious, to try to specify Milton's "sources." The most profitable result of reading earlier versions of his fable is the realization that in all essentials, in imaginative and artistic power, he was greatly original, and was indeed celebrating—to quote the line he borrowed from Ariosto—"Things unattempted yet in Prose or Rhime."

Parallel principles legitimized the use of classical materials in a Christian poem. If sanction was needed, beyond immemorial veneration for the classics, it was provided by two age-old doctrines, the allegorical* reading of classical myth and the idea (a first aproach to comparative mythology*) that such myth was a refraction of the true history recorded in the Old Testament—as in the obvious likeness between Eden and the Golden Age or between the story of Noah and that of Deucalion and Pyrrha surviving a universal flood. Thus in his two accounts of Noah's flood (*PL* 11. 719–901) Milton freely combined details from the Bible and Ovid* (*Metam.* 1. 253ff.) and perhaps Sylvester. With allegorical reading Milton (after *Mask*) had little to do; Orpheus, for instance, in *Lyc* and in *PL* (notably in 7. 32–39) is not, as he was in Giles Fletcher's* *Christs Victorie, and Triumph* (3. 7), a "type" of Christ, but simply the archetypal poet, done to death by a hostile mob. Nor—whatever he thought—does Milton take much account of "refraction": one reference of that kind is to "*Eurynome,* the wide-/ Encroaching *Eve* perhaps" (10. 581–82); the more memorable allusion to Mulciber is noticed below. (The latest, fullest, and most learned study of the whole subject is Don C. Allen's *Mysteriously Meant* [1970].) Milton did make use of the patristic tradition that the rebellious angels became the gods of heathenism. Behind the great figure of Satan we may see Prometheus, Odysseus, Achilles, Turnus, and others, but the important thing is that Milton contrasts the heroism of the classical warrior-chieftain (and even that perverted in Satan) with the true heroism fully possessed by the Son and finally understood by Adam. To some of the older—or unregenerate younger—critics, Milton's God has appeared unpleasantly close to Zeus or Jupiter, but any such resemblance was not, of course, intentional; so far as it goes, it is only an external result of the epic conception and structure.

Echoes of miscellaneous poetry and prose, ancient and modern, have been assembled by generations of editors and commentators; these will be most fully collected in the forthcoming *Variorum Commentary* upon *PL.*

The Milton of the earlier tracts had shown the religious, ethical, political, and social optimism of an idealist exulting in the aims and growing achievements of the Puritan revolution. The sustained eloquence—and incidental wit—of *Areop* had expressed high confidence in man's religious and rational capacity to discern and to follow righteousness, to attain true virtue by facing the manifold temptations in the midst of which God had placed him:

> many there be that complain of divin Providence for suffering *Adam* to transgresse, foolish tongues! when God gave him reason, he gave him freedom to choose, for reason is but choosing; he had bin else a meer artificiall *Adam,* such an *Adam* as he is in the motions [puppet shows]. (4:319; cf. *PL* 3. 98–128, etc.)

When Truth and Falsehood grapple, "who ever knew Truth put to the wors, in a free and open encounter"? (4 : 347).

Milton's first tract, *Ref* (1641), had ended with a fervent prayer in which he invoked Christ as "the Eternall and shortly-expected King" who would "put an end to all Earthly *Tyrannies*" and proclaim his "universal and milde *Monarchy* through Heaven and Earth" (3 : 78–79). In the same paragraph he had imagined a poet—such as himself, no doubt— "offering at high *strains* in new and lofty *Measures* to sing and celebrate thy divine *Mercies,* and *marvelous Judgements* in this Land throughout all Ages." But the tract boldly, indeed rashly, published on the very eve of the Restoration, *Way* (1660), was a cry of despair for *"the good Old Cause"* (6 : 148). During many years before that Milton had seen Truth often put to the worse, had grown more and more disillusioned with the mass of men and many of their leaders. The Restoration finally extinguished the vision that had long inspired and absorbed his energies (and had cost his eyesight as well)—the vision of a holy community, a Christian state governed by Puritan saints (as philosopher-kings), a sort of interregnum before Christ's second coming. Now, in 1660, the grand new reformation had become a mirage; and, especially in the latter half of *PL,* it is seen as fulfilled only after the Day of Judgment, when fire has made all things new.

Thus Milton's desire in *PL* to "assert Eternal Providence, / And justifie the wayes of God to men" is not mere conventional piety; it is the effort of a devout Christian who, more than most men, had maintained and must maintain his faith in Providence in the face of all the public and private shocks it had undergone. And wholehearted faith in Providence requires understanding, constancy, and divine help. In *Educ* (1644) Milton had, along with a secular definition of education, given a less familiar one that assumes man's responsibilities and religious striving:

> The end then of Learning is to repair the ruines of our first Parents by regaining to know God aright, and out of that knowledge to love him, to imitate him, to be like him, as we may the neerest by possessing our souls of true vertue, which being united to the heavenly grace of faith makes up the highest perfection. (4:277)

But the opening lines of *PL* dwell much less on salvation than on sin. The relative emphasis on "Mans First Disobedience" and on tragic loss is fully borne out by the title and the poem as a whole, even though it is a "divine comedy." Thinking again of *Areop* and Milton's early confidence in man's rational dignity and power of choice (which, to be sure, are reasserted in *PL*), we can hardly help feeling that public and private experience has lessened his trust in reason* and heightened his concern with humble faith and obedience*. In *PL* (as in *PR* and *SA*) the poet's faith rests only on God and the capacity of individual souls, aided by grace, to achieve regeneration. *PL* was a personal testimony and a tract for the times as well as a beautiful work of art. We must consider, however briefly and baldly, some patterns of belief and thought that constitute the foundation or foreground or background of Milton's vision of human history and destiny. While it is axiomatic that a great artist's vision of life is timeless, it is no less axiomatic that it is conditioned by his own age and its inherited traditions. There is no short-cut to modern reinterpretation (as directors of Shakespearian plays so often assume there is), and we must read *PL* with bifocal lenses. Our first effort must be to understand what the author believed and thought and felt and said. If it is argued that such an effort is difficult or impossible for many or most modern readers, the obvious answer is that readers of any literature of the Christian past must bring unprejudiced historical, imaginative, and emotional sympathy to beliefs and ideas that they themselves may not hold; if they cannot do that, their stunted sensibility should turn elsewhere.

Further, we must not view *PL* as clouded by the old label, "the Puritan epic," a label unhappily not yet dead and buried although, in fact, Puritan elements in the poem are so few and small as to be almost invisible. C. S. Lewis pronounced the doctrine of *PL* "overwhelmingly Christian, . . . not even specifically Protestant or Puritan," except for a few isolated passages (*A Preface to Paradise Lost* [1942], p. 91). Going somewhat beyond Lewis, a Roman Catholic scholar, Sister Miriam Joseph, argued that *PL* is "capable of being read as a poem embodying theological doctrines in conformity with those of the Catholic Church" (p. 249 in *Laval théologique et philosophique* 8 [1952] : 243–84). In the latest full study of Milton's beliefs, C. A. Patrides, quoting and opposing this conclusion, holds that *PL* "is not a Christian poem generally; it is, rather, a Christian *Protestant* poem. . . ." (*Milton and the Christian Tradition* [1966], p. 5). Modern readers, whether religious or secular in outlook, may be indifferent to such distinctions, but they can or must approach *PL* as a grand archetypal "myth" or paradigm of the human condition as it appeared to a poet of grand Christian imagination and much-tried faith.

Neither in his treatise nor in his poem does Milton offer what could be called a metaphysical explanation of that supreme crux of traditional religious thought, the existence of evil*. Satan, the first rebel against divine order, whom Michael denounces as "Author of evil" (*PL* 6. 262; cf. *CD* 1 : ix), is a character in a poem, a superhuman dramatic embodiment of human pride. Milton's concern is with evil as a fact of life, a perpetual challenge to man's conscience, reason, and integrity; it exists, by God's permission, because man must possess freedom of will* and choice. But if the true Christian faces perpetual temptation and hazard, at the same time he is assured that God will supply free grace* and has provided for the ultimate defeat of evil. If the non-Christian's imagination cannot stretch to the final victory of good, he can at least accept the idea of everlasting war between good and evil in the individual soul and in the world at large.

Adam and Eve, united with each other and with God in love and joy, created perfect but not immutable, endowed with free will and reason and responsibility, and given a home of ideal beauty, disobey God's one prohibition, a test of their fidelity (*PL* 4. 428; 8. 325; *CD* 1 : x). Eve is tempted by Satan, Adam by Eve. Their sin, as Milton says in *CD* (15 : 181–83), and says or implies in the poem,

> comprehended at once distrust in the divine veracity, and a proportionate credulity in the assurances of Satan; unbelief; ingratitude; disobedience; gluttony; in the man excessive uxoriousness, in the woman a want of proper regard for her husband, in both an insensibility to the welfare of their offspring, and that offspring the whole human race; parricide, theft, invasion of the rights of others, sacrilege, deceit, presumption in aspiring to divine attributes, fraud in the means employed to attain the object, pride, and arrogance.

This catalogue, however, seems to level all degrees of significance. In *PL* there are two main causes of the Fall, of disobedience : "presumption in aspiring to divine attributes," "pride" (in the religious sense), and Eve's weakness of reason along with Adam's weakness of will in abdicating his own responsibility and putting loyalty to Eve before loyalty to God and right.

Milton's subtle development of these

themes will be outlined below and can here only be summarized in general terms. Pride* was the traditional motive of Satan's revolt against God, and Eve, tempted by Satan to become a goddess, to seek superhuman knowledge and power, virtually reenacts his sin: "for inferior who is free?" (9. 825). A hint of similar pride appears in Adam's colloquy with Raphael, when he is warned not to let astronomical curiosity displace his prime concern, the right conduct of life. This is not obscurantism on the part of the poet who, much more than most earlier humanists, had stressed the value of science* in education, who had in *Areop* named Galileo* as a martyr to astronomical truth, and who cites him more than once in *PL*. But, however limited Milton's reading in his later years, he could hardly be unaware of growing scientific and skeptical rationalism (he was certainly aware of Hobbes*), since throughout his century many thoughtful Christians were troubled over excessive "curiosity" and pleaded for temperance in knowledge (see Howard Schultz, *Milton and Forbidden Knowledge* [1955]). To quote only one witness, Ralph Cudworth, the eminent Cambridge Platonist*, in his famous sermon of 1647 to the House of Commons, had thus summed up the attitude we find in *PL*:

> We think it a gallant thing to be fluttering up to Heaven with our wings of Knowledge and Speculation: whereas the highest mystery of a Divine Life here, and of perfect Happiness hereafter, consisteth in nothing but mere Obedience to the Divine Will.

Or, as Milton says, "obedience and love are always the best guides to knowledge" (*CD* 14:25; cf. *PL* 12. 583–85). The central importance of the hierarchy of knowledge—of "priorities," as we say—is attested at the very end of *PL*, when Adam, now wiser, confesses his error in seeking to rise above human limits and declares his Christian faith and humility, and Michael replies:

> This having learnt, thou hast attaind the summe

> Of wisdome; hope no higher, though all the Starrs
> Thou knewst by name, and all th'ethereal Powers,
> All secrets of the deep, all Natures works,
> Or works of God in Heav'n, Aire, Earth, or Sea,
> And all the riches of this World enjoydst,
> And all the rule, one Empire. . . .

If there is any theme in *PL* that should appeal directly to us, it is this, since our age has become so increasingly disturbed, indeed horrified, by the outward and inward sway of science and technology and—along with its immense benefactions—its anti-human power over life and death.

For a general statement covering the motives of Eve's and Adam's disobedience*, a reminder of their traditional essence, there is Richard Hooker (*Of the Laws of Ecclesiastical Polity,* 1. 7. 6–7, in *Works,* ed. Keble, Church, and Paget, 7th ed. [1888], 1 : 224):

> Reason therefore may rightly discern the thing which is good, and yet the Will of man not incline itself thereunto, as oft as the prejudice of sensible experience doth oversway.
> Nor let any man think that this doth make any thing for the just excuse of iniquity. For there was never sin committed, wherein a less good was not preferred before a greater, and that wilfully; which cannot be done without the singular disgrace of Nature, and the utter disturbance of that divine order, whereby the preeminence of chiefest acceptation is by the best things worthily challenged. . . . sometimes the subtilty of Satan inveigling us as it did Eve, sometimes the hastiness of our Wills preventing the more considerate advice of sound Reason.

What Hooker calls the disgrace of Nature and the disturbance of divine order Milton takes account of after each sinner has eaten the fruit (9. 782–84, 1000–1004). His comments are not mere rhetoric*, and the transformation of the ideal world of nature into ours (10. 648–715) is not mere fancy; they reflect the unity and hierarchical order of the divine cosmos (see M. Y. Hughes, *ELH: A Journal of English Literary History* 36 [1969]:

193–214). And man's hierarchy of faculties is likewise upset (9. 1127ff., quoted below).

If the modern secular mind rebels against Milton's emphasis on the disobeying of God's command, we may remember —and perhaps even accept—the doctrine that he shared with other philosophic Christians, that true freedom can be enjoyed only by the good, that obedience to God—or love of goodness, if we prefer that phrase—is the natural choice of uncorrupted human reason. And that brings us to the traditional and cardinal principles of "Christian Liberty"* and "Right Reason." The Reformation doctrine of Christian liberty was the charter and basis of the salvation open to fallen man, and Milton was one of its most earnest exponents. The Mosaic law, with its countless prescriptions and its animal sacrifices, was adequate for a people at the Hebrews' early stage of religious and moral development, but for the Christian Milton it is abolished (except insofar as elements in it accord with right reason). The finest passage in Book 12, apart from the conclusion, and a great example of the impassioned poetry of ideas, is the triumphant contrast drawn between the Old Testament and the New, the Covenant of Works and the Covenant of Grace (12. 285ff.). Christian liberty means that the regenerate Christian, aided by grace, is an independent, self-governing being, freed from all subservience to external religious authority—a doctrine that did not need much extension to be revolutionary. And the inner voice of conscience is a higher authority than the Bible itself (*CD* 16 : 281).

Right reason is at once an ally and a curb of Christian liberty, As Michael tells Adam (12. 83ff.),

Since thy original lapse, true Libertie
Is lost, which alwayes with right Reason dwells
Twinn'd, and from her hath no dividual being.

Earlier, praising the faithful Abdiel, God in significant terms condemns the rebel angels

who reason for thir Law refuse,
Right reason for thir Law, and for thir King
Messiah, who by right of merit Reigns.
(6. 41–43)

The concept of right reason, implicit at least in Plato and Aristotle, was fully formulated by Stoic moralists and was readily assimilated into Christian thought: it meant that all men, pagan and Christion alike, have a God-given apprehension of the basic moral principles, and the collective right reason of mankind issues in the binding doctrines of natural law. As Hooker said, in words that may sound startling from an Elizabethan divine,

The general and perpetual voice of men is as the sentence of God himself. For that which all men have at all times learned, Nature herself must needs have taught; and God being the author of Nature, her voice is but his instrument. (*Eccles. Pol.* 1. 8. 3; *Works* 1 : 227)

Or, to quote Milton, as distinguished from the written law of God,

The unwritten law is no other than that law of nature given originally to Adam, and of which a certain remnant, or imperfect illumination, still dwells in the hearts of all mankind; which, in the regenerate, under the influence of the Holy Spirit, is daily tending towards a renewal of its primitive brightness. (*CD* 16 : 101)

But Christian liberty and right reason cannot prevent frail man from falling into sin, because true freedom must include freedom to err. Spiritual death

consists, first, in the loss, or at least in the obscuration to a great extent of that right reason which enabled man to discern the chief good, and in which consisted as it were the life of the understanding. (*CD* 15 : 207)

Thus, in and after the Fall, the hierarchical order of faculties in Adam and Eve is turned upside down (*PL* 9. 1127ff.):

For Understanding rul'd not, and the Will
Heard not her lore, both in subjection now
To sensual Appetite, who from beneathe
Usurping over sovran Reason claimd
Superior sway.

To move from earth to heaven, in traditional orthodoxy the three persons of the Trinity* are coessential and coequal. Milton had been a Trinitarian (witness the prayer at the end of his first tract, partly quoted earlier), but in the later strictly biblical theology of *CD* (1. ii–vi) God, the Son, and the Holy Spirit form a descending hierarchy. It is plain that in *PL* the Son* is everywhere represented as inferior in authority to the Father*, that —invested with the Father's power—he is the executive agent in the war in heaven, in the work of creation*, in the colloquy with Adam on the latter's need of a companion, and in the passing of judgment on Adam and Eve; in the last three passages he is called "God" and "Universal Lord" and in 8. 403ff., he speaks of himself as God. Such assignment or fusion of powers helps to explain why Milton's chief "heresy" awakened no or few misgivings in generations of pious readers, including the clerical editors Newton* and Todd*. Above all, however, the Son as mediator is the voice of love and mercy, and his supreme act is his voluntary sacrifice of himself as man's redeemer. Although at times the pamphleteer had perhaps seemed to approach Pelagian* confidence in man, "There are few opinions that Milton held more sincerely or more consistently than his view of the Atonement" (Patrides, p. 141). *See* ARIANISM.

Up at least through *Areop* Milton had considered himself a Calvinist* (there were kinds and degrees of Calvinism), but in *PL,* as in *CD* (1, iv), he explicitly rejected arbitrary predestination* and equated "the elect" with all true believers. In the heavenly council God foresees but in no way determines man's disobedience (a knotty theological point); he has made man "just and right, / Sufficient to have stood, though free to fall" (3. 98–99). When the Son asks if mankind is then to be damned, God replies that he will freely grant grace to all those who are earnest in faith, repentance, and obedience. Yet the sin of disobedience and "Affecting God-head" must be atoned for (3. 209–12) :

He with his whole posteritie must dye,
Dye he or Justice must; unless for him
Som other able, and as willing, pay
The rigid satisfaction, death for death.

This pronouncement has especially alienated many readers, who have charged Milton with abhorrent Puritan legalism. But it is manifestly unfair to condemn him for sharing, in Protestant terms, a view of the Atonement* held by many Christian spokesmen over many centuries (Patrides, pp. 130–42). Of such witnesses we can hear only one, the saintly Bishop Andrewes* (whose death the young Milton had lamented in his third Latin elegy):

Fond men! if He would quit His justice or waive His truth, He could; but His justice and truth are to Him as essential, as intrinsically essential, as His mercy; of equal regard, every way as dear to Him. Justice otherwise remains unsatisfied; and satisfied it must be either on Him or on us. (*Ninety-six Sermons* [Oxford, 1841] 1 : 784–85)

Some other questions concerning God and the Son will be considered later.

The doctrines so far noticed had more or less support in tradition, although Milton's degrees of emphasis were his own. He was much less traditional in his understanding of the grand concept historically expounded in Arthur O. Lovejoy's *The Great Chain of Being* (1936). When we think of the earlier Milton's Platonic dualism, particularly the ethical, we are hardly prepared for his metaphysical* monism, his conception of matter as created "good" and not fundamentally different from spirit (*PL* 5. 469ff.; *CD* 15 : 17ff.). It is highly significant that this is the first piece of instruction that Raphael imparts to Adam —significant too that the angel is here called "the winged Hierarch." A further distinctive feature of Milton's scale of nature* is that it is not static (as it is in Pope's *Essay on Man* 1. 233ff.) but dynamic, that the world is a world of becoming, matter perpetually passing upward into spirit (5. 469–500). Whatever repeated shocks Milton's faith in men underwent, his monism is a form of metaphysical optimism. It is of course a part of his unshakable faith in God, and in *PL* he looks forward again and again to that eternity when "God shall be All in All" (3. 341).

At the top of the hierarchy of being is the creator and sustainer of the world, the source of all life and good, of reason and law and love. God's most metaphysical account of Himself is given as He sends forth the Son to create our world in the midst of Chaos, "the Deep" (7. 168ff.):

Boundless the Deep, because I am who fill
Infinitude, nor vacuous the space.
Though I uncircumscrib'd my self retire,
And put not forth my goodness, which is free
To act or not, Necessitie and Chance
Approach not mee, and what I will is Fate.

This God is not the brute will seen by some critics from Sir Walter Raleigh to F. R. Leavis and William Empson; that idea, if usable at all, fits Calvin better than the anti-Calvinistic Milton. For Milton, as for his contemporary Henry More, the Cambridge Platonist, and for Newton also, God fills infinite space, although, in the lines quoted, He has not yet put forth His creative power upon Chaos. It is logical therefore that Milton denies the view that our world was created out of nothing and maintains that God created it out of his own substance (*CD* 15 : 17ff.). He is "uncircumscrib'd" (*Non circonscritto*, in Dante's* less metaphysical phrase in *Purgatorio* 11. 2) because he is free to act or not. Hence he is not to be confused with pagan or skeptical ideas of "Necessitie and Chance" and "Fate"; as a rational Deity, he creates a rational world.

The vast universe of Milton's imagining is both a spiritual and a spatial hierarchy, each reflecting the other. At the top is heaven*, the perfect abode of God, the Son, and the angels; below is Chaos*, the sea of raging elements, in the midst of which the newly created world (the Ptolemaic world of spheres) hangs from heaven by a golden chain; at the bottom is the newly created hell*, the fiery prison of Satan and his fellow rebels. These four regions are not completely separated; good and bad angels, and the Son and Sin and Death, move up and down from one to another, with some obvious restrictions. (The relations of spiritual and spatial and the patterns of movement have been developed by Isabel G. MacCaffrey and J. I. Cope.) The supreme movement is that of God down to His creatures and of the creatures toward God (N. Frye, *The Return of Eden* [1965], p. 50). A miniature of the whole dynamic design is the morning canticle of Adam and Eve (5. 153–208) —based chiefly on Psalm 148—in which the sun, the stars, mists and showers and winds, beasts and birds and fish, all are rising or falling, walking, creeping, flying, gliding, all participating in and celebrating the divine universal harmony (J. H. Summers, *The Muse's Method* [1962], pp. 71–86). The same energy of movement and growth animates the pictures of the creation in Book 7. Milton fully shares the traditional belief, represented by Aquinas* and Calvin alike, that "in contemplation of created things / By steps we may ascend to God" (5. 511–12).

In answer to Adam's questioning, Raphael (8. 66ff.) presents two theories of the physical world, the geocentric and the heliocentric (he omits the Tychonic compromise). Here as elsewhere Milton is noncommittal; but his use of the Ptolemaic scheme had the advantage of keeping "the sedentarie Earth" and its human pair in the middle of both the spatial and the spiritual world. Moreover, Milton shows no trace of disquiet over the Copernican view; and he is not—as the religious and scientific Pascal was—appalled by the eternal silence of infinite space, because, as we have seen, God fills it. Nor is Milton in the least disturbed by the revival of an ancient idea that caused perhaps more religious concern than Copernican doctrine, the idea of a plurality of inhabited worlds (3. 565–71; 8. 140–58). He had always responded with fervor to thoughts of both plenitude and control. The ordinarily nonmystical poet is kindled into half-mystical ecstasy by contemplation of "Holy Light" and the "Starry dance" of the planets in their everlasting order —which he invokes as a parallel to the "Mystical dance" of the angels before God's throne (5. 618–27). Thinking of the unity and harmony of this vast ordered universe, in which all creatures and things are related and interdependent, we understand why earth and nature groan when ideal order is disrupted by the sin of Adam and Eve.

Such elements of belief and thought as have been touched on here must be recognized by readers of *PL* (just as readers of Yeats and Eliot and Joyce do not grudge the necessity of homework). But the modern impact of the poem at once subsumes and transcends particulars. Modern readers, accustomed to an outer and inner world of confusion and disorder, are or should be well qualified to respond to Milton's presentation of confusion and disorder partly overcome, not without suffering and loss. However remote his beliefs and postulates may be from ours, he does not impose a factitious order upon human experience. His characters represent in various forms and degrees the weaknesses and the true or fallacious strengths that make up human beings in all ages. If for some readers Milton's archetypal myth of the human condition is disabled by its Christian frame, it may still be said that his vision remains potent in combining a passion for freedom with a passion for discipline, in proclaiming both the dignity and the responsibility of individual man. The religious conception of "pride," as treated in *PL*, needs no great extension to embrace the modern scientific *hubris* from which even scientists have been turning away (some time after other people). A number of modern writers and some events of modern history have brought back to life ideas of the Fall of man, of damnation and hell, not as an obsolete dogma but as a fall continually reenacted, a hell continually re-created; and that is what Milton himself saw, in his way, a perpetual fall but also a possible recovery. Hell, Chaos, Eden, and Heaven are not merely places but states of mind, and hell can be felt in Eden. We may pass by here the old question of the hero of *PL* —whether the Son or Adam or both together; Milton's assertion of eternal Providence becomes a "mythic" parable of the nature and achievement of true heroism, and that keeps the poem, for all its vast range and apparent remoteness, at the center of human experience.

PL has such simplicity and complexity, such unity in multiplicity, that both the grand design and narrative details completely and minutely embody and express the controlling theme; it follows that various critics' diagrams of the structure have an inevitable basic agreement. Arthur Barker, invoking neoclassical theory of the epic as drama, has seen the ten-book *PL* of 1667 falling logically into five acts of two books each. (We may remember that the third of Milton's early drafts for an allegorical drama was divided into five acts.) Barker suggests that the twelve-book structure gave more prominence to man's restoration and changed "a tragic pattern into the threefold pattern of a divine comedy, underlining the intention expressed in the opening invocation by throwing into clearer relief the adaptation and modification of the Virgilian pattern," that is, "three movements of four books apiece," turning respectively on Satan, the Son, and Man (*Philological Quarterly* 28 [1949]: 17–30; repr. in *Milton: Modern Essays in Criticism,* ed. Barker [1965]). A. S. P. Woodhouse saw "the crisis of the human action, which is the subject of the poem, . . . framed by the narrative of the past and the narrative of the future," so that "we have the patterned series: Satan defeated in heaven by Christ, Satan victorious on earth over Adam, Satan defeated at last by Christ, who is the second Adam" (*University of Toronto Quarterly* 22 [1952–53]:109–27). Isabel MacCaffrey sums up "the main configuration of the poem" as "from deep Hell up to the Mount of God, and down again to the 'subjected Plaine' of fallen earthly life" (*Paradise Lost as "Myth"* [1959], p. 59; cf. N. Frye, *The Return of Eden*

[1965], pp. 18–21; J. T. Shawcross, *Studies in Philology* 62 [1965]: 696–718, and his essay in *New Essays on Paradise Lost,* ed. T. Kranidas [1969]; E. Sirluck, *Paradise Lost: A Deliberate Epic* [1967], pp. 11–13).

The rapidly multiplying books of modern criticism have ample space for sophisticated discussion of the inexhaustible subtleties of *PL,* but here perhaps the best or the only course is the simplest: to follow the story as it unfolds, with occasional pauses over some main features. We may start, however, with what is chronologically the earliest event, as given in Raphael's recital to Adam: God's proclamation of His Son as His "great Vice-gerent" to whom "shall bow / All knees in Heav'n" (5. 600–615). On the literal plane the proclamation is a dramatic device to inaugurate the epic action; metaphorically, it is a manifestation to the angels of their own creative principle, the Word (N. Frye, p. 33). It stirs envy and anger in the archangel Satan, who "thought himself impaird" (like Macbeth at King Duncan's naming his son Malcolm as Prince of Cumberland). Pretending commands from God, Satan draws off "the third part of Heav'ns Host" to his seat in the north and rouses them (all but the faithful Abdiel) to rebellion. The ensuing three-day battle is ended by the Son, who, sent forth in "The Chariot of Paternal Deitie," embodies divine order and power. The rebel angels are driven through a gap made in the wall of heaven and fall through Chaos into the hell prepared for them. Milton's hell is far from its traditional place inside the earth.

Following the epic method of the plunge *in medias res,* the poem, after the invocation and exordium, begins when Satan and "his horrid crew" have for nine days and nights been "rowling in the fiery Gulfe / Confounded though immortal." Satan—fully pictured as he moves to the burning shore—rallies and reviews his legions, whose leaders are described in terms of their future roles as heathen deities. "Thir Glory witherd," they are still loyal to "thir great Sultan"

(a significant word), and he feels deep compassion for the fate he has brought upon them. But his speech to them, like his previous speeches, is a defiance of God and an exhortation to revenge. Mulciber (Hephaestus, Vulcan) directs the magical building of the palace of Pandemonium*, an edifice which, with its artifice and glitter, is a meretricious imitation of heaven. The leaders' grand debate yields diverse proposals, from direct renewal of war to passive acceptance of their lot. The debate is wholly pragmatic; there is no recognition that evil has been overcome by good. Earlier, in his second speech to Beelzebub (1. 162–65), Satan had acknowledged the true nature of the conflict and, in avowing his own aims, had indirectly declared God's, and also, in part, Milton's own view of his theme:

> If then his Providence
> Out of our evil seek to bring forth good,
> Our labour must be to pervert that end,
> And out of good still to find means of evil.

In the debate, the final proposal, put forth by Beelzebub but devised by Satan, is the most subtle kind of revenge, to corrupt the inhabitants of God's new creation, the earth. Satan alone is brave enough to volunteer for such a perilous expedition into the unknown; and he does not minimize its dangers.

His first stop is at the gates of hell, guarded by the foul monsters Sin and Death. Here begins the poem's one thread of allegory (as distinguished from symbolism). When Satan, in heaven, conceived of revolt, Sin had sprung from his head (obviously and ironically like the goddess of wisdom—and war—in Greek myth); and Death was the offspring of Satan's amorous dalliance with her (cf. James 1:15: "Then when lust hath conceived, it bringeth forth sin; and sin, when it is finished, bringeth forth death"). This allegory—to be continued later in the poem—was censured by such neo-classical critics as Addison, Voltaire*, and Johnson*, but for moderns it is a startling success: it shows the "heroic" Satan in his real setting and relations and, especially, it is a grisly counterpart to the Trinity and the generation and enthronement of the Son—as in Sin's triumphant anticipation, with its delayed and shocking adjective: "I shall reign / At thy right hand voluptuous." Meanwhile Satan's followers divert themselves with "epic games" or song or vain philosophic debate or exploration of hell; both their restless activities and the physical scenes reflect "A Universe of death," inward and outward. These first two books, in narrative, description, and dramatic speeches, are a magnificent display of the poet's sustained energy of imagination, language, and rhythm. And the preeminent figure is at once a grandly "heroic" leader and the embodiment of egoistic pride and passion, a spurious deity strong only in evil; the two books as a whole expose a false substitute for the harmony, joy, and true freedom of heaven.

The great invocation to Light (Bk. 3) establishes the blind poet's claim to tell of things invisible, effects a transition from the lurid darkness of hell to the radiant purity of heaven, and creates an atmosphere of holy awe that prepares for the heavenly council, an obvious contrast to the council in hell. We have already taken some account of God's outline of man's situation and destiny, his freedom, his fall, and—through the self-sacrifice of the Son—his redemption. Milton's whole presentation of God has offended many of his readers—although the finest critic among them, Coleridge*, thought his strong biblical anthropomorphism "very wise" (*Coleridge on the Seventeenth Century*, ed. R. F. Brinkley [1955], pp. 590–91; *The Romantics on Milton*, ed. J. A. Wittreich [1970], p. 278). Some critics, invoking Dante for contrast, have thought it a strategic blunder to make the Deity a speaking character at all, though God would seem to be, in a poem on the epic pattern, the inevitable expounder of His own authority and judgments. To the complaint that, in the midst of the poetic richness of *PL*, God's speeches are singularly flat and prosaic, the cogent answer is that Milton's rev-

erence for God and Christian truth required the Deity's utterance to be bare, unadorned statement—a principle noted by Coleridge and developed by various modern critics, for example, Arnold Stein (*Answerable Style* [1953], pp. 127–29); Irene Samuel (*Publications of the Modern Language Association* 72 [1957]; repr. in *Milton*, ed. Barker); T. Kranidas (*The Fierce Equation* [1965], pp. 130ff.); Stanley E. Fish (*Surprised by Sin: the Reader in Paradise Lost* [1967], pp. 57ff.); I. G. MacCaffrey, on the theme of Book 3 (*New Essays on Paradise Lost*, ed. Kranidas [1969]). Yet Milton is quite able at times to suggest the mystery and majesty of God—"Dark with excessive bright thy skirts appeer" (3. 380). Evil characters, of course, are always much easier to draw than good ones, and it was still more difficult, even for a God-intoxicated poet, to render the dynamic perfection of heaven, although, along with the loving heroism* of the Son, much is achieved through the use of light and movement and ecstatic song, the beauty of harmonious order.

Of God's legalism something was said above, but a little more is necessary here, at the point in the poem where it chiefly appears. We must remember that God is the source not only of life and good but of moral law, partly revealed, partly discovered by the right reason of man, and law has an inherent degree of rigor. As for Milton's method, he did some harm to his God by creating celestial drama, by dividing the attributes of Deity between the Father and the Son: God is the Absolute, the Unmoved Mover, while the Son—the dramatic antagonist of Satan—is the voice of love and mercy, and his speeches have a distinctive tone and rhythm (Summers, *Muse's Method*; cf. C. A. Patrides, *Journal of English and German Philology* 64 [1965]; H. Mac-Callum, on the role of the Son, in *Paradise Lost: A Tercentenary Tribute*, ed. B. Rajan [1969]). The effect of such a division, at least on minds averse to any notion of absolutes, is to make God seem merely harsh in contrast to the Son—and

Milton takes pains to have God express agreement, prior agreement, with the Son's compassion for sinful man. To come back to the heavenly council and the satisfaction of justice, the Son alone volunteers to die for man's redemption, as Satan alone had volunteered to compass man's ruin. "So Heav'nly love shall outdoo Hellish hate." God glorifies His Son's self-sacrifice and looks forward to his ultimate reign as king, to his judging mankind at the last day; after that there will be no need of kingship.

From the heavenly council we turn back to the voyaging Satan. Landing on the outer shell of the newly created world, he flies down through spheres and stars to the sun and thence to the earth. There he bitterly apostrophizes the sun, whose light recalls the lost glory of heaven (and Milton's very different apostrophe to light in the opening of Bk. 3). Here, for once, Satan's character is given a tragic dimension. In contrast with his earlier "heroic" harangues to his followers, he is now, when alone, tortured by a conscience. In a soliloquy—which partly reminds us of Marlowe's Faustus—Satan condemns his revolt as severely as God himself could have done; and whereas he had earlier boasted of the freedom of hell and his sovereignty there, he now finds himself a prisoner: "Which way I flie is Hell; my self am Hell"—a pregnant reminder of Milton's supreme concern with states of mind and soul. However, pride forbids repentance, and, with the simple and terrible resolve, "Evil be thou my good," be makes his way into Eden. Although he has revealed tragic possibilities, they are to be dissolved by his further self-degradation; at most he may perhaps be called "a tragic villain" (Stein, p. 50).

It was a grand stroke of irony that Milton should delay his picture of the earthly paradise until we enter it with Satan and view it with his malevolent eyes and our own. The scene and symbol of man's happy innocence, which, in a "straight" presentation, might have been only a lush pastoral vision, lies from the start under the shadow of its destroyer.

But this is only one arresting example of a comprehensive way in which Milton's epic goes beyond its predecessors : since —like Sophocles and others—he is telling a story universally known, he can envelop his two groups of opposed characters in dramatic irony on a grand scale (to be distinguished of course from the conscious ironies of various speakers; and heavenly beings remain above the author's irony). Thus, although Satan, chiefly in the soliloquy already noticed, can recognize the difference between good and evil, as a rule he and his fellows rebel and fight and plan revenge without any understanding that God and goodness are ultimately invincible—even though the corrupt Satan does succeed in corrupting man. If the poet's depiction of the doomed Satan in his heroic postures is harshly ironic, he is compassionate in his ironic depiction of Satan's victims; Adam and Eve likewise are ignorant of the future, and we register the various results of their failures of insight, constancy, and action, which multiply as they approach their Fall. A further idea, present to Addison and Johnson, has been strongly urged by Fish (*Surprised by Sin*) : that Milton's irony takes in his readers too, that their spiritual and moral capacity is being tested at the same time as Adam's and Eve's, since they may reveal their fallen state by sharing impulses and ideas that they should reject. Certainly many of Milton's older critics, and a few modern ones, might stand as conspicuous examples.

To return to Satan's entry into Eden, the successive animal and other similes that attend his progress are not at all a new and deliberate debasement of a grand figure; they are, like his involvement with Sin and Death, reminders of his real self, now shorn of the half-spurious grandeur he had displayed in hell. All his base passions are kindled by the sight—which is also our first real sight—of Adam and Eve, and he turns into something between Richard III and Iago as, while pretending pity, he gloats over his prey and enjoys his own sardonic irony (4. 375ff.) :

League with you I seek,
And mutual amitie so streight, so close,
That I with you must dwell, or you with me
Henceforth . . . ; Hell shall unfold,
To entertain you two, her widest Gates,
And send forth all her Kings. . . .

The problem of preparation for the Fall is handled with great skill : Adam and Eve must preserve their ideal innocence and yet must be shown as vulnerable, so that the Fall, when it comes, will seem a logical climax, not a surprise. To that end Milton supplies hints of increasing significance. Eve in her first speech is the ideal wife, but, in recalling her first experience of living, she tells how she had (like Narcissus) admired her own beauty as reflected in a pool (4. 460ff.). She recalls too—with another veiled echo of Ovid, this time of Apollo and Daphne—how Adam had pursued her. Both Eve's vanity and Adam's passion are quite natural and innocent, but the possibility of weakness is registered. Ideal love in an ideal world is celebrated in Eve's pastoral speech (4. 635–58); and Milton goes out of his way to stress the purity and rightness of their physical relations in contrast with romantic and promiscuous lust. From overhearing their talk of the forbidden tree Satan has already (4. 512ff.) formed a plan of campaign : he will appeal to the desire for knowledge that will make the pair "Equal with Gods." And the poet's benediction on their nuptial sleep ends with a compassionate wish : "O yet happiest if ye seek / No happier state, and know to know no more"—an echo of Virgil's praise of humble Italian farmers who are content with their lot (*Georg.* 2. 458). With all his upholding of conscious, rational righteousness, Milton reveals at times a nostalgic yearning for a world of unconscious, primitive innocence.

Beginning his campaign, Satan, "Squat like a Toad, close at the eare of Eve," sets about infecting her mind with ambition. In the morning she tells Adam of a disturbing dream (5. 28ff.) : obeying a voice she thought Adam's, she had gone forth, soon found herself at the forbidden tree, saw its fruit eaten by an angel-like figure who exhorted her to eat and become a goddess, and, doing so, she had soared aloft with him. Awake, she is relieved to find it a dream, and she is soothed by by Adam's lecture on dream psychology. But the drama, apparently Milton's invention, is a significant step toward the Fall : it is or should be a warning to both; it involves the main motive of ambition and the minor one of appetite and is an involuntary mental preenactment of the Fall; and, though Eve's waking reaction attests her present conscious innocence, in her uncensored dream her initial horror had given place to full enjoyment—without Adam—of her supposedly godlike exaltation.

At this point Milton combines two epic conventions best exemplified in the *Aeneid* : the retrospective account of events that preceded the opening of the poem and the divine admonition delivered to the protagonist. Raphael is sent from heaven expressly to warn Adam that continued happiness depends on obedience to God; his will, though free, is mutable and exposed to temptation. The naked, innocent pair rejoice in entertaining their celestial visitor at a picnic, and the question of angelic substance and digestion leads into the important metaphysical statement noticed above. Raphael's narrative of the past, in satisfaction of Adam's curiosity, opens with the first of several apologies—really the poet's—for the rendering of heavenly things in terms accommodated to human minds : in other words, the stories of the war in heaven* and the creation are more mythic and symbolic than literal.

The cause and outcome of Satan's revolt we observed at the start. The war is described in concrete epic terms. Satan appears both as a wicked pretender to divine authority ("Th'Apostat in his Sun-bright Chariot sate / Idol of Majestie Divine"; 6. 100–101) and, in his punning* exchanges with Belial about the artillery he has invented. as a cynical professional soldier. Apart from its grand climax, the onset of the Son, the war has often been censured as too unrealistic for an epic and too realistic for a spiritual symbol. But in one persuasive interpretation the war is seen as a kind of monstrous burlesque in which realism or materialism plays a grotesque and ironic part (A. Stein); it has also been taken as a typological "shadow of things to come, and more particularly . . . of this last age of the world and of the Second Coming of Christ" (W. G. Madsen, *From Shadowy Types to Truth* [1968], p. 111). Certainly, for both Adam and the reader, the war is an object lesson on the violence unleashed by the egoistic lust for power that would overturn divine order, all order.

After heaven has been purged of destructive anarchy, Milton, at this central point in the poem, turns to the great work of peace, the creation of our world and man. Raphael again reminds Adam of the difficulty of describing divine acts and warns him against intemperance in the quest for knowledge. He then proceeds with his account of the six days' work. As Satan had created evil out of good, God creates good out of evil. The Son, as usual, is God's executive agent, though presented as the triune Godhead, "The King of Glorie in his powerful Word / And Spirit coming to create new Worlds." The description of order imposed upon Chaos is one of Milton's most impressive passages, and hardly less so is the quieter picture of the Son's triumphal return to heaven after he has accomplished his task "Answering his great Idea" (the Platonic word is significant). In his account of creation Milton takes in another epic or semi-epic genre, the hexaemeral, but his version stands alone. The theme of fecundity had always stirred his imagination; he had already given it full expression in his description of Eden and distilled it in the exuberant lines on Raphael's arrival there (5. 291ff.): "A Wilderness of sweets; . . . / Wilde above Rule or Art; enormous bliss." So the picture of creation, abundantly expanded from Genesis, is filled with the poet's sensuous excitement in the manifold burgeoning of life. Raphael ends with a

repetition of his earlier warning: God's worshipers, created in his image, will be "thrice happie if they know / Thir happiness, and persevere upright."

Raphael's final phrase, as he invites further questioning—"not surpassing human measure"—is warranted by what follows in Book 8. The structure of the world leads Adam—with what may be called a touch of presumption, in comparison with his hitherto exemplary humility—to question the divine economy: would it not be better for the tiny earth, with its two inhabitants, to revolve instead of getting its light and darkness from the revolutions of the vast firmament? Raphael's scientific answer, while appropriate in an epic of cosmic scope, is much less important than his injunction about temperance in the quest of knowledge, the necessity of keeping first things first, that is, the conduct of life. Then Adam's story of his experience, while a natural sequel to Raphael's story of creation, reinforces, from a very different angle, the point that issued from astronomy and constitutes another stage in the preparation for the Fall. Adam ends with a eulogy of Eve which, in its mounting extravagance, must make any understanding reader anticipate Raphael's frown. Eve, says Adam, aroused new and overpowering passion: has Nature—that is, the Creator—failed in making him so subject to a being admittedly inferior, mentally and physically, to himself? In thus abdicating his higher responsibility ("Authority and Reason on her waite"), in putting a creature between himself and God, Adam is guilty, if not of idolatry, at least of intemperance. A man's love for his wife, much more than astronomical knowledge, is commendable in itself, but Adam has got his priorities confused; and his defensive response to the angel's rebuke does not annul the effect of his previous confession. He is right-minded, but his vulnerability is far more apparent than it was before.

In Book 9 Satan, who had been expelled from Eden by Gabriel, returns to carry out his plan. Just before he enters the serpent he has a midnight soliloquy that we link with his earlier address to the sun. Now, in self-pity, he finds ease only in evil, though he recoils from "foul descent" into a serpent, "This essence to incarnate and imbrute, / That to the hight of Deitie aspir'd" (the word "incarnate" recalls the Son, particularly 3. 315). As for Adam and Eve, they develop the most sustained drama in a notably dramatic epic : in their mode of speech, as in their thoughts and feelings, they become less and less regal, more and more human, as their first disagreement warms up. Trouble begins with Eve's self-willed proposal that they work apart and accomplish more, without amorous interludes—a proposal not in accord with their appointed way of life and love. Adam's overprotectiveness rouses Eve to somewhat shrill insistence on her ability to look after herself. Adam, now more tactful, says that her presence is a support to him. But Eve grows still more self-assertive; she misapplies the argument of *Areop*, which was written in and for a fallen world, and, as Adam tells her, she is disregarding God's will and warning. Indeed, Adam anticipates what is to happen, that reason may be deceived by "some faire appeering good." However, he surrenders and she goes off, "like a Wood-Nymph light" (the word "light" may be deliberately ambiguous), and the poet breaks out in pity for "much deceav'd, much failing, hapless *Eve*." Thus the serpent, luckily for him, finds her alone. In a beautiful variation on the earlier allusion to Proserpine (quoted below), she is described as upstaying the flowers, "Her self, though fairest unsupported Flour, / From her best prop so farr, and storm so nigh." Her beauty disarms even Satan, for the moment. Then, catching her attention, he addresses her with a sonneteer's flattery. Eve's astonishment at his ability to speak gives him his cue : from a wondrous fruit he has gained new powers. Led to the forbidden tree, Eve, "yet sinless," recoils, citing God's prohibition. Satan, "with shew of Zeale and Love / To Man," cunningly apostrophizes the "Sacred, Wise, and Wisdom-giving Plant,"

from which he has not suffered death but won new life : God only wants to keep his creatures low, when they might become "as Gods / Knowing both Good and Evil as they know."

The "credulous" Eve, soliloquizing, is completely taken in by Satan's arguments. She plucks and greedily gorges on the fruit, with "expectation high / Of knowledg, nor was God-head from her thought," "And knew not eating Death." (Celebrating God's exaltation of the Son, the angels had quaffed "immortalitie and joy" : 5. 638.) In this state of *hubris* and corruption, Eve goes on to practical reflection : perhaps "Our great Forbidder" has not seen her; shall she share her "change" with Adam or make herself his equal, or even superior, by keeping "the odds of Knowledge" to herself, "for inferior who is free?" (This was the motive of Satan's revolt.) But what if God ends her life and Adam lives on with another Eve? For wholly selfish reasons, she decides to have Adam share with her "in bliss or woe." So subtle is Milton's portrayal of Eve that we read her conclusion—"So dear I love him, that with him all deaths / I could endure, without him live no life"—with arresting uncertainty as to how far she is telling the truth, how far deceiving herself.

Paying to the tree the reverence she had denied to God, Eve returns with a bough of fruit to Adam (who has woven a garland of flowers to adorn her hair), and shows her acquisition of godlike knowledge by beginning with a lie : "Thee I have misst, and thought it long. . . ." She has, of course, been having the time of her life. As, "with Countnance blithe," she pours out her tale and, with false reasons, urges him to eat, Adam's garland "Down drop'd, and all the faded Roses shed." His first horror gives place, in his mind, to the resolve to die with her. All readers feel, as Milton felt, the anguish in Adam's imagining lovely Eden as, without Eve, "these wilde Woods forlorn." Then, addressing her, he argues, in her and Satan's way, that God may not punish them, that they may become gods; at any rate he will live or die with her. The declaration evokes from Eve a fine stroke of the poet's irony, "O glorious trial of exceeding Love"—a line that, in itself, would at once suggest Christ's self-sacrificing love for man (indeed, Milton had so used "exceeding love" in his early *Circum*). Adam is easily persuaded to eat the fruit, "Against his better knowledge, not deceav'd, / But fondly overcome with Femal charm" (cf. 1 Tim. 2 : 14). Good liberals applaud Adam's human loyalty to Eve and condemn Milton (not to mention Milton's God) for implicitly condemning it; but such liberals would be the first to condemn the same lack of principle in the political sphere—"My country, right or wrong."

The "intoxicated" pair now

> swim in mirth, and fansie that they feel
> Divinitie within them breeding wings
> Wherewith to scorne the Earth.

(The image of wings may parody the Platonic ascent of the virtuous soul : cf. *Mask* 374ff., *Phaedrus* 246ff.) But supposedly superhuman knowledge engenders only subhuman lust. Recalling the beauty of "Wedded Love" in their days of innocence, we can hardly repress a shudder at the levity with which Adam now sees Eve as only a sexual object—and she him likewise; and Milton ends Adam's speech (9. 1029–33) with a conscious echo of the sensual invitations of Paris to Helen and Zeus to Hera in the *Iliad* (3 and 14).

Waking from gross sleep, the one-time "Lords of the World" move from shame and remorse to angry recriminations. There is sorrow in heaven for the fulfillment of what had been foretold, and the Son is sent down to pass judgment; here Milton somewhat expands Genesis with little change. Sin and Death, now freed from hell to prey on earth, build a causeway through Chaos to make passage henceforth easy for themselves and the fallen engels—a parody of Creation. Satan, entering Pandemonium "In shew Plebeian Angel militant / Of lowest order" (the dictator's flair for the theatrical, as Tillyard said), gives a self-glorifying report of his success. There follows an anticlimactic and more than Ovidian metamorphosis : Satan, and then his followers, are transformed into hissing serpents, which feed on fruit that turns to ashes. In the universe above, the world of eternal spring, which had felt the wounds of the primal sin, is changed to our world of cold and heat and storm, of war and death among beasts, birds, and fish. Nature is fallen as well as man. This change, following the humanization—or degradation—of Adam and Eve, is a large step from the golden age into history.

In a long soliloquy (10. 720–844) the despairing Adam, stretched on the cold ground, laments his lot, his alienation from God and the curses his posterity will heap upon him; he arraigns divine justice for imposing "terms too hard" and longs for immediate death. But finally, absolving God, he blames only himself and "that bad Woman." Being thus wrought up, when she appears he bitterly repels her first "Soft words." Milton had a problem in the presentation of Eve : she must be the first sinner and the seducer of Adam, yet she must not fall too low to be restored to her dignity as mother of the human race. Much of that restoration is accomplished by her initiating reconciliation as she had initiated sin, by the penitent words and faltering rhythm of her first speech, the rhythm, as Joseph Summers says, of the Son, the voice of love. In tears she

> at his feet
> Fell humble, and imbracing them, besaught
> His peace, and thus proceeded in her plaint.
> Forsake me not thus, *Adam,* witness Heav'n
> What love sincere, and reverence in my heart
> I beare thee, and unweeting have offended,
> Unhappilie deceav'd. . . .
>
> (10. 911–17)

She will appeal to God that His sentence may light on her alone.

Deeply touched, Adam is reconciled, and would, if he could, take all blame upon himself; they can only strive "In offices of Love, how we may light'n /

Each others burden in our share of woe." Thus the pair, humanized and estranged by sin, are humanized and reunited by a love sadder but richer than their idyllic honeymoon had been; but full regeneration is still to come. Eve, "recovering heart," proposes two solutions for their plight : either to nullify their legacy of woe to posterity by abstaining from intercourse ("which would be miserie / And torment less then none of what we dread" —a remarkable testimony to Milton's understanding of the strength of desire), or to frustrate "A long days dying" by suicide. Adam, though struck by Eve's sublime "contempt of life and pleasure," shows, as always, more religious concern and insight than Eve, whose concern is always with him. Evasion, he says, will not serve; they must go back to the place where sentence was passed and offer penitential prayers. So, under the working of "Prevenient Grace" (11. 3), they end Book 10 with a first upward step, an ending very different from the "mutual accusation" that ended Book 9. This lengthy outline of the Fall, however inadequate any outline is, may emphasize the fact that Milton did not spend his main interest or all his powers on the Satan of the early books.

God decrees (as in Genesis) that the remorseful but guilty and unreliable pair must be expelled from Eden, lest they eat of the Tree of Life and live forever in a fallen world (Frye, p. 81); and he despatches Michael to "send them forth, though sorrowing, yet in peace." Meanwhile Adam and Eve, as they go out to work, feel that their prayers have met with favor, but they see signs of an altered world, perhaps ill omens for them. Their reactions to Michael's message are typical : Eve is stricken by the loss of home and objects of her daily care, Adam by the loss of his accustomed communication with God. To Eve Michael says that she should think her native soil to be wherever her husband abides; to Adam he gives assurance that God is present not in one place but everywhere, "still compassing thee round / With goodness and

paternal Love." To confirm this, and to teach faith and patience, he has been sent to unfold the future : "good with bad / Expect to hear, supernal Grace contending / With sinfulness of Men." So, putting Eve to sleep, Michael takes Adam to the top of the highest hill in Paradise and presents things to come in a series of visions. This is the last large epic convention that Milton adapts to his special purposes, one that belongs to both the traditional heroic poem (as in the *Aeneid* 6 and 8 and *Gerusalemme Liberata* 17) and the hexaemeral genre. And it becomes a Christian parallel to the classical myth of decay after the golden age, though it does not end there.

The continuance of the original sin is shown in Cain's murder of Abel; in the pains and fatal diseases brought on by "ungovern'd appetite"; in the sensual allurements of a bevy of fair women who ensnare "the Sons of God"; in rapine and war and conquest, against which the righteous Enoch pleads in vain (11. 665ff.); then in the licentious corruptions of peace, which Noah cannot curb; and finally the flood overwhelms the multitude of the wicked. (Milton recalls Heb. 11 : 1–7, on Abel, Enoch, and Noah—men of faith in the line of Abdiel.) But Book 11 ends with the rainbow, a perpetual reminder of God's covenant :

> Day and Night,
> Seed time and Harvest, Heat and hoary Frost
> Shall hold thir course, till fire purge all things new,
> Both Heav'n and Earth, wherein the just shall dwell.

In Book 12, pausing "Betwixt the world destroy'd and world restor'd," Michael shifts from vision to narrative, mainly no doubt because the saving illumination to come must be more directly impressed upon Adam. Some time after the flood the spirit of conquest and tyranny revives in Nimrod. But with Abraham Israel emerges as God's chosen people; and then God delivers the Law to Moses. Throughout, Adam's misjudgments have been corrected by Michael, and his linking of many laws with many sins brings the fervent exposition of the superseding of the Law by the Gospel (12. 285ff.). The ultimate triumph of good in the birth, ministry, and death of Christ leads Adam to wonder—echoing a traditional paradox—if perhaps his Fall was fortunate in evoking this supreme manifestation of divine love.

Adam can now comprehend such love; but the idea of a fortunate fall as the climax of the epic argument gets more support from numerous recent critics than from Milton. Some other critics do not take Adam's exclamation—impulsive and oversimple, like his earlier judgments—as expressing the poet's view, which, as Books 11 and 12 amply show, is much more complex. In *PL* as in *Areop,* Adam fell into the "doom"—not the felicity— "of knowing good by evil" (*PL* 11. 84ff.; 4 : 310–11). God will ultimately bring good out of the evil of the Fall, but man, the good man, however cheered by the promise of redemption, must face trial and tribulation with Christian fortitude before he "is raised to a far more excellent state of grace and glory than that from which he had fallen" (*CD* 15 : 251). Even Christ's church will grow corrupt (12. 507ff.). Lines 535ff. are a grim picture of life in the Christian era, of a world "To good malignant, to bad men benigne," a world to be changed only at Christ's second coming. Adam's response is a statement of the true and sufficient knowledge he has received, a statement quietly moving in its substance and rhythm, of faith in obedient love of God and trust in His providence, in the practice of righteousness, humility, and constancy. This, replies Michael, is "the summe / Of wisdome," far beyond knowledge of nature or wealth or political power : if he acts in accord with the Christian virtues, especially love, "the soul / Of all the rest," Adam, though leaving Paradise, will possess a paradise within him, "happier farr."

Michael's instruction to Adam has been found long, heavy, and dull by a number of critics, from C. S. Lewis to Louis Martz, but what Lewis called "an untransmuted lump of futurity" has also had many able defenders. (Lists are given by two recent ones : John Reesing, *Milton's Poetic Art* [1968], p. 184; B. Rajan, *The Lofty Rhyme* [1970], pp. 168–69. Two other recent defenses are by Mary A. Radzinowicz, in *Approaches to Paradise Lost,* ed. Patrides, and G. M. Muldrow, *Milton and the Drama of the Soul* [1970]). If Milton's narrative and descriptive method here owes something to the scenes on the shields of Achilles and Aeneas (*Iliad* 18. 483–608; *Aeneid* 8. 620–728 : the latter are prophetical), the debt is small. His style for the most part is deliberately plain and bare, but his imaginative reason is deeply engaged; for these two books sum up all that the frustrated idealist had learned of the meaning of life and death, of the faith and fortitude and righteous happiness within the reach of fallen man. We have noted earlier that the view that the change from ten to twelve books had the effect of emphasizing the process of regeneration. Throughout the first ten books Milton had been able to relate his grand *exemplum* directly to the later life of man only through brief incidental allusions, similes, and comments. Now, the story becomes —apart from the survey of false religions in 1. 376ff.—the first segment of human history, and the reader identifies his knowledge and experience with that of Adam and his posterity. Moreover, Michael's presentation and his correcting of Adam's many failures of understanding constitute Adam's spiritual, moral, and social education, the process of illumination that, as we see from his last speech, makes him the first Christian. But the reader is also, however unconsciously, made to share the poet's experience and vision, and without the historical survey he would not know and feel the profound pessimism that Milton's own faith in Providence had to conquer and did conquer. Finally and most immediately, the marvelous conclusion would fail of its effect if it had come, say, at the end of Book 10, without the picture of the world into which Adam and Eve are to go—a revelation very far from the glorious prophecy Anchises gave to Aeneas; and of course here the climactic figure is not Augustus—or Astraea—but Christ.

The ending of the poem is the finest achievement of the master of perfect endings. Michael brings Adam down from the hill and awakens Eve, in whom his power had inspired comforting dreams: she can say to Adam "now lead on" in a spirit wholly different from the "Lead then" she had addressed to the serpent. The Cherubim, descending, glide over the plain as an evening mist "gathers ground fast at the Labourers heel / Homeward returning"—a homely, "un-Miltonic" simile that anticipates the daily toil of Adam and his sons. Led away by Michael, who disappears,

They looking back, all th' Eastern side beheld
Of Paradise, so late thir happie seat,
Wav'd over by that flaming Brand, the Gate
With dreadful Faces throng'd and fierie
    Armes:
Som natural tears they drop'd, but wip'd
    them soon;
The World was all before them, where to
    choose
Thir place of rest, and Providence thir guide:
They hand in hand with wandring steps and
    slow,
Through *Eden* took thir solitarie way.

Without venturing upon vain analysis, one may say that these simple narrative and pictorial lines suggest through every word and phrase the most subtle and moving interplay of sorrow and fear, hope and love. Adam and Eve are again "hand in hand," as in the days of happy innocence. Providence is their guide, yet they are alone, dependent on each other, going into an unknown world, a humble pair who have, in some measure, defeated Satan. "*Eden*"—a paradise within—is to be "rais'd in the wast Wilderness" (*PR* 1. 7). (The actual paradise will be swept away by the flood, to become "an Iland salt and bare, / The haunt of Seales and Orcs, and Sea-mews clang": *PL* 11. 834–35.) Even this bald outline of *PL* gives some notion of one prime and dynamic structural principle, the continual use of contrast, concrete or abstract, literal or

symbolic: good and evil, light and darkness, the Son and Satan, love and hate, creation and destruction, eternity and human time, life and death, humility and pride, obedience and disobedience, order and anarchy, liberty and servitude, reason and passion, love and lust, grace and nature, nature and artifice....

Although Milton's choice of the epic over the dramatic form gave him the full scope he needed, his subject involved difficulties that had not existed for Homer, that were somewhat troublesome for Virgil, and that became much more formidable for a biblical epic in the scientific and rationalistic climate of the later seventeenth century: that is, the use of the traditional mold of the heroic poem, concrete in its very nature, for themes of increasing abstraction. The everlasting war between good and evil, the Fall of Man and his means of redemption, and the significance of both for the temporal and eternal destiny of the human race, imposed new strains on the resources of the heroic poem, although for the most part Milton triumphantly surmounted them.

This epic development from Homer through Virgil to Milton brings up another but related kind of progressive change. Homer's narratives may be called impersonal and objective—in a relative degree of course, since complete objectivity could not operate in poetry of any kind. But the *Aeneid,* as countless readers and critics have felt, clearly reflects the temperament and philosophy of its author—"Thou that seëst Universal Nature moved by Universal Mind;/ Thou majestic in thy sadness at the doubtful doom of human kind." And in *PL,* as Anne Ferry in particular has fully shown (*Milton's Epic Voice: The Narrator in Paradise Lost* [1963]), the masterful personality, the strongly held beliefs and values, the controlling voice, stern, compassionate, exultant, of the poet are everywhere apparent, from the total theme down to the smallest detail, are felt, indeed, in every word—notably in the repetition of such key words as *fruit, taste, woe, merit, seed.*

Recent criticism, while it has brought new insight to the substance and art of *PL,* seems to have largely taken for granted the basic adaptations of the classical pattern and conventions; but these adaptations, however commonplace, are too central to be passed over. Milton's whole poetic career demonstrates both his instinct for working within an established convention and his instinct and power to re-create it. In *PL* he may be most original when he may seem to be merely imitating Virgil or Homer. While the form of *PL* was governed by Milton's subject and avowed purpose, and while the poem has many incidental Homeric echoes, in structure it is much closer to the *Aeneid* than to any other epic. (Some references were given above. Many adaptations of Virgil are discussed by D. P. Harding, *The Club of Hercules: Studies in the Classical Background of Paradise Lost* [1962]; cf. M. A. Di Cesare in *Milton Studies* 1 [1969].) *PL* is, even more than the *Aeneid,* a closely coherent story that never loses sight of its theme and its goal. One general parallel (whether or not Milton thought of it) is that, as the *Aeneid* depicts the fall of an old world in the east and the defeated hero's creation of a new world in the west, so in *PL* fallen man is enabled to rise again, to move toward salvation; "as in the *Aeneid,* the ending is the starting point renewed and transformed by the heroic quest of Christ" (N. Frye, p. 20).

The various structural conventions (partly noticed already) are also closest to those of the *Aeneid,* though some belong to epic tradition in general. All are given a new significance. Milton's Muse, Urania—the ancient Muse of astronomy had been elevated, especially by Du Bartas, into the Muse of religious poetry—is "Heav'nly," and Milton's several invocations, far from being literary formalities, are earnest prayers for divine inspiration. (The "Spirit" of 1. 17, etc., commentators have often taken as the Holy Spirit, the third Person of the Trinity, but Milton says—in *CD* 14 : 393–95—

that the Holy Spirit may not be invoked. Unless he is violating his own doctrine, his "Spirit"—to bypass numerous discussions—would seem to be "a personification of the various attributes of God the Father," as M. Kelley says in *This Great Argument,* p. 117; cf. *CD* 15 : 13.) Moreover, whereas Homer and Virgil had one major invocation at the beginning and occasional brief ones later, Milton's (except 1. 376) are all elaborate and have varied thematic and structural functions. The opening one arouses portentous expectations in linking the story to be unfolded with the creation of the world, and it links the poet with the author of Genesis. The invocation to Light (Bk. 3) heralds the change of scene from hell and the infernal debate to heaven and sets the tone for the heavenly council. Further, the idea of "Holy Light" elicits the poignantly personal lines on Milton's blindness, his continuing love of the classics and, above all, the Bible; but the personal is submerged in the impersonal, dramatic utterance of "the blind poet" who prays for the compensation of inward light. The prelude to Book 4, while not an appeal to the Heavenly Muse, is an anguished cry of horror and compassion evoked by Satan's approach to Eden. The invocation of Book 7, following the war in heaven, introduces the peaceful creation of the world, in particular the earth and man; and the poet, in the evil days of the Restoration, thinks of the fate of Orpheus. The invocation of Book 9, contemplating the Fall "and all our woe," contrasts that truly heroic theme with the martial and mundane themes of traditional epic and romance.

Plunging into the middle of things had of course been an epic device from Homer onward, but Milton's giving of his first two books to his cosmic villains, Satan and his fellows, was a highly original stroke. It was also, as critical history has shown, a hazardous one, although—not to mention Satan's age-old infamy—the poet had from the first moment presented his "heroism" as governed by evil pride and passion; he had no reason to anticipate the long sway of "Satanist" misinterpretation. It might not be overstrained to see a partial parallel (which Milton need not have had in mind) with the episode of Dido in Virgil's first and fourth books, since Dido is in some sense equivalent to Satan in leading the protagonist from the way of righteousness and providential design. At any rate, both poets have at times been charged with divided sympathies that have divided some readers' sympathies also.

Two large parts of the first two books illustrate Milton's enrichment of epic conventions. One is the roll-call of the fallen angels in 1. 376–521. The catalogue of ships in the second book of the *Iliad* is commonly skipped by modern readers. In *Aeneid* 7. 641ff. Virgil made such a roll-call more vivid through his embroidery of local associations, and more functional because his warriors are the followers of Turnus, the leader of resistance to Aeneas and to the divine plan; so Milton describes the chief devils, God's enemies, by anticipating their later roles as heathen deities, and his catalogue becomes a survey of the spread of idolatry through Palestine and the Middle East. As for the second convention, Milton's handling of the infernal debate has dwarfed the dozens of epic councils in the works of all his predecessors, including Virgil and Homer, thanks to his dramatic staging and the realistic and strongly differentiated characters revealed in the arguments, feelings, diction, syntax, and rhythm of his speakers. And since, apart from the superior though limited comprehension of Belial, they are all reasoning in ignorance of the real issue, the conflict between good and evil, the total effect of the debate is ironic.

We noticed before two other conventions, which have complementary functions and which, in Milton's treatment, occupy about a third of the poem. One is the narrative of earlier events. Here again there is an obvious progression: Odysseus's relating of his personal adventures; Aeneas's account of the fall of Troy and his company's wanderings in search of their destined home, a national theme; and, in *PL,* the story of the war in heaven and the Creation, told by an angel—whose message of warning to Adam and Eve links him with the celestial messengers of Homer and Virgil, particularly Hermes (Mercury), to whom Milton alludes (5. 285). The second convention, the prophetic survey of the future, is personal in the *Odyssey,* national and imperial in the *Aeneid* (6. 756–853, 8. 626–728), and, in *PL,* is the revelation to Adam of the course of Providence and the way of salvation.

One conspicuous element of the classical epic and of *PL* is the elaborate heroic simile. Similes in Homer, though they often picture violent actions, are perhaps most memorable when they give us vignettes of normal peaceful life as we read of war and death and perilous voyaging. Milton's similes are drawn from the most heterogeneous sources: his personal awareness of nocturnal hoodlumism and burglary in London and books of travel and history, nature and traditional folklore and the observations of Galileo*. Such items are occasional but important links between the remote fable and the actual world. They may give semi-realistic authenticity, or heightened mystery, to the unfamiliar or unknown, and they may carry or imply a moral judgment on character and action. And while Homeric similes may bear a loose general resemblance to whatever they are brought in to illustrate, Milton's commonly have an organic relevance, even in details, a relevance that may extend far beyond the immediate context.

We may note a few examples, simple and complex. In the pictures of Satan in the burning lake and moving toward the shore (1. 192ff.), his huge stature and power are at once validated and ironically undercut by allusions to those enemies of divine order, the Titans and Giants, and to the biblical Leviathan or whale (in medieval fables the devil, mistaken by mariners for a safe island); and traditional general comparisons—a shield like the moon, a spear like a mast—have specific particulars added (1. 286ff.). But these external similes, apart from latent irony, are much less imaginatively and emotionally charged than more original and dramatic ones that follow—as when the "Arch Angel ruind" is grand enough to be compared with the sun misted or partly eclipsed (1. 589ff.). Earlier, enveloped in fiery heat, the dauntless leader

> stood and call'd
> His Legions, Angel Forms, who lay intran'st
> Thick as Autumnal Leaves that strow the Brooks
> In *Vallombrosa,* where th' *Etrurian* shades
> High overarch't imbowr.
> (1. 300–304)

Milton's allusion to fallen leaves outdoes those of Homer, Virgil, and Dante, partly because the beauty of the "shady valley" Milton had seen in Italy, intensified by visual and rhythmical effects, makes an ironical contrast with the burning lake and its shore. Then the idea of a weltering multitude of warriors is reinforced by a much more elaborate simile, which piles up images of destruction and confusion in a picture of the Egyptian pursuers of the Israelites—a forcible reminder of God's punishment of the wicked.

For a total contrast in substance and impact, there are the mythological allusions that alone can evoke the incomparable loveliness of the earthly paradise, of the first unspoiled innocence of nature and man. Yet, as we have seen, the whole description of the garden is poignantly ironic because Satan is already there, and irony is concentrated in the most famous of all Milton's similes (4. 268–72):

> Not that faire field
> Of *Enna,* where *Proserpin* gathering flours
> Her self a fairer Floure by gloomie *Dis*
> Was gatherd, which cost *Ceres* all that pain
> To seek her through the world. . . .

Here an inspired conceit—Proserpine gathering flowers, herself a fairer flower gathered by the prince of darkness—becomes an unspoken anticipation of the fate of Eve; but no one can analyze the suggestions of beauty and frailty and loss

and "all that pain."

For Milton, as for Shakespeare and countless others, classical mythology provided what no other source could provide, concrete images of superhuman power or evil or perfection or beauty, images rich in accumulated meaning and associations. In the Christian context of *PL* such allusions may appear, as in secular poetry, without comment, or may often be branded as pagan fiction —though Milton the artist remains uninhibited. One superb example is the fall of Mulciber (Hephaestus, Vulcan) in 1. 738ff.:

> and how he fell
> From Heav'n, they fabl'd, thrown by angry *Jove*
> Sheer o're the Chrystal Battlements; from Morn
> To Noon he fell, from Noon to dewy Eve,
> A Summers day; and with the setting Sun
> Dropt from the Zenith like a falling Star,
> On *Lemnos* th' *Ægaean* Ile: thus they relate,
> Erring. . . .

The lines follow the pagan myth even while declaring its falsity, and they are a marvel—a gratuitous marvel—of pictorial art and still more of expressive changes in rhythm; the passage comes from the heart of a lover of beauty and it is quite remote from its half-comic source in Homer (*Il.* 1.590–94) in its romantic seriousness and idea of vast space. And "romantic" may be applied, along with "reductive" or "antiheroic," to the picture of the fallen angels crowding into the newly built palace of Pandemonium (1. 777ff.), where Milton blends reminiscences of classical myth, of the *Aeneid* (6. 451–54), and of *A Midsummer Night's Dream.* Mythological allusion is a kind of imaginative and moral shorthand in which Milton surpassed all other English —perhaps all other—poets.

A few old and a few modern critics have damned Milton's "grand style*" as if it were a kind of artificial and uniform brocade, mere magniloquence; and in or between the lines of the modern complaints lurks the assumption that all good poetry has been and should be colloquial in diction, syntax, and rhythm, an assumption that, of course, will not bear a moment's scrutiny. More perceptive critics, from C. S. Lewis to Christopher Ricks, have shown the real character of Milton's grand style. Obviously *PL* required—from a poet capable of achieving it—a style appropriate for a religious epic that embraced the whole history and destiny of man and a vast imagined universe, and whose characters were all divine and angelic except Adam and Eve. The texture of *PL* is stylized, as any long poem must be and as, in their different ways, the *Iliad, Odyssey,* and *Aeneid* are; but at the same time it is—often within a single passage—a mosaic of various styles, in keeping with the various characters and situations (including the comic). At its fullest and best, critical analysis cannot get very far into the essence of Milton's power, and here only a few headings can be set up; what matters is the sensitive reader's experience, however inarticulate.

To glance at a few obvious variations, the first book, dominated by Satan, is rich in vague images of lurid darkness and more precise images of martial and architectural splendor; in the second, the styles of the debaters range from the blunt forthrightness of Moloch the warrior to the sinuousness of Belial the intellectual. We noted above the contrast between the bare expository speeches of God, of Moral Law, and the compassionate tenderness of both language and rhythm in those of the Redeemer. In the sensuous descriptions of Eden and the process of Creation, of natural beauty and fecundity, pictorial energy partakes of religious delight in the divine handiwork. Adam and Eve at first address each other with a syntactical amplitude that betokens enjoyment of their power of speech and, above all, complete contentment and security—the ceremony of innocence. But when they begin to disagree, and when Eve, under the sway of the tempter, feels new desires for new experience, her exploratory debate with herself proceeds in short syntactical units and plain, direct language; her corruption can be measured by the distance between this mode of thought and her weaving and unweaving of an intricately ordered pastoral pattern in the asseveration of her love for Adam (4. 639–56). And their quarreling after the Fall is far from majestic. Finally, plainness of narrative style is the staple of Books 11 and 12, the outline of human history, much of it condensed from the Bible. Thus "stylization," while it does describe the poem as a whole, loses half its meaning when it permits such diversities of functional level and tone.

The grand style and devices for attaining it had been discussed and practised by Italian poets and critics (F. T. Prince, *The Italian Element in Milton's Verse*), and both in his sonnets, spread over some thirty years, and in his often impassioned and exalted prose Milton gave many signs of his mastery of such devices, of his approach to the style or styles perfected in *PL*. Perhaps the chief thing is the breaking up of the ordinary word order of prose, and this phrase, of course, covers an infinity of ways and degrees. Such deliberate "disorder" becomes, in Milton's hands, the most forceful and arresting kind of order. It includes the placing of words, phrases, and clauses for shades of emphasis, for parallelism or contrast, and such functional dislocation may be carried out with the freedom of an inflected language. (Janette Richardson has seen in such devices the strong influence of Virgil [*Comparative Literature* 14 (1962) : 321–31].) Along with this goes elliptical and muscular compression, which may disregard syntax for the sake of expressiveness. And there are other elements, such as allusive periphrasis, which is almost never mere inflation but rather is used to make a suggestive point, often one that adds an idea or a judgment. All these and other devices for achieving sublimity can succeed only when they become the natural mode of a supreme artist, and, as Dr. Johnson said, Milton's "natural port is gigantick loftiness." However, we must not forget that contrast is an instinctive principle of Milton's imagination and style, that much of his epic utterance is more or less straightforward, and that many of his most complex and sublime effects—as in the last lines of *PL*—are attained through the utmost simplicity of means.

The idea of hierarchy, of the great chain of being, which is so central in Milton's cosmic, religious, and ethical thought, works in his style also. Whereas poets in our time, in describing nature, strive for images and epithets never thought of before, Milton enjoys and seeks to share the high pleasure of recognition, of seeing every creature and thing performing its appointed function in the divine and universal order. Large examples are the pictures of Eden and the Creation, and smaller ones range from the morning canticle of Adam and Eve (5. 153–208) to the ascending list of sights denied to the blind poet (3. 40–44), which concentrates a total view of man and life in the culminating phrase, "human face divine." If in much neoclassical verse the principle of "general nature" yielded tame flatness, it does not in Milton, who, with or without added particulars, feels and communicates vitality. As F. T. Prince remarks (apropos of the swan in 7. 433–40), Milton gives a "triumphant demonstration, a conscious exhibition of the true nature of things" (*Approaches to Paradise Lost,* ed. Patrides, p. 59). Or, as Anne Ferry puts it, "The language of Satan and of fallen man unnaturally disjoins the unities of God's creation, while the metaphors of the inspired narrator, so to speak supernaturally recreate those unities" (p. 121).

One impressionistic prejudice, repeated for generations, is that the diction* of *PL* is so heavily Latinate that we sink under it. That is simply not true, as even the brief excerpts quoted here might serve to suggest. (E. M. Clark gave a precisely statistical refutation of the stubborn fallacy in *Studies in Philology* 53 [1956].) The occasional use of English derivatives in their original Latin sense had been an element in the language of poetry since

Spenser (to go no further back), and it appears in the supreme model of English English, Shakespeare—as in "Th' extravagant and erring spirit hies / To his confine." Moreover, Milton's Latinate words have various positive values. Thus "error," used of paradisal brooks (4. 239), means not only "wandering" but the prelapsarian purity of "rightness in wandering" (A. Stein, p.66; C. Ricks, pp. 110ff.). Abstract nouns may have far more power than concrete words : for example, "Magnificence" (2. 273), or "the Tree / Of prohibition" (9. 644–45 : Ricks, p. 76). Such words range from the mock-heroic ("expatiate," 1. 774) to the terms of Satanic or postlapsarian technology (6. 512ff., 10. 1070ff.). What gives Milton's English its supposedly un-English cast is rather, we have observed, his wresting of word order and syntax to manifold expressive purposes. Instead of administering dogmatic, schoolmasterish rebukes, hostile critics might better have been grateful that, as a stylist, Milton revealed a new world of resources in the language. And—as such critics do not recognize— in *PL* as in his other poems the meaning (whatever its latent subtleties) is almost never in doubt, whereas it very often is in Shakespeare.

The use of blank verse* for a heroic poem was in itself a bold innovation (which Milton defended in his short preface), and the blank verse of *PL,* in keeping with the style, created a new world of expressive rhythm. One main characteristic was what Milton in his preface spoke of as "the sense variously drawn out from one Verse into another." Thus the opening sentence of *PL* is of sixteen lines, only a few of them end-stopped. Throughout the poem—except where the flow is deliberately disturbed— we feel what C. S. Lewis described as "the enormous onward pressure of the great stream on which you are embarked" (*Preface,* p. 45). It is quite idle to contrast—to Milton's disadvantage—the blank verse of an epic with the blank verse of Shakespearian dialogue. Milton's epic orchestration, like his verbal texture, is stylized, but with the same wide range of flexibility. Within the frame of the decasyllabic line Milton took every conceivable liberty. Except for the purpose of illustrating such liberty, we must not scan his lines in terms of conventional metrical feet. While the norm is iambic, words and syllables are stressed or slurred or elided, speeded or retarded, singly or in bunches, in accordance with the intended sense and feeling. Thus in the first line, "Of Mans First Disobedience, and the Fruit," the second, third, fourth, sixth, and tenth syllables carry the stresses that emphasize the theme; or syllabic stresses may be evened out to suggest steady flight : "All night the dreadless Angel unpursu'd" (6. 1). The number of stresses is normally five but varies from four to the relentless eight of "Rocks, Caves, Lakes, Fens, Bogs, Dens, and shades of death" (2. 621). Because stresses and pauses vary in number, weight, and position, the variations and the underlying norm provide a continual interplay of surprise and recognition. A caesura may occur anywhere, even after the first syllable : in the invocation to Light, after "Seasons return, but not to me returns" (3. 41), the next line begins with "Day," poised by itself—a position and a pause that compel us to realize its full meaning. (Further, as Donald Davie has remarked, the word comes as a surprise, since we expect a season to be named.) The lines on Mulciber quoted above are a great example of change of pace (and "Dropt" illustrates Milton's frequent use of a forceful monosyllabic verb as the first word of a line : cf. 1. 45, etc.). Another superb example of change of pace is the passage in which the Son leaves heaven for the work of Creation : "They view'd" the turbulent sea of Chaos (an instance, by the way, of what Keats* called Milton's "stationing" of figures) and after the turbulent lines the Son imposes order: "Silence, ye troubl'd waves, and thou Deep, peace" (7. 216); and then a strong smooth flow of verse—not like the account of Satan's voyage—as the divine designer rides "Farr into *Chaos,* and the World

unborn." Such manipulation of rhythm and examples can only begin to suggest the aural sensitivity a reader must cultivate, and the best thing he can do is to read *PL* aloud. In no poem in the world is rhythm a more active and essential element of meaning. [DB]

PARADISE REGAINED. In 1671 Milton's *PR* was published together with *SA* in a slim octavo volume of 220 pages, by the same publisher, John Starkey, who had brought out Milton's *Brit* the previous year. No manuscript of the poem survives, so that this first (and only) edition published in Milton's lifetime constitutes the authoritative text.

By 1671 Milton had had the satisfaction of knowing that his longer epic had found an audience, whether fit or unfit, numerous enough to buy up the full issue of 1300 copies. It is not recorded whether Milton received for his new volume of poems a sum of money approaching the £10 he was paid for *PL*, but his nephew Edward Phillips testifies (*Life of Mr. John Milton,* 1694) that then as now *PR* had difficulty finding its own fit audience, being "generally censur'd to be much inferiour to the other." Phillips also records Milton's irate repudiation of such judgments—"He could not hear with patience any such thing when related to him"—and offers his own opinion that "possibly the Subject may not afford such variety of Invention, but it is thought by the judicious to be little or nothing inferiour to the other for stile and decorum."

There is no firm evidence establishing the circumstances and date of composition of *PR,* though surviving contemporary records indicate a general belief that the poem was written just after *PL*. Edward Phillips assigns its composition to the period 1667–1670, though as a matter of inference rather than evidence : "*Paradise regain'd* . . . doubtless was begun and finisht and Printed after the other was publisht, and that in a wonderful short space considering the sublimeness of it." If we may believe the often-repeated tale of the inception of the poem recounted by Milton's friend Thomas Ellwood* in his autobiography, *The History of the Life of Thomas Ellwood* (1714), the period of composition must fall between 1665 and 1670. Ellwood states that after reading the manuscript of *PL* late in 1665 he had observed to Milton, "Thou hast said much here of paradise lost, but what hast thou to say of paradise found?" To this statement Milton reportedly made no answer but "sat some time in a muse." Ellwood further reports that at some unspecified time after he returned to London upon the cessation of the plague in 1666 Milton showed him *PR* (whether printed or in manuscript is not clear) and "in a pleasant tone" said to him, "This is owing to you; for you put it into my head by the question you put to me at Chalfont, which before I had not thought of." The story, with its dubious exaltation of Ellwood as surrogate for Milton's muse, has a somewhat apocryphal quality. Yet there is no reason to believe that the incident was invented out of whole cloth; at the very least it provides additional evidence of contemporary opinion as to the date of composition.

Most modern Milton scholars have accepted this dating and many of them (e.g., James Holly Hanford, *Studies in Philology* 15 [1918]: 244–63; E. M. W. Tillyard, *Milton* [1930]; Douglas Bush, *English Literature in the Earlier Seventeenth Century, 1600–1660* [1962]) find that *PR* presents a culminating statement of the great themes and issues that exercised Milton for a lifetime—temptation, the true heroism, the paradise within. But the traditional dating has been challenged by some scholars. On the basis of certain statistically tabulated prosodic tests—for example, use of terminal and medial pauses, treatment of polysyllables, percentage of feminine or pyrrhic endings— John Shawcross has concluded (*Publications of the Modern Language Association* 76 [1961]: 345–58) that the main speech sections of Books 1, 2, and 4 of *PR* were written before *PL,* and the induction

to Book 1 and Book 3 added later, as the work was revised for publication. Without appealing to statistics but rather to the preponderance of dramatic speech in *PR* as compared to *PL,* as well as to some few inconsistencies in the text, Parker, *Milton,* has speculated that *PR* was first conceived as a drama and begun probably about 1656–1658 before Milton started to write *PL* as an epic, and that it was then revised as a narrative poem sometime within the period 1665–1670.

But arguments for chronological development based upon observed trends in prosodic and stylistic features without consideration of the demands of genre and theme have not met with widespread acceptance. Indeed, insisting that statistics on prosody must be read with attention to the interrelation of form and matter, Ants Oras has elaborated and extended his own seminal statistical study (*SAMLA Studies in Milton* [1953]) in a new monograph that strongly reaffirms the traditional chronology, *Blank Verse and Chronology in Milton* (1966). He finds that Milton's use of adjectives and adjectival participles, syllabized and unsyllabized "-ed" endings, placement of monosyllabic and other adjectives before and after nouns, use of metrical pauses, and use of polysyllables all combine to reinforce a credible pattern of artistic evolution from largely Elizabethan beginnings in *Mask,* to Milton's creation of a distinctively magnificent epic style in *PL* 1–6, to the gradual emergence of a more austere, less ornamented style in the final books of *PL,* culminating in a further development and extension of this last style in *PR* and *SA.*

The only major source for *PR* is the biblical account of the Temptation* of Christ in the wilderness, recounted in a few short verses in Matthew 4:1–11, Mark 1:12–13,, and Luke 4:1–13. Probably in part for dramatic effectiveness, Milton followed Luke's sequence of Christ's three major temptations (stones, kingdoms, tower) rather than the more often cited Matthew sequence (stones, tower, kingdoms). Moreover, Luke, and also Mark, provide some basis for the poem's nonbiblical temptations by intimating that Christ was tempted throughout the full forty days, an intimation that led Calvin* and some other exegetes to the conclusion that Christ underwent many temptations, of which only the most important were recorded in the Gospels. On this slender basis Milton constructed an extended narrative account of Christ's temptation in four books, 2,070 blank verse lines.

In contrast to the abundance of poems and dramas about the Fall of Man*, there were very few literary treatments of the temptation of Jesus that could provide Milton with suggestions or topics for elaborating the biblical story. The episode was treated in some mystery play cycles, most suggestively in the *Ludus Coventriae* in which a Council in Hell consisting of Satan, Belial, and Beelzebub discusses the problem of Christ's identity and determines upon a strategy of tempting him by means of the three root sins of mankind (as below); a soliloquy in which Christ complains of his severe hunger pangs; and an impressive panorama of the ancient and modern kingdoms offered to Christ in the kingdoms temptation. The temptation episode constitutes the third part of the Anglo-Saxon* narrative *Christ and Satan* (9th century) attributed to Caedmon and just possibly known as Milton in the Junius manuscript; its three parts treated, respectively, Christ's battle with Satan in heaven, his harrowing of hell, and (in fragmentary form) his temptation by Satan in the wilderness. Christ's temptation also received brief and very summary treatment in biblical poems spanning several centuries, which treat the whole life of Christ or else focus specifically upon his passion and death —for example, Juvencus's *Evangeliorum libri quattuor* (ca. 330), Marcus Hieronymus Vida's* *Christiad* (1535), Nicholas Frénicle's *Jésus Crucifié* (1636). But in only two narrative poems did the incident receive extended literary development: Jacobus Strasburgus's *Oratio Prima* (1565, ca. 800 hexameters), the only

"brief epic" that takes Christ's temptation as its subject, and the second book of Giles Fletcher's* *Christ's Victorie, and Triumph* (1619), whose four books treat, respectively, the Parliament in Heaven adjudicating the Fall of Man, the Temptation of Christ, the Passion and Crucifixion, and the Harrowing, Ascension, and triumphal procession of the saved to heaven. In both works the temptation episode is presented in allegorical* terms. Strasburgus (whose poem Milton can hardly have known, although some elements of it are suggestive for his conception) describes the episode as a "duel" waged in dialogue between the Satanic forces and Christ, a "young warrior" learning the rudiments ("*rudimentum*") of the great warfare he is to wage at the Harrowing (cf. *PR* 1. 155–62); the temptation itself is a psychomachia in which Christ is attacked by the Furies of Hell and certain personified vices —Avarice, Glory, Ambition, etcetera, which his virtues resist and ultimately defeat. Fletcher's poem, which Milton probably did know, presents Christ in the wilderness encountering along with Satan the allegorical figures of Famine, Despair, Presumption, and Pangloretta— this last presiding over a Spenserian* "Bowre of Bliss" that incorporates all worldly pleasures and honors.

Although there are no obvious literary sources for Milton's poem, and very few analogues for it, one can identify "sources" of another kind in the materials that provided the basis for the conceptual framework and the interplay of ideas in the poem. Elizabeth Pope ("*Paradise Regained*": *The Tradition and the Poem* [1947]) was the first to call attention in this regard to the paramount importance of the biblical exegetical tradition, pointing to the identity which that tradition established between Christ's three temptations, the three temptations leading to Adam's fall, and the root temptations of mankind enumerated in 1 John 2 : 13; these primary temptations constituting the so-called Triple Equation are sensuality (in Protestant versions, distrust), avarice or ambition, and vainglory. In *Milton's Brief Epic* (1966), Barbara K. Lewalski has examined the source material in biblical commentary more fully, pointing to the basis it provides for Milton's treatment of the temptation as Christ's initiation into his threefold office as Prophet, King, and Priest, as well as for his poetic typological* exploitation of various Old Testament types of those functions. Classical philosophy is also an important source of moral ideas and concepts in the poem—notably Plato*, as Irene Samuel has established in *Plato and Milton* (1947), or Plato as modified by the Ciceronian emphasis upon the "cardinal" virtues* of Justice, Fortitude, Temperance, and Wisdom, according to Arnold Stein's formulation (*Heroic Knowledge* [1957]).

The question of the genre of *PR* and the further question of the poem's relation to *PL* have been much disputed among modern Milton scholars. The matter seemed obvious enough, however, to eighteenth-century critics and editors of the poem, who took it to be an epic* and an intended sequel to *PL*. In this vein the earliest essay on the poem, Richard Meadowcourt's* *Critique on Milton's Paradise Regain'd* (1732) observes that the poem's exordium deliberately imitates the *Ille ego qui quondam* widely attributed to Virgil* as the proem to the *Aeneid;* Meadowcourt's tract as well as Charles Dunster's* 1795 annotated edition of *PR* are now available in Joseph Wittreich's facsimile edition (1971). Wittreich's preface analyzing trends in eighteenth- and nineteenth-century criticism points out that the general assumption of the poem's epic character often led to invidious censure of it in comparison with *PL* on such grounds as the narrowness of its plan, the paucity of its action, the lack of variety in its parts, and the slightness as well as theological inappropriateness of the temptation of Christ as an epic subject. In an effort to account for the disparity between the two epics and the incomplete or truncated epic apparatus of the second, Thomas Newton* observed

in his edition of 1752 that the poem must have been written in haste. At the end of the eighteenth century these observed differences were given a more positive emphasis, as in William Hayley's* argument (*Life of Milton,* 1794) that *PR* created a new kind of epic embodying "the true heroism, and the triumph of Christianity." The real breakthrough, however, occurred in Charles Dunster's edition which, although it described the poem as an intended and necessary sequel to *PL*, nevertheless used Milton's own distinctions in *RCG* to identify it as a brief epic distinct from the "diffuse epic" of *PL* and modeled "in great measure" upon the Book of Job.

Several modern critics, however, have found in the significant structural and stylistic differences between *PL* and *PR* grounds for assigning the latter poem to some other generic classification. E. M. W. Tillyard (*The English Epic and Its Background* [1954]) complains that the poem is "too short, confined, and simplified for the necessary epic variety and . . . quite lacks choric character"; elsewhere (*Milton*) he had observed that "it is not an epic, it does not try to be an epic, and it must not be judged by any kind of epic standard," being more appropriately seen as a moral allegory in the medieval mode. Howard Schultz (*Publications of the Modern Language Association* 67 [1952]: 790–808) approaches the poem primarily as an ecclesiastical allegory in which the words and actions of Christ stand for and refer to the situation of the Christian church *vis à vis* its historical and contemporary enemies. Some other critics (in addition to Shawcross and Parker) have described the poem as a drama : Douglas Bush (*English Literature in the Earlier Seventeenth Century*) refers to it as a "closet drama with a prologue and stage directions," and Arnold Stein (*Heroic Knowledge*) views it as a psychological drama staged in the hero's mind. Looking to yet another generic tradition Irene Samuel (*Plato and Milton*) has argued the work's mimesis of Platonic dialogue, and Kenneth Muir (*John Milton* [1955]) approaches it as rhetorical argument, "nearer in genre to Dryden's *Religio Laici* than . . . to *Paradise Lost*." More recently Louis L. Martz (*ELH: A Journal of English Literary History* 27 [1960] : 224–25) presents the poem as a formal meditation on the Gospel account of Christ's temptation, which at the same time has strong affinities with Virgil's *Georgics* by reason of its bare, unadorned style and its ethical theme of the temperate, disciplined, frugal life.

Despite all this, a large number of modern critics still consider *PR* to be an epic according to some definition, and have addressed themselves to the discovery and clarification of that definition. In a seminal article (*Studies in Philology* 35 [1938] : 35–62), Merritt Y. Hughes described the impact of medieval and Renaissance romances and epics upon Milton's poem, indicating that their heroes paved the way for the allegorical Christ of *PR* by redefining heroic virtue or magnanimity in terms of the qualities of patience, endurance, and renunciation. Also assuming the poem's epic character, John Steadman (*Milton and the Renaissance Hero* [1967]) shows how Milton in both epics undertakes a critique and redefinition of the traditional epic values of fortitude, sapience, leadership, love, and magnanimity. More recently, Donald L. Guss (*Studies in Philology* 68 [1971] : 223–43) has defended the poem's epic purpose on the ground that it has the appropriate epic focus upon the historical situation of the hero and upon his extraordinary virtue in resisting Satan's plausible lures, and that it creates thereby the appropriate epic effect, astonishment and wonder. He argues moreover that it is a brief epic in that it avoids the use of episodes, which Renaissance epic theory sanctioned in the "diffuse epic" as a means of producing variety. Ralph W. Condee (*Yale Review* 59 [1969–70] : 356–75) has discussed *PR* as the most complete realization of Milton's own epic theory, defined in *PL* 9. 13–44 by means of a harsh critique of traditional epic données. *PR* is accordingly a poem in

which traditional epic elements are included but turned to very different account : the great adventure here is not a heroic journey but a patient standing; here a great worldly kingdom is not founded but refused; here armies are displayed but no battles occur; here romance lords and ladies appear, but as waiters and waitresses at a Satanic banquet; here Christ achieves his final victory not by heroic combat but by simple restraint, standing still; here instead of the hero's emerging from obscure beginnings into glory he concludes his epic adventure still obscure, unknown, private.

Milton's Brief Epic, already mentioned, endeavors to establish a more precise generic identity for the poem by examining contemporary theory relating to the "brief epic" as a kind. The study begins by assuming, even as Charles Dunster had in 1795, that Milton's rather puzzling reference in *RCG* to "that Epick form whereof the two poems of *Homer,* and those other two of *Virgil* and *Tasso* are a diffuse, and the book of *Job* a brief model" is a serious statement of generic theory with direct applicability to *PR.* Investigation of the poem in terms of this statement has led to two literary traditions that furnished assumptions, materials, and methods for Milton's brief epic : (1) a tradition of biblical exegesis and literary treatment of the Job story as epic and epic model, which flourished from patristic times to Milton's own, and (2) a long tradition of theory and practice relating to the brief biblical epic as a special literary category with distinctive characteristics.

Some bases for the view of Job as epic have been studied by Charles M. Jones (*Studies in Philology* 44 [1947]: 209–27) and Israel M. Baroway (*ELH: A Journal of English Literary History* 2 [1935] : 66–91) : (1) the idea of the great antiquity of the Book of Job, thought in the seventeenth century to be among the first literary productions of mankind; (2) the idea of its uncertain authorship and possible oral transmission, which links it to early folk epics of other nations;

(3) the supposed hexameter verse form of most of the work, relating it to classical epic—an often-repeated error introduced into the mainstream of Jobean exegesis by St. Jerome*. In addition to these links, Lewalski's investigation reveals a traditional conception of Job as an epic subject. Though many Reformation and modern exegetes tended to approach the book as drama or as philosophical discourse, the dominant patristic and medieval tradition of Origen*, Chrysostom*, and Gregory the Great—carried on by many Catholic and Protestant exegetes in the sixteenth and seventeenth centuries (Juan de Pineda, Balthazar Corderius, Joseph Caryl*, John Diodati*), and developed in such poetic versions as Henry Oxenden's *Jobus Triumphans* (1656) and Helie Le Cordier's *Job* (1667)—interprets the episode as a heroic combat of cosmic significance between Satan, the Adversary of God and man, and Job, God's designated champion, warrior, athlete, and wrestler. The generic formula implicit in this reading provided a model for at least one other seventeenth-century brief epic on another subject, Robert Aylett's *Joseph, or Pharoah's* [*sic*] *Favourite* (1623) in five books (ca. 2,950 lines).

Milton's poem signals its relation to the Book of Job through a tissue of references and allusions: the character Job is named on six occasions (1. 147, 369, 425; 3. 64, 67, 95), the Book is quoted twice (1 : 33–34, 368), and either the Book itself or the tradition of commentary on it is alluded to on at least ten other occasions. The poem begins with Satan still in his Jobean character as Adversary continuing his Jobean wanderings to and fro upon the earth; he comes now to another "assembly," Christ's Baptism, where he again hears God's high commendation of a superlative hero (Job 1: 6–12; *PR* 1. 30–39). In both cases God's acclaim provokes Satan's determination to tempt the hero, in both the hero is displayed as God's champion in the encounter, and in both the conditions of the combat are set forth in two supernatural

councils—two councils in heaven in the Book of Job, and in *PR* Satan's council in mid-air followed immediately by God's heavenly council. Moreover, God's comment indicates that Christ's trial will be of the same order as Job's and will serve (in part) to display Christ's merit* as an "abler" Job :

> he [Satan] might have learnt
> Less over-weening, since he fail'd in *Job,*
> Whose constant perseverance overcame
> Whate're his cruel malice could invent.
> He now shall know I can produce a man
> Of female Seed, far abler to resist
> All his sollicitations, and at length
> All his vast force. . . .
>
> (1. 146–53)

The structure of Milton's poem is also modeled in part upon the "epic" conception of Job's trials and challenges—loss of goods and children, afflictions in his flesh, and then as his most arduous trial the steady, remorseless arguments of the three friends set on by Satan to lead him to false estimations of his own virtues and finally to despair. So in *PR*, Christ is first shorn of all material support, then assailed in his flesh by hunger, and then bombarded by Satan with a relentless stream of arguments intended to undermine his conception of himself and his mission. God's address to Job from the whirlwind, often interpreted as an apparent rather than a real rebuke intended as a further test of Job's faith and humility, has its counterpart in the storm scene of *PR,* which Satan interprets to Christ as a portent of God's displeasure. The ending of the Book of Job was construed by the commentators as setting forth God's proclamation of Job's complete triumph over all temptation, and Job's enjoyment of the reward appropriate to a heroic victor—the twofold multiplication of all his former goods. So, in *PR*, Christ's victory is proclaimed by the heavenly host, and all the goods he refused to receive at Satan's hands are given or promised to him in more exalted form. (For a critique of this designation of the Book of Job as a generic model for *PR,* see Robert H. Stein's article in *Anglia* 88 [1970] : 323–33.)

Milton's Brief Epic also links *PR* generically to a European tradition of brief biblical epics—Neo-Latin, Italian, French, and English—extending over several centuries, thereby setting Milton's poem in a broader generic context than that supplied by the seventeenth-century English biblical poems studied by Burton O. Kurth (*Milton and Christian Heroism* [1959]). Poems comprising the brief epic category are about 1,500 to 4,000 lines, often in three or four books, and often on New Testament subjects. Among particularly influential examples are Juvencus's *Evangeliorum libri quattuor* (ca. A.D. 330, 3,226 hexameters); Sedulius's *Carmen Paschale* (ca. A.D. 430, 4 books, 1,768 hexameters); the fragmentary Caedmonian *Christ and Satan* (ninth century, 733 lines); the *Mariana* of Giovanni Battista Spagnuoli, called Mantuan (1481, 3 books, ca. 1,500 hexameters); Jacopo Sannazaro's *De Partu Virginis* (1526, 3 books, ca. 1,450 hexameters), Marcus Hieronymus Vida's *Christiad* (1533, 6 books, ca. 6,000 hexameters), Du Bartas's* *Judit* (1574, 6 books, ca. 2,000 lines); Robert Aylett's *Susanna* (1622, 4 books, ca. 1,470 lines) and *Joseph* (1623, 5 books, ca. 2,950 lines); Giovanni Battista Marino's *La Strage de gli Innocenti* (1610, 4 books, ca. 3,230 lines); Giles Fletcher's *Christ's Victorie, and Triumph* (1610, 4 books, ca. 2,120 lines); and Jacques de Coras, *Samson, Poëme Sacré* (1665, 5 books, ca. 2,470 alexandrines). Such poems customarily claimed epic status in proems or prefaces or critical treatises on the following bases: (1) the theory that parts of the Bible are already epic poetry and so can supply epic subject matter; (2) the definition of a hero as one whose virtues and spiritual conquests merit eternal fame in heaven; (3) the analogous virtues and actions of some biblical and classical heroes such as Samson and Hercules; and (4) the assertion that the true biblical subject has far greater nobility and excellence than have pagan fictions inspired by false muses.

PR uses the données of this generic tradition in an imaginative and highly original way: it is, not surprisingly, the crowning achievement of the kind. Of the three basic formulas devised for the biblical brief epic—the standard patristic format of a panoramic subject presented sequentially, the usual medieval model in which a sequence of episodes or scenes is linked together typologically, and the predominant Renaissance structure wherein a single action or episode is expanded and given broader epic dimension by the use of allusions, prophecies, recitals, and iconographical* descriptions often based upon typological symbolism—Milton used the Renaissance formula. Though he does not employ the simplest and most common Renaissance strategy for giving an epic aura to the poem by thick-sowing it with Virgilian diction, epithets, and echoes, and he also eschews the often-imitated neoclassical structure of Vida's* *Christiad*. But he does adapt a number of the expected generic topoi: an *in medias res* beginning with Christ's baptism; two "infernal" councils now held in mid-air rather than in hell; a council in heaven wherein God addresses Gabriel and makes references to his earlier employment as angelic nuntius at the Annunciation (1. 138–40); a prophecy of Christ's immediate and ultimate victory over Satan spoken by God before the encounter; two transformed epic recitals —Christ's meditation about his youthful experiences and aspirations, and Mary's reminiscences about the great prophecies and promises atending the hero's early life; an epic catalogue of the kingdoms of the world; a transformed prophetic vision in which the hero, instead of viewing his own destined kingdom, sees and rejects all those kingdoms which are not his; an epiclike, martial pageant of Parthian warriors; and a passage dealing with the education or learning of the hero (the learning temptation).

Within the brief epic tradition Milton's greatest conceptual debt may well be to Sannazaro's *De Partu Virginis,* in which the apparently unlikely "epic" subject of the incarnation and birth of Christ is not treated structurally as a truncated *Aeneid,* but (primarily through the use of typological symbolism) as the true nucleus or epitome of a vast epic action. For Milton the similarly unusual choice of the temptation episode as subject no doubt suggested itself as a complement to the temptation in *PR,* but beyond this, it is the one episode in Christ's life (except for the Harrowing of Hell which Milton's mortalism* kept him from using) that is peculiarly suited to the format of the brief epic, in that it could be treated as a transmutation of the single combat of hero and antagonist—traditionally, the focal, climactic event of a long epic. Milton accordingly presents the temptation as an epitome of the perpetual battle of the Son and Satan throughout all time, and uses martial imagery to associate the permutations of the argument with the thrust and parry of a great duel. He does not present this duel as an allegorical *psychomachia* (as Giles Fletcher and Jacobus Strasburgus had done), but rather as an inordinately subtle and complex mental combat in which hellish wiles must be conquered by wisdom. Milton also took over the common brief-epic technique of using typological allusion to extend historical perspective and achieve epic dimension for the subject chosen, though by incorporating such reference into the debate between Christ and Satan he gave the technique unprecedented dramatic power. Through such allusions Milton presented the temptation episode against the panorama of all previous history, and displayed Christ as the epitome and fulfillment of all earlier patterns of heroism.

Accepting in part Louis Martz's account of the poem as an exercise in formal meditation, Stewart A. Baker (*Comparative Literature* 20 [1968] : 116–32) finds that Milton's poem transmutes the military themes of the classical epic to the spiritual values of Christianity primarily by means of an interplay of epic and pastoral motifs and vocabularies. He also finds Sannazaro's *De Partu Virginis* to be the most suggestive model for *PR,*

noting that, like Sannazaro, Milton employs pastoral motifs to assimilate "the historical themes of epic into the consciousness of the individual," and that he does this primarily by establishing the pastoral landscape as the symbolic setting for meditations upon the typological figures and events of Christian history. Pointing to the inverted pastoral* landscape of the poem (a wilderness instead of the "happy Garden" of earlier epics) Baker notes the structural and thematic importance of several true and perverted pastoral elements in the poem : a wilderness "dusk with horrid shade" in which Jesus' presence creates something like the conventional pastoral landscape of hill and shady vale; true and false examples of the *locus amoenus;* the piscatory apostles with their complaint. Moreover, Jesus' rejection of the courtly glories of the world is an affirmation of the pastoral value of inner harmony over the epic values of material wealth, conquest, political power.

Such recognition that *PR* derives from a somewhat different generic tradition than *PL* invites the conclusion that it is a companion poem to the long epic rather than (as is often assumed) a sequel or postscript. *Milton's Brief Epic* urges that the focus of *PL* is upon the condition of mankind manifested in and extending from the story of Adam, and that the subject is the Fall and the redemption of man; whereas in *PR* the focus is upon Christ the hero, and the subject is his heroic achievement and mission in its deepest significance and broadest ramifications. The distinction seems mirrored in the stance of the epic narrator. In *PL* he presents himself as one of Adam's progeny, insisting in image and statement upon the inner darkness and spiritual blindness that dooms him to failure in his difficult task unless the Spirit will act upon him. In *PR* by contrast the narrative voice is easy and confident, since the narrator now sees himself not as fallen but as redeemed man, sharing in Christ's victory and therefore confidently expecting the Spirit's assistance in triumphing over the difficulties of his theme. The narrator's identification with Christ's perspective, and his constant activity in interpreting the poem for the reader and commenting upon the views expressed by the various characters is explored further by Roger H. Sundell (*Milton Studies* 2 [1970] : 83–101).

The chief reason why *PR* has not been a notable favorite with the critics is their dissatisfaction with the hero, Christ. Some have complained about the negative, restrictive values (Puritan or Stoic) that he seems to embody—in sharp contrast to the gentleness and love such readers expect to find associated with the Savior of mankind. So H. J. C. Grierson protested (*Criterion* 7 [1928] : 254), "the restrictive virtues in themselves are somewhat cold and negative. . . . We miss in Milton's Christ the note of passionate, self-forgetting love. He is too serene and forbidding, if noble and imperturbable." In somewhat different terms, Tillyard (*Milton*) declared Milton's hero to be "in fact partly allegorical, partly Milton himself, imagined perfect." Northrop Frye (*Modern Philology* 53 [1956] : 227–38) asserts that Christ becomes increasingly unsympathetic as the poem develops—"a pusillanimous quietist in the temptation of Parthia, an inhuman snob in the temptation of Rome, a peevish obscurantist in the temptation of Athens."

Another kind of complaint is directed to the static, undramatic character of the hero, necessitated by the fact that he must perforce be presented as divine, or as perfect man unable to fall. Elizabeth Pope finds Milton conforming to the dominant interpretation of the temptation story throughout the centuries—the view that Jesus underwent the temptation as a man, with his divine power held in abeyance so as to teach mankind how to withstand temptation, but that he was nevertheless fully conscious of his divinity and even (some commentators held) that he deliberately mystified Satan about it through his ambiguous answers. Such a view is the basis for Allan Gilbert's comment (*Journal of English and Germanic Philology* 15 [1916] : 606) that Christ, as the only-begotten of God, had no need for the human means offered by Satan, and of Douglas Bush's observation (*English Literature in the Earlier Seventeenth Century*, p. 412) that "the sinless divine protagonist of *Paradise Regained* cannot falter, much less fall." Other readings emphasize that the divine hero is also an allegorical representative of human perfection and on that score also an undramatic figure : in Hughes's conception (*Studies in Philology* 35 [1938] he is an "exemplar Redeemer, the Word of St. John's Gospel, as it fused with the craving of critics and poets of the late Renaissance for a purely exemplary hero in epic poetry."

Other critics have recognized some genuine dramatic conflict and some real development of Christ's character in the poem, though they do not agree upon the course this development takes or upon the conception of Christ's nature that makes such development possible. Some see Milton's Christ as exercising only his human intellect and will throughout the temptation, and therefore as capable of dramatic conflict : M. M. Mahood (*Poetry and Humanism* [1950], p. 211) describes him as "the perfect man, as yet scarcely aware of His divine progeniture," and Northrop Frye (*Modern Philology* 53 [1956]) finds that he withstands the temptations as a human being until the tower episode, at which point the omnipotent divine power "takes over" the now fully proved human will. Arnold Stein (*Heroic Knowledge*) sees the work as a kind of drama of consciousness, finding that Christ's answers project a true action, a positive process of self-definition even as Satan also drives on to the ultimate self-definition he has chosen. Yet all these recognize the problem created for dramatic action by a perfect hero who cannot be moved, Stein arguing that Milton's chief solution for the difficulty was to shift much of the dramatic weight to Satan's temptation activity, his anguished consciousness, his desperate uncertainty about Christ's true identity.

Beyond this, however, several critics have discussed the identity motif as giving dramatic interest to the role of Christ as well as to that of Satan. Edward Cleveland (*Modern Language Quarterly* 16 [1955] : 232–36) argues that Christ withstands all the temptations as exalted man until the tower assault, at which time he dramatically and gloriously reveals his divinity. A. S. P. Woodhouse (*University of Toronto Quarterly* 25 [1955–56] : 173) declares that Christ gains from his experience in the wilderness "a progressively deeper insight into his own nature as well as into God's purpose," and actually advances from human beginnings to a full realization of his divinity in the tower scene. John Steadman (*University of Toronto Quarterly* 31 [1962] : 416–30) presses this insight further, to assert that Christ really does learn through the dialogue with the devil, beginning at a stage of limited knowledge and "gaining an ever-clearer and more comprehensive insight into God's will in the course of his wilderness ordeal." In *The Harmonious Vision* (chap. 6 [1954]) Don. C. Allen finds still greater dramatic potential in a hero who fluctuates throughout the poem between the divine and human natures, giving evidence of this alternation by the striking tonal differences of his various speeches.

Milton's Brief Epic explores the identity motif in the poem more fully and examines the theological basis for it, attempting to show that Milton achieves genuine dramatic tension and movement by exploiting this motif. Obviously, as Satan later remarks, the divine title "bears no single sence" (4. 517); Satan himself can claim with some justice, "The Son of God I also am, or was, / And if I was, I am; relation stands; / All men are Sons of God" (4. 518–20). Milton works out the dramatic potentialities inherent in the conventional conception of a puzzled and self-deluded Satan seeking to determine throughout the temptation whether Christ is indeed divine, but he especially exploits his own Christology, according to which this incarnate Christ undergoes a kenosis* that involves a true emptying out of his divine understanding and will, not merely an obscuring or covering over of his divinity. See in this regard Milton's discussion of the Incarnate Christ in his *CD,* Book 1, chapters 3, 5, 14, 15, 16. For different interpretations of Milton's doctrine of the Incarnation* *see* THE FALL AND RESTORATON OF MAN; MESSIANIC HUMILIATION AND EXALTATION; THE SON). Such a Christology provides a basis for presenting Christ in the poem as a dramatic character undergoing a true test or temptation, in that he is (theoretically at least) able to fall, capable of growth, and genuinely (not just apparently) uncertain of himself. Having undergone such a kenosis, he meets the temptation as a man, gaining back only gradually and through God's progressive illumination as he merits it, his awareness of his Divine Nature.

Satan's address to his forces in the first Consult and Christ's meditation as he goes forth into the desert make clear that hero and antagonist begin their duel at approximately the same level of knowledge : both are cognizant of the prophecies, both saw the signs at the recent Baptism, both are ignorant of the identity between this Son of God and the "first-Begot." Christ has learned what he knows of himself through his mother's tales of the miraculous prophecies attending his birth, and through the Scripture writings, which have convinced him that he is the promised Messiah. He is now led to the desert—"to what intent / I learn not yet"—obviously conscious of his limited human knowledge but conscious also of the guidance of the Spirit : "For what concerns my knowledge God reveals" (1. 291–93). The debate-duel between Christ and Satan develops as a battle of wits in which both hero and tempter strive for the advantage which accompanies superior understanding. To succeed in perverting Christ Satan has to understand him perfectly, but he himself is the victim of imperfect knowledge and naiveté concerning Christ's nature and mission. To withstand Satan's temptations

Christ must refuse all inadequate, partial, or erroneous versions or parodies of himself and his mission, which Satan presents to him out of his vast store of firsthand experience with human weakness throughout all time. Though Christ knows such things only at second hand through his wide reading in Scripture and secular history, he has the special advantage of being able to merit* the gift of divine illumination, which seems to be granted him after he has withstood each of the major temptations in terms of his own human powers. Their different modes of apprehension yield vastly different results as both Christ and Satan attempt to cope with the ambiguities of Christ's title, Son of God, and with the metaphorical prophecies about Christ's role. Christ comes to an imaginative realization of the full, spiritual meaning of such terms whereas Satan remains cunning, brilliant even, but ultimately literal-minded, unable to fathom God's metaphors.

Dramatic tension in the poem also develops in terms of one great central paradox that virtually transmutes activity and passivity into each other. Satan appears to do all the acting, dancing about Christ in a fever of motion and trying one scheme after another, one argument after another, whereas Christ seems to be impassive, immobile. Yet it is in Christ's consciousness, not Satan's, that true change and growth take place: Christ progresses through somewhat uneven stages and partial climaxes of understanding and revelation to full comprehension and definition of himself and the various aspects of his role in the grand climax on the tower. Satan, for all his feverish activity, cannot resolve the puzzle about Christ's identity and mission until that same climactic moment, which forces upon him the recognition of his long-time antagonist, and with that recognition, his own defeat and fall.

The fundamental themes of the poem have been variously defined, and the various definitions have implications for the way in which the poem's structure is understood. One approach finds the thematic center to be the presentation of some paradigm of heroic virtue by Christ the exemplary hero : such paradigms are commonly seen as revaluations in Christian terms of classical patterns of virtue and heroism. This reading usually takes the kingdoms temptation to be the essence of the poem, with the temptation of the stones treated as prologue and the tower temptation as climactic epilogue. Allan Gilbert (*Journal of English and Germanic Philology* 15 [1916]) laid the groundwork for this approach to the structure by sharply dissociating the stones-into-bread temptation from the banquet temptation despite their common concern with food, arguing that the Satanic banquet is the first of the glories of the world offered to Christ as gifts. From another point of view Roy Daniells (*Milton, Mannerism and Baroque* [1963], pp. 194–208) has described the structure of the poem in terms of late baroque* architecture, with the first and last temptations subordinated as if they were small side passages flanking the expanded central element, the splendid and elaborate panoramas of the kingdoms.

Tillyard (*Milton*) understands the theme of the poem as the quasi-allegorical confrontation of reason (Christ) and passion (Satan). In terms of structure, he finds that the various Satanic offers that constitute the principal temptation of the kingdoms are "carefully graded according to the subtlety and inwardness of their appeal," and are climaxed by the offer of philosophic learning; the tower scene he takes to be no temptation at all but the brief rout of Satan. Recognizing that Christ at one point (2. 483) refers his renunciation of kingdoms to magnanimity, Merritt Y. Hughes (*Studies in Philology* 35 [1938]) discusses the poem's theme in relation to the redefinition and Christianization of that Aristotelian* virtue in terms of constancy, patience, *contempus mundi,* and the fusion of the active and contemplative lives. From a somewhat different point of view Frank Kermode (*Review of English Studies* n.s. 4 [1953]: 317–30) sees the theme of the poem as the definition of Christian heroism, which Christ exemplifies by confuting or transcending even the most exalted classical heroic ideals : an Ovidian banquet of sense, Scipio's embodiment of true earthly honor; Rome as the sum of pre-Christian civilization with its wealth, glory, and military power; Athens (Socrates) as the sum of natural wisdom. Though he does not address the question of structure, John Steadman (*Milton and the Renaissance Hero* [1967]) also sees Milton's primary theme in *PR* to be the definition of Christian heroism in its total perfection, which involves a critique and revaluation of the traditional epic values of fortitude, sapience, leadership, love, and magnanimity.

Also concentrating almost entirely upon the second temptation, Irene Samuel defines the theme of the poem as "the winning of happiness," achieved by progressive affirmation of and at length transcendence of Platonic ethical values. The temptations ascend according to the Platonic scale of the goods desired by various kinds of men and governments: pleasure, wealth, fame (true fame for Plato is defined as the praise of virtue by the judicious and by Milton as heavenly glory). Ethical knowledge or wisdom, the highest good for Plato, is transcended in *PR* by God's revelation of spiritual truth, and the place of wisdom at the pinnacle of Plato's scale of goods is taken by that loving trust in God which alone can regain human happiness and paradise. Arnold Stein (*Heroic Knowledge*) also finds that the Platonic scale of goods and the Platonic tripartite soul (appetitive, passional, rational) form the basis for the central theme of the poem, a dramatic definition of "heroic knowledge" that is a "preparation for acting transcendence in the world, by uniting intuitive knowledge with proved intellectual and moral discipline." But in his reading, this scale (and so also the structure of the poem) is modified by the hero's manifestation of the Platonic *unity* of the virtues, and by the antagonist's disposition to leapfrog forward and then retreat

backward along the scale according to dramatic necessities and opportunities. This reading also enables Stein to take account thematically and structurally of the first and third temptations, interpreting the first as an initial "transcendence" that subsumes much that is to follow in the kingdoms temptation by its invitation to excessive trust in material goods, and the temptations of the storm and tower as the ultimate transcendence —a mythic enactment of the "way of death" that produces more abundant life, and a climactic translation into action of the heroic knowledge that the hero has gained.

Emerging from this interpretive tradition, but with the significant difference of combining a structural emphasis upon Christ's exemplification of certain virtues with a dramatic reading of the poem's action, is Gary Hamilton's recent study (*Philological Quarterly* 50 [1971] : 567–81). Hamilton sees the Christ of the poem regaining in the course of its action that Paradise Within promised to Adam and his progeny in *PL* 12. 575–87, by exemplifying precisely those virtues denominated by Michael as the conditions for its attainment—in the first temptation (Book 1) Faith; in the banquet and riches temptations (Book 2) Temperance; in the offer of Parthia (Book 3) Patience; and in the offers of Rome and Athens (Book 4) that "sum / Of wisdom" which Michael proclaimed to be greater than all earthly riches or earthly knowledge. This schematic arrangement also functions dramatically, Hamilton argues, since what we see in *PR* is "a human Christ in the process of raising himself up 'under long obedience tri'd,' " and thus in some sense performing here his redemptive mission for Adam's sons; only after this achievement does he again assume on the tower his Divine nature and begin that redemption as a public mission.

A second major approach to the theme and structure of the poem accounts for the nature and sequence of the temptations in terms of the traditional identification of Christ as Second Adam. In her

1947 study Pope demonstrated Milton's significant use of the so-called Triple Equation, which has been mentioned. She also pointed out Milton's alteration of this traditional exegetical pattern in response to trends in contemporary Protestant exegesis, and also the demands of his own artistic conception. Thus he conceived the stones-into-bread temptation in Protestant terms as a temptation to distrust, and identified the temptation to appetite (the banquet) as Protestants did with the kingdoms temptation, though he incorporated in his banquet scene the full range of fleshly sins usually encompassed in the medieval reading of the first temptation. Moreover, for dramatic climax Milton reworked the tower temptation as a temptation by violence and an identity test, removing its usual associations with vainglorious presumption and assimilating these to the second temptation also. In Pope's reading Milton's poem is structured so as to set forth each day a different kind of temptation : temptation by necessity, based upon the Protestant version of the stones-into-bread; temptation by pleasures and gifts (the whole range of worldly goods, including carnal delights, vainglory, kingdoms and their glories); and temptation by violence, a special Miltonic conception not usual in treatments of the temptation, though susceptible of interpretation as the specific temptation of the Devil.

Woodhouse (*University of Toronto Quarterly* 25 [1955–56]) also finds that the primary theme of the poem concerns Christ as Second Adam and that a secondary identity theme is implied in the statement that the glorious Eremite will be brought forth from the desert "By proof th' undoubted Son of God." In his view, Milton made some general use of the Triple Equation in developing the primary theme, but took special care to work out parallels with his own story of Adam : thus he invented the Belial proposition, "Set women in his eye," in order to provide a parallel for his own Adam "fondly overcome with Female charm," and he surrounded the kingdoms

offer with two invented "contemplative" lures—the banquet temptation, which moves on the level of the senses to recall "the crude Apple that diverted Eve" (2. 349), and the Temptation of Athens, which works on the level of the intellect to parallel the apple as the fruit of the Tree of Knowledge. Much more complexly, Burton J. Weber (*Philological Quarterly* 50 [1971] : 553–66) argues that the patristic reading of the Triple Equation as involving temptations to sensuality, ambition, and vainglory defines the fundamental structure of the thre-days' trial; that these temptations relate to the parts of the Neoplatonic* tripartite soul—sense, reason, and intellect (from which springs will); and that, moreover, "Milton turns each day's temptation, and each subsection of each day's temptation, into a test of the full neo-Platonic tripartite soul." Another recent study, Robert E. Reiter's University of Michigan dissertation, "In Adam's Room : A Study of the Adamic Typology of Christ in *Paradise Regained*" (1964), affirms that the Adam-Christ typological parallels and contrasts make up the principal thematic and structural elements of the poem. And as a minor aspect of the Second Adam theme H. H. Petit (*Papers of the Michigan Academy* 44 [1959] : 365–69) points up Milton's suggestive treatment of Mary as Second Eve—nurturing Christ in his office whereas Eve enticed Adam to man's Fall and patiently enduring her uncertainties over Christ's absence whereas Eve, similarly puzzled by God's ways, rebelled. The link is reinforced in the ending of Milton's two epics : Adam and Eve go forth from Eden calmly together, and Christ returns home "private" to his mother's house.

Still another critical approach defines the theme of the poem in terms of Christ's redemptive office or mission, conceiving that role as both broader and more precisely related to Christ's own unique situation than either the Triple Equation or Second Adam motif admits of. Schultz has argued (*Publications of the Modern Language Association* 67 [1952] and

Milton and Forbidden Knowledge, pp. 222–35) that Christ is not tempted in his private but in his official capacity (that is, as prophet, priest, and king of his Church) and that accordingly all of the temptations are ecclesiastic in their frame of reference, not moral : "Milton meant the Head of the Christian church to set a pattern not primarily for the Christian layman, but for the church and its ministers." Accordingly, Christ's refusals have relevance only to the special responsibilities laid upon the church as Christ's spiritual kingdom. Schultz takes the stones-into-bread temptation as an offer of false guidance to Christ the prophet of the Gospel; the banquet temptation as an offer of Popish idolatry, a pervasion of the Church's true worship; and all of the other temptations as worldly props and aids that Christ's wholly spiritual kingdom, the Church, may not use.

In a different vein Northrop Frye (*Modern Philology* 53 [1956]) takes the thematic center of the poem to be the presentation of the temptation episode as Christ's second agon with Satan, looking back to the first, the Battle in Heaven, and forward to the final battle to come at the end of time. He argues that the episodes of the poem present Jesus not only as antitype of Adam, but also of Israel wandering in the wilderness en route to the Promised Land, so that some of the temptations concern the ways in which the Gospel is to annihilate and fulfill the Law—as in the abjuration of all force in Christ's Kingdom, and in the adumbration of the forthcoming destruction of the Temple in Satan's fall from its tower. Michael Fixler (*Milton and the Kingdoms of God* [1964]) also finds typology to be of primary importance in developing the fundamental themes of *PR*. Though he associates the temptations with the threefold office of Christ as prophet, priest and king, his primary focus is upon the ways in which Satan uses Jewish messianic speculation and especially contemporary echoes of it in Puritan millenarianism* to promote a false chiliastic version of Christ's king-

dom. He discusses, moreover, how various temptations subtly challenge Christ to distinguish precisely how and when the Law is to be replaced by the Gospel, notably the banquet scene wherein, as Fixler elsewhere shows (*Modern Language Notes* 70 [1955] : 573–77), Satan disingenuously includes foods forbidden by the Law among the banquet's plenty, even while explicitly denying that he has done so.

In *Milton's Brief Epic* Lewalski has argued that the poem's theme and structure are ordered to display (through the three conventional temptations) a precise and progressive development and testing of the three functions of Christ's office —prophet, king, and priest. Many Protestants regarded Christ's baptism and temptation in the wilderness as his formal entry or initiation into his mediatorial office, and Milton incorporates this idea through two references in the poem's induction (1. 28, 189). Since these functions are assumed to continue forever in Christ's Church, Milton can permit reverberations of the future to be heard above the dramatic exchanges in the Christ-Satan encounter, and so can subsume within the temptation episode the entire course of Christ's life, the experience of his Church throughout Christian history, and even the anagogic fulfillment of these roles at the end of time. The poem also develops its theme through a pervasive typological perspective, by means of constant reference to Adam, Job, Moses, Elijah, David, Daniel, Judas Maccabeus, Hercules, Socrates, and many other recognized Old Testament (and even classical) types of Christ. Such typological references are made to function dramatically, in that Satan's constant temptation strategy is to invite Christ to accept inferior types of his redemptive action in place of those major Old Testament types whom he has seized upon as worthy models, or else to identify with these major types in their literal signification and thereby fail to fulfill them spiritually, as his mission demands. Christ must engage throughout with the difficult intellectual problem of how he ought to relate himself to history, how far the past is to provide a model for his actions, and wherein he must redefine its terms in order to become himself the model for the future. The typological allusions also enhance the epic scope of the poem by projecting the episode of Christ's temptation against the panorama of history, with Christ becoming the summation, the compendium, the completion of all the earlier heroes. Through such use of typological reference and such projection into the future of Christ's office, this particular encounter between Christ and Satan is placed in the double perspective of the past and the future, as indeed the turning point between the past and the future: it is the center and epitome of all history.

As a test of the prophetic role, the first temptation sets in opposition truth and falsehood, using physical bread as metaphor. Christ identifies God's Word as his proper spiritual food (1. 349–51) and declares of Satan, "lying is thy sustenance, thy food" (1. 429). As founder of the new law, Christ associates himself on the basis of a common forty-day fast with two recognized types of his prophetic office—Moses and Elijah—while Satan in shepherd disguise offers Christ his own guidance, parodying Christ's role as Good Shepherd and making his own claim to oracular prophecy. Concluding this incident, Christ asserts unequivocally his claim to be the living oracle who will teach the final word of God, making all inferior prophecy cease. The motif of the prophetic role extends into Book 2, for the lavish banquet is in one dimension a diabolic parody of the heavenly manna and of the temperate repasts offered to Elijah. It is thus an invitation to Christ to identify himself literally with those prophetic types, Moses and Elijah, who were fed in the same desert by God: since God has not provided for Christ in the wilderness, the Devil will provide. In line with this, Satan's false claim that the banquet in no way violates the dietary provisions of the Law poses Christ the dilemma of whether in refusing it he

would seem to subject himself (and his Church) to such ceremonies, but his authoritative affirmation of lordship over nature* and Pauline "Christian Liberty*" (2. 379–84) asserts with new force his function as prophet of the New Testament, fulfilling and superseding the Law and the Prophets.

The banquet temptation also introduces the kingdoms sequence, which Satan undertakes in a new guise, "As one in City, or Court, or Palace bred" (1. 300); that is, he now takes up his role as Prince of this world, condescending to a naive and inexperienced Christ. The banquet-wealth-glory sequence constitutes Milton's own special version and use of the Triple Equation: Christ overcomes here just those temptations which defeated Adam, and thereby displays that kingship over the self which Milton saw as the basis for any kind of public role or dominion. The banquet is an analogue of Eve's first temptation to carnal appetite and the parallel is further developed by the circumstance that some of the banquet foods are forbidden—unclean under the Law and forbidden to Christians insofar as the Devil's Table is always synonymous with idolatry. Eve's temptation to avarice and ambition has its parallel in Satan's effort to promote in Christ an inordinate desire for kingly dominion, with the offer of wealth as the only means to achieve it. And Eve's temptation to vainglory and pride in desiring to be "as Gods" is paralleled in Satan's offer of glory to Christ. In response to this offer Christ disparages the glory-seeking world conquerors whom Satan has proposed to him as types—Alexander, Caesar, Scipio— affirming that glory "to God alone of right belongs" (3. 141). At the end of this sequence Christ names Socrates, the teacher of mankind and willing sufferer for truth's sake, as the noblest classical type of himself, identifying thereby the source of many of the ethical principles he has enunciated throughout this primarily ethical sequence. But he exalts Job even above Socrates as an exemplar of ethical wisdom and moral virtue.

By the statement, "But to a Kingdom thou art born, ordain'd / To sit upon thy Father *David's* Throne" (3. 152–53), Satan shifts the terms of discourse from the kingdom within to the public realm, now challenging directly Christ's divinely ordained kingly role. In the first brief exchange Satan urges Christ to recapitulate the zeal and duty shown by his Old Testament type Judas Maccabaeus by taking up arms at once to seize his rightful kingdom, but Christ replies that zeal and duty consist first in waiting upon God's time. Presenting then a magnificent vision of Parthian armed might, Satan builds upon Christ's recognition of himself as heir to David's throne to suggest that Christ become literally a second David, seeking after David's physical kingdom, Israel, by David's means, armed might. Denouncing such means, Christ shows himself "*Israel's* true King," that is, the true, peaceful king of the new Israel, the invisible church. The Roman Empire next presented to him in glorious panorama is symbolically the great Antichrist—at once the Kingdom of this World and (as often in Protestant polemic and exegesis) the Roman Catholic Church; it is thus a substitute kingdom—"all the world"— offered in place of Christ's own spiritual kingdom, and in renouncing it Christ refers to the metaphors of Daniel's tree and stone to indicate that his spiritual kingdom will at length conquer and subdue all worldly kingdoms whatsoever.

At this point, just when the reader is sure that Satan has exhausted all his skill in displaying Roman grandeur, Satan offers Athens to Christ in all of its fourth- and fifth-century glory as the compendium of classical learning. He equates this with wisdom*, and presents it as precisely the nonmaterial good needed for Christ's accomplishment of all the lofty ideals and functions he has himself just defined—the kingly office of "ruling by persuasion," the prophetic role of teaching true wisdom, and the completion of the kingdom within the self. Christ's refusal of the offer identifies true wisdom as deriving only from above, and removes his church from any necessary reliance upon the world's wisdom.

In the final storm-tower sequence Christ endures with a patience surpassing that of Job the ultimate test of the kingdom within—violence and the threat of death. In addition, the false portents invoked to interpret the storm challenge Christ's prophetic role, and the prediction of difficulties to come for his kingdom threatens that function. But Milton especially contrived the storm-tower sequence to foreshadow and epitomize Christ's passion and death, the essence of his sacrificial priestly office, while at the same time, as has been noted, the tower episode functions as the ultimate identity test. Placing Christ upon the pinnacle of the tower where without miracle he cannot stand, Satan supposes that he has allowed for all the possibilities : if Christ is a mere man he must fall from the spire; if he is divine he will save himself by miracle; if he is uncertain he may cast himself down to test himself and God. But what happens is that Christ shows his divinity not by miraculous escape on Satan's terms but by calmly maintaining the impossible posture into which Satan has thrust him, imaging forth the passive endurance he will display at the Crucifixion. As he will then, Christ is now permitted to turn this very passion into a dramatic act of conquest over Satan, so that Satan "smitten with amazement" falls even as Christ receives and manifests full consciousness of his Divine Sonship.

Still other thematic and structural patterns have been discerned in the poem. Arthur Barker (in *Essays in English Literature from the Renaissance to the Victorian Age, Presented to A. S. P. Woodhouse,* ed. Millar McLure and F. W. Watt [1964]) has argued that the poem's structure does not depend upon balanced sequences of hierarchial temptations; indeed, that the temptations are hardly even of negative significance, so thoroughly confused is Satan about the Law, and even about pagan wisdom. He finds the essence of the poem to be its treatment of Christ's response to the true call sounded beneath the confused Satanic parodies of it, together with the treatment in each of the four books of some significant aspect of natural and supernatural renovation and of the resultant Christian liberty. Mason Tung (*Seventeenth Century News* 24 [1966] : 58–59) discerns two interlocking patterns of temptation in the poem, involving the five main modes of temptation pointed to in the song of the Angelic choir (1. 178–79) : one pattern shows Satan attempting to "seduce," "allure," and "terrify" Jesus into revealing his mere humanity, and the other shows him endeavoring to "tempt" and "undermine" Christ into disclosing his divinity. These motives and methods are then related to the specific temptations. A structural division based upon the two fundamental biblical conceptions of sin—error, relating to the intellect (explored in the first two books), and rebellion, relating to the will (explored in the last two books), is advanced by Mother Mary Christopher Pecheux in *Calm of Mind: Tercentenary Essays on "Paradise Regained" and "Samson Agonistes,"* ed. J. A. Wittreich, Jr. [1971], pp. 49–65); she finds further that the themes of man's universal slavery to sin in both kinds, and Christ's total victory over both are emphasized in the tower scene and the concluding angelic hymn. A more formalistic structural study is that of Alexander H. Sackton (*University of Texas Studies in English* 33 [1954]: 33–45), which calls attention to elements of rhythmic repetition, balance, symmetry, and parallelism in Milton's poem, such as the three accounts of Christ's baptism presented from different perspectives, the variations on the theme of doubt and distrust throughout Book 1 and in the induction to Book 2, and the parallelism of the diabolical banquet and the angelic banquet.

The richness and the complexity of structure of *PR* are perhaps best seen in an overview. Basic of course is the tripartite structure provided by the three biblical temptations, in each of which Christ as private man withstands a characteristic human vice and exhibits its contrary virtue : in the first temptation, doubt and despair; in the second, the intemperance, avarice, and vainglory to which Adam and Eve succumbed; in the third, the fear and terror promoted by Satan's violence. Similarly, as public figure Christ in these three temptations learns about and is exercised in the three functions of his mediatorial Office and by that same token defeats Satan in the three aspects of *his* public role; the True Prophet overcomes the Father of Lies; the True King of the church and the world dethrones Satan, Prince of this World; the suffering Priest exposed in darkness and in air overthrows the Prince of Darkness and the Prince of the Air. In counterpoint to this, one may distinguish four rather than three basic structural components of the poem, since the private and public themes develop concomitantly in the first and third temptations but sequentially in the kingdoms temptation, with the shift to the concerns of the public office of kingship pointed by the words, "But to a Kingdom thou art born." Still another structural counterpoint within the kingdoms temptation is its organization according to the traditional tripartite scale of ethical goods—*voluptaria* (Belial's proposal of women and the banquet scene), *activa* (wealth, glory, kingship over Parthia and Rome), and *contemplativa* (classical learning and poetry)—as Howard Schultz notes in *Milton and Forbidden Knowledge* (pp. 224–27). Furthermore, the division into four books provides an additional counterpart, each book emphasizing its own thematic motif : Book 1 is wholly concerned with challenges to faith; Book 2 explores the motif of intemperance, either as related to bodily enjoyments or to external possessions and honors; Book 3 adumbrates the concepts of *time* and *force,* as related either to personal glory or to the public mediatorial kingdom; Book 4 presents a series of climaxes, each outdoing the last in scope and effect—Rome, Athens, and then the final victory and revelation on the tower. The tower scene shows Christ victorious in all three roles : as suffering Priest he sustains the violence of Satan, Sin, and Death and overcomes all three; as True Prophet, Second Oedipus (as the epic simile suggests) he puts down the riddling tempter who would devour all mankind; as King he fulfills that aspect of his public kingly role which involves the destruction of Satan and all his works.

Until quite recently, stylistic commentary on *PR* has amounted chiefly to comparison, often invidious, between the dense, richly textured, evocative style* of *PL* and the bare, unadorned, austere style of *PR*. As a concomitant of such comparison, critics often posit some falling off in Milton's poetic powers, or else apologize for his choice of an unfortunate subject for poetic treatment. These strictures have found recent restatement in W. W. Robson's article (*The Living Milton,* ed. Frank Kermode [1960]), which argues that the entire poem takes color from Christ's verbal style—strangely colorless and toneless, flat, laconic, terse, brusque, dry, and dull, though marked by gravity and formality. The result is an overall style that is inelastic and mannered, save where Satan's speeches evoke a broader range of feeling and deeper resonances.

The style, of course, has its defenders, who point out that its muted, chastened quality is entirely suited to its epic subject. David Daiches (*Milton* [1957]) observes that Christ's simplicity of diction and quietly assured style contrasts with the almost parodic uses of grand rhetorical* eloquence and ornament in Satan's speeches, especially in his presentation of Parthia and Rome. Martz (*ELH: A Journal of English Literary History* 27 [1960]) has identified the style as georgic —dignified, modest, somewhat latinate, reminding us of *PL* at a distance but deliberately muted; Martz calls attention also to the battle of rhetorical modes within the work, as this chastened style used by the narrator and the hero plays off against Satan's high oratorical style. Confirming these impressions, Ants Oras (*Blank Verse and Chronology in Milton*) has documented statistically Milton's use

in *PR* of "a more austere style, less orotund, less reverberant and ornamental, briefer in its rhythms, shorter in the words it used," reserving his earlier epic style of grandeur and magnificence only for special purposes—as in Book 3 when Satan attempts to convert Christ to worldliness through gorgeous pageants and magniloquent rhetoric. Donald L. Guss (*Studies in Philology* 68 [1971]) locates one source of *PR*'s modest style in Augustine's* characterization of the style of the Bible as noble and grave, though not studiously ornamented, and Cassiodorus's description of it as "casta, fixa, verax," (chaste, piercing, truthful). Milton, Guss believes, undertook in this poem to imitate the style of Scripture through such devices as ellipses of verbs and subjects, use of parallelism and coordinate syntax, and epigrammatic texture created by sonorous short phrases, antithetical words, and verbal repetitions. A small dissenting voice to this general line of defense of the brief epic's style has been raised by Christopher Ricks (*Modern Language Notes* 76 [1961]:701–4) who challenges the description of it as muted and chastened, pointing rather to several repetitions and weak periphrases suggestive of some flagging in Milton's usual taut stylistic control.

Detailed studies of various components of the style of *PR* have been undertaken in John Carey's introduction to *PR* in the Carey-Fowler edition of Milton's poems (1968), in several special articles, and also in *Milton's Brief Epic,* which argued that *PR* employs many of the same verbal, syntactical, and sound patterns characteristic of *PL,* although in lesser profusion and with a restraint dictated by the demands of the subject. For example, wordplay, evoking multiple meanings and resonances, is a prominent feature of the style of *PR* (even as of *PL*) and it is equally characteristic of Satan, the narrator, Christ, and the Father. Among the most common kinds are etymological metaphors, which call forth an older and more vividly pictorial sense of a word along with a modern sense (e.g., Satan described as being "Nigh Thunderstruck" by God's voice); puns*, which also are often based upon etymology (Satan's description of Christ in the wilderness as "deserted"); and verbal reflections or echoes, often ironic, as in Satan's sardonic use of the term *rudiments* in reference to Christ's supposed rusticity, harking back to the Father's observation that the temptation will exercise Christ in the "rudiments" (first principles) of his great warfare against Satan, Sin, and Death. Satan's particular interest in ambiguity is manifested throughout the poem in his questioning of and laying claim to the title Son of God.

Several studies have explored imagery and image patterns in the poem. Lee S. Cox (*ELH: A Journal of English Literary History* 28 [1961]:225-43) has discussed in detail one such pattern, opposing Christ the Living Bread, the true food from heaven offering life, to Satan the false food, whose sustenance is lies; this pattern also opposes physical food supporting the life of the senses to the spiritual food that is God's Word. Identifying another significant range of imagery, Cooper R. Mackin (*Explorations of Literature,* ed. Rima D. Reck [1966]) argues that *PR*'s aural imagery—the harpies' wings, the vocality of Satan, the tempest—functions as a metaphor for the ultimate meaning of Satan's temptations as a disruption of harmony. *Milton's Brief Epic* calls attention to several other patterns : Christ as rock opposing Satan as Spirit of the Air; a pervasive light-darkness pattern identifying Christ as source of light in conflict with Satan as the power of darkness; and extensive martial imagery establishing the submerged metaphor of the temptation as a duel or single combat between the hero and his antagonist. Carey has discussed another feature of the imagery, the interesting permutations from remoteness and abstraction to concreteness in the descriptions of landscape and scene; he notes that the pageants of the banquet, the Parthian army, Rome, and Athens grow successively more specific, actual, and

concrete, so that Athens, though least gorgeous, is most fully visualized. Carey calls attention also to specific Miltonic devices for creating remoteness—the concessiveness of the description of the banquet in which the repetitions "or . . . or" permit us to make up our minds rather than forming a defined image of what we have seen, and the total inclusiveness of phrases such as "All Fish from Sea or Shore," which promotes the generality of the generic. He notes also the interpenetration of desert and forest scenes, arising from Milton's attempt to amalgamate the allegorical "woody maze" and the bare, rocky desert—which later grows green as Christ seems in some measure to raise Eden "in the waste wilderness."

Poetic figures as such are not present in great abundance in the poem, though it is interesting to remark, as Carey has, that simple similes increase steadily in number as the poem proceeds. Christ's comparison of Satan to "a fawning parasite" is the only example in the first book, Books 2 and 3 have scarcely more, whereas in Book 4 there are many: Christ's comment on the pedants, "collecting toys, . . . / As Children gathering pibles on the shore" (328-30); his scornful characterization of an ornamented style when the matter is false, "swelling Epithetes thick laid / As varnish on a Harlots cheek" (343-44); the description of Satan's fall from heaven "like an Autumnal Star / Or Lightning" (619-20), and several others. There are several epic catalogues in *PR* as well—briefer than those in *PL* but achieving the same exaltation of language by massing together evocative and sonorous names : the catalogue of the places where the disciples sought Christ after his baptism; of the classical nymphs seduced by Belial and the classical gods he impersonated in doing so; of the nymphs and knights attendant at the Satanic banquet; of the various ancient kingdoms subsumed in the Parthian empire; of the places from which the Parthian horsemen came; and of the places near and far now tributary to the Roman Empire.

The epic similes of the poem have also received some critical attention. Kingsley Widmer (*ELH: A Journal of English Literary History* 25 [1958]: 258–69) has argued that the similes in this poem as in *PL* function to point up the incommensurability of Christian and classical views of heroism and evil, that they generally compare "small things with greatest," and that they work together to suggest a "fascinating and shocking master simile," the world as evil and virtue as renunciation. *Milton's Brief Epic* notes that five of the six epic similes in *PR* occur in the last book and hence help to heighten the style of the poem as it rises to epic climax; moreover, this classical epic device helps develop the theme of the higher heroism, being wholly restricted to descriptions of Satan or of the Satanic values. The five similes in Book 4 all characterize Satan in defeat: three of them make up a finely graded sequence of comparisons for Satan's now compulsive temptation behavior, offering first a human analogue, then one in the animal kingdom, and finally one in inanimate nature, thereby imaging in the sequence itself Satan's steady disintegration and loss of control (4. 10–21). The two longer epic similes compare Satan's defeat by Christ to Antaeus's defeat by Hercules and to the Sphinx's destruction by Oedipus (4. 563–76).

Turning to syntactical and sound patterns as an aspect of style, we observe that these elements are less spectacular in the brief epic, yet produce a highly effective tenseness and terseness. The sentence length is decidedly abbreviated: the average in *PR* is seven lines, as Carey points out, with only two examples extending to 25 lines or over, a common enough unit in *PL*. Brevity of sense unit and laconic expression frequently characterize Christ's retorts: "Who brought me hither / Will bring me hence, no other Guide I seek" (1. 335–36); "Mee worse than wet thou find'st not" (4. 486). Monosyllabic lines, rare in *PL*, are relatively plentiful here, used for instance for Christ's parries but also in Satan's appeal

for Christ's compassion (3. 204–24). *Milton's Brief Epic* defends the decorum of such syntactical devices as follows: Christ uses the terse, pointed sentences to image the precision and rigor of his mind, and the narrator as redeemed man properly models his style upon Christ's. Satan also endeavors much of the time to imitate Christ's own reasonable, precise mode of speech so that his proposals will sound like the objectification of Christ's own thoughts, the discourse of his alter ego. Satan can of course use the long period for special effects, as when he presents the entire panorama of Athens as a single sentence of 48 lines.

PR also makes significant use of the fluid or liquid syntax that Christopher Ricks has found to be so characteristic of *PL*—constructions that introduce subtle nuances and ambiguities of meaning by admitting of more than one reading, as when verbs and adjectives connect with more than one object or noun. For example, the description of famous world conquerors as "Rowling in brutish vices, and deform'd, / Violent or shameful death thir due reward" (3. 86–87) permits "deform'd" to adhere to "vices," suggesting perversion, and also to "death," suggesting physical misshapenness. A similar technique utilizes the slight hesitation of the voice at the end of the poetic line to convey a fleeting suggestion of a meaning other than that indicated by the completed syntactical unit. This device produces an ironic overtone in Satan's observation that the demons now "Must bide the stroak of that long threatn'd wound, / At least if so we can, and by the head / Broken be not intended all our power / To be infring'd" (1. 59–62). The slight hesitation after "power" invites first the reading that the metaphorical wound means destruction of all the devils' power but then Satan adds the verb "infring'd" to control "power," thereby blurring his momentarily accurate perception of his desperate situation. This device also reinforces the metaphor of John the Baptist as a herald with trumpet opening the lists between Satan and Christ: "Now had the great Proclaimer with a voice / More awful than the sound of Trumpet, cried / Repentance (1. 18–20); the brief withholding of the word *Repentance* by the line-ending enables the jousting metaphor to create its effect before we are brought to concentrate on the literal story.

Certain other syntactical devices, which create a sense of balance and stasis in the poem appropriate to the cerebral combat and the immobility of the hero, are enumerated by Carey. One such is the use of participles rather than other parts of the verb—often past participles that freeze action into posture, for example, "on him baptiz'd" (1. 20), "by the head / Broken" (1. 60–61), "whom he suspected rais'd" (1. 124), "Or torn up sheer" (4. 419), "With sound of Harpies' wings and Talons heard" (2. 403). This device often defines characters by reference to their more stable past conditions rather than to their present uncertain roles, for example, "King of *Israel* born" (1. 254), "the new-baptiz'd" (2. 1). The present participle is often used to reduce the swift or sudden to the continuous or gradual, for example, "on him rising / Out of the water" (1. 80–81), "the Spirit leading" (1. 189), "Appearing, and beginning noble deeds" (4. 99), "men divinely taught, and better teaching" (4. 357). Another device establishing balance and stasis by suggesting leisure and expansiveness as opposed to brisk action is the almost pleonastic pairing of adjectives, nouns, and verbs: "defeated and repuls't," "agast and sad," "path or road," "obscure, / Unmarkt, unknown," "Unhumbl'd, unrepentant, unreform'd," "Cottage, Herd or Sheep-cote" (1. 6, 43, 322, 24–25; 3. 429; 2. 288).

Finally, both Carey's introduction and *Milton's Brief Epic* discuss the poem's important use of rhetorical schemes, especially iterative schemes—figures that derive their force from both sound repetition and word order, and that affect both sound and sense. Through structural balance and sound repetitions they elevate and stiffen the language, providing the impression of a patterned verbal duel

analogous to a single combat. It is noteworthy that Satan's speeches are no more marked by such rhetorical figures than Christ's or the narrator's. *Ploce* (repetition of the same word with some few words interspersed) is the most common figure and *traductio* (repetition of the same root word in various grammatical forms) comes next: both are habitual weapons in the Christ/Satan exchanges (e.g., 3. 44–120), where Christ, picking up Satan's five uses of "glory" and "inglorious" in the previous speech, replies with "glory" or "glorious" eleven times, and Satan follows with "glory" or "glorious" eight times. Other constantly used figures are terminal or medial rhyme (true and slant), antithesis, *anaphora* (repetition of the same word or words at the beginning of successive poetic lines), *epizeuxis* (repetition of the same word immediately, with no intermission), and *epanalepsis* (repetition of the same word or words at the beginning and end of a line of verse).

Interestingly enough, however, these devices of sound patterning also contribute to the impression of spontaneous speech, a progressive and dramatic working out of meanings and understandings as Christ and Satan talk. More paradoxical still, those speeches which most critics have singled out as containing the greatest measure of emotional realism are among those contrived with the greatest rhetorical art, for example, Satan's despairing description of his own condition (3. 204–24). One of Milton's most remarkable achievements in the poem is precisely this, the creation of a patterned language that suggests a stylized verbal duel, but that is in no way antithetical to psychological realism or dramatic intensity.

Students of *PR* have also addressed a variety of special topics, too numerous to discuss here. The reader should consult Schultz's essay (*ELH: A Journal of English Literary History* 32 [1965] : 275–302) for an excellent survey and evaluation of recent scholarship on the poem. The following remarks focus upon topics of particular significance, either because they have attracted extensive critical comment or because they mark out important new directions in criticism.

The most puzzling, distressing, and for that reason most frequently discussed single episode in *PR* is the so-called learning temptation, in which Satan offers Athens to Christ as a kingdom embodying precisely that nonmaterial good—classical learning—which seems best suited to his nature and requisite for his office of teaching and ruling by persuasion. The difficulty is that Christ renounces so categorically all the realms of knowledge, sometimes in a tone of matter-of-fact analysis, often in a tone of harsh denunciation. Classical philosophy is "false, or little else but dreams, / Conjectures, fancies, built on nothing firm (4. 291–92); the classical poets are greatly inferior to the Hebrew poets since they sing "The vices of thir Deities, and thir own," and are, once one removes their "swelling Epithetes," found to be "Thin sown with aught of profit or delight" (4. 340–45); the classical orators are far below the Hebrew prophets in teaching "The solid rules of Civil Government" (4. 358). Such language has provoked some critics to rage against Christ's harsh repudiations, and others to condescending pity for what they take to be Milton's subconscious tensions about his earlier love of learning. R. M. Adams (*IKON: John Milton and the Modern Critics* [1955]) sees in Christ's speech only a "provincial contempt of the classics," and "a feeling for the Christian dispensation as not only supplementing but cancelling pagan reason." W. B. C. Watkins (*An Anatomy of Milton's Verse* [1955]) declares that Milton here "negates learning like an Alexandrian bonfire" and "rips to shreds the passion of fifty years." Douglas Bush (*The Renaissance and English Humanism* [1939]) finds it painful "to watch Milton turn and rend some main roots of his being." George Sensabaugh (*Studies in Philology* 43 [1946]: 258–72) explains these "strange pronouncements" as stemming from a "deep Disillusion." And E. M. W. Tillyard (*Milton*) senses in the passage a mood of "mortification or masochism" in which

Milton "goes out of his way to hurt the dearest and oldest inhabitants of his mind: the Greek philosophers—his early love Plato included—the disinterested thirst for knowledge, the poets and orators of Greece and Rome."

Defenses of the learning temptation and efforts to clarify Milton's intentions in it have been mounted from several bases. For one thing, several critics have observed that the offer of Greek learning is tainted by the terms in which Satan conceives and presents it. Irene Samuel has observed (*Publications of the Modern Language Association* 64 [1949]: 708–23; *Plato and Milton*, pp. 122–29) that Satan reveals himself in this temptation as an arch-sophist, offering Jesus universal knowledge as a means to universal power ("As thy Empire must extend, / So let extend thy mind o'er all the world," 4. 222–23), and as an infallible weapon for universal persuasion. The claim that "Error by his own arms is best evinc't" (4. 235) is also sophistical; both Socrates and Jesus believe that only truth can conquer falsehood. Further, *Milton's Brief Epic* argues that by the terms of his offer Satan makes wisdom a wholly mundane thing, so that Athens, like Rome, becomes a compendium of the earlier worldly enticements—though highly refined. Here the ambition proposed is not for simple dominion over Athens but for such association with its intellectual richness as will lead to domination of the mind "o'er all the world"; the glory offered is the opportunity to "Be famous . . . / By Wisdom" (4. 221–22); and replacing the grove containing the Epicurean banquet is the "Olive Grove of *Academe*" (4. 244), filled with sensory delights directed to a much more judicious taste. Continuing this line of argument Phillip McCaffrey (*Milton Quarterly* 5 [1971]: 7–13) observes that Satan sees in Athens only another mode of power and fame, that he shows no appreciation of Athens' strictly intellectual and artistic accomplishments for their own sake—praising Plato chiefly for the attractiveness of his "retirement"; Aristotle as the "breeder" of world conquerors;

Socrates for his great influence on later schools; Homer for the envy Apollo (really a devil) showed for his poem; Demosthenes for his ability to promote war. Satan thus does not offer learning, much less wisdom to Christ, having little appreciation himself for the best Athens can offer even in strictly humanistic terms.

Recognition of Satan's perversity does not, however, account fully for the completeness and vehemence of Christ's rejection of learning, and several other justifications of the episode have been developed in relation to various specific conceptions of the poem's hero and theme. In Samuel's reading the temptation is addressed to Jesus as exemplar hero and model for every Christian, so that Jesus' reply is not to be explained by reference to his divine nature or his special role; rather, it only reaffirms Milton's consistent understanding of wisdom as deriving from Plato and Socrates, and modified by the Christian faith. The principles Jesus affirms are, Samuel asserts, the "adequacy of the human spirit, with or without particular books, in the quest of all knowledge essential to the good life"; the denial of independent value either to learning as such or to any particular branch of it, save as it is used to help achieve the good life; the idea that learning is simply a tool for purging the sight whereas wisdom, the vision of truth, comes finally through faith that unites the spirit with its Maker. This last is a conversion of Plato's precept that when reason beholds the Good, every part of the soul finds its appropriate satisfaction. Arnold Stein is in essential agreement with this reading, but he focuses upon the dramatic acting out of this definition by Christ, who in the temptation itself is manifesting that useful knowledge and that inspiration and illumination of the "spirit and judgment" by which alone we may know the truth about God and man.

A radically different approach is that of Howard Schultz (*Milton and Forbidden Knowledge* [1955]), which resolves the problem of accounting for Jesus' harsh rejection of learning by denying the relevance or application of such rejection to the Christian everyman, referring it strictly to an ecclesiastical context in which Christ as head of the church enunciates counsels of perfection meant only "for the church and its ministers." In this interpretation, Christ's repudiation of learning means simply that he and the ministers of his church have no need of human learning to perform the offices of teaching and ruling the church, and the learning temptation is a precise analogue to the argument concerning the education of ministers outlined in Milton's anti-tithe tract, *Hire*.

The reading of this episode advanced in *Milton's Brief Epic* takes Jesus to be a dramatic character rather than an exemplary or allegorical model either for the Christian Everyman or for the Christian minister, and argues that the dramatic terms of Satan's offer precludes limitation of its reference either to the private moral realm or to that of Christ's kingdom, the Church. Satan indeed proposes classical learning as necessary to the accomplishment of Christ's kingly office of "ruling by persuasion," and to his prophetic (teaching) office of refuting the gentiles' "Idolisms, Traditions, Paradoxes." But he also offers it as requisite to achieve the wisdom appropriate to the life of contemplation for which Christ showed an early propensity, as well as the kingdom "Which every wise and vertuous man attains" within the self—"These rules will render thee a King compleat / Within thyself" (4. 283–84). What Satan is doing is offering Christ his own version of wisdom, which is knowledge of all things "in the world" and knowledge relating to moral virtue (ethics*). This is a much too limited definition of wisdom even for the Stoics and Plato, and it is entirely foreign to Christians in the Augustinian tradition who, following Augustine, called the first sort of knowledge *scientia* rather than *sapientia,* labeled the second sort *prudentia* or else a variety of *scientia,* and held that true wisdom, *sapientia,* comes only from above. Augustine's exegesis of Job 28 : 28,

"Behold, piety, that is wisdom; but to depart from evil is knowledge," provided a basis for such distinctions by defending wisdom as discourse about divine things and knowledge as human ethical teaching. Augustinian Christians such as Filelfo, Nicholas of Lyra, John Colet, and a long line of commentators on the Book of Job enumerated the errors of the classical schools and contrasted Greek ethical knowledge with Job's wisdom in terms closely resembling Christ's language in *PR*; a particularly close analogue to the Miltonic passage has been traced by Edna Newmeyer (*Bulletin of the New York Public Library* 66 [1962] : 485–98) to Theodore Beza's* *Job Expounded.*

Dramatically, then, the episode develops in these terms : at the conclusion of the banquet-wealth-glory sequence Christ has appealed to both Socrates and Job as teachers and exemplars of the highest moral and ethical knowledge, proclaiming Job as the more nearly perfect. Later, in the learning temptation, Satan, using his accustomed strategy, invites Christ to identify himself with the lesser type, Socrates, and changes the terms of the discourse so as to equate the moral knowledge (*scientia*) for which Christ had earlier honored Socrates, with true wisdom from above (*sapientia*), which alone can achieve the life of contemplation, the perfection of the kingdom within, and the realization of the prophetic and kingly offices. In answer, Christ disparages as lacking in wisdom the same classical philosophers whose ethical knowledge he had before praised, associating himself rather with the more adequate Jobean conception of wisdom. He seems to allude also to that special status of which he himself is not yet fully aware—his own role as the true oracle, image of the Father's wisdom, unique recipient and exponent of the "Light from above, from the fountain of light" (4. 289).

With a fine sensitivity to dramatic nuance and interplay Balachandra Rajan (in *The Lofty Rhyme* [1970]) has provided a defense of the learning temptation in terms of Christ's emerging perception of his particular redemptive role in history. He sees the learning temptation as developing strictly out of the logic of combat rather than out of Milton's psyche, so that Satan at this point in the interchange cleverly offers Christ what heretofore he had seemed to be talking about, a kingdom not of this world. Christ refuses the offer, not in his capacity as perfect man but as the historic Christ whose destiny it is to bring down into history a power of grace* beyond the light of nature*. As Christ observes, in accents of compassion rather than scorn, the light of nature cannot show the truth about man's creation, Fall, and redemption by grace, and thus the philosophers must remain "Ignorant of themselves, of God much more" (4. 310) despite their pursuit of self-knowledge. The reader, also knowing these things, is expected to understand that Christ, who is to bring the higher wisdom into history and redeem nature by grace, cannot accept the lower knowledge as a substitute.

Another topic of particular interest to critics is the special significance of historical time* in *Paradise Regained.* In *ELH: A Journal of English Literary History* 26 (1959) : 297–513 Jackson I. Cope contrasts the dominant spatial orientation of *PL* with the flat, dimensionless world of *PR*. In his view the spatial visions of the kingdoms in the latter poem turn into evocations of history* : space becomes time. He does not, however, conclude from this that the hero acts dramatically in the particular historical circumstances, but rather concludes that there is no real temptation in *PR,* only the "exfoliation of the eternally given into time." This last perception is pressed further in Cope's article (*Milton Studies* 1 [1969] : 51–65), which argues that the time emphasized in the poem is ritual time, giving us no sense of drama but rather of a prediction fulfilling itself, a story that remembers its end in its beginning, an action that is in no place or time because in every place and time. By contrast, Laurie Zwicky (*ELH: A Journal of English Literary History* 31 [1964] : 271–77) finds that the motif of the "appointed time" operates to heighten dramatic tension in the poem as the Christian sense of *kairos,* the divinely appointed moment of special revelation or action, plays off against Satan's concept of eternally recurrent cycles. Jesus' knowledge of the time prefixed is incomplete, yet he patiently waits upon it, whereas all Satan's temptations urge Christ to "seize the day" and act before his time. From a somewhat similar perspective Lewalski's article (in *The Prison and the Pinnacle,* ed. Balachandra Rajan [1973]) argues that the juxtaposition and confrontation of various perspectives—the Father's, Satan's, Christ's—on time and history is a dominant structural element in the poem and a source of its dramatic tension. Satan's cyclical concept of time and his fixed historical categories render him unable to conceive of anything he has not seen before : hence his insistence that Christ must repeat one or more of the historical patterns Satan proposes to him. Christ, however, with his stance of openness to divine revelation, can perceive and accommodate new departures, and so makes re-creation possible—new men, new lives, a new kingdom. As Christ works out his philosophy of history, what has been is the appropriate starting point but not the fixed definition of what will be. The historical process is seen to be linear, not cyclical, its course shaped by Divine Providence and human will. And Christian typology is shown to involve patterned repetitions that can at the same time accommodate progress, redefinition, and re-creation.

Finally, some efforts to treat *PR* in terms of affective criticism may be noted. One such study, a long chapter in Jon S. Lawry's *The Shadow of Heaven: Matter and Stance in Milton's Poetry* (1968), identifies two opposed stances in the poem, one at Jordan of annunciation and promise, where the persons of the drama gather to witness a seeming union of God and man; and the second in the sterile desert, where that promise is apparently lost but actually realized. Lowry finds that the reader's stance is established at Jordan with the chorus of Christ's followers who watch and wait, so that the reader participates in their discovery and enactment of patience. In relation to the desert stance, the reader shares the largely solitary, internal pressure of the dialectic, and must acknowledge his taste for "fallen" literary and intellectual heroics like those of Satan. The tower revelation shifts the stance to annunciation again, relieving the audience for its long patience at the edge of Jordan and permitting it to experience in some degree the exaltation the Son now enjoys and the paradise he has regained. Analyzing reader response in rather different terms, Lawrence A. Hyman (*Publications of the Modern Language Association* 85 [1970]: 496–508) argues that Milton, as a means of building dramatic interest and tension, deliberately evokes and uses the inevitable disagreement and lack of sympathy fallen readers must feel toward Christ. His point is that "the contrast between our feelings, our human desires for the glories of this world, and the rejection of these desires by Christ is the emotional center of the poem," leading us to apprehend imaginatively the terrible price that must be paid by Christ to accomplish his (and our) victory.

Also focusing sharply upon reader response but arguing that the poem works finally upon the reader in more positive ways, Stanley Fish (*Calm of Mind,* ed. Wittreich, pp. 25–47) invokes terms somewhat analogous to those he employed for *PL* in *Surprised by Sin.* Fish defines two basic patterns in *PR*—a dramatic pattern in which the sphere of activity of the hero is progressively narrowed until his will is wholly subsumed in God's, and a verbal pattern in which the complexity and volubility of language is progressively diminished in the hero until his individual voice is heard no more. Both of these movements reach their respective climaxes of inaction and silence on the tower. These two patterns generate in the reader expectation, disappointment, and perplexity, frustrating again and again his mounting desire for some kind of activity or at least full explanation on the hero's part. However, if the reader can learn to subordinate his own will to the terms of the poem in a manner analogous to the hero's subordination of all assertive action and self-expression to his obedience to God, the reader can be led from impatience and frustration to understanding and approval of the Son's stance and of the poem's values.

Though *PR* has received much less critical attention than *PL,* the dimensions uncovered by those who have studied the work are already sufficient to support Coleridge's* tribute to its consummate art when he described the poem as "in its kind . . . the most perfect poem extant." The perfection is not merely formal : perhaps the greatest distinction of *PR* is the large measure of success it achieves in incorporating, evaluating, and ordering the complex of classical-Judeo-Christian values, which constitute the heritage of Western man. The particular ordering vision, like all human things, is partial. But the poem's dramatic situation —Christ's search in the wilderness to comprehend his nature and discover his mission; his subsumption of the past but rejection of its dead literalisms; his abjuration of the many evil or ignoble or imperfect or less perfect modes of action, which would preclude attainment of the highest concept of personal excellence and mission—presents a myth of human striving toward ideals of comprehension and order, of wisdom and noble action, that must remain relevant and powerful as long as such ideals hold any meaning whatever for us. [BKL]

PARADOX. That Milton's own attitude to paradoxes is itself paradoxical is not surprising. As the OED points out (*s.v. Paradox*), the connotations of this term during the seventeenth century are sometimes unfavorable ("as being discordant with what is held to be established truth") as well as favorable ("as a correction of vulgar error").

Renaissance dictionaries often define *paradox* as a statement contrary to common opinion or as a rhetorical* figure.

According to Elyot's *Dictionary* (as augmented by Thomas Cooper, London, 1559) the noun signifies "a sentence contrary to the opinion of the more parte," while the adjective denotes "a thing mervaylous strange contrary to the most commune opinion." Robert Estienne's influential *Thesaurus Linguae Latinae* (Basel, 1576) declares that the Greek word means "wonderful" (*admirabilis*) and signifies something "praeter opinionem, & inauditus." He quotes Cicero's* *Paradoxa* and *De Finibus* as authority for rendering the Greek word *paradoxa* as *admirabilia*. Estienne further defines paradox (*paradoxon*) as a rhetorical scheme, citing the authority of Julius Rufianus. Because "this figure suspends the sense and appends something beyond the expectation of the audience" (Rufianus declares), it is called *sustentatio* (suspense) or *inopinatum* (unexpected). As a rhetorical scheme, paradox is also known as *hypomone* (*sic*). Puttenham similarly classifies *paradoxon* "or the wonderer" under the "figures sententious, otherwise called rhetoricall," observing that "Many times our Poet is carried by some occasion to report of a thing that is marvelous, and then he will seeme not to speake it simply but with some signe of admiration. . . ." As an example, Puttenham cites Cato's remark on a "yong unthrift" who had sold the "salt marshes" near Capua that he had inherited as his patrimony (*Arte of English Poesie,* ed. Edward Arbor [1869], pp. 233–34) :

Now is it not, a wonder to behold
Yonder gallant skarce twenty winters old,
By might (mark ye) able to doo more?
Than the mayne sea that batters on his shore?
For what the waves could never wash away,
This proper youth hath wasted in a day.

Milton's nephew, Edward Phillips, likewise defines paradox as a rhetorical figure (*OED*): "something which is cast in by the by, contrary to the opinion or expectation of the Auditor, and is otherwise called *Hypomene*." This definition closely resembles Rufianus's statement as quoted in Estienne's *Thesaurus.*

In Renaissance usage, this term could be applied alternatively to seriously argued philosophical propositions contrary to popular opinion (such as Zeno's paradoxes of motion and Cicero's *Stoic Paradoxes*) or to mock encomiums and burlesque demonstrations of deliberate absurdities. Like Erasmus's* *Moriae Encomion,* Isocrates' orations in praise of Helen and Busiris could be regarded as paradoxes; and Synesius's *De laudibus calvicii oratio* was translated into English by A. Fleming as *A paradox, proving by reason and example, that baldnesse is much better than bushie haire* (London, 1579). Ortensio Landi's *Paradossi, cioè, sententie fuori del comun parere* (Lyons, 1543) was imitated by Charles Estienne in *Paradoxes, ce sont propos contre le commune opinion: debatus, en forme de Declamations forenses: pour exerciter les jeunes advocats, en causes difficiles* (Poitiers, 1553). In a later edition of Landi's book (1563), the author published a *Confutatione,* in three distinct orations, of his own *Paradossi.* Donne's *Paradoxes and Problems,* John Hall's *Paradoxes* (London, 1650), and a book of *Paradoxes, or Encomions in the praise of being Lowsey. Treachery . . . Blindnesse. The Emperor Nero. Madnesse.,* ascribed to "S.S." (1653) belong to this tradition of the burlesque or comic paradox. For fuller discussion, see Rosalie Colie, *Paradoxica Epidemica* (1966), and the introduction by Don Cameron Allen to the reprint of Hall's *Paradoxes* (1956).

The more serious Renaissance conception of paradox, on the other hand, is fairly close to Aristotle's* notion of *thesis.* In the *Topics* he defines the latter as "a supposition of some eminent philosopher that conflicts with the general opinion; *e.g.* the view that contradiction is impossible, as Antisthenes said; or the view of Heraclitus that all things are in motion; or that Being is one, as Melissus says : for to take notice when any ordinary person expresses views contrary to men's usual opinions would be silly. Or it may be a view about which we have a reasoned theory contrary to men's usual opinions, *e.g.,* the view maintained by the sophists that what is need not in every case either have come to be or be eternal. . . ." A

thesis is also a problem, "though a problem is not always a thesis," and practically "all dialectical problems . . . are now called 'theses'" (*Topics,* trans. W. A. Pickard-Cambridge, in *Basic Works of Aristotle,* ed. Richard McKeon [1941], p. 197).

"How wilt thou reason with them, how refute / Thir Idolisms, Traditions, Paradoxes?" Satan inquires of the hero of *PR.* "Error by his own arms is best evinc't" (4. 235). This is Milton's only explicit reference to paradox in his poetry; and, as in his prose, he employs the term pejoratively. When he applies it to the arguments of his political and ecclesiastical opponents in his controversial treatises, or in his theological and logical works, he uses it as a virtual equivalent of "contradiction" or "absurdity"; the term becomes a weapon of defense and offense against his adversaries, complementing and underlining his method of *reductio ad absurdum* in attacking their arguments.

In *Ref* he dismisses the affirmation "*No Bishop, no King*" as a "trimme Paradox," and proposes to "fetch you the Twin-brother to it out of the Jesuites Cell . . ." (3 : 46–47). In *DDD* he ridicules his opponents' interpretation of Matthew 9 : 8 ("*the hardenesse of your hearts*") as "a paradox never known til then, onely hanging by the twin'd thred of one doubtfull Scripture, against so many other rules and leading principles of religion, of justice, and purity of life" (3 : 432). In *Tetra* he expresses his contempt for their views on the same text as "the most grosse and massy paradox that ever did violence to reason and religion, bred onely under the shadow of these words, to all piety and philosophy strange and violent, that God by act of law drew out a line of adultery almost two thousand yeares long . . ." (4: 152–53). Cicero "declares it publicly as no paradox to common ears, that God cannot punish man more, nor make him more miserable, then still by making him more sinnfull" (3 : 442). In *Bucer,* on the other hand, Milton complains that he himself has been "esteem'd the deviser of a new and pernicious paradox" by men "of whose profession and supposed knowledge I had better hope . . ." (4 : 13).

According to the chapter on the Son of God in *CD*, it is self-evident that "the Father alone is a self-existent God, and that a being which is not self-existent cannot be God"; the contrary view, Milton insists, involves a *"paradoxum aliquod absurdissimum."* It is "wonderful," he observes, "with what futile subtleties, or rather with what juggling artifices, certain individuals have endeavored to elude or obscure the plain meaning of these passages; leaving no stone unturned, recurring to every shift, attempting every means, as if their object were not to preach the pure and unadulterated truth of the gospel to the poor and simple, but rather by dint of vehemence and obstinacy to sustain some absurd paradox from falling, by the treacherous aid of sophisms and verbal distinctions, borrowed from the barbarous ignorance of the schools" (14: 209). If "the Son be of the same essence with the Father, and the same Son after his hypostatical union coalesce in one person with man, I do not see how to evade the inference, that man also is the same person with the Father, an hypothesis which would give birth to not a few paradoxes" (14 : 313). In *Logic* he condemns several "paradoxes of the theologians" as contradictory or contrary to reason—that is, the dogmas that *"Christ can have a human nature and an infinite body"*; that *"In the Lord's supper an accident can exist without a subject"*; and that the statement *"The Father alone is true God"* does not exclude the Son and the Holy Spirit (11. 315, 317). In *Hire* Milton's prefatory epistle to Parliament alludes to his earlier defense of Parliament's actions in the civil war and the execution of King Charles: ". . . it suffic'd som years past to convince and satisfie the uningag'd of other nations in the justice of your doings, though then held paradoxal . . ." (6 : 44).

If one were to judge by these statements alone, one might infer that Milton had been safely innoculated against the seventeenth-century epidemic of paradoxes and that (unlike Sir Thomas Browne) he was no more "paradoxical" in philosophy than subservient to "the great wheel of the Church" in divinity, "not reserving any proper Poles or motion from the Epicycle of my own brain" (*Religio Medici*, pt. 1). In actuality, however, the reverse is true. In his poetry he delights in oxymoron ("darkness visible," "precious bane," "Courtly Stable," "lowliness majestic," "Exaltation to Afflictions high"). In verse and prose alike he exploits the paradoxes of the Christian tradition : strength in weakness and weakness in strength, the better fortitude of patience and heroic martyrdom, the paradoxes of the Virgin Birth and the Incarnation ("wedded Maid, and Virgin Mother," the "Infant God" who in his "swaddling bands" can "control the damned crew" of demons, the "Heav'n-born child . . . meanly wrapt in the rude manger"), the paradox of the blind seer, the liberty of the captive slave, the freedom of the servant of God, the paradox of good out of evil and life out of death, the paradox of the *felix culpa* and the fortunate fall. At the end of *PL* Adam hails the goodness infinite "That all this good of evil shall produce, And evil turn to good" as "more wonderful" than the first creation of light out of darkness. He hesitates whether to repent of the sin he has committed and occasioned or to rejoice that "much more good thereof shall spring. . . ." He learns that God overcomes evil with good, accomplishes great things by small, subverts "worldly strong" by things deemed weak and "worldly wise / By simply meek"; he learns that "suffering for Truth's sake / Is fortitude to highest victory, / And to the faithful Gate of Life. . . ."

Milton does not refer to these contrasts as paradoxes; instead, he usually designates them as mysteries or as miracles. They belong to the traditional Christian marvelous, and he frequently expoits them (as the Christian *concettisti* of the seventeenth century exploited the paradoxes of the faith for the effect of *admiratio*). They enhance, affectively as well as intellectually, the power and wisdom of the Deity;

and they hinge, in many instances, on the contrast between divine truth and human opinion. The wisdom of the world is mere folly in the sight of God, and vice versa. The paradoxes of the faith, like those of the classical philosophers, are often truths that appear absurd because contrary to common opinion and vulgar belief. Milton's paradoxes and oxymorons frequently depend on the contrast between truth and the deceptive appearance of truth, on the distinction between divine vision and secular error, on the diverse (and often contrary) epistemologies of flesh and spirit.

In his prose treatises, Milton exploits many of these paradoxes as arguments, though he refers to them by other names than that of paradox. "For who is there almost that measures wisdom by simplicity, strength by suffering, dignity by lowliness?" he demands in *RCG*. "Who is there that counts it first to be last, something to be nothing, and reckons himself of great command in that he is a servant?" God has "sent Foolishnes to confute Wisdom, Weaknes to bind Strength, Despisedness to vanquish Pride. And this is the great mistery of the Gospel made good in Christ himself, who . . . came not to be ministered to, but to minister. . . ." (3: 243). The "mighty weakness of the gospel" can "throw down the weak mightiness of man's reasoning." It is the "mysterious work of Christ, by lowlines to confound height, by simplicity of doctrine the wisdom of the world. . . ." (3 : 248). Or again, in *2Def*: "There is, as the apostle has remarked, a way of strength through weakness . . . in proportion as I am weak, I shall be invincibly strong, and in proportion as I am blind, I shall more clearly see. O! that I may thus be perfected by feebleness, and irradiated by obscurity!" [JMS]

PARAEUS, DAVID (1548–1622), a Calvinist* theologian and exegete, who taught at Heidelberg from 1584 until his death. He was well known in England for his interpretation of Romans 13, which he read as giving to those with power to establish rulers the power to restrain them or pull them down as well. A young Oxford divine named Knight was so ill-advised as to preach this opinion in 1622. When summoned before James I* to explain himself, his plea was that he had been misled "by *Pareus* a Divine of *Heidelberg*." The King pardoned the preacher but ordered that the offending *Commentary on the Epistle to the Romans* "should be publickly burnt." It was, at both universities and in London.

Milton refers to Paraeus a number of times in his prose works, though not always to agree with him. Thus his opinion is cited in *DDD* (3 : 391), where Milton argues from Genesis 2 : 18 that the chief end of marriage is "a meet and happy conversation" of man and wife. Nevertheless Milton rejects Paraeus's view that Christ revoked the permission for divorce* given under the Old Testament. This, says Milton, would make the Gospel of grace harsher than the Mosaic law (3: 451–53). Nor does he agree with Paraeus that Moses permitted divorce for wives only, since, as Milton says revealingly, "a husband may be injur'd as insufferably in marriage as a wife" (3 : 475). In *Tenure* (5 : 49), Milton quotes Paraeus on Romans 13 with approval. Paraeus's division of the Apocalypse in the manner of a tragedy* is cited by Milton to disarm Puritan criticism of the arts in *RCG* (3: 238) and in the preface to *SA*. The influence of Paraeus's commentary on the Apocalypse on these passages and on *PL* is discussed by Michael Fixler in *New Essays on Paradise Lost,* edited by Thomas Kranidas (1969). [JAD]

PARKER, SAMUEL (1640–1688), Anglican controversialist. He was born at Northampton, into a strong Puritan family. His background was reinforced by his education at Northampton Grammar School and at Wadham College, Oxford (B.A., 1660), and Trinity College, Oxford (M.A., 1663). He was ordained in 1664. In 1662 or 1663, according to comments made in 1673 by Andrew Marvell*, he apparently visited Milton from time to time and often discussed with him the course of action he should take in the face of the restored episcopacy. Ultimately Parker decided to abandon the Nonconformists. He was made Archdeacon of Canterbury in 1670.

Having conformed to the Church of the Restoration, Parker, in a series of works beginning with *A Discourse of Ecclesiastical Polity* (1671) and culminating with a defense of Bishop John Bramhall* (1672), made himself the "terror of the Non-Conformist world." These works prompted a rejoinder from Marvell, a satire entitled *The Rehearsal Transpros'd* (1672). In the course of the bitter controversy that ensued, Parker and his supporters turned some of their spleen on Milton. Milton was denounced as an obscene mountebank, his pamphlets and *PL* were ridiculed, and Marvell was designated as a fellow-journeyman to the blind schoolmaster. The major opponents to Marvell in this controversy were the author of *The Transproser Rehears'd* (1673), probably Richard Leigh*, though also attributed to Parker, and Parker in *A Reproof to the Rehearsal Transpros'd* (1673). Marvell brought a dignified end to the argument in *The Rehearsal Transpros'd: The Second Part* (1673), in which he accused Parker of gratuitously betraying Milton, a man who had befriended him. He reminded Parker that he, too, had been a partaker of the king's clemency, and that Milton had long since expiated himself in a retired silence. Insisting that Parker could easily have discovered that Milton had had no hand in *The Rehearsal Transpros'd,* Marvell concluded by declaring that Parker had acted inhumanely and inhospitably, like "a man that creeps into all companies to jeer, trepan, and betray them."

Parker was made Bishop of Oxford in 1686, and, by mandate of James II, president of Magdalen College in 1687. He died at Oxford on March 12, 1688. [JLG]

PARKER, WILLIAM RILEY (1906–1968), scholar who left Princeton University for a position at Ohio State University; then he moved to New York University, where he remained until 1956 as professor. During this time he was secretary of the Modern Language Association and of the American Council of Learned Societies. Upon completion of these assignments he moved to Indiana University, where he remained until his death, serving for a time as chairman of its English Department.

Besides these public activities, which earned him several honorary doctorates, Parker never abandoned his interest in Milton. Developing an idea suggested to him by Charles G. Osgood* at Princeton, he first explored the background of *SA* in classical drama : *Milton's Debt to Greek Tragedy* (Baltimore, Ohio, 1937). Most of the rest of his active career was devoted to biographical studies which resulted first in his *Milton's Contemporary Reputation* (1940), with facsimile reprints of five pamphlets directed against Milton during his lifetime, introduction and notes, and finally in the two-volume *Biography* (1968), the first exhaustive one since Masson*, a detailed and indispensable collection of information. A completely independent scholar, Parker was never satisfied with unproved if traditional assumptions. Thus he raised such questions as whether Milton's last sonnet were not addressed to Mary Powell rather than to Katherine Woodcock and whether *SA* should not be dated in the 1640s or 50s rather than after *PL* and *PR*. At the time of his death he was editing *SA* for the Variorum commentary of the poetry. [WBH]

PARODIES. "Parodies of Milton's Poems," wrote Walter Hamilton, "are neither numerous, nor particularly amusing . . ." (*Parodies of the Works of English and American Authors,* vol. 2 [1885]). Nevertheless they exhibit considerable diversity, ranging from close imitation of specific verses to comparatively free imitations of the poet's style, from occasional verbal or thematic allusions to burlesques of extended passages or even an entire poem.

Like Homer* and Virgil*, Milton invited parody on a variety of grounds and from admirers as well as detractors. As "classics" all three authors were sufficiently well-known to make parodic allusion to them intelligible. (Since the enjoyment of this genre depended largely on an audience's familiarity with the work parodied, a widely known author would normally be a fitter subject for burlesque than an obscure writer; as the popularity or notoriety of its model decayed, the point and edge of the parody usually lost their keenness.) Moreover, as exemplars of epic magnificence or majesty or sublimity, all three poets served as models for the high style; and it would be appropriate, therefore, for writers of mock-heroic or "high burlesque," as well as serious imitators, to turn to them for epic* conventions and motifs. Even when the heroicomic poet's primary aim lay elsewhere than in direct parody of these authors, he might (in varying degrees) form his style and construct his poem after their example, introducing extended passages of oblique allusion or direct parody. From serious to jocose imitation was an easy stage—especially for writers who had learned their art through close study and judicious imitation of ancient and modern "classics" —and the same poet who consciously followed Virgil or Milton in serious compositions might conveniently do so in burlesque.

Parody has been defined (*OED*) as "A composition in prose or verse, in which the characteristic turns of thought and phrase in an author or class of authors are imitated in such a way as to make them ridiculous, especially by applying them to ludicrously inappropriate subjects; an imitation of a work more or less closely modelled on the original, but so turned as to produce a ridiculous effect." Though this definition is applicable to many of the burlesque treatments of Milton's poems, it is not, in the strictest sense, applicable to "serious" parodies like George Herbert's "Souls joy, when thou art gone." Here the intent (as Hutchinson rightly observed) was not "to travesty the original, but to convert the profane to sacred use." In such sacred parodies of secular love

songs, the ridiculous had little place; nor was it always present in secular parodies of the poetry of sacred love.

Critical discussion of parody—and of its relationships with burlesque, mock-heroic, and travesty—has suffered from ambiguous terminology. For the problem of definition, the reader should consult George Kitchin, *A Survey of Burlesque and Parody in English* (1931); Albert H. West, *L'influence française dans la poésie burlesque en Angleterre entre 1660 et 1700* (1931); and Richmond P. Bond, *English Burlesque Poetry 1700–1750* (1932).

According to Victor Fournel, parody changes the condition (or social rank) of the personages in the works it travesties, whereas the burlesque finds a new source of the comic in the perpetual antithesis between the rank and the words of its heroes. Paul Lehmann, on the other hand, restricts the term parody to works that "formally imitate or quote . . . some text assumed as familiar" or else "present points of view, manners, . . . events, and personages, . . . with apparent fidelity," while deliberately caricaturing and perverting them. For Kitchin, in turn, parody denotes the "direct imitations of an individual work with humorous or critical intention," whereas burlesque refers to the "wider species in which an author's work generally or that of the school to which he may be attached is imitated with comic intention." In West's definition, travesty reproduces a serious work under a comic guise, and it differs essentially from parody. In the true parody, the subject and the original personages are changed, but the language and style are not deformed. In the travesty, however, the subject and personages remain substantially the same; only the language and style are metamorphosed. West further regards the heroicomic as the contrary of the burlesque. The former invests a vulgar person or episode with the dignity and amplitude of the epic language; the latter depicts an august and great action in the jargon of the markets. Nevertheless (he adds) "this important distinction between the burlesque and the heroicomic" was not observed in seventeenth-century England; here the word *burlesque* denoted two different comic genres.

Whereas A. F. B. Clark distinguishes the mock-heroic from the burlesque and W. M. Dixon employs "*mock-heroic* as a generic word," R. P. Bond prefers to treat *burlesque* "as a generic term," subdividing it into high and low burlesque and their subspecies. Defining burlesque in terms of "the use or imitation of serious matter or manner, made amusing by the creation of an incongruity between style and subject," he associates the travesty and the Hudibrastic with the low or "diminishing" burlesque (which "places the subject above the style"), and assigns the parody and the mock poem to the high or "magnifying" burlesque (which "fixes the style above the subject"). Travesty (Bond observes) "lowers a particular work by applying a jocular, familiar, undignified treatment, and the Hudibrastic poem uses the same procedure on more general matter. . . ." Parody "mimics the manner of an individual author of a poem by substituting an unworthy or less worthy subject. . . ." The mock poem "copies the manner of a general class of poetry without specific reference to a poet or poem. . . ."

In classical Greek the term *parōidía* signified "*a song or poem in which serious words become burlesque, a burlesque parody*"; it was derived (according to Liddell and Scott) from *parōidós* ("*singing indirectly, obscurely hinting*"). According to Aristotle's* *Poetics*, Hegemon was the first to write parodies: "Homer makes men better than they are; Cleophon as they are; Hegemon the Thasian, the inventor of parodies, and Nicochares, the author of the Deiliad, worse than they are" (*Poetics* 1448a, trans. Butcher). Hegemon's works included a *Gigantomachia* in hexameters (Gerald F. Else, *Aristotle's Poetics: the Argument*).

In antiquity (according to Gilbert Highet, *The Classical Tradition*), parody was particularly common among skeptic and cynic philosophers, who attacked Homer's authority by parodying "his greatest lines." Short interludes of parodic verse frequently occur in Menippean satire; and the Greek satirist Timon of Phlius composed a mock-heroic poem depicting a battle of philosophers and entitled *Silloi* ("Squints"). Juvenal's fourth satire contains a grandiose description of a council held by Domitian on "a ridiculously trivial subject," but mock-heroic episodes in other Roman satires are comparatively brief. Since the comic or burlesque epic *Margites* ascribed to Homer has not survived, the "only ancient poem which could be called a comic epic is *The Battle of Frogs and Mice. . . .*" In Highet's opinion, epic parody "began again in the Renaissance as soon as men became really familiar with the *Aeneid. . . .*" He regards Tassoni's *La Secchia Rapita* ("The Ravished Bucket") as an "epic parody"; and E. R. Curtius (*European Literature and the Latin Middle Ages*) applies the same term to Teofilo Folengo's macaronic Latin epic *Baldus* (1517).

In the preface to *Annus Mirabilis* Dryden* contrasted the images and effects of heroic and burlesque poetry, and their modes of imitating or adapting the classics. In the preface to Juvenal ("A Discourse Concerning Satire"), he extended this discussion specifically to parody. The descriptions or images that he had borrowed from Virgil—his "master in this poem" of the *Annus Mirabilis*—are "the adequate delight of heroic poesy" inasmuch as they "beget admiration, which is its proper object. . . ." Conversely, "the images of the burlesque, which is contrary to this, by the same reason beget laughter; for the one shows nature beautified, as in the picture of a fair woman . . . ; the other shows her deformed, as in that of a lazar, or of a fool with distorted face and antic gestures, at which we cannot forbear to laugh, because it is a deviation from nature."

According to Dryden's definition, parodies are "verses patched up from great poets, and turned into another sense than their author intended them." The *silli* composed by the Greek satiric poet Timon were full of such parodies. Such, among the Latin writers, was "the famous *Cento of Ausonius; where the words are Virgil's, but by applying them to another sense, they are made a relation of a wedding-night; and the act of consummation fulsomely described in the very words of the most modest amongst all poets. Of the same manner are our songs, which are turned into burlesque, and the serious words of the author perverted into a ridiculous meaning. Thus in Timon's *silli*, the words are generally those of Homer and the tragic poets; but he applies them, satirically, to some customs and kinds of philosophy which he arraigns" (ed. George Watson).

Inconsistent though they often were, these theoretical distinctions are historically significant, inasmuch as they entered the critical discussions of Addison*, Johnson*, and others or conditioned the parodists' own conceptions of their genre. As Bond observes, Samuel Johnson quoted Edmund Smith's views on the superiority of "the great burlesque . . . to the low," inasmuch as it is "much easier to make a great thing appear little, than a little one great" and because the author of "lofty burlesque" must not only "find out and expose what is ridiculous" but also "raise and elevate."

The pleasure of parody (like that of burlesque in general) sprang from a conscious violation of the rules of logic and of art. In making the great appear small, or vice versa, the burlesque poet resembled the sophist; and in describing the trivial in magnificent language or relating the sublime in ridiculous style, he was (as he usually realized) breaking the fundamental rule of decorum (that "grand master piece to observe") and the sacrosanct ratio between *res* and *verba*, matter and style.

For parodies of Milton, the reader should consult Hamilton (pp. 217–36); Kitchin; Bond; and Raymond Dexter Havens, *The Influence of Milton on English Poetry* (1922). A register of burlesque poems published in England between 1700 and 1750 appears in Bond, pp. 233–453. Haven (pp. 573–697) quotes apparent borrowings from Milton by later English poets, in addition to extensive bibliographical lists of poems influenced

by *PL, L'Al* and *Il Pen, Lyc, Nat, Mask,* and other poems. West (pp. 186–93) lists parodies and burlesque poems published in France between 1644 and 1825 and English parodies and burlesque imitations published between 1650 and 1825. For the more comprehensive category of serious imitations and paraphrases of *PL,* such as Hopkins's "Milton's *Paradise Lost Imitated in Rhyme* (1699), Mme. Du Boccage's *Le Paradis terrestre, poème imité de Milton,* and Robert E. Clark's *Paradise Lost: In Rhyme* (a version of Book 1 [1867]), see Havens; John Martin Telleen, *Milton dans la littérature française* (1904); and Earl R. Wasserman, *Modern Language Notes* 58 (1943). Ann Gossman, in "Milton Trickt and Frounc't," *Notes and Queries,* n.s. 2 (1955) : 100–102, discusses rhymed versions of passages in *PL,* published in 1738 and 1740.

First published in 1701 as *Imitation of Milton,* John Philips's* *The Splendid Shilling* won Addison's praise as the finest burlesque poem in English, Goldsmith's admiration as the best English parody of Milton, and Johnson's grudging commendation for the novelty achieved by degrading Milton's "sounding words and stately construction" by applying them "to the lowest and most trivial things. . . ." Bearing the Miltonic epigraph :

"Sing Heavenly Muse,
Things unattempted yet in Prose or Rhyme,
A Shilling Breeches, and Chimera's dire"

this mock poem describes the miseries of "griping Penury"—the dun, the catchpole, hunger and cold—in Miltonic blank verse*. Though it begins with a Horatian* echo ("Happy the Man, who void of Cares and Strife"—cf. Epode 2, "Beatus ille qui procul negotiis," and Maren-Sofie Røstvig, *The Happy Man,* 1954–1958), it contains lines and images reminiscent of passages in *PL,* including echoes of the ship image near the end of Book 2 and of the autobiographical references near the beginning of Books 3 and 7. Like the historical Milton, the narrator in *The Splendid Shilling* solaces himself in evil days with a tobacco pipe :

Then Solitary walk, or doze at home
In *Garret* vile, and with a warming puff
Regale chill'd Fingers, or from *Tube* as black
As *Winter's Chimney,* or well-polish'd Jett,
Exhale *Mundungus,* ill-perfuming Smoak.
Not blacker *Tube,* nor of a shorter Size
Smoaks *Cambro-Britain* (vers'd in Pedigree,
Sprung from *Cadwalader* and *Arthur,* ancient
    Kings,
Full famous in Romantick tale) when he
O're many a craggy Hill, and fruitless Cliff,
Upon a Cargo of fam'd *Cestrian* Cheese,
High over-shadowing rides, with a design
To vend his Wares, or at the *Arvonian* Mart,
Or *Maridunum,* or the ancient Town
High *Morgannumia,* or where *Vaga's* Stream
Encircles *Ariconium,* fruitful Soil. . . .

Philips's shilling had been wisely invested. Within a few years it had brought in rich returns in small cash and commodity: copper farthings, suet puddings, strong English ale, and solid English homilies. Many of these imitations begin with the *Beatus ille* formula that Philips had adapted from Horace; they are "Miltonic" chiefly in their use of blank verse instead of rhyming couplets and in distant echoes of Miltonic diction and syntax. Taking Philips rather than Milton as their stimulus and model, they are (not surprisingly) much closer to *The Splendid Shilling* than to *PL* in style. They form a prolific, though minor, subspecies in the tradition of Miltonic parody:

Happy the boy, who dwells remote from
    School,
Whose pocket or whose rattling-box, contains
A Copper Farthing!
          (Mrs. Pennington, *The Copper
                Farthing*)

Happy the man who in his pot contains
A suet dumpling; . . .
          (*The Suet Pudding*)

Happy the man! whose well-stor'd shelf
    contains, . . .
A set of goodly sermons.
          (*The Curate's Caution*)

As for "Ale irriguous," Thomas Warton composed "A Panegyric on Oxford Ale," in emulation of the "matchless bard" who had sung "The SPLENDID SHILLING's praise" and "Whose steps in verse Miltonic I pursue,/ Mean follower. . . ."

Philips's followers celebrated puddings, apple dumplings, and potatoes with equal gusto, or rejoiced in the numismatic bliss of Birmingham halfpennies and crooked sixpences. A "poem in Miltonics" entitled *The Empty Purse* appeared in 1750; Havens has traced Phillips's influence on works like Maurice's *School-boy,* Lardner's *College Gibb,* and Woty's *Campanalogia,* and on poetry of "low estate" such as *The Old Shoe, The Sweepers,* and *The Bugs.*

The anonymous *Cerealia* (1706) in praise of ale has also been ascribed to Philips. More doubtful is Philips's authorship of a burlesque originally printed in 1713 and reprinted in *The Bee: or, Universal Weekly Pamphlet,* no. 11 (1733) under the title *Chloe's Chamber-Pot. A Poem in Imitation of Milton.* Nancy Lee Riffe ("An Early Miltonic Burlesque," *Notes and Queries* n.s. 11 [1964]: 296) notes that this work was first attributed to John Philips in *The London Magazine* in February 1754.

Gay's *Wine, A Poem* (1708) parodies the proposition and invocation of *PL,* invoking the assistance of the god of wine:

Of Happiness Terrestrial, and the Source
Whence human Pleasures flow, sing *Heavenly*
    Muse,
Of sparking juices, of the enliv'ning Grape,
   . . .
Bacchus Divine, aid my advent'rous Song,
That with no middle flight intends to soar.
Inspir'd, Sublime on *Pegaseon* Wing
By thee upborn, I draw *Miltonic* Air.

After an apotropaeic formula ("Drive hence Rude and Barb'rous Dissonance / Of Savage *Thracians,* and *Croatian* Boors"), the poet describes a convivial drinking party at a tavern, invests doorman and hostess and butler with epic dignity, and reports the several toasts to queen, notables, and mistresses. He concludes with a final Miltonic echo:

Thus we the winged Hours in harmless
    Mirth,
And Joys Unsulli'd pass, till Humid Night
Has half her Race perform'd, . . .

Fanscomb Barn, a blank-verse burlesque by Anne, Countess of Winchilsea, followed in 1713. Among the English translations of Edward Holdsworth's *Muscipula* (1709)—a mock-heroic poem describing the invention of a mouse trap— R. D. Havens recognizes "unrimed burlesques of *Paradise Lost*" by Daniel Bellamy, John Hoadly, and an unidentified translator. Borrowings from Milton are also prominent in Bishop Warburton's English translation of Addison's Latin poem on the battle of the cranes and pigmies (1724). Francis Fawkes, R. Jephson, William Woty, William Shenstone, and John Armstrong also parodied Milton's poetry. William Somervile produced a *Hudibras and Milton Reconciled* as well as a burlesque of Milton's style in *Hobbinol, or the Rural Games* (1740). Samuel Wesley* composed *The Descriptive, a Miltonic, after the Manner of the Moderns*. Cowper's* "Verses Written in his 17th Year, on Finding the Heel of a Shoe" burlesques *PL*, while the opening lines of his longer poem *The Task* adapt passages from both of Milton's epics to a eulogy of the sofa. An anonymous political satire in blank verse describing the duel between William Adam and Charles James Fox appeared in 1780 under the title *Paradise Regain'd, or the Battle of Adam and the Fox*. (See Havens for fuller discussion of these burlesque poems.) *A Description. In Imitation of Milton* (1721), subsequently reprinted as *The Bog-House*, treats (as R. P. Bond observes) "the lowest possible subject, a description of a toilet and the process of purging" in "high diction with some Miltonic tricks." *Bartholomew-Fair: or, a Ramble to Smithfield* (1729) was described as "a Poem in Imitation of Milton." A poem on gin entitled *Geneva* and ascribed to "Alexander Blunt, Distiller" appeared in 1729; noting the parody of Milton in this work, Bond quotes the following variation on the *psychostasia* motif :

> Her golden scales *Astraea*, then
> Uprais'd; in one, *Geneva's* merits plac'd;
> The merits of *Malt Liquor*, t'other held;
> '*The latter, quick flew up, and kick'd the beam!*'

Bond also comments on the parody of Milton's style in Andrew Brice's *Freedom* (1730), *An Epistle from Oxon* (1731), *Gin, A Poem, in Miltonick Verse* (1734), *A Panegyric on a Louse, in the style of Milton* (1737), James Bramston's *The Crooked Sixpence* (1743), and *A Bacchanalian Rhapsody* (1746).

Burlesque exploitations of Miltonic themes and conventions occur in American poetry along with serious imitations of his verse. (See INFLUENCE ON AMERICAN LITERATURE.) George F. Sensabaugh, *Milton in Early America* (1964) calls attention to an early burlesque of *Paradise Lost* in the *American Magazine and Historical Chronicle* (1743). In *Sawney, An Heroic Poem, Occasion'd by the Dunciad*, James Ralph employed Miltonic motifs, including the scales image from Book 4 of *PL*. Francis Hopkinson's *Dirtilla* utilized Miltonic echoes for his mock encomium of dirt, but (unlike Ralph and Trumbull) he lacked (as Sensabaugh observes) the "talent to fashion humorous verse from the grand style" of *PL*. In Trumbull's *M'Fingal*, a mock-epic on Whig and Tory rivalries, Sensabaugh notes the extensive use of Miltonic imagery and echoes of *PL* and *PR*, in addition to the influence of Butler's *Hudibras* and allusions to Homer and Virgil. In *The Porcupine, Alias the Hedge-Hog: Or, Fox Turned Preacher* (1784), Sensabaugh finds a burlesque of the conversation between Eve and Satan before the Fall.

In France, Voltaire* ridiculed Milton as "cet atrabilaire,/ que d'Olivier fut un temps sécretaire" both in poetry and in prose, but (as Telleen observes) "La parodie du *Paradis perdu* la plus grave se trouve dans la *Pucelle*." Though this burlesque version of the life of Jeanne d'Arc was chiefly directed against Chapelain's sacred epic *La Pucelle*, Voltaire borrowed elements of the Christian marvelous and other "choses bizarres" from *PL* in order to make his hagiographical travesty seem more ridiculous. Saint Denis blushes like Milton's Raphael, mounts a beam of light as though it were a horse, and "sans dire une parole,/ Pique des deux, et par les airs s'envole." Voltaire also burlesques such epic (and Miltonic) motifs as the psychostasia and the celestial arsenals, and converts the battle of angels into a combat between saints of rival nations, Saint Denis and Saint George.

The principal French parody of *PL*— *Le Paradis perdu* (1805) of Viscount Évariste Désiré de Forges de Parny—was (as Telleen suggests) partly inspired by Voltaire's *Pucelle* but carried the element of farce to a more ludicrous extreme. Parny's poem, composed in the context of the years following the French Revolution and the consolidation of Napoleon's power, utilized the Christian marvelous to ridicule the Christian faith. In addition to this parody of Miltonic epic, Parny composed other anti-religious burlesques, such as *La guerre des dieux* (a mock-heroic poem in ten cantos), *Les Rosecroix,* and *Les Galanteries de la Bible.*

In many of these parodies, the spirit of rivalry—with other parodies, as well as with Milton himself—is not far from the surface. Several of the more successful examples were inspired less by the parodist's reaction to Milton than by contests sponsored by various nineteenth- or twentieth-century journals. In 1880 *The World* offered prizes for poems composed on the theme "The Opening of Parliament" and written in the style of Book 2 of *PL.* John Foote of Kensington won first prize with a burlesque account of parliamentary debate between Onslow, Granville, and Beaconsfield :

> . . . mute and perplexed
> Sat all the Peers, awaiting who appeared
> To second, or oppose, or undertake
> The perilous attempt, till Onslow, raised
> Alike by merit and the Premier's choice
> To that bad eminence, in glib-set speech
> Began. . . .

Granville, the leader of the opposition ("in act most graceful and humane / Of all who fell from office") replies to Onslow's address, "breathing forth / Hatred implacable" and denouncing "Revenge, and dissolution dangerous / To less than Peers." His "sentence pleased,/ Counsel-

ling revolt," until Lord Beaconsfield (the curl of Vivian on his forehead thinned by years but "Majestic still in ruin") rises and addresses the Peers of the Empire as their "chief" :

> . . . for still to me the popular vote
> Inclines, here to continue, and build up here
> A growing Empire, so with Freedom joined;
> . . .

> Well have ye judged of old, and still
> Ye shall judge well, discerning to avoid,
> By me advised, shameful dismemberment
> Of this great realm.

In the same competition Mr. H. Hamilton of Holloway won second prize with a parody on the opening lines of Book 2 (see below).

As John Robert Moore points out in *Studies in Philology* 48 (1951) : 1525–25, the infernal council was the "one part of *Paradise Lost* best suited to the most urgent literary needs of the Augustans," for it could "serve as a pattern for satire against rival chieftains. . . ." According to report Wharton's Hell-Fire Club consciously imitated the infernal council. In an ode *On Rebellion* Defoe* attempted to supply Milton's omissions in the devil's story with verses of his own : "*Satan,* with hideous ruin thus supprest. . . ." Noting the "direct line of descent from *Paradise Lost* through *Absalom and Achitophel* to *Faction Display'd* (1704), *The Dyet of Poland* (1705), and all the teeming host in the Age of Anne," Moore calls attention to imitations or echoes of Milton's infernal council in the works of Richard Blackmore, John Dennis*, William Shippen, in Luke Milbourne's *The Moderate Cabal* (1710), and in *The Junto* (1710) and other early eighteenth-century poems. Thomas B. Stroup (*Journal of English and German Philology* 46 [1947]: 165–67), detects echoes of Milton's infernal scenes in Gay's play *The Mohocks* (1712).

The infernal council also served as a model for political satire in eighteenth-century America. *The Demos in Council: or 'Bijah in Pandemonium. Being a Sweep of the Lyre, In close Imitation of MIL-*

TON was published at Boston in April 1799, "when the Federalists and Antis were at daggers drawn, and personalities of the fiercest sort were daily interchanged" (see the reprint in *The Magazine of History with Notes and Queries, Extra No.* 106 (1925), pp. 55–70). A quotation from Milton's description of Hell (transferred to the Anti-Federalists or "Jacobins") serves as epigraph :

> They "breed
> Perverse, all monstrous, all prodigious things,
> Abominable, unutterable; and worse
> Than fables yet have feign'd."

Beginning with a parody of the opening lines of Book 2, the poem describes the consultation of Anti-Federalist politicians during the incarceration of 'Bijah, then relates his release and the exultation of his followers, whose celebrations are finally disrupted by a sheriff's posse. Of the speakers in this parody of Milton's infernal conclave, 'Bijah has been tentatively identified as Samuel Adams, Honee as Austin, Junius as Jarvis, and Tummas as Thomas Edwards. Though there are few Miltonic allusions in the latter part of this burlesque, the parodic imitation in the first half of the poem is fairly close. 'Bijah's address from the throne may serve as an example of the anonymous poet's techniques of parodic adaptation:

> Cits, lawyers, doctors, brother Jacos all,
> For since this gaol, within its walls can hold
> Me but a month, tho' sad, oppress'd and fall'n,
> I give not all for lost. From this abode,
> Our Gallic virtues bursting, will appear
> More glorious and more dread than from no fall,
> And trust themselves to fear no second fate.
> Me, tho' just right, and the sole laws we own'd,
> Did first create your equal, next, free choice,
> Consent unanimous, so that I should meet
> The force of bench and bar, me eminent
> Establish, in a safe unenvied throne.
> Distinguish'd rank among the Fed'ralists
> So dread, which follows dignity, might draw
> Envy from each inferior; but who here
> Will envy, whom the highest place exposes
> Foremost to stand your bulwark, and condemns
> To greatest share of constant pain?
> . . . Where there is no good
> For which to strive, no strife can come up there

From faction. . . . With this advantage then
To union, and firm faith and firm accord,
More than can be 'mong Fed'ralists, we now renew
Our custom'd work of opposition.
. . . By what best way,
Whether of open war or covert guile,
We now debate. Who can advise will speak.

The next speaker, Honee, "pen-ful wight," wears the borrowed rhetoric of Moloch. The "lankest yet the fiercest man / Of all the club," he is "now fiercer by despair" :

> His trust was with the senate to be rank'd,
> Uplift in power; but would be any thing,
> Rather than not to be at all. Now all
> Hope lost, he dauntless look'd. Juries and bars,
> Fines and imprisonments, pill'ries and ropes,
> He reck'd not. . . .
> My sentence is for open war; of wiles
> More inexpert, I boast not. . . .
> For while we sit contriving, shall our friends,
> Myriads that stand in arms, and longing wait
> The signal to come o'er, sit ling'ring there
> Lean, hungry; and this land, their proffer'd place
> Instead of, hang on noble *Talleyrand,*
> Who finds it plaguy hard to get 'em rhino?
> . . . No let us rather choose,
> Arm'd with French flames and fury, all at once land
> O'er this fair land to force resistless way.

Junius, "in act more graceful, and humane," echoes Belial's misgivings :

> . . . But could we break our way by force,
> And at our heels our *Sans Culottes* could come
> With blackest insurrection to confound
> The light we war against, yet our enemies
> Could cut us down like rotten trees before
> The whirlwind's sweep.

Tummas counters these "words cloth'd in reason's garb" with arguments inherited from Mammon :

> Either to o'erturn the government, so dread,
> We war, if war be best, or to regain
> Our own rank lost.

The debate is terminated by Democritus, who possesses the "grave aspect," "Atlantean shoulders," and language of Beelzebub :

> Why sit we here projecting peace and war.

. . . And what peace can we return, . . .
Yet ever plotting, how the Fed's may least
Enjoy their conquest, . . .

After a chronographia describing the "rosy steps" and "Orient pearl" of morning, thé poet turns to Milton's Hell-gate for imagery :

Now *Hartshorn* from his side the fatal key,
(Sad instrument of 'BIJAH'S woe) he took,
Then in the key-hole turns
Th' intricate wards. . . . On a sudden open fly,
With impetuous recoil and jarring sound,
The prison doors, and on their hinges grate
Harsh thunder!

At this point his friends, "waiting his coming forth" in "mobbish-wise," bear him on their shoulders, "High in the midst, exalted as a god," and "Idol of *French* magnificence!"

Since the opening lines of Book 2 of *PL* appear to have been a favorite model for burlesque imitation, a few examples, ranging from Dryden to Edgar Lee Masters, may help to indicate the variety of ways in which parodists might exploit this passage. In Dryden's *MacFlecknoe,*

The hoary prince in majesty appeared,
High on a throne of his own labors reared.

In Pope's* *Dunciad* the imitation of Milton is closer : Book 2 of the burlesque begins with an imitation of Book 2 of the divine epic. Milton's arch-devil abdicates his throne in favor of Pope's arch-dunce —Lewis Theobald in the earlier version, and Colley Cibber in the later revision :

High on a gorgeous seat, that far out-shone
Henley's gilt tub, or Fleckno's Irish throne,
Or that where on her Curls the Public pours
All-bounteous, fragrant Grains and Golden show'rs,
Great Cibber sate. . . .

In *The Pediculaiad, or Buckram Triumphant* (1770), a mock-heroic account of warfare between a flea and a louse, William Woty introduces his heroic tailor in lines reminiscent of Milton's Satan :

High on his shop-board in exalted state
Pre-eminent sat *Buckram*, . . .

The American poet Thomas Godfrey echoed the same passage twice in his juvenalia (see Sensabaugh's discussion) :

High in the midst, rais'd on her rolling throne,
Sublimely eminent bright FANCY shone.

High on a shining seat with rubies grac'd,
Cupid, the God of am'rous thoughts, was plac'd.

Another American poet, James Ralph, similarly turned to Pandemonium's throne for his model :

High on a pompous throne, with glitt'ring gems
Emblaz'd, the lordly tyrant sits sublime.

The anonymous Federalist sympathizer who wrote *The Demos in Council* (see above for discussion) achieved a closer imitation of Milton's description of Satan enthroned :

High in a room of legal state, which far
Outvied the strength of *Dedham* or of *York,*
Or e'en the *Concord,* which with heavy hands
Clanks on her slaves her barb'rous chains and bars,
'BIJAH exalted sat, by merit rais'd
To that bad eminence; and from despair,
Insatiate to pursue vain war with laws,
His proud imaginations thus displayed: . . .

H. Hamilton's burlesque on the opening of Parliament (published in *The World* in February 1880) rebuilt Pandemonium in high Victorian, translating Satan's polity into the higher imperialism :

High on a throne of Royal state which well
Beseemed the rule of Britain, and of Ind,
In sable vested, save for lustrous star
And circlet bright of gleaming gem and gold,
Victoria proudly sat by lineage raised
To that fair eminence. . . .

Summoned by the usher to the House of Lords, the commons come "trooping to the bar"—only to share a fate like that of the plebeian angels in Satan's capitol :

Behold a wonder! They, who in their place
Were pompous in their port as any peer,
Now fight and jostle for a standing-room;
Their self-importance breathless and collapsed
As Aesop's fabled frog.

Meanwhile, like Milton's infernal peerage, the "noble lords—dukes, earls, and smaller fry"—sit "far above, / And at their own convenience,"

Quaint demi-gods, in crimson robes and hats
Shiny and tall.

Thereupon Cairns discloses "the Royal thoughts / And Beaconsfield's concoc--tions":

"Despite our loss
In Zululand, and Chelmsford's blundering,
Imperium et Libertas will appear
More glorious to the Jingoes than no war,
With what besides in Parliament or field
Hath been involved in failure. To this, then,
Our policy of old we now return—
How best we can contrive, by force or guile,
To filch our neighbours' lands, and keep our own."

Mention also may be made of *Paradise Lost: or, the Great Dragon Cast Out* by "Lucian Redivivus" (1872), a hostile parody in Hudibrastic couplets attacking Christianity by way of Milton's Christian poem. The poem begins with the War in Heaven* and goes on to describe Adam— "our poor, diddled, naked great-grand-papa," according to the Preface, p. 11— in disparaging terms. As for the creation of Eve, although

some blockheads have gainsaid it,
The job did great Jehovah credit.
Not only was she made up neatly,
But Adam's side was healed completely . . .
And great, no doubt, was his surprise,
When first he waked and rubbed his eyes,
To find so choice a piece of *goods*
Close by him, and without her *duds*.

The author elaborately annotated his text in the manner of contemporary editions of Milton. For this quotation he observes,

No doubt but poor Adam stared like a stuck pig when his peepers were first unbuttoned to find his rib (a tempting piece of goods, no doubt) quite naked, as well as himself! But as the pippin was nibbled, it was most likely he saw the cocks and hens, and tups and ewes, &c., all busy in the family way, or, as Cotton says, "hard at it," which must have given him a bit of a notion, if his head was ever so thick. (p. 64)

Oddly enough "Lucian" assumes, unlike Milton, that sex was unknown until Adam "made free / With great Jehovah's apple tree." The rest of the poem details the Fall* and ends, like *PL*, with the expulsion from the Garden.

In *The Spooniad* (1914) Edgar Lee Masters transfers the Satanic throne and the motif of rebellion to an American setting (see Havens for an account of other parodies of Milton in this poem):

High on a stage that overlooked the chairs . . .
Sat Harmon Whitney, to that eminence,
By merit raised in ribaldry and guile, . . .

One of the more skillful burlesques of Milton's style belongs to the twentieth century. In 1931 *The Week-end Review* proposed a contest to supply Milton's "regrettable omission of any reference to tooth-brushing in the description of Adam and Eve retiring for the night" in *PL*, Book 4. Sir Edward Marsh's contribution (to be inserted between lines 740 and 741 of the original: "These troublesome disguises which wee wear" and "Strait side by side were laid") began with the following description:

Yet pretermitted not the strait Command,
Eternal, indispensable, to off cleanse
From their white elephantin Teeth the stains
Left by those tastie Pulps that late they chewd
At supper.

Thereupon Eve, "our general Mother," having "insorb'd" the "pure Lymph" from a "salubrious Fount," cleanses her "gumms impearl'd" with "tart juices . . . on sprigs of Myrtle smeard, / (Then were not Brushes). . . ." (See Sir Edward Marsh, *A Number of People* [1934]).

Among the minor poems, *L'Al* and *IlP* were favorite objects for parody. *The Garrulous Man* (1777) begins by banishing "blubbering Melancholy" ("Of the blue devils and book-learning born, / In dusty schools forlorn; / Amongst black-gowns, square caps, and books unjolly") to some "college cell, / Where muzzing quizzes mutter monkish schemes, / And the old proctor dreams. . . ." Invoking instead that "baggage fat and free, / By gentles called Festivity, / And by us rolling kiddies, *Fun*,"—daughter of Harlequino and Mother Shipton, or, "as some deeper say," child of Jack Pudding and Jenny Diver—the anonymous author echoes Milton's conclusion :

> Freaks like these if thou canst give,
> Fun, with thee I wish to live.

Horace Twiss's *Fashion* (1814), a paraphrase of *L'Al*, banishes "loth'd vulgarity, / Of Ignorance and native Dullness bred," invokes the "nymph of slender waiste, / Known early by the name of Taste, / And now denominated Fashion," and ends with the promise :

> These delights if thou canst give,
> FASHION, with thee I wish to live."

Mundy's "The Hare Hunter" parodied various parts of both *L'Al* and *IlP* ("Hence, Fox-hunting! thou fiend forlorn, / Of Uproar wild and Tumult born"). *Gradus ad Cantabrigiam* (1824) by "a Brace of Cantabs," parodied the opening lines of *L'Al* in much the same manner as the author of *The Garrulous Man* :

Hence, loathed MATHEMATICS !
Of lecturer and blackest tutor born,
In lecture-room forlorn,
Mongst horrid quizzes, bloods, and bucks
    unholy. . . .

An "Ode" composed on Burns's centennial birthday by "an ardent admirer of MILTON" began with a parody of *L'Al*:

Hence, chroniclers of Time,
Makers of almanacs and strange predictions,
  . . .

while the anonymous author of "Football" (1883) dismissed "hateful idleness," child of Ennui and Vice, to invoke the goddess Sport, offspring of Leisure and Health.

Parodies of Milton's lyric on Shakespeare appeared in *Punch* (1856, 1863). Dryden's epigram on Milton was a popular subject for parody. It was selected by the editor of *Truth* as the "model for a parody competition" in 1884, and

several of the numerous examples have been reprinted by Hamilton.

As the Miltonic elements in the mock-heroic poetry of Dryden and Pope have been investigated elsewhere, it would be superfluous to reexamine this problem in detail. For the influence of *PL* on Dryden's *MacFlecknoe* and *Absalom and Achitophel* the reader should consult *i. a.* Anne Davidson Ferry, *Milton and the Miltonic Dryden* (1968); Ian Jack, *Augustan Satire* (1952); Morris Freedman, "Dryden's Miniature Epic," (*Journal of English and Germanic Philology* 57 (1958) and "Satan and Shaftesbury," *Publications of the Modern Language Association* 74 (1959). For Miltonic parody, imitation, and allusion in *The Rape of the Lock, The Dunciad,* and other poems by Pope, one should consult the standard editions by John Butt, Aubrey L. Williams, and others; Reuben A. Brower, *Alexander Pope, The Poetry of Allusion* (1959); the dissertation by June M. Bostich, "The Fallen Sublime : A Study of Esthetic and Moral Decay in the *Dunciad*," *Dissertation Abstracts International* 32 : 2632A–33A (Univ. of California, Riverside, 1971). [JMS]

PASSION, THE. A fifty-six line fragment, *Passion* appeared in both the 1645 and 1673 editions of Milton's poems. In its opening lines, Milton alludes to *Nat,* which he had written in December 1629. Possibly he planned to write a series of poems around the major feast days of the Christian calendar, and his success with the ode encouraged him to compose *Passion* the following March. A note that he appended to it tells us, however, that he found the subject "to be above the yeers he had, when he wrote it, and nothing satisfi'd with what was begun, left it unfinisht."

Milton's lack of satisfaction with his work was justified. His failure was not due to lack of technical proficiency, for the stanzaic form he used was the same one that he had successfully employed in the proem of *Nat*—six lines of iambic pentameter plus an Alexandrine, with a rhyme scheme of ababbcc. Utilizing this form, he created competent verse despite some minor imperfections, for example, employing the same rhyme sounds in the concluding couplets of his first, second, and fifth stanzas. His real failure lies at a deeper level: the stanzas, quite simply, do not go anywhere.

They tell us what he has been writing (*Nat*), what he has been reading (the *Christiad* of the Italian poet Vida*), and what he intends to write (an elegy on Christ's death in contrast to Vida's epic treatment of his life). They do not in any sense fulfill that intention. Neither an appeal to "night best Patroness of grief" nor a journey in Ezekiel's chariot to "where the Towers of *Salem* stood" enables the poet to come to terms with his proposed subject. Extravagant descriptions of his grief suffice only to carry him through two more stanzas before he breaks off, temperamentally incapable perhaps of writing on Christ's Passion. Indeed, the extant stanzas constitute only a proem to a poem, whose envisioned form we can not guess.

Temperamental incapacity at least is the explanation of James Holly Hanford for the poem's failure: "The truth is that the crucifixion was not a congenial theme to him at any time. Even this early he seems to have felt instinctively that man's salvation depends upon himself and that he needs Christ as a guide and model perhaps more than as a redeemer" (*A Milton Handbook*, 5th ed., p. 115). More moderate is William Riley Parker's view that the young Milton "lacked the experience of life to make a poem upon so tragic and triumphant a theme" (*Milton*, p. 72). However one explains it, the poem is a failure, though not perhaps without its significance. From it, Milton may well have realized the danger of overextending himself in tackling subjects for which he was not yet emotionally and artistically ready. [ERG]

PASSIONS, THEORY OF THE: *see* SCIENCE, MILTON AND.

PASTORAL POETRY. The history of pastoral poetry begins with Theocritus*, who was born in Sicily and wrote on the island of Cos and in Alexandria in the first half of the third century B.C. Theocritus invented what we think of as the genre of pastoral poetry, borrowing techniques from epic and drama as well as from folk songs and drawing upon his knowledge of country life in Sicily and on Cos. Theocritus was a sophisticated poet appealing to the attraction of urban readers for a simpler life, but he did not romanticize the country. His herdsmen are vigorous, coarse, and sometimes humorous figures who complain of their trials in love and engage in singing matches; only occasionally, as in *Idyll* 1, are they idealized. The poetry reveals a genuine regard for the realities of country life, which are often presented in ironic perspective.

With Virgil* pastoral poetry became a more self-consciously literary art; he was imitating Theocritus and thus working with materials that he regarded as traditional. Virgil gave his shepherds exotic names and placed them in a fictitious Arcadia (the real Arcadia is a rocky, barren region in central Greece, thought to be the birthplace of Pan) that offers a life of delight and ease. Virgil's Arcadia reflects the moods of its inhabitants; one is conscious of a harmony between man and the landscape. The shepherds that populate the *Eclogues* display a more refined sensibility than those of Theocritus and are capable of greater emotional range. T. G. Rosenmeyer (*The Green Cabinet: Theocritus and the European Pastoral Lyric* [1969]) points to Virgil's transformation of Theocritus's naive and comical Polyphemus (*Idyll* 11) into the melancholy Corydon of *Eclogue* 2, who longs for death as a release from the sufferings of love. Virgil not only enlarged the emotional range of pastoral poetry, he gave it a new dimension by admitting political concerns. In the background of the first eclogue are harsh facts about the dispossession of farmers; the dead shepherd Daphnis, lamented in the fifth eclogue, may be Julius Caesar; the fourth (or "Messianic") eclogue, subsequently interpreted as a veiled prophecy of the coming of Christ, looks to the advent of a new Golden Age of peace and justice with the birth of an unnamed consul. Virgil begins this eclogue by announcing his intention to treat a higher theme ("paulo maiora canamus").

Although Theocritus introduced many of the motifs that became a part of pastoral tradition and remained an important influence, Virgil did more to shape the course of subsequent pastoral poetry. In the medieval period the pastoral eclogue developed in the direction suggested by Virgil, toward the figurative treatment of serious themes. E. W. Tayler (in *Nature and Art in Renaissance Literature* [1964]) has discussed the way pastoral convention and pastoral imagery drawn from the Bible fused to provide a vocabulary through which Carolingian eclogues treated allegorical* subjects far removed from actual rustic life. An unrelated medieval pastoral form, the *pastourelle*, typically describes a knight's seduction of a country maid.

From the time of Virgil, at least, pastoral poetry contained the seeds of satire*. It is not surprising that his successors began to anatomize the evils that they excluded from Arcadia. Petrarch* used the eclogue to attack the corruption of the papal court in Avignon. Baptista Spagnuoli, known as Mantuan, wrote ten moralizing eclogues that were widely read and imitated. In *Spenser, Marvell, and Renaissance Pastoral* [1970] Patrick Cullen uses the term *Mantuanesque* (as opposed to *Arcadian*) for pastoral poetry that is primarily satirical and didactic. The Mantuanesque strain is pronounced in a number of the eclogues of *The Shepheardes Calendar*, among them "May," in which Spenser* attacked the Catholic clergy with what his annotator E.K. called "Satyrical bitternesse." The allegorical tradition of Renaissance pastoral furnished ample precedent for St. Peter's denunciation in *Lyc* of bad shepherds who neglect their flocks.

By the time Spenser published *The Shepheardes Calendar* (1579) pastoral had come to be regarded as a well-defined genre in which a poet could, as Puttenham put it in *The Arte of English Poesie,* "under the vaile of homely persons, and in rude speeches . . . insinuate and glaunce at greater matters." The example of Virgil suggested that young poets should prove themselves in pastoral, which called for a low style, before proceeding to the worthier and more challenging task of writing an epic. In *The Shepheardes Calendar* Spenser was self-consciously trying out his poetic skills, showing his ability to assimilate pastoral tradition and to handle the functions that the eclogue had assumed (love-complaint, elegy*, satire, panegyric). But it was natural for him to aspire to higher flights, as he does in the October eclogue. He knew that the oaten pipe had only so many tunes.

The story of pastoral in England embraces much more than the eclogue. The popular anthology of pastoral lyrics, *England's Helicon* (1603), provides a measure of the vogue for pastoral by the end of the sixteenth century; the editors even doctored some poems to give them a pastoral coloring. The pastoral impulse can be seen everywhere in the literature of the period; in masques (such as Jonson's* *Pan's Anniversarie*), in romances (Sidney's* *Arcadia*), in the drama (Shakespeare's* *As You Like It* and *A Winter's Tale,* Fletcher's* *The Faithful Shepherdess,* and Jonson's *The Sad Shepherd,* to name a few), and even in epic* (the Pastorella interlude in Book 6 of *The Faerie Queene*). Several important Italian models fostered the taste for pastoral in England. Sannazaro's *Arcadia* (1504)—influenced by the Greek prose romance, *Daphnis and Chloe,* by Longus—did a great deal to popularize the idealized world that Virgil had invented. Influential pastoral dramas by Tasso*, *Aminta* (1573), and Guarini, *Il Pastor Fido* (1590), presented complicated love plots in an Arcadian setting.

Despite the enormous variations in intention and form of Renaissance pastorals, it is possible to generalize about the Arcadia that its shepherds and shepherdesses typically inhabit (allowing for such exceptions as Shakespeare's realistic Forest of Arden). Pan is often acknowledged as the ruler of this imaginary country, and numerous nymphs and deities are at home there. Although Arcadia may assume English forms, with Daphnis or Sincero (Sannazaro's languid poet-hero) giving way to Colin Clout, it remains an essentially pleasant place that offers freedom from the cares of the larger world of court and city. It may have overtones of the Golden Age described by Ovid* and others, when spring was eternal and man was spared the burdens of commerce and the disorders of war. A famous chorus in the *Aminta* presents the Golden Age as a time where love was free and natural. Arcadian leisure is the sign of a profound state of contentment that the Roman poets called *otium* (its opposite, *negotium*, suggests business and, by implication, any kind of difficulty). This *otium* should not be seen as reflecting a kind of escapism inherent in pastoral but rather as a calm that allows the life of the soul to flourish, manifesting itself in contemplation, love, and friendship.

Interest in Arcadia had waned by the time that Milton began to write, to the point that pastoral appealed mainly to those writers who looked back nostalgically to simpler times under Elizabeth. Nevertheless, Milton's 1645 book of poems displays a "pervasive atmosphere of Greek and Roman pastoral," as Louis Martz has commented (*The Lyric and Dramatic Milton*, ed. Joseph Summers [1965], pp. 3ff.). Although Milton only twice attempted a classical pastoral form—in his two major elegies—he drew easily upon the resources of pastoral tradition. Virgil's seventh eclogue supplied the motto for the title page, and Virgilian names (Thyrsis, Amaryllis, and the rest) occur in a number of the poems. The background to the portrait of Milton that serves as a frontispiece for the volume reveals a shepherd piping under a tree, an appropriate emblem for a young poet who described his *Nat* to his friend Charles Diodati* (in *El* 6) as simple strains meditated on his native pipes and in *Ep Dam* announced his farewell to pastoral, and Latin poetry, by promising to hang his pipe on a pine tree.

Milton's *Nat* is sometimes characterized as pastoral, but its pastoralism consists of little more than an indebtedness to Virgil's fourth eclogue and a reference to Christ as Pan, a commonplace association by the time of the poem. *L'Al* and *IlP*, particularly the former, raise more interesting questions. *L'Al* recalls the cheerful mood of much Elizabethan pastoral poetry, particularly that of Nicholas Breton and such admirers of Spenser as Michael Drayton, George Wither, and William Browne of Tavistock. Joan Grundy (*The Spenserians* [1969]) cites passages in Browne's rambling *Brittania's Pastorals* that offer a view of rural English life very like that presented in *L'Al;* Milton's own copy of this work survives, with his annotations. Yet Milton's view of country life is on the whole more generalized than Browne's. *L'Al* gives the impression of being a genre study of actual rustic scenes while in fact creating an idealized pastoral world. Milton's shepherds and milkmaids are representative figures, not the particularized rustic characters that T. S. Eliot* would have preferred, and they are animated by an unfailing spirit of mirth. Such "secure delight" is possible where "youthful Jollity" banishes "Wrincled Care," thus keeping time at bay. Its pleasures are "free" and "unreproved" because innocent, like those in the Arcadian world of Tasso's *Aminta*, where anything that pleases is considered lawful. The key to this innocence in *L'Al* is simplicity, the simplicity of dancing in the checkered shade and eating dinners of "Herbs, and other Country Messes" (Corydon and Thyrsis could be illustrations for Meliboeus's defense of the simple life in Book 6 of *The Faerie Queene*). *IlP* is less obviously pastoral, though Rosenmeyer finds its melancholy and the kind of peace it offers consonant with much in pastoral tradition.

In *L'Al* Milton replaced pastoral *otium* with a sense of festivity and avoided turning the English countryside into a version of Arcadia. In *Arc,* his first venture in the masque form, he domesticated classical pastoral by imagining Arcadian shepherds journeying to England and acknowledging the Dowager Countess of Derby as their Queen. John M. Wallace (*Milton: Modern Essays in Criticism,* ed. Arthur Barker [1965], pp. 77ff.) regards the masque as an index of growing dissatisfaction in the seventeenth century with the Arcadian ideal. Whatever Milton's attitude toward Arcadia (one can argue that he was merely using the fiction here to pay an elegant compliment), he made its shepherds and nymphs serve a higher ideal than the classical Pan. Their new "rural Queen" is a radiant figure who merits comparison with Latona and Cybele and is worshiped by a Genius of the Wood who can hear the music of the spheres.

Mask represents a more ambitious venture in a mode not so clearly pastoral but indebted both to pastoral drama and to the masque. In discussing the pastoralism of *Mask* Rosemond Tuve (in *Images and Themes in Five Poems by Milton* [1957]) remarks that "pastoral imagery had found a natural home in the masque." The highly literate audience for whom Milton wrote his masque would not have been troubled by references to Pan or by the appearance of a river goddess with her attendant nymphs. No doubt the Earl of Bridgewater* readily accepted the fiction by which Henry Lawes*, his children's tutor, became the shepherd Thyrsis. Milton of course put pastoral machinery to new uses, complicating the action of the masque and enlarging its frame of reference. Thyrsis is also a Platonic* daemon who defines for the audience a heaven where virtue is rewarded, and both he and Sabrina suggest the operation of Christian grace*.

In their different ways Thyrsis and Sabrina confirm the existence of a natural world that is "most innocent," as the Lady describes it, and even benevolent. Both illustrate a fundamental harmony between man and nature : Thyrsis, who can "still the wilde winds when they roar" with his "soft Pipe," and Sabrina, who protects the shepherds and is celebrated by them at their festivals. References to these shepherds—similar to the rustics of *L'Al* but Virgilian enough to play oaten flutes—dimly outline a pastoral world that surrounds the dark wood of Comus and the castle of the Earl of Bridgewater, symbolic poles of the action of the masque. In this humble pastoral world the Lady and her brothers feel secure. It would take only the sound of "folded flocks" or the light of a rush candle to relieve the uncertainty of the brothers. But they have strayed beyond the limits of such familiar landmarks into the labyrinthine wood, which represents for them a new region of experience.

Comus can be regarded as an antipastoral figure who perverts the innocence of the natural world by making the wood "hideous" and threatens the orderly life of the countryside and the court. For him "The Star that bids the Shepherd fold" signals the beginning of revelry instead of announcing the peaceful close of the shepherd's day, as it often does in the pastoral eclogue. The "barbarous dissonance" that he and his troop produce disrupts the tranquil evening piping of Thyrsis. Comus's creed of sensuous gratification, acted out in his Bacchic rites and given a theoretical basis in his argument for exploiting nature's abundance, challenges the ideal of living by nature's "sober laws" expressed by the Lady. Milton gives enough hints of rustic life to suggest that the shepherds embody such an ideal on one level. They live simply, not rioting in nature's abundance but relying on their labor and the good offices of Sabrina to ensure a modest prosperity. The country dances at the end of the masque, far from being the "ill manag'd Merriment" of drunken hinds that the Lady fears initially, constitute wholesome "play" that demonstrates the well-being of all those in the domain of the Earl.

Sabrina represents Milton's most imaginative use of pastoral tradition in the masque. Her function resembles that of the river god in *The Faithful Shepherdess* and, as Grundy has observed, that of the river god in Book 1 of *Britannia's Pastorals*, but Milton made her a more important and engaging figure than either of these. Although one can "explain" Sabrina by making her an instrument of grace, she remains a mysterious presence who suggests a power for goodness in nature that cannot be fully understood. Her miraculous appearance greatly diminishes the stature of Comus, by comparison no more than a dealer in illusions.

The paradisal realms described in the epilogue of *Mask*, whatever their precise origins and significance, present a higher order of pleasure and repose than one could find in any earthly Arcadia. Milton shows nature perfected in a heavenly paradise from which night and the "Shrewd medling Elfe" are excluded; Thyrsis and Sabrina are no longer necessary to unlock the healing powers of the natural world. One gains access to this paradise only through the sharp contention of virtue with evil in a fallen world. The freedom that may be enjoyed there, unlike the freedom of Arcadia, must be earned through such trials.

In *Lyc* and *Ep Dam* Milton adapted the pastoral elegy to his own complex needs. The best study of Milton's debt in *Lyc* to the conventions of the pastoral elegy remains James H. Hanford's pioneering article in *Publications of the Modern Language Association* 25 (1910): 403–47. Translations of the most important classical and Renaissance elegies can be found in *The Pastoral Elegy*, ed. T. P. Harrison and H. J. Leon, and *Milton's "Lycidas"*, ed. Scott Elledge (1966). In *Lyc* Milton paid tribute to Theocritus and Virgil (by invoking the rivers Arethusa and Mincius) and assimilated from them and their Renaissance imitators the conventions that would serve his purposes, among them the description of fellowship in pastoral terms, the mourning of nature, the questioning of the nymphs, and the ritual of decking the hearse with flowers. Such deliberate use of literary artifice provoked a memorable outburst from Samuel Johnson* : "Passion plucks no berries from the myrtle. . . . where there is leisure for fiction, there is little grief" (*Life of Milton*). Modern critics have challenged Johnson's implicit assumption that sincerity demands plain statement, showing how Milton's use of convention enabled him to express not only his grief for King* but deep concerns about poetry and justice (see especially Tuve).

Milton extended the range of the pastoral elegy in *Lyc*, reaching beyond the limits of the pastoral world because its personae could not provide the answers to his insistent questions. The poem strains toward epic* in seriousness and scope, introducing Apollo, St. Peter, and ultimately the figure of the resurrected Christ in the process of establishing a larger spatial and temporal frame of reference. Yet Milton was able to stretch the form of the pastoral elegy to accommodate his doubts and their resolution. After the voice of Apollo quiets the shepherd singer's anxiety about his calling and again after the "dread voice" of St. Peter promises vengeance on the corrupt clergy, the poem returns to the pastoral vein. Its triumphant consolation, fusing Christian and pastoral imagery in a vision of Lycidas being received into a pastoral heaven, offers what Isabel McCaffrey has called "a pastoral mode deepened and reconfirmed" (*Lyric and Dramatic Milton*, pp. 65ff.). This consolation takes account of "tears" and the unpredictable violence suggested by the "whelming tide," as the metaphoric description of King and Milton as shepherds did not. In its transcendent pastoral world the music of the oaten flute becomes the richer music of the "unexpressive nuptial Song," and the friendship of two young poets gives way to the joyous fellowship of all the saints. This glimpse of the "blest Kingdoms" drives out nostalgia, the dominant emotion of much pastoral poetry, and replaces it with vibrant hope.

In *Ep Dam* Milton again drew upon a variety of pastoral elegies (Castiglione's* *Alcon* is perhaps the most important) and at the same time disengaged himself from the pastoral mode. Ralph Condee (*Studies in Philology* 62 [1965] : 577–94) takes the poem as evidence that the tradition of the pastoral elegy was wearing thin. He sees Milton as moving beyond the normal limits of this tradition in the kind of anguish over the human condition he expressed, in his concern with plans for an epic, and in a conclusion that is an "ecstatic hymn" rather than an adaptation of the conclusion of the pastoral elegy.

More sympathetic critics than Dr. Johnson have objected to the elaborate pastoral machinery of *Ep Dam,* yet the force of the poem depends upon it. Milton developed the pastoral world of *Ep Dam* as fully as he did in order to show the inadequacy of its consolations. Thyrsis assumes the conventional posture of the shepherd singer under a familiar tree, yet he sings of how he wanders alone through solitary places ("pererrans" and "oberro" anticipate the suggestive use of "wander" in *PL*). The refrain, instructing the sheep to go home unfed because there is not leisure to feed them, testifies to a loss of the *otium* that is normally at the heart of pastoral life. Such a sense of disruption is not unusual in the pastoral elegy, but Milton's emphasis on the estrangement of the singer—from the pleasures of the landscape and the company of nymphs and shepherds—is. In *Ep Dam* nature does not mourn generally. Only Thyrsis's fields decay, and then only as a result of his neglect. In his solitary grief Thyrsis, like Adam in the immediate aftermath of the Fall, seeks the deepest shadows. Instead of allowing Zephyrus to lull him back to contentment, he listens to the melancholy sounds of Eurus (the southeast wind) in the trees and to the more threatening "malus auster" (the south wind) as it assaults his elm tree. This sense of isolation leads Thyrsis to the recognition that men live essentially alone ("aliena animis"). Thus he rejects the assumption of easy fellowship that underlies most pastoral poetry.

Milton's subsequent description of his Italian journey*, in pastoral terms, serves as a pleasant interlude, an intimation that life might have continued in the old way. His account of imagining tranquil days by the waters of the Colne with Damon constitutes a kind of "false surmise," ended abruptly by the fact of death. The pastoral vein virtually dries up when Milton dismisses the landscape he has created ("vos cedite silvae") and announces his epic plans, in effect shedding the role of Thyrsis to assert a new poetic identity. In his brief enumeration of British themes and the subsequent description of scenes on the cups given him by Manso*, one gets a glimpse of his imagination ranging more freely than it could within the confines of pastoral poetry.

Milton's most significant adaptation of pastoral tradition appears where one might least expect it, in the epic toward which so much in his early career pointed. Where previous epics had included episodes that could be called pastoral—for example, the visit of Aeneas to Evander's kingdom in Book 8 of *Aeneid,* Erminia's sojourn among the shepherds in *Jerusalem Delivered,* and Calidore's comparable sojourn among the shepherds in *The Faerie Queene*—Milton used a Christian pastoralism to embody values and conditions of life that serve as a critique of traditional epic assumptions about the proper ends of human activity. To suggest the innocence of Adam and Eve, Milton placed them in an earthly paradise that has many of the characteristics of Arcadia. The harmony of Adam and Eve with their natural surroundings, the rhythm of their days, the purity of their love, and the *otium* that they enjoy all point to pastoral tradition. Eve's statement of her love for Adam in Book 4, which begins "With thee conversing I forget all time," is perhaps the loveliest of all English pastoral lyrics. Rosenmeyer finds certain passages, especially those in which Adam and Eve praise God, the best examples of "pastoral eulogy" in the language. For a fuller discussion of pastoral elements of *PL,* see John R. Knott, Jr., *Milton's Pastoral Vision* (1971).

In *PL* Milton raised the pastoral mode to a new level of seriousness by making it embody a simplicity intended for man by God. This simplicity depends upon the obedience of Adam and Eve and is the key to their bliss. It includes a sense of the harmony of all created things in the service of God, obviously a larger and more profound harmony than that of the traditional Arcadia. Milton sanctified the life of Adam and Eve ultimately by making Eden the "shadow" of a pastoral heaven in which the angels alternate between praise of God and repose on flowery banks.

In an article in *New Essays on Paradise Lost*, ed. Thomas Kranidas (1969), pp. 86ff., Barbara Lewalski stresses the dynamic character of life in Eden, arguing that Adam and Eve, like the Garden itself, continue to grow. To talk about the *otium* of Adam and Eve is not to deny the dynamism of Eden but to place one's emphasis elsewhere, upon the underlying peacefulness of this life and the simplicity that makes it possible. As Rosenmeyer has pointed out in an illuminating chapter on the subject, *otium* implies a calmness that allows for liveliness and play. Schiller characterized it as "the calm of perfection, not the calm of idleness; a calm which derives from the equilibrium of forces, not from their paralysis."

One can better appreciate the repose that the Garden affords after seeing the confusion into which Adam and Eve fall. The historical vista that Michael opens up for Adam reveals a life that increases in complexity and turmoil as man moves away from his original state of communion with God. The consolation is that Christ will bring man back through the world's wilderness to the "eternal Paradise of rest." Through scenes offering glimpses of heaven and apocalyptic prophecies revealing the bliss that awaits the saints, Milton suggested the peace and joy of this heavenly paradise much more fully in *PL* than he could in *Lyc*. In the Garden itself the traditional *otium* becomes a reflection of the peace of God. The "loss of Eden" that Milton describes in *PL* comprehends many kinds of "loss," but none is more fundamental than the loss of this peace. [JRK]

PATIENCE: *see* FORTITUDE.

PAULET, JANE, MARCHIONESS OF WINCHESTER (1607–1631). She married John Paulet in 1622; Paulet succeeded his father as Marquis of Winchester in 1629. Her death, during pregnancy, resulted from a recent operation, and her second child was born dead. The Earl of Holland, close friend and kinsman of the Marchioness, was Chancellor of Cambridge, and some of the students wrote elegies for her, which were apparently not printed, although they probably circulated in manuscript. Besides Milton's elegy *EpWin,* poems by Ben Jonson*, William Davenant*, Walter Colman, and William Camden* survive. Lines 31–34 of Milton's elegy imply that he heard only the public account of her death, attributing it to pregnancy, not the actual account, which was known to people close to the Marchioness (which information survives in a letter to the Duchess of Buckingham). An earlier version of the epitaph, preserved in a manuscript in the British Museum, suggests acquaintance in earlier days. [WM]

PAULUS DIACONUS, Italian historian of the eighth century and one of the major historians of the Middle Ages. Paulus's chief works are a *History of the Lombards* and a continuation of the Roman history of Eutropius. Eutropius had constructed a history, in ten books, based upon Livy, Suetonius, and others, covering a period from the founding of Rome to the accession of the emperor Valens (364); it was titled *Breviarium ab urbe condita*. Paulus continued the *Breviarium* to the time of Justinian II (711), in eighteen books, called the *Historia Romana*. It was then carried forward to the year 806 by Landulph the Wise, in twenty-four books, called the *Historiae miscellae*. It was this last named to which Milton apparently referred twice in *Brit* concerning Roman expeditions, and with which he associated the name Paulus Diaconus. Ruth Mohl (Yale *Prose* 1 : 430, 432) notes that Milton's page references in *CB* indicate that he consulted a 1603 edition of the *Historiae miscellae* printed in Ingolstadt, Bavaria. [JAR]

PEARCE, ZACHARY: *see* BENTLEY, RICHARD.

PECK, FRANCIS (1692–1743), antiquary. A graduate of Trinity College*, Cambridge, and a minister, Peck was elected a fellow of the Society of Antiquarians on March 9, 1732, and held the prebendal stall of Marston St. Laurence in Lincoln Cathedral from January 1738 until his death. He wrote an imitation of Milton's blank verse* in 1719, "Sighs upon the Never Enough Lamented Death of Queen Anne. An Imitation of Milton," but his important writing achievements were *Desiderata Curiosa: or, A Collection of Divers Scarce and Curious Pieces; Memoirs of the Life and Actions of Oliver Cromwell, As Delivered in Three Panegyrics of Him, Written in Latin: The First as said by Don Juan Roderiquez de Saa Meneses, Conde de Penaguiao, the Portugal Ambassador: The Second, as Affirmed, by a Certain Jesuit, the Lord Ambassador's Chaplain: Yet Both, it is thought, Composed by Mr. John Milton (Latin Secretary to Cromwell) as was the third. With an English Version of Each. The whole illustrated with a large historical preface; many similar passages from the Paradise Lost & Other Works of Mr. John Milton; & Notes from the Best Historians;* and *New Memoirs of the Life and Poetical Works of Mr. John Milton.* The first is a curious accumulation of materials lacking clear arrangement and sometimes obvious significance, and two original papers. Volume 1 appeared in 1732; volume 2 in 1735; and it was reprinted in one volume in 1779. In volume 2 Peck quotes the (erroneous) date of Milton's death (November 15) from Richard Smyth's "Obituary" (British Museum, Sloane MS 886, f. 73v; published 1849). In the second (1740; rpt., 1755), as the title page relates, are first of all two documents (erroneously) assigned to Milton, given in Latin and English. Peck

has numerous notes to these pieces that cite Milton and his works; they indicate the relationship between Milton's tracts and contemporary issues, thus providing some further background to a study of Milton the public servant. In the preliminary material and the Preface are significant references to Milton passim. Specifically the state letter to the Portuguese Agent (now dated December 19, 1650), given as around June 1652 (*CM* State Letter no. 16), is reproduced on pp. 3–4; the state letter to the king of Portugal (now dated July 25, 1654), given as around July 10, 1652 (*CM* State Letter no. 65), is given on p. 10; and Sonnet 16 to Cromwell is quoted on p. 46. But the most noteworthy item in the collection is Peck's publication of the panegyric remarks on Cromwell in *2Def,* given here in Latin on pp. 37–47, and in the first English translation of part of the work on pp. 115–29.

The *New Memoirs* (1740) is likewise a curious collection as the Table of Contents on the title page evidences: I. An Examination of *Milton's* Stile; II. Explanatory & Critical Notes on divers Passages of *Milton* & *Shakespeare*; III. *Baptistes*: A Sacred Dramatic Poem, in Defence of Liberty; as, written in *Latin,* by Mr. *George Buchanan*; Translated into *English,* by Mr. *John Milton*; & first published in 1641; IV. The Parallel, or Archbishop *Laud* & Cardinal *Wolsey* Compared: a Vision, by *Milton;* V. The Legend of Sir *Nicholas Throckmorton* . . . By (his nephew), Sir *Thomas Throckmorton;* VI. *Herod* the Great; a Poem: By the Editor; VII. The Resurrection, a Poem in Imitation of *Milton*: by a Friend; and VIII. A Discourse on the Harmony of the Spheres: by *Milton.* The first item (pp. 105–32) is the first attempt to categorize Milton's poetic style; for example, no. XVI of the types reads, "He often places the substantive between *two adjectives,* which is very classical. As, *Bitter constraint* & sad occasion deare. Lycidas 6," and gives five more examples. The second item (pp. 132–208 [Milton] and 222–54 [Shakespeare]) illustrates language and meaning by extracts from various authors, including contemporaries; for example, for "curfew" (*Mask*, 435) Peck notes its etymology, the historical use of curfew by William the Conqueror, and its appearance in *King Lear* and *The Tempest*. The third (pp. 265–428), sometimes found separately bound in libraries, has unfortunately been noted by people who have taken Peck's enthusiastic but far-fetched ascription as valid. Peck presents an extensive and detailed argument for authorship; he includes Milton's prose outline for "Baptistes" in *TM* (pp. 278–79). In addition there are notes on the play in the nature of his explanatory and critical observations on Milton and Shakespeare. Item four (pp. 429–37) is not, of course, Milton's, despite Peck's Preface. He does not connect items five and six (in two separate sets of pagination) in any way with Milton, making their inclusion in the volume that emerged from his studies odd. Item seven (new pagination) imitates Milton by use of blank verse, language and style* (e.g., line 67, "Rock, fountain, flow'r, the human face, the kid"), and, the author probably thought, the subject. The eighth item (also new pagination) reprints *Prol* 2 in Latin together with an English translation by Peck. On pages 209–21 Peck prints 1) lists of editions* of *PL, PR,* and *SA,* and the minor poems; 2) the contents of *TM;* 3) a list of corrections for the common texts of the three major poems as found by comparison with the original editions; and 4) "*A Table of all* MILTON'S *English* Poems, *set down as near as possible in the very order of time they were wrote.*" (Pages 255–64 give a listing of Shakespeare's works.)

The kind of antiquarian and scholarly attention observed in the sections of *New Memoirs* already cited is lavished also in a kind of "life" prefacing these sections (pp. 1–105). Just as Peck erred in certain ascriptions, so he errs here in making guesses and reporting information that have proved untrue. But the "life" is nonetheless important for many things that it does report from various sources and for its observations. Peck reports, for example, that Milton's mother was a Haughton from Haughton-Tower, Lancashire, his source being a letter from Roger Comberbach of Chester to William Cowper, Clerk of the Parliament, dated December 15, 1736. Although this is not accurate, Milton's mother was apparently related to Haughtons. Peck is also the first to note Milton's burial record in St. Giles, Cripplegate. The "life" includes critical analyses of poems, quotations from various other critics, Lawes's* letter on *Mask,* the plans for *PL* and other subjects from *TM,* a list of translations of Milton's work, a Latin epitaph by Peck, and a discussion of eight representations of Milton (one is not of Milton). The volume is illustrated by a portrait from a half-length picture then owned by Peck, given to him by Sir John Meres (it is not of Milton, however), and an engraving of the medal struck by William Benson. [JTS]

PELAGIANISM, an early fifth-century heresy especially combated by St. Augustine*, denied that mankind was innately sinful and asserted instead that man has the power within himself apart from divine grace* to do good; indeed, unassisted man could lead a sinless life. Orthodox Christianity ultimately rejected this man-centered system because it provided no significant place for Christ's atonement or for any divine activity on earth.

Milton believed with the Arminians* that man has freedom to choose between good and bad, and accordingly he has sometimes been classed with the Pelagians. But he never held that unassisted man could make such choices, and he attacks the Pelagians as heretics in *Eikon* (5 : 224) and *Animad* (3 : 126). Rather, he believed that God freely bestows His grace upon everyone; this action permits each recipient to will to do good if he so chooses, but he may resist and so turn to evil ways. This position, shared with the Remonstrants against the Calvinists*, has certain affinities with semi-Pelagianism, an attempt to harmonize the Pelagian and Augustine positions. [WBH]

PENN, JOHN: *see* ADAPTATIONS.

PERKINS, WILLIAM (1558–1602), one of the best-known and most influential Anglican divines of his time, probably surpassing even Hooker* in the extent of his fame. Born at Marston Jabbett in Warwickshire, he apparently spent a profligate and drunken youth before experiencing a sudden conversion. He matriculated at Cambridge in 1577, but showed at first no particular theological bent, being interested rather in the study of mathematics, astronomy, and magic. But as an undergraduate he was in contact with men of religious leanings like his tutor Laurence Chaderton, one of the leaders of the group of moderate Puritans at the university, and doubtless such influences gradually made themselves felt. In 1584 Perkins was elected a fellow of his college, Christ's* (later to be Milton's college too), and it was at this time that he began his career as a highly successful preacher, becoming lecturer at Great St. Andrew's Church. On his marriage in 1594 he gave up his fellowship at Christ's but throughout his short life he was never far from Cambridge, and he was buried there in his church of St. Andrew's.

Perkins's reputation as a preacher was considerable among both the learned and the simple. Fuller* says of him in *The Holy and the Profane State* that "his sermons were not so plain but that the piously learned did admire them, nor so learned but that the plain did understand them." The same is true of his many treatises. His influence and fame rested upon the practical and helpful clarity with which he deals with moral and theological questions; he was a learned man who devoted himself to clarifying the often very abstruse matters of conscience* with which the ordinary Protestant of the sixteenth and seventeenth centuries found himself compelled to struggle. Fuller compares his achievement in moral theology to that of Socrates in philosophy: "so our Perkins brought the schools into the Pulpit, and unshelling their controversies out of their hard school-terms, made thereof plain and wholsome meat for his people." His works are wide-ranging, but his central concern is always to provide guidance for the Christian who wishes, and needs, to relate all the practical details of moral conduct to the will of God.

One important aspect of this concern is the effort to develop a specifically Protestant casuistry or "practical divinity," the relating of moral theory to moral practice in particular instances. One of the most famous of the treatises, *The Whole Treatise of the Cases of Conscience,* is devoted, as its title suggests, to an examination and resolution of the difficulties of particular "cases." Its purpose is to demonstrate the methods by which the layman may reach a decision in instances where moral duties may be hard to relate to general principles, or where apparent conflict of principle may arise. Though in the Roman Church casuistry was well established, the Reformed Churches had lacked such guidance, and Perkins's clear, sensible, practical thinking on issues of moral conduct met a genuine need of his time. It also strengthened the position of Protestantism against the strictures of Rome, and this too would have been close to Perkins's heart. It was a common Roman claim that the Reformed doctrine of justification by faith alone encouraged a carelessness of ethical conduct; works like Perkins's, demonstrating to the layman the ways by which he could solve for himself problems of behavior, and identify his moral duty, went far to counter the accusation.

Perkins was also a more direct supporter of the Puritan cause within the Anglican church, so far as that cause could in his day be distinguished from Anglicanism as such. He was no extremist, but, moderate though he was, like so many divines of the period he could not escape being to some degree a polemicist. The necessary connection between the impulse to provide guidance through practical divinity and the need to support the tenets of Calvinism* is seen in the title of one of the treatises: *A Case of Conscience, the*

Greatest that ever was: how a man may know whether he be the child of God, or no, on the vexed question of assurance of election. Perkins was a firm opposer of the Roman church and of such remnants of Roman practice as might still be detected in the Church of England, and he was involved in some controversy on this issue, but his supporters and his opponents alike recognized the ability and the candor with which his views were expressed. An important contribution to the discussion of how far reform should be carried, and where it was essential that lines between the churches should be drawn is his *A Reformed Catholike: or, A Declaration shewing how neere we may come to the present Church of Rome in sundrie points of Religion: and wherein we must for ever depart from them,* a work whose brilliance spread Perkins's reputation throughout Europe.

Perkins, then, dealt clearly and cogently with many of the most vital issues in the Christian life of sixteenth- and seventeenth-century England, and his prestige and authority were considerable. Some of his works were, very early, translated into other vernaculars, and some into Latin; and in England they were reprinted very frequently during his lifetime and for three decades after his death. Throughout the seventeenth century he was regarded with respect as an authoritative spokesman for English Protestantism. His treatises seem to have been normal reading for people of cultivation and piety, and thirty years after his death Phineas Fletcher* wrote in a short poem "Upon Mr. Perkins his printed sermons" of the life that "Perkins (our wonder)" still enjoys in his works. A number of distinguished churchmen, both orthodox and of a more Puritan cast, referred to him as an authority, and his influence extended to the New World.

It is not surprising, therefore, that Milton knew Perkins's works, and called upon them on occasion to support his own arguments. Not only was Perkins a generally influential force in English Protestantism; he was, more specifically,

interested in matters of the same kind as those for which Milton's prose works show such passionate concern, "cases of conscience" involving the particular application of moral principles as revealed in the Bible. One of the subjects on which Milton felt very strongly was that of divorce*; and to persuade his countrymen that divorce for reasons other than adultery was in keeping with Christian morality, it was good strategy to call upon the work of a respected authority on practical divinity. Not, of course, that Perkins had himself advocated that divorce be permitted in the case of minds ill-matched. Rather, Milton strives to show that such permission is a logical result of some of Perkins's arguments, to force the posthumous assent of the great Protestant casuist to the moral and logical inevitability of the case. Thus in *DDD*, Milton can be seen as it were wrestling with Perkins to compel his support in spite of himself. Arguing (against those who claim that Mosaic divorce was "a meer judicial Law") that divorce is "a Law of moral equity," he calls upon Perkins to show that the Christian should still be subject to such Old Testament laws, for Christ came not to abrogate the Mosaic law but to cleanse it of its abuses: "*Perkins* in *A Treatise of Conscience* grants, that what in the judicial Law is of common equity, binds also the Christian" (3 : 467).

The passage referred to in *A Treatise of Conscience* is one in which Perkins differentiates between those of Moses' judicial laws which are of particular equity (that is, relating to the particular circumstances of the Jewish state) and those which are of common equity, "made according to the lawe or instinct of nature common to all men" [*The Workes of . . . Mr. William Perkins* (London, 1612), 1 : 520]. These are moral laws that bind the consciences of all men, not of the Jews only; and such a law, Milton claims, is the Old Testament permission to divorce where nature "vehemently seeks to part." Perkins's view of the nature of Mosaic divorce law does not in fact agree with Milton's. In *A Godly and Learned Exposition of Christ's Sermon in the Mount* he defines Moses' law, which allows a man to divorce his wife *"because hee hath espied some filthinesse in her"* as being not moral but "civill, or politicke, for the good ordering of the Common wealth" (*Workes*, 3 : 68), tolerating an evil in order that a greater evil may be avoided. Certainly Perkins here as elsewhere not only concedes but insists that, as Milton puts it, "our Saviour heer confutes not Moses Law, but the false glosses that deprav'd the Law" (3 : 470). He uses the same phrase, *false gloss* (*Workes*, 3 : i), for the corruptions of the Scribes and Pharisees. But he does not, of course, proceed to the idiosyncratic conclusion that according to Milton follows naturally upon this insistence. Milton goes on :

> which being true, *Perkins* must needs grant, that somthing then is left to that law which Christ found no fault with; and what can that be but the conscionable use of such liberty as the plain words import? So that by his owne inference, Christ did not absolutely intend to restrain all divorces to the onely cause of adultery.
>
> (3 : 470)

Perkins's conclusion from the same premises is the quite different one that Christ's intention was to free Moses' law from the corrupt Pharisaic interpretation that allowed a man to divorce his wife "by any light occasion." Thus two vigorous thinkers, both Protestant, both ardently moral, both in general agreement on the matter of the relation of Christ's law to that of Moses, and both referring to the same biblical texts, reach totally contrary conclusions : a state of things far from unusual in the period, and an interesting comment on the nature of biblical interpretation and the natire of casuistry. [KW]

PERRINCHIEF, RICHARD: *see* ANTAGONISTS.

PETER MARTYR (1500–1562), Protestant theologian. Pietro Martire Vermigli was the son of devout Florentines of status, followers of Savonarola. He entered the Augustine Order, studied at Padua, and earned a brilliant reputation as teacher, preacher, and administrator. He read the works of the reformers, and became associated with Juan de Valdés, Bernardino Ochino, and other liberal clerics. Summoned to examination, he fled Italy in 1542, going to Strasbourg where he was welcomed by Martin Bucer* and made professor of theology. In 1547 he accepted Cranmer's invitation to become Regius Professor of Divinity at Oxford. He was consulted about the Book of Common Prayer, and participated in disputations on the nature of the eucharist. On the accession of Mary Tudor (1553), he found it advisable to retire to the Continent, where he eventually became professor of Hebrew at Zurich. Peter Martyr belongs to a small group of Protestant theologicans from whom Milton derived particular support for his various views. Milton cites Peter as authority in the divorce tracts, in *1, 2,* and *3Def,* and in *CD*. In *Tenure* he speaks of Peter as "a divine of foremost rank." He alludes most often to Peter's commentaries on Corinthians and on the Book of Judges. The citation from the latter in the *CB* (18 : 185), dated 1642–1644 (?), concerns the people's right to bring tyrannic officers to account or to demote them. [PS]

PETRARCA, FRANCESCO (1304–1374), Tuscan poet and humanist. Born at Arezzo, Petrarch studied law at Montpellier and Bologna, took minor orders, and served at the papal court at Avignon in the entourage of Cardinal Giovanni Colonna and subsequently as secretary to Pope Clement VI. Traveling extensively on diplomatic missions, he divided his life between Avignon and Italy. His friends included Giacomo Colonna, the brother of the Cardinal; Azzo da Correggio, who extended patronage in Parma; the Visconti family in Milan; King Robert of Naples and Sicily; Giovanni Boccaccio*; and, for a brief time, Cola de Rienzo. Like Cicero*, whose *Letters to Atticus* he rediscovered and transcribed, he wrote numerous familiar letters to various friends; and, like Cicero, he praised the delights of private studies in rural solitude as well as the performance of public duties. He retired frequently for literary recreation to the village of Vaucluse on the river Sorgue and devoted his *De vita solitaria* to the pleasures of the contemplative life. His admiration for the moral and political stature as well as the literary excellence of the ancients appears in his *De viris illustribus,* biographies of famous men of antiquity, and in his *Africa,* a heroic poem on the defeat of Hannibal by Scipio Africanus the Elder. He possessed a manuscript of Homer; but, despite his Greek studies with a Calabrian monk, Bernard Barlaam, he never attained sufficient mastery of the language to understand the Homeric epics. His *Secretum,* a spiritual autobiography presented in the form of a dialogue between Petrarch and Saint Augustine* reflects the influence of Augustine's *Confessions.* His other Latin compositions include verse epistles, eclogues, a book *On Memorable Things,* letters to dead authors, a treatise on prosperity and adversity (*De remediis utriusque fortunae*), and attacks on the neglect of classical learning and poetry, the arrogance of the Averroists, and the corruptions of the papal court at Avignon. The oration he delivered on the occasion of his coronation with laurel at Rome in 1341 extols the office of the poet and the stimulus of personal glory.

His most influential vernacular works were his *Canzoniere* or *Rime,* a collection of sonnets and *canzoni* in praise of Laura, and his *Trionfi.* Though the identity of Laura has been a controversial issue, and many critics have regarded her as an allegorical rather than a historical personage, the sixteenth-century scholar Alessandro Vellutello recorded an Avignon tradition associating her with the de Sade family, but nevertheless preferred to identify her with Laura Chiabaud, baptized near Vaucluse. Morris Bishop supports the identification proposed by the Abbé de Sade, who identified Petrarch's lady as Laura de Noves, wife of Hugues de Sade. According to the *Canzoniere,* the poet encountered his lady at the church of Saint Clare in Avignon on April 6, 1327; on the same day at the same hour exactly twenty-one years later, she perished in the Black Death of 1348. The poems in her honor have been divided into two groups *in vita Laura* and *in morte Laura.*

In a brief survey of Renaissance Petrarchism, Ernest Hatch Wilkins observes that "each of the three divisions of [Petrarch's] work"—his Latin writings, his *Trionfi,* and his *Canzoniere*—produced a "specific wave of influence," and these reached their peaks at different times. In Italy and in other European countries, these waves tended to follow the same sequence: first the Latin works, then the *Trionfi,* and lastly the *Canzoniere.* Centering his study specifically on the influence of the *Canzoniere,* Wilkins defines Renaissance Petrarchism as "the writing of lyric verse under the direct or indirect influence of Petrarch in a period beginning in his lifetime and ending about 1600." Its chief manifestations, in his opinion, are "the use of Petrarchan words, phrases, lines, metaphors, conceits, and ideas, and the adoption, for poetic purposes, of the typical Petrarchan experiences and attitudes" (see *Studies in the Life and Works of Petrarch* [1955], pp. 280–82). On the problem of Laura, see Edward H. R. Tatham, *Francesco Petrarca, The First Modern Man of Letters,* (1925), 1 : 224–53; Morris Bishop, *Petrarch and his World* (1963), pp. 62–70, 379–80.

Milton's allusions to Petrarch in his pamphlets and familiar letters are largely conditioned by the subject he is discussing. In writing to his Florentine friend Benedetto Bonmattei*, who was currently writing a book on the Tuscan tongue, Milton appropriately praises the beauty of the *lingua hetrusca* and its literature, especially for men who have little knowledge of Latin and Greek. He himself, who has "not wet merely the tips of my lips with both these tongues, . . . can yet sometimes willingly and eagerly go for a feast to that Dante of yours, and to

Petrarch . . ." (12 : 35). In apologizing to Carlo Dati* for the "rather harsh sayings against the Pope of Rome" in some of his own Latin poems (in his 1645 edition), Milton begs "the indulgence you were wont to give, I say not to your own Dante* and Petrarch in the same case, but with singular politeness to my own former freedom of speech . . ." (31 : 51). Carlo Dati, writing to Milton in the autumn of 1647, quotes from Petrarch's *Trionfi* (31 : 299). In *CB*, under the heading "De legibus [,] earum dispensationibus et indulgentiis," Milton refers to the Life of Petrarch by Thomasinus of Padua, "in which young Petrarch is reluctant to study law" (18 : 191). This is an allusion to *Petrarch redivivus* by Giocomo Filippo Tomasini*, Bishop of Città Nuova, published at Padua in 1635; the volume also contained a brief account of Laura ("Accessit nobilissimae foeminae Laurae brevis historia").

In *Ref* Milton cites Petrarch's condemnation of the Donation of Constantine* and the effect of "ill got wealth" on the church in "his 108. Sonnet which is wip't out by the Inquisitor in some Editions; speaking of the Roman *Antichrist* as meerely bred up by *Constantine*" (3 : 26, 27). Later in the same treatise he returns to Petrarch's protest against the encroachment of the papacy on Caesar's empire : "the next time you shall see him a Woolfe, a Lyon, lifting his paw against his raiser, as *Petrarch* exprest it, and finally an open enemy, and subverter of the Greeke Empire" (3 : 43,44). In *Apol* Milton defends himself against accusations of unchastity by proclaming his preference for chaste poets like Dante and Petrarch, "the two famous renowners of *Beatrice* and *Laura* who never write but honour of them to whom they devote their verse, displaying sublime and pure thought, without transgression" (3 : 303). Again in *Apol* he ridicules the charge of "blasphemy" by comparing it to the similar accusation made against Petrarch on grounds just as absurd : "Thus did that foolish Monk in a barbarous Declamation accuse *Petrarch* of blas-

phemy for dispraising the French wines" (3 : 309). See Yale *Prose* 1 : 895n, on Petrarch's *Apologia contra Gallum.*

For Milton's use of Petrarchan themes, such as the *donna angelicata,* and his indebtedness to the Petrarchan sonnet, *canzone,* and madrigal, see John S. Smart, *The Sonnets of Milton,* 1921, E. A. J. Honigmann, *Milton's Sonnets* (1966), and F. T. Prince, *The Italian Element in Milton's Verse* (1954). [JMS]

PHILARAS, LEONARD (known also as Villeré, Villaré, Villeret, etc.) (ca. 1590–1673), diplomat, scholar, translator and aspiring revolutionist. He was like John Milton in his range of interests, his extraordinary mixture of the scholarly and the practical, the politically present and the visionary. Unlike Milton, he lacked genius and a native political base.

Philaras was educated in Athens in his early years and later at Rome. In Rome he attended St. Athanasius College, the "Greek College" founded by Loyola in 1572 as one of a number of national schools intended to train and use as proselytizers the young men of the Protestant nations and of Eastern Christianity. The curriculum was carefully constructed to instill loyalty to Rome and it was partly successful in its efforts to use young Greeks to attack the Eastern church. Often, however, the efforts were wasted. Philaras is one of a number of young Greeks trained at St. Athanasius who seemed, despite important gestures toward uniting Eastern and Western churches, more interested in freeing than in converting Greece. The pages of this period of Greek intellectual history are filled with dramatic cases of intellectual-political adventurers who reached important positions of influence and then used this influence to attempt the liberation of Greece. Men like Philaras, Johann Cottounios, and Kyril Loukaris attained positions of authority and from those positions tried to revive the nation, which they saw as now prostrate and poor but glowing with the spirit of its past and its potential for the future.

Philaras was at St. Athanasius as student and teacher from 1613–1617, when he received the doctorate in theology. In 1619 he joined and took a leading role in the proposed Crusade of Charles Gonzaga, Duc de Nevers, for the recovery of Greece (Berger de Xivrey, *Tentative d'insurrection organisée dans le Magne de 1612 a 1619 au nom du duc de Nevers* [1841]). Despite impressive support, including that of the philhellene Capuchin Père Joseph, the *eminence gris*, the Crusade never embarked, its ships burning at Venice, where they had been collected for the proposed war.

Philaras never gave up. A letter to Milton was only one of several attempts to gain support, expertise, or encouragement for his lifelong ambition. In 1633 he dedicated his Romaic Greek translation of Bellarmine's *Christine Doctrine* to Cardinal Richelieu, and, following a plea for the union of Eastern and Western Christianity, he urges the regeneration of "that brave nation which was in former times the salt and the sun of the universe." It was doubtless Milton's political potential that led Philaras to send his respects via the Parliamentary Agent Renée Augier, and his portrait "with the eulogium full worthy of your merits." A copy of the portrait—looking rather like Descartes—is in the possession of Professor C. Th. Dimaras of the Sorbonne. It is clear from Milton's letter that Philaras had tendered enough informed praise, suggestion of his own worth and of the worth of his interests, to strike from Milton one of his best familiar letters.

In Letter 12, dated June 1652 (12:55–59) Milton thanks Philaras for his high opinion of *1Def,* for his greetings, his portrait, and his "most gracious letter." The second paragraph starts with "conventional" praise of the Greeks, but we cannot dismiss it as pure convention since the same note appears in *2Def,* where the praise of Philaras, representing "Greece herself—Athens the eye of Greece" (8 : 191) is cited along with the praise of Queen Christina* for Milton's *1Def*. The letter proceeds to assure Phil-

aras that he, Milton, would gladly "call forth our army and navy to free Greece, land of eloquence, from the Ottoman Tyrant." But first Philaras must become like Milton :

> There is, however, something else besides to be tried and in my judgment far the most important: namely that some one should, if possible, arouse and rekindle in the minds of the Greeks, by the relation of that old story, the old Greek valour itself, the old industry, the old patience of labour.

Milton's deepest convictions and formulas, about eloquence and action as well as on personal and political liberty, are stirred by the letter from Philaras. The relationship was a brief one but emblematic of the English poet's deep affinities for things Greek and for men libertarian. It also suggests a steady sense of political reality, about past and present, that informed and tempered his vision.

The second letter to Philaras is concerned with Milton's blindness*. It followed more than two years later and after Philaras had visited Milton. It can be noted here that Milton reiterates his feeling for Greece and addresses Philaras as "one of the most loving friends' (12 : 67).

The ideas that brought Milton and Philaras together were liberty, national identity, and a respect for, and skill in, eloquence. The career that enabled Philaras to travel and to learn was that of diplomat. From 1640 to 1656, initially under the sponsorship of Cardinal Richelieu, he was envoy from Odoardo Farnese, Duke of Parma, to the French court. He appears to have been a well-known figure whose temporary disgrace in 1654 (upon the death of Odoardo) is noted in the Thurloe *State Papers* (2 : 246). Among Philaras's effects when he was arrested was "a letter of civility Mr. Milton had writ." Masson conjectures that Milton's letter helped Philaras; there is no evidence either way on its effect. In 1656 he returned to Parma as Secretary of State, and later that year he was also appointed Ambassador to Venice, where he stayed until 1661. Philaras was next appointed librarian of St. Marks; that he was unable to take up the position in Venice has been finally proved by A. E. Karathanases (*Ho Eranistes* [1970] 8: 76–78).

The last report we have of Philaras is in a letter of Cornelius Magnus, December 15, 1674, recalling the distinguished figure who had died the preceding year:

> I saw him in Venice carrying out his last embassy for the Duke of Parma. He sat in the place of honor in the midst of scholars because of his knowledge of [classical] Greek and his profound study of the Church Fathers.

It is not an unattractive last report. Cornelius goes on to speak of the dispersal of Philaras's fine library, an intriguing possibility for Renaissance scholars.

The published works of Leonard Philaras are as follows: Three editions of Διδασκαλία Χριστιανική (translations into Romaic Greek and Latin of Bellarmine's *Dottrina Christiana;*) Rome 1616, Paris 1633, Rome 1637; Ode on the immaculate conception, Paris 1644; *In Laudem Venetorum Respublicae de . . . defensione a suis facta contra turcos in obsidione . . . metropolis Crete,* 1688. In addition, there are some scattered epigrams and the published portrait, as well as a version in manuscript of the *Greek Anthology* in the Bibliotheque Nationale (Coislin 352); vast numbers of his state letters in Italian, French, and Latin are in the Archivo de Stato in Parma. The best bibliographic source is still Emile Legrand, *Bibliographie Hellénique du 17e siècle,* 3 : 407ff. A convenient survey of an area little known to American and British scholars is *The History of Neo-Hellenic Literature* by C. Th. Dimaras, translated by Mary P. Gianos (Albany, State University of New York Press). Two essays on Philaras are those by B. Knös, "Ho Leonardos Ho Philaras," in *Prosphora ek Stilpona Kyriakiden (Offering for Stilpon Kyriakides)* (Salonica, 1953), pp. 345–57 and including a bibliography, and T. Kranidas, "Leonardos Philaros, Sygenes Athenaios (Leonard Philaras, Noble Athenian)," in *The Fulbright Forum in Cyprus* (n.d.) pp. 13–19. Except where noted in the text, the material in this article is drawn from these two essays. [TK]

PHILIPS, JOHN (1676–1709), poet. Remembered by students of Milton for his poem "The Splendid Shilling," which Addison* termed "The finest burlesque poem in the British language" (*Tatler,* no. 249), Philips also wrote other pieces in imitation of his favorite author, Milton. "The Splendid Shilling" was first published as "In Imitation of Milton" twice in 1701 : 1) *A Collection of Poems: viz. The Temple of Death: by the Marquis of Normandy.* [etc.] *With Several Original Poems, Never Before Printed,* pp. 393–400 (reissued, 1702); 2) [Charles Gildon, ed.], *A New Miscellany of Original Poems, on Several Occasions,* pp. 212–21. It reappeared in *Apollo's east: or, Wits Entertainment* (1703), pp.147–50. In 1705 it was published under the title *The Splendid Shilling. A Poem In Imitation of Milton. By the author of Blenheim,* apparently without Philips's consent, for within a month appeared *The Splendid Shilling. An Imitation of Milton. Now First Correctly Publish'd.* It frequently was reprinted, usually with other poems by Philips or in various miscellanies and poetic collections. A Latin version by Thomas Tyrwhitt was called "Splendeus Solidus" and published in *Translations in Verse* (Oxford, 1747); another by Edward Popham, "Nummus Splendidus," appeared in *Selecta Poemata* (1776), 3: 101–7, and was reprinted. In *The Altar of Love. Consisting of Poems, and Other Miscellanies. By the Most Eminent Hands* (1727; various reprints) is found the anonymous "An Imitation of Mr. John Phillips's Splendid Shilling," pp. 53–59. The poem also spawned such further parodies* of Milton as James Bramston's "The Crooked Six-Pence," which was published with Philips's poem in *The Crooked Sixpence. With a Learned Preface Found Among Some Papers Bearing Date the Same Year in which Paradise Lost was Published by the late Dr. Bentley*

(1743). Philips's burlesque, in blank verse supposedly with the tone, diction, and style* of that in *PL,* presents the miseries of one in debt, fearing collectors, and without even a shilling to buy tobacco, wine, food, or clothes.

The celebrity of the poem brought Philips to the attention of Robert Harley and Henry St. John, who employed him to write verses on the battle of Blenheim as a Tory view countering Addison's "The Campaign." The poem is imitative of Miltonic verse, but less noteworthy than its predecessor; it appeared in 1705 and was frequently reprinted. His next poem, *Cerealia: An Imitation of Milton. Petronius* (1706), also evidences Philips's ability to parody style. It was reprinted in poetic collections though not in editions of Philips's works. The first book of another imitation, "Cyder," had been written earlier when Philips was at Christ Church, Oxford, but did not appear until January 1708 after Jacob Tonson* had made an agreement with him for two books: *Cyder. A Poem. In two Books. With The Splendid Shilling. Paradise Lost, and two Songs, &c.* "Cyder" appears on pp. 2–40; "The Splendid Shilling," with an epigraph partially from *PL* 1. 6–8, on pp. 41–45; and "To a Lady with Milton's *Paradise Lost,*" on p. 45. The poem was frequently reprinted or reissued separately or in collections. An edition of the poem in 1791 has "Notes Provincial, Historical and Classical, by Charles Dunster," with references to Milton throughout. It was translated into Italian by Lorenzo Magalotti in 1749 as "Il Sidro." The poem, also written in imitation of Virgil's "Georgics," discusses the cultivation of the apple tree and the manufacture of cider, while partaking of features of topographical poetry. The anonymous *Milton's Sublimity Asserted: In a Poem. Occasion'd by a late celebrated piece, entituled, Cyder, a Poem; in Blank Verse, by Philo-Milton* (1709) attacks Philips's production as Samuel Johnson* was to do later. Various parodies also occur, such as John Gay's *Wine A Poem* (1708), which has an allusion to Milton on p. 3, and

thus they are likewise parodies of Milton's alleged style. A poem attributed to Philips, but probably only imitative of him, is *A Poem on the Memorable Fall of Chloe's P - - S Pot, Attempted in Blank Verse* (1713); it thus parodies "Miltonic" style.

George Sewell's *The Life and Character of Mr. John Philips* (1712) included reissues of the poems; other editions of the life and poems, with various title pages, occur in 1715, 1720, 1744, and 1763. There are references to Milton in the *Life* and the epitaph on the monument to Philips in Westminster Abbey (erected 1710), which also refers to Milton, is given on p. 34. The epitaph has been attributed to Robert Friend and to Francis Atterbury, among others. Philips's good friend Edmund Smith published a *Poem to the Memory of Mr. John Philips* in 1710 (it was frequently reprinted); there are two specific allusions to Milton in it. Thomas Tickell, editor of the 1720 edition of Milton's *Poetical Works,* compared the two poets in *Oxford. A Poem* (1707): Philips "equals the poet, and excels the man."

As a poet Philips is important as a reaction against the dominance of the heroic couplet as poetic vehicle and as a forerunner in "Cider" of James Thomson, but his fame in his own time and after has been entwined with his imitations of Milton's style, language, and blank verse. His work thus advanced a general public acquaintance with *PL* and helped formulate often invalid views of Milton's verse and diction. [JTS]

PHILLIPS, EDWARD (brother-in-law); *see* PHILLIPS FAMILY.

PHILLIPS, EDWARD (nephew) (1630–1696?), the elder of the two sons of Edward and Anne Milton Phillips who survived infancy. He was a pupil, an amanuensis, and a biographer of his uncle, the poet. Born in August 1630 (our only information is the note in John Milton's family Bible*) in the Strand near Charing Cross (according to Anthony Wood), he was sent to study with Milton in 1640 after Milton's return from his grand tour and remained with the poet until about 1646. In his *Life of Milton* he summarizes the curriculum and pedagogy of this tutelage, which correlate fairly well with Milton's *Educ*. He matriculated in Magdalen Hall, Oxford, November 19, 1650 (possibly first attending Westminster School), and left the University in 1651.

He then became a citizen of Shrewsbury (1651–1655), where he figured in transfers of several properties that descended to him after the death of his mother and his father's mother. He made visits to London, serving as amanuensis* to Milton in writing a letter to Herman Mylius* for the poet February 13, 1652, and attending some of Henry Lawes's* concerts. He may also have visited friends or family in Lincoln and Oxford during this period. In Shrewsbury he became acquainted with Gilbert and Joseph Sheldon.

He became tutor to (1) John Evelyn, son of the diarist (1663–1665); (2) Philip Herbert, son of the Earl of Pembroke and Montgomery (1665–1669?); (3) Isabella Bennett, daughter of the Earl of Arlington (1677–1679?). He translated and transcribed materials for the use of Elias Ashmole (1662–1664), then preparing his work on the Order of the Garter. He acted as an amanuensis for Milton in transcribing portions of *PL*.

He married a widow with several children (so Wood) and kept a school in the Strand. He assisted both Aubrey* and Toland*, giving them information that they incorporated in their studies of Milton's life. Thomas Agar*, his step-father, left £200 to Edward Phillips for an annuity in his will (October 27, 1673), provided that in the meantime he could not secure for Phillips the position of engrossing of appeals to be passed under the Great Seal; presumably the £200 came to Phillips. He received from Milton's widow many of his uncle's papers.

He helped to support himself by publishing several items, from commendatory poems to dictionaries. His *Life of Milton*

(1694) is one of the earliest biographies of the poet and a valuable source, even though it is marred by careless chronology, some name-inaccuracies, and some ambiguities. His writings include: (1) "To his Honour'd Friend, Mr. *Henry Lawes*, upon his Book of *Ayres*," 1653; (2) trans., Juan Pérez de Montalván, *The Illustrious Shepherdess*, 1656; (3) trans., Juan Pérez de Montalván, *The Imperious Brother*, 1656; (4) ed., *Poems by that Most Famous Wit, William Drummond of Hawthornden*, 1656; (5) *The New World of English Words*, 1658, 1662, 1671, 1678, 1696; (6) *The Mysteries of Love & Eloquence*, 1658, 1685 [a second issue of the second edition carrying the title *The Beau's Academy*, 1699]; (7) ed., Sir Richard Baker's *A Chronicle of the Kings of England*, 1660, 1665, 1670, 1674, 1679, 1684, 1696; (8) ed., John Buchler's *Sacrarum Profanarumque Phrasium Poeticum Thesaurus*, 1670, 1679; (9) *Theatrum Poetarum*, 1675; (10) ed., John Speed's *The Theatre of the Empire of Great Britain*, 1676; (11) *Tractatulus de Modo & Ratione Formandi Voces Derivativas Linguae Latinae*, 1682; (12) *The Minority of St. Lewis*, 1685; (13) *A Treatise of the Way and Manner of Forming the Derivatives of the Latin Tongue*, 1685; (14) trans., John Milton's *Letters of State* with *Life*, 1694.

[REH]

PHILLIPS, JOHN (October 1631–1706?), the younger of the two sons of Edward and Anne Milton Phillips who survived infancy. Like his elder brother, Edward (II), he was a pupil and an amanuensis* of the poet and produced several publications of varying quality throughout his adult life. We do not know where he was born, the time of birth coming to us alone from the entry in Milton's family Bible*: "John Phillips is a year younger [than Edward (II)] about Octob. [1631]."

John Phillips was the first of the brothers to be placed under Milton's tutelage, apparently boarding in his uncle's house, and was the last to leave. He was with Milton twice as long as was his brother. He was exposed to the same course of study that his brother Edward pursued, study that fairly correlates with Milton's proposals in *Educ:* languages, choice graded reading materials, divinity, singing.

Wood* wrote John Phillips off as a scorner of religious systems ("accounted by those that knew him well to have little or no religion"; "atheistical"), an opportunist ("A man of very loose principles"), and anarchistic ("having early imbib'd in a most plentiful manner the rankest antimonarchical principles, from that villanous leading incendiary Joh. Milton his uncle"); Aubrey* considered him "very happy at jiggish poetrey." John Phillips was never a man of Milton's stripe.

Milton may have employed John Phillips during Commonwealth days in a secretarial function, to judge from remarks in Edward Phillips's Life of Milton. Certainly John Phillips undertook with Milton's guidance the preparation of *Responsio ad Apologiam Anonymi cujusdam tenebrionis pro Rege & Populo Anglicano infantissimam* (1652). Milton may also have had young Phillips in the way of becoming an intelligencer. A letter sent from Wales by a John Phillipps to John Gunter, London, on February 15, 1654, reports on the anti-Cromwellian opinions and practices of certain Welshmen. Milton's friend from Cambridge days, Andrew Sandelands*, wrote from Scotland April 11, 1654, of a similar employment of "Mr. Philipps (Mr. Milton's kinsman)." John Phillips was also a signatory to deeds in Shrewsbury pertaining to ancestral property on November 26, 1653, and November 25, 1654, along with his brother Edward.

He was arrested and fined April 25, 1656, for his part in *Sportive Wit*, considered scandalously libidinous to Commonwealth men. At the time his residence was in Westminster. He may have been in debtors' prison in 1674. He entered the Titus Oates controversy in 1678. In 1684 he was apprehended for "seditious and dangerous pamphlets and libels." He became acquainted with John Toland*, who acknowledged his aid in the preparation

of his *Life of Milton* (1698).

He married, but whom? Wood alleges that John Phillips "forsakes his wife and children, makes no provision for them." The time of his death is not known for sure, nor the place.

His writings include : (1) *Responsio ad Apologiam Anonymi cujusdam tenebrionis pro Rege & Populo Anglicano infantissimam*, 1652; (2) commendatory poem to Henry Lawes's* *Ayres and Dialogues*, 1653; (3) *A Satyr against Hypocrites*, 1655, 1661, 1671, 1674, 1677, 1680, 1689 (one 1661 issue has the title *The Religion of the Hypocritical Presbyterians in Meeter;* a manuscript copy of the first edition is in the Bodleian Library); (4) trans., Bartolomé de las Casas, *The Tears of the Indians*, 1656; (5) *Wit and Drollery, Jovial Poems*, 1656, 1661, 1682; (6) *Sportive Wit*, 1656; (7) *Montelion, 1660*, 1659; (8) *Montelion, 1661*, 1660?; (9) *A Letter from the King of Denmark to Mr. William Lilly occasioned by the Death of His Patron the King of Sweden*, 1660; (10) *Pantagruel's Prognostication*, 1660; (11) *Montelion, 1662*, 1661; (12) *Montelion's Introduction to Astrology*, 1661, 1664; (13) *Don Juan Lamberto: Or, a Comical History of the Late Times*, 1661; (14) trans., *Paul Scarron's Typhon: Or, The Gyants War with the Gods*, 1665; (15) *Montelion's Predictions*, 1672; (16) *Maronides or Virgil* [Bk. 5] *Travestie*, 1672; (17) epigram in Matthew Locke's *Observations upon a Late Book*, 1672; (18) "Duellum Musicum" in Locke's *The Present Practice of Music Vindicated*, 1673; (19) *Maronides or Virgil* [Bk. 6] *Travestie*, 1673; (20) *Mercurius Verax*, 1674; (21) continuation of James Heath's *A Chronicle of the Late Intestine War*, 1676; (22) trans., de Scudéry's *Almahide*, 1677; (23) trans., La Calprenède's *Pharamond*, 1677; (24) trans., J. B. Tavernier's *The Six Voyages*, 1677, 1684; (25) *Jockey's Downfall*, 1679; (26) trans., Tavernier's *A Collection of Several Relations*, 1680; (27) *Dr. Oates's Narrative of the Popish Plot Vindicated*, 1680; (28) *Mr. L'Estrange Refuted*, 1681; (29) *News, from the Land of Chivalry*, 1681; (30)

The Character of a Popish Successor, Part the Second, 1681; (31) *Speculum Crape-Gownorum*, 1682; (32) *New News from Tory-Land*, 1682; (33) *A Pleasant Conference upon the Observator and Heraclitus*, 1682; (34) *Horse-Flesh for the Observator*, 1682; (35) trans., Job Ludolph's *A New History of Abessinia*, 1682, 1684; (36) *An Anniversary Poem on the Sixth of May*, 1683; (37), trans., W. J. Grelot's *A Late Voyage to Constantinople*, 1683; (38) trans,. La Framboisière's *The Art of Physick*, 1684; (39) trans., "Concerning Musick" and "Concerning the Fortune or Vertue of Alexander the Great in Two Orations" from Plutarch's *Morals*, 1684, 1691, 1694; (40), trans., "Concerning the Procreation of the Soul as Discours'd of in Timaeus" from Plutarch's *Morals*, 1684, 1691, 1694; (41) trans., "Plutarch's Conjugal Precepts Dedicated to Pollianus and Euridice" and "Wherefore the Pythian Priestess Now Ceases to Deliver Her Oracles in Verse" from Plutarch's *Morals*, 1685, 1690, 1691, 1694; (42) *An Humble Offering to the Sacred Memory of . . . Charles II*, 1685; (43) trans., Cervantes' *Don Quixote*, 1687; (44) *Modern History, or a Monthly Account*, 1687–1690; (45) *A True and Exact Relation of the Earthquake*, 1688; (46) *Advice to a Painter*, 1688; (47) trans., Du Vignan's *The Turkish Secretary*, 1688; (48) *Sam.Ld. Bp. of Oxon, His Celebrated Reasons*, 1688; (49) trans., *The Dilucidation of the Late Commotions of Turkey*, 1689; (50) *The Present State of Europe*, 1690–1706 (?); (51) trans., "Concerning Such Whom God Is Slow to Punish," "Of Garrulity or Talkativeness," and "Of Love" from Plutarch's *Morals*, 1691, 1694; (52) trans., "Which Are the Most Crafty : Water-Animals or Those Creatures That Breed upon the Land" from Plutarch's *Morals*, 1691, 1694; (53) *The General History of Europe*, 1692; (54) trans., Marie-Catherine Le Jumel de Barneville's *The Present Court of Spain*, 1693; (55) "On the Peruvian Bark," "Upon His Majesty's Going into Flanders," "Horace's 34th Ode, Book I," "To Phillis" in *The Gentleman's Journal*, 1694; (56) *In Memory of Our Late Most Gracious Lady, Mary Queen of Great-Britain, France, and Ireland*, 1695; (57) *Augustus Britannicus*, 1697; (58) commendatory poem to John Blow's *Amphion Anglicus*, 1700; (59) *The Vision of Mons. Chamillard*, 1706. [REH]

PHILLIPS FAMILY. The Edward Phillips of Shrewsbury "who coming up Young to Town, was bred up in the Crown-Office in Chancery, and at length came to be Secondary of the Office under Old Mr. Bembo [John Benbow]" was able, as appears from the records of the Heralds' Visitation of 1623, to trace his lineage back for five generations. He was, like his father before him, an eldest son. His mother was Katherine (died 1650), the daughter of John Prowde of Salop; the parents were married in 1597, the date of the still-surviving document pertaining to their marriage settlement. Dorothy Prowde, first wife to John Benbow, and Lewis Prowde of Lincoln's Inn were related to Katherine.

Edward the Secondary married Anne Milton, the only sister of the poet surviving infancy, at St. Stephen's, Walbrook, on November 22, 1623. The clergyman who married them was Thomas Myriell*, the author of *Tristitiae Remedium* (1616), which contained musical compositions by the elder Milton. Five days after the marriage, the scrivener, three of his apprentices, an agent, Edward Phillips, and the younger John Milton signed their names to tripartite indentures arranging the marriage settlement between the two families. Then it was that the "considerable Dowry [£800]" was given with Anne to Phillips by the scrivener. Properties that figured in the Phillips-Prowde settlement are also included in the 1623 settlement.

Edward Phillips witnessed the will of John Benbow June 14, 1625, and after Benbow's death October 7, 1625, was promoted to the position of Deputy Clerk of the Crown Office.

The home of Edward and Anne Phillips was in the Strand near Charing Cross, in the parish of St. Martin in the Fields. The parish registers contain entries of the baptisms and burials of three of their children : John (baptized January 16, 1625; buried March 15, 1629); Anne, the "Fair Infant" (?) (baptized January 12, 1626; buried January 22, 1628); and Elizabeth (baptized April 9, 1628; buried February 19, 1631). Two sons, whose time of birth is known only approximately from entries in John Milton's family Bible*, were also born to these parents : Edward* (born August 1630) and John* (born, posthumously, October 1631). These two sons were to be John Milton's pupils and amanuenses.

Edward and Anne signed their names to a Shrewsbury lease January 18, 1628. By this time Edward's father had died. He himself was buried at night on August 25, 1631, having died probably from the plague. On August 12, 1631, he had made out his will, "being weak in bodie"; the elder Milton and his apprentice Henry Rothwell witnessed the signing of this will. The widow was named executrix, and the will was proved September 12, 1631. No mention is made in the will of his only surviving child and namesake nor of the expected child. His main concern seemed to center in his four living brothers and sisters. To them he instructed his wife to give after his mother's death the goods and chattels that were in her use, and in the event that these portions did not average twenty pounds each, he desired his "loving wife Anne to make it upp soe much." The rest he left to Anne.

Among the friends of Edward and Anne Phillips was Thomas Agar*, described by Milton's nephew as the "Intimate Friend" of Edward Phillips of the Crown Office in Chancery. He not only "worthily Succeeded" his friend in the place of Deputy Clerk, he also became the second husband of Anne Milton Phillips, probably early in 1632. [REH]

PHILO JUDAEUS. Born in Alexandria of wealthy and prominent parents, Philo (fl. 20B.C.–A.D.40) was a Hellenized Jew, educated in both Judaism and Greek philosophy. Most of his writings are philosophic discourses on topics from Hebrew Scripture, in which he attempts to interpret Scripture in terms of Greek philosophy and to revise Greek philosophy in the light of these scriptural traditions. As a commentator on Plato*, and particularly on the *Timaeus,* Philo began a revisionist tradition in which Plotinus* and Proclus figured most prominently. He originated the phrase *intelligible world* to describe the two stages of the Logos, which he defined as the Thoughts (or Ideas) of God and the creation of these Thoughts as Real Beings. In the history of philosophy, Philo's ontological speculations are among the most important aspects of his work, but Milton seems not to have been impressed by them, since he cites Philo not for his Platonic commentaries but for his method of allegorizing* Scripture and for his views on divorce* and government.

Milton mentions Philo by name four times, alluding either to Philo's *Special Laws (De specialibus legibus)* or to *Allegories of the Law (Legum allegoria).* *DDD* refers to Philo's allegorical interpretation of Exodus 17 : 11, in which "by symbols," Philo says, God shows how the Israelites were victorious over the Amalekites "just as heaven holds kingship in the universe and is superior to earth." Milton is attacking the canon laws that forbade divorce and seeks to show the law as accomplice to sin when it prohibits divorce. "If the Law allow sin," he says, "it enters into a kind of covnant with sin, and if it doe, there is not a greater sinner in the world then the Law it self." His reference to Philo is only vaguely relevant, apparently used to invoke an authority for allegorizing Scripture, and he seems to be aware of it: "The Law, to use an allegory something different from that in *Philo Judaeus* concerning *Amaleck,* though haply more significant, the Law is the *Israelite* . . . and hath this expresse repeated command *to make no cov'nant with* sin *the Canaanite,* but to expell him lest he prove a snare." The significance of this reference is that it shows Milton fully capable of allegorizing Scripture when it suits him and that his choice of Philo as an authority for doing so is particularly apt, since Philo was among the best-known of the ancient philosophers for his method of finding the Scriptures "intended symbolically rather than literally."

Milton's two references to Philo in *Tetra* are used to support his arguments for the basis of a true marriage (of souls as well as of bodies) and for divorce. Philo was cited by various authorities as supporting divorce, and Milton seems to be doing the same thing rather uncritically. "*Philo* in his book of speciall laws," Milton says, would allow a husband to keep a childless wife—"esteems him only worth pardon that sends not barrennes away." Milton's point actually obscures Philo's point, which could have been turned to much better purpose. According to Philo, husbands of childless women had a duty to put them away, but could be pardoned from not doing so on the grounds of "familiarity, that most constraining influence," a "charm of old affection imprinted on their souls by long companionship."

Milton refers to Philo a second time in *Tetra* to support his view that divorce, among the Pharisees, might be granted "for every cause . . . , for every accidental cause, any quarrell or difference that might happ'n." Milton is evidently thinking of Philo's *Special Laws* (3. 5), in which Philo takes account of women who have been divorced by their husbands. But Philo's text does not fit Milton's purposes very well, and one suspects that Milton cites Philo more for the widely held view that Philo supported divorce for any cause than for any particular regard for what Philo actually said.

In *1Def*, Milton undertakes to show that in Deuteronomy 17 "it appears by God's own witness that all nations and peoples have always possessed free choice to erect what form of government they will, and also to change it into what form of government they will." He uses Philo as "another solid authority" (*Special Laws* 4. 185) to support his argument that Deuteronomy 17 "releases the king from

the law no otherwise than as an enemy may be said to be so released." Milton tries to reinforce his point by citing Philo's *Allegories of the Law* (3. 79–80), though he mistakes the correct book : "In the second book of the *Allegories of the Law,* 'A king,' says he [i.e., Philo], 'and a tyrant are contraries.' And a little after, 'A king not only commands, but also obeys.' " Milton's second quotation does not appear in Philo's *Allegories,* and it is extremely doubtful that Philo would have written it at all, as William J. Grace notes in the Yale *Prose,* "for Philo looked upon kingship as of divine origin, and upon the king as the representative of God upon earth, subject only to the laws of God and nature, a point of view entirely foreign to the words which Milton attributes to him."

In spite of his evident carelessness with the Philonic texts, it is clear that Milton recognized the authority and importance of Philo's writings and the use to which they could be put in highly polemical disputations. He approves what he takes to be Philo's views of government, and although skeptical about Philo's allegorical readings of the Scripture as in his disregard for them in his employment of the images of Aaron's Breastplate (*PR* 13. 13–15) or Jacob's Ladder (*PL* 3. 510ff.), he is willing to employ Philo's method when it suits his purpose. [PEB]

PHILOSOPHUS AD REGEM. This five-line Greek epigram appeared in both the 1645 and 1673 editions of Milton's poems. It is essentially undatable, with estimates ranging from his days in grammar school at St. Paul's* (before 1625) to 1642–1645. William Riley Parker assigned it to the end of 1634 or the early part of 1635. His reasons were its position in the 1645 text, which he believed to be in chronological order, and a possible relationship to Milton's Greek paraphrase of Psalm 114, which he probably sent to his former teacher at St. Paul's, Alexander Gill*, along with a letter dated December 4, 1634. In the letter, Milton stated that he had written no Greek verse since he had left Gill's school; Gill, Parker surmises, "like a good schoolteacher encouraged the former Pauline to write more in Greek." The poem then may have been Milton's response to that encouragement, although Parker also notes the possibility that it may have been composed much later (*Milton*, 1 : 144).

The poem's full title, which is quite long, is in Latin and Greek : "A king, finding by chance, among men deeply guilty, a philosopher, whom he did not know at all, and who was wholly innocent, condemned the philosopher to death. As the philosopher was going along the road to death, he suddenly sent these verses to the king." This sets up the situation that the words of the epigram illuminate. In addressing the king, the philosopher is more interested in the good of the commonwealth than in his own life; he observes that the king can kill him easily enough, but that in doing so, he will destroy one of his city's "far-famed bulwark[s] of defence."

Assessments of possible topical significance in the poem depend upon the date to which it is assigned. If one follows the suggestions of Parker noted above, then "the poem may have been suggested by Gill's unfortunate clash with Laud* and the Star Chamber, and his subsequent pardon by King Charles on 30 November 1630" (*Milton*, 1 : 144). If, on the other hand, one follows David Masson*, who dated it between 1642–1645, it may be that Milton was casting himself in the role of the philosopher and Charles I in that of the king (*Poetical Works* [1890], 1 : 308). Neither suggestion is entirely satisfactory. Against the first is the time lapse between the events and the poem that supposedly alludes to them. Topical works generally refer to events that are currently newsworthy, and by 1634 Gill's troubles with the government were hardly that. Against the second is Milton's designation of the men among whom the philosopher was found as "deeply guilty." This does not accord with Milton's known estimate of his Puritan colleagues and makes it difficult to know how to take the poem that follows.

"Philosophus ad regem" is an epigram, that is, a brief poem that attempts to capture the essence of a situation or action. The genre originated in antiquity, and indeed John T. Shawcross notes that the "verses sound like a paraphrase of a classic epigram, [though] no source has been determined" (*Complete English Poetry* [1963], p. 116). A number of scholars (Hughes, Le Comte, Carey) have, however, related line five to *The Great Didactic* of the Moravian educator, Comenius* (1592–1670). In the closing pages of his work, Comenius quotes Luther as saying : "A good and wise man is the most precious treasure of a state, and is of far more value than palaces, than heaps of gold and silver, than gates of bronze and bars of iron" (trans. M. W. Keatinge, 2d ed. [1910], p. 301). John Carey also notes the praise of a wise man in Proverbs 24 : 3–6 (*Poems of John Milton* [1968], p. 13).

"Philosophus ad regem" is interesting as one of only three Greek compositions of Milton's that have survived. It has done little, however, to augment Milton's reputation as a student of the classics, for classicists (Burney, Butcher) have given it low marks as an example of Greek verse. [ERG]

PHILOSOPHY, MILTON'S. Among traditional philosophies, the Neoplatonism* of Plotinus* (ca. A.D. 204–270), Porphyry (233–ca.306), Iamblichus (d. about 330), and other late followers of Plato still had some prestige. Throughout the Middle Ages Plato* himself had been known chiefly through the *Timaeus*, the most mystical of his dialogues, and Neoplatonism—most conveniently approached through the *Enneads* of Plotinus—was also essentially mystical. At its root lay a profound skepticism of empirical knowledge, which came through senses believed to be untrustworthy. The system therefore relied entirely on mind and in its later forms courted divine revelation through ecstatic union with God. That it did not appeal to Milton is suggested by the absence from his writings of frequent allusions to Neoplatonists. Astonishingly, he nowhere mentions either Plotinus or Iamblichus, though he must, in his wide reading, have run across innumerable references to them. Dionysius the Pseudo-Areopagite* (fifth century?), a late Neoplatonist, although surely known to Milton is not mentioned either. Unless a reference in *1 Def* (7 : 45) is to him, Bernardus is ignored, as is Witelo. Porphyry and Proclus are mentioned together twice in nonphilosophical passages of *Areop* and *Brit* (4 : 302, and 10 : 88), and Porphyry once on a logical definition (*Logic* 11: 241). Lucius Apuleius (second century), author of a prose story called *Metamorphoses* or *The Golden Ass,* and reputed because of his interest in magic to have been a Neoplatonist, appears once, but only as characterized by "gay ranknesse" (*Apol* 3 : 347). Otherwise the Neoplatonism of late antiquity leaves no clear traces in the eighteen volumes of *CM.*

Renaissance Neoplatonism was qualitatively different and requires separate treatment. It had, also, a considerable vogue in Milton's time and offered one of the two main philosophical options, the other being a modified Aristotelianism*.

The movement was provoked by the recovery of virtually all Plato's writings and their translation into Latin by Marsilio Ficino (1433–1499), a Tuscan who headed the Florentine Academy under the sponsorship of Cosimo and Lorenzo de' Medici. Ficino saw Plato through the eyes of Plotinus, Porphyry, Proclus, Apuleius, Iamblichus, and Psellus, all of whom he also Latinized or edited; and he was influenced too by Hermes Trismegistus*, whose supposed writings, brought to Florence in 1460, were at once entrusted to him for translation.

Circumstances were peculiarly favorable for a Neoplatonic renaissance. After centuries of dominance, the Aristotelian philosophy of the schools had lost its original energy and was becoming wearisome. The fall of Constantinople in 1453 brought Byzantine scholars to the West, sometimes with precious documents known only by reputation or wholly unknown.

Among these were Gemistus Pletho and Johannes (or Basilius) Bessarion, both vigorous Platonists; and John Argyropolos, by teaching Greek at Florence, brought within the young Ficino's reach a linguistic skill not achieved by Petrarch* or Boccaccio* in the preceding century. What resulted, and for long was known as "Platonism," was a curious mixture of philosophy, mysticism, and superstition drawing upon many sources; though most of these dated from late antiquity, some were believed to be immemorially ancient. Although the influence was late in reaching England, a specifically English school of "Cambridge Platonism"* flourished in Milton's time, and Henry More, perhaps its most distinguished member, was still publishing in 1668.

To this complex of notions Milton was drawn only slightly, and not for long. In *IlP* (88) he mentions "thrice great *Hermes*" as astronomer or astrologer, and in the same poem he alludes (93–94) to "those *Daemons* that are found / In fire, air, flood, or under ground," spirits of the four elements (fire, air, water, and earth) which had a partly Hermetic source as well as a partly popular one. Hermes appears a second time by name in the Latin *Idea* (33). For the rest, his name does not appear. The concept of a universal harmony, in contrast, was obviously pleasing to Milton. Harmony alone "Could hold all Heav'n and Earth in happier union" (*Nat* 108) and is "ninefold" (*Nat* 131) because each of the nine spheres produces its distinctive note (*see* MUSIC OF THE SPHERES). *Sol Mus* is drenched with the idea; *Prol 2* is given over entirely to it; and *CM Index* has, altogether, thirty-five references to "Harmonies," "Harmonious," and "Harmony." The explanation lies in Milton's eager interest in and susceptibility to music. Otherwise—unless Sears Jayne is right in his interpretation of *Mask* as Neoplatonic (*Publications of the Modern Language Association* 74 [1959] : 533–43) and Purvis E. Boyette in "Milton's Eve and the Neoplatonic Graces" (*Renaissance Quarterly* 20 [1967] : 341–44)—an influence either of Renaissance Neoplatonism or any of its direct or indirect representatives requires much subtlety to find. Many of the best-known Neoplatonists— Bruno Campanella, Faber Stapulensis (Jacques Lefèvre d'Étaples), Ficino himself, Patrizzi, Pico, Symphorien Champier, Trithemius—are nowhere mentioned. Orpheus* appears sixteen times in the *Index,* but only as mythological figure and poet. Zoroaster is totally missing, as is Roger Bacon (died ca. 1294), often appealed to as a notable magician. (The marginal note on Ariosto* [18 : 334] is not Milton's.) Agrippa also is absent. The conclusion is inescapable that Milton had no deep intellectual or temperamental affinity with the dominant philosophical mysticism of his period.

The reasons for the incompatibility may be guessed at. For one thing, both Neoplatonism and Renaissance esotericism generally had an Italian origin and were predominantly Roman Catholic. The detestation of religious ceremony and symbolism by the Puritans of Milton's time derived at least partly from the obvious relationship of Catholic and Anglican High Church practices to the magic rigamaroles described by men like Agrippa. In the same way, Ficino's talismans, Agrippa's mystical seals and amulets, and whatever else was erroneously thought to constrain either daemonic forces or the divine power were repugnant to anyone who believed the best access to God to be through the reading of Scripture, instruction by preaching, and public and private prayer. A copious seventeenth-century writer who except for two neutral references in *Logic* made only three possible allusions to astrology, all unfavorable (*Mask* line 359; *Ref* 3 : 50; *Apol* 3 : 342), is unlikely to have been impressed by what he read of the Neoplatonists. Although Milton was capable of elevation and in his early writings—for example, at the end of *Ref*—sometimes rises to a mood not far from ecstasy, he was basically hardheaded. His *materialism,* which involved a belief that the soul itself was material and died with the body, to achieve consciousness again only at the Resurrection,

was at the opposite extreme from the Neoplatonic insistence that the substructure even of matter was mind. (For a different view, see Walter Clyde Curry, *Milton's Ontology, Cosmogony, and Physics* [1957], as well as Denis Saurat, *Milton: Man and Thinker* [1925]).

With regard to true Platonism the situation is different. The conclusion of both Herbert Agar's brief *Milton and Plato* and Irene Samuel's more detailed *Plato and Milton* is that Milton was deeply affected by his readings in Plato and that his views reflect Plato's influence in regard to cosmology*, music*, politics*, rhetoric*, and, especially, ethics*. Milton was, indeed, "one of the first scholars in modern Europe to penetrate the mists of Neoplatonism and come face to face with the master" (Agar, p. 23). For a full investigation of the subject the reader must go to these two studies; here it is possible only to list some conclusions. Apart from the Pythagorean harmonies, Greek thought of the pre-Socratic period appeared to Milton insignificant (Samuel, p. 31). Socratic and post-Socratic thought was a different matter, for the educational plan detailed in *Educ* was, Milton said, "what I can guess by reading, likest to those ancient and famous Schools of *Pythagoras, Plato, Isocrates, Aristotle,* and such others" (4 : 287). Samuel's inference is that "Milton's view of education was 'Socratic,' his concept of rhetoric largely 'Academic' [i.e., based on the rhetoric of Plato and his followers], and his ethical theory almost entirely 'Platonic' " (p. 32). The Pythagorean influence seems to have been limited to the notion of celestial harmonies and the importance of music in education; but the latter was also **Platonic.**

According to Samuel, Milton's cosmology derived from Plato's *Timaeus* its theories about "The ordering of the world out of elementary chaos, the figure of God as father of the created universe, of formless space as the mother, [and] the institution of the dance-like planetary changes to serve man's reckoning of time and draw his mind by contemplation to the worship of their maker" (ibid., p. 39; but see also

Edward Chauncey Baldwin, *Publications of the Modern Language Association* 35 [1920]: 210–17). In politics, the influence appears to have been limited to what Agar calls "The analogy between the soul and the state, and . . . the belief that the ideal condition for both soul and state is one of harmony, in which each part fulfils its own function and does not interfere with any other part" (*Milton and Plato*, p. 15). Milton's republicanism was, however, in other respects sharply different from the totalitarianism recommended by Plato's *Republic* and implied by his *Laws*. Milton's rhetorical principles, if partly Academic, drew also from other sources. In *Educ* he recommends "a gracefull and ornate Rhetorick taught out of the rule of *Plato, Aristotle, Phalereus, Cicero, Hermogenes, Longinus*" (4 : 286); but Quintilian*, omitted here, appears fourteen times in *CM Index*. Aside from his interest in archetypal ideas, which is as much Aristotelian as Platonic (compare the playful treatment of these in *Idea*), the chief remaining influence from Plato appears to have been ethical and to have consisted chiefly in an emphasis on "that act of reason which in *Ethics* is call'd *Proairesis* [i.e., the deliberate choice of one thing over another] : that they [the pupils of his projected school] may with some judgement contemplate upon moral good and evil" (*Educ* 4 : 284). The crucial importance of moral choice in Milton's major poetry requires no elaboration, and the role of free will is clear. For the rest, a distrust of appetite and a strong distaste for all varieties of hedonism—Epicurean, Cyrenaic, and other—although continuous with Christian asceticism has filiations leading back to Plato and beyond. The views of divorce argued in four tracts may, as Samuel believes, depend on "the Platonic dichotomy of the world into two realms : the material, or that which affects the body, and the spiritual, or that which affects the soul" (*Plato and Milton*, p. 157). The distinction, however, is too commonplace to have required a Platonic source. Milton's most unmistakably Platonic writing is surely *Mask,* in which (lines 437–68) the praise of chastity implies ascent of the "Platonic ladder" from grosser to more spiritual objects : a progression reported from Diotima in the *Symposium.* Although the idea had been taken up by Ficino and other Neoplatonists and had been developed rapturously in the fourth book of Baldassare Castiglione's *Courtier,* its impact on Milton could have been direct. More generally, the Platonic yearning for an understanding of the good, the true, and the beautiful is implied by much that Milton wrote, and he evidently found Plato's style enchanting and his moral tone admirable. Yet he was, after all, a Christian, so that in *PR* all pagan speculation is condemned as frivolous (see especially 4. 272–321).

Two more ancient philosophical systems must be noticed before considering contemporary influences. Of Epicureanism, which like the typical modern Milton associated with a search for pleasure ("In corporal pleasure he, and careless ease . . ." —*PR* 4. 299), not much need be said. Epicurus himself is alluded to seven times by Milton, four times unfavorably and three neutrally. The sect itself is referred to three times with distaste; "Epicureans" appear once neutrally and twice negatively. The Epicurean poet Lucretius* comes off somewhat better, no doubt because of his literary skill and warm sympathy for human troubles. In *Educ* Lucretius is recommended for the study of youths (4: 284); in *Areop* he is referred to as a good poet (4 : 301); and in *Marginalia* to Aratus he is cited as having remarked that we are all born of heavenly seed and have the same father (18 : 325–26). For the rest, a number of Lucretian echoes have been detected in *PL*. Some of these are doubtful, others relatively certain (e.g., in 10. 1071ff., and 11. 565ff., where the discovery of fire and the smelting of iron and brass are described). Although also a materialist, Milton was not much concerned with the atomic substructure of matter, and he believed the origin of the cosmos to have resulted not from the accidental swerving of atoms but from the divine *fiat.*

To Stoicism, revived by Justus Lipsius (1547–1606) and reinforced by the Renaissance popularity of Seneca, Milton's debt is somewhat greater. The moral toughness of men like Cato, often alluded to admiringly by Stoics, and the quiet earnestness of Epictetus and Marcus Aurelius were well suited to evoke sympathy in a reader of Milton's temper. Yet his judgment of Stoicism too was preponderantly negative. Since Stoicism—usually combined with Christianity—was a real option in Milton's time, its tenets will be examined briefly.

Stoicism, usually associated with the patient bearing of affliction, was actually more complex. It included a physics and a logic as well as an ethics and deserved inclusion with Socrates, Plato, the Skeptics, the Peripatetics, and the Epicureans in the list of Greek schools given by Christ in *PR* (4. 293–321), where, however, it is treated severely ("The Stoic last in Philosophic pride, / By him call'd vertue . . . Alas what can they teach, and not mislead; / Ignorant of themselves, of God much more"). The founder of the school, Zeno of Citium (ca. 336–ca. 264 B.C.), had begun as a Cynic and remained a materialist, a nominalist, and a rationalist. His follower Chrysippus (died ca. 206 B.C.) elaborated Zeno's ideas, especially by extending to physical nature the Cynic notion of a tension or strain in man's ethical strivings. The strain in the corporeal mind was merely one manifestation of a strain universally present in matter, and this was responsible for the Heraclitean "flux." Chrysippus was responsible also for the development of a Stoic logic, which had the reputation of being dry, formal, and technical—a sort of protoscholasticism.

As a whole, the system was materialistic, dynamic, and either monist or pantheist. Its materialism resulted from the positing of a *pneuma* (wind, air, breath), which had emanated from a World-Soul and existed in various states of concentration. Hence the apparent, but ontologically unreal, difference of corporality and incorporality. Plato and Aristotle, in contrast, believed that ultimate reality had

the character of mind. The dynamism involved the presence in all substance (*ousias*) of a passive principle that caused it to respond to contacts and an active principle or tension that made it capable of initiating motion. The sole cause—which substituted for Aristotle's efficient, material, formal, and final causes (mentioned in *Logic* 11 : 33 : "by which, from which, through which, or on account of which")—was the efficient cause, defined as physical contact. The monism or pantheism of the system was logically necessitated by its materialism. The human soul too was simple, not compound, and was dominated by reason, which was the source of all just human laws. Since all rational men assent to these, the Stoic ethic was cosmopolitan or universal and emphasized justice and friendship. For many Stoics, religious feeling encouraged the offering of prayers but required worship at no shrines or temples. Polytheism was, however, sometimes defended on the ground that the heavenly bodies, which were also rational, had divinity; or, again, the popular myths might be saved by reading allegory into them. Among the Romans, whose bent was more practical, the doctrine became less speculative, and of this later Stoicism the popular understanding is less inadequate. In his human dealings, the Stoic was thought to be marked by a special gravity and sternness and by a devotion to duty.

Milton's references to Stoicism and Stoics are relatively numerous. Apart from the excerpt already cited from *PR*, Miltonists will recall the mention, in *Mask*, of "those budge Doctors of the *Stoick Furr*" to whom it is "foolishness" to lend one's ear (lines 705–6). But there are many others. In *Apol* "*Stoick apathy*" is referred to in a pejorative context (3 : 322). Because he had edited Epictetus, the French controversialist Salmasius* is twice scornfully called a Stoic (*1Def* 7 : 481 and 531) and once twitted for inconsistency : "A Stoic of the severest . . . who considers 'an island swimming in luxury' to be happy !" (ibid., p. 287). In *CD* (17 : 253) Stoicism is called an opposite to the virtue of patience: "sensibility to pain, and even lamentations, are not inconsistent with true patience." In *PL* (2. 564–65), when the fallen angels are discussing philosophy, they consider "Passion and Apathie, and glory and shame, / Vain wisdom all, and false Philosophie." In the *Prol* 6 (12 : 223) Milton speaks contemptuously of persons who think themselves Catos. Elsewhere he attacks the Stoics for believing that all sins are equally grave (*CD* 15 : 201), for accounting reason "the common *Mercury*" who will guide truly those who submit to him (*Apol* 3 : 318), and for teaching that virtue and vice are the gifts of divine destiny—an allusion specifically to Chrysippus (*DDD* 3 : 441). The remaining citations are all in the *Logic* and are neutral. These number eight and have to do either with competing logical principles or with the assigning of principles to proponents. The logician Chrysippus therefore shares with Marcus Aurelius the moralist—mentioned six times—pride of place among the Stoics whose names appear in the *Index*. The founder of the school, Zeno, is cited twice favorably (*1Def* 7 : 287, and *Epistol* 12 : 15), but such other notable Stoics as Aristo of Chios, Panaetius of Rhodes, Cleanthes of Assus, Cornutus, and Posidonius not at all. Clearly Milton's Christian principles made unpalatable to him the notion that firmness unassisted by divine grace sufficed to make men moral; and other Stoic doctrines seemed to him tainted by this fault.

We come at last to a consideration of modern influences, confining our attention to the three most innovative philosophers of the period, René Descartes (1596–1650) on the Continent and Francis Bacon* (1561–1626) and Thomas Hobbes* (1588–1679) in England. Other influential thinkers—for example, Niccolo Machiavelli* (1469–1527) and Michel de Montaigne (1533–1592), who were noted for such qualities as moral realism and skepticism—cannot be discussed here because they were not technically philosophers. There will then remain to be considered only Aristotelianism, which despite the effervescent Neoplatonism continued to dominate formal education and hence to exert strong pressures.

The rationalism of Descartes stood sharply apart from the empiricism of Bacon because it deflected attention from sensory data to sheer cogitation. One's jugment of a possible influence of Descartes on Milton must be negative. His name does not appear in the *Index,* and no scholar has felt it worth while to investigate Milton's indebtedness to him. Here, as elsewhere, the absence of references of course need not imply total ignorance. Nevertheless, the impact of Descartes's thought on the poet was negligible or nonexistent.

That Milton knew something of Hobbes is certain. "His widow," John Aubrey* wrote, "assures me that Mr. Hobbes was not one of his acquaintance, that her husband did not like him at all, but he would acknowledge him to be a man of great parts, and a learned man. Their interests and tenets did run counter to each other—vide Mr. Hobbes *Behemoth.*" The relationship has been explored by Don M. Wolfe (*Studies in Philology* 41 [1944]: 410–26). According to Hobbes, the universities "had planted in men's minds the seeds of sedition, feeding their fancies with the ideal of mixed monarchy and the virtues of the ancient commonwealths" by stuffing them with Cicero*, Seneca, Cato, Aristotle, and other classic writers who were unfriendly to monarchy. Aristotle, says Hobbes, "seldom spake of kings but as of wolves and other ravenous beasts." The rise of Presbyterianism* and the private reading of Scripture tended to the same effect (cf. ibid., pp. 411–13). Since Milton looked instead for political guidance to natural law, which "he conceived as a code of absolute justice derived both from man's natural reason and his reflections upon Christian principles" (ibid., p. 418), the incompatibility was complete. Between the man who of all the Royalists had been quickest to exile himself in France and the defender of the regicides both in England and—in Latin—on the Continent there could be no sympathy.

In his detestation of Hobbes Milton was not alone. Except among the most uncompromising absolutists, Hobbes was in fact the terror of his age. When *Leviathan* appeared in 1651, the exiled Charles II's advisers were appalled by it; and in 1666, when the royalist Parliament ordered an investigation of books tending toward atheism, blasphemy, or profaneness, the same work was mentioned as especially requiring examination. Although Hobbes wrote much, unsoundly, on mathematics, published a treatise called *De Corpore,* and analyzed the causes and progress of the Civil War in *Behemoth,* he was notorious chiefly as an atheist (he denied the charge but believed that since the cessation of miracles religion should be defined and regulated by the state) and for his pessimistic view of human nature, which he judged to be unalterably vicious and motivated solely by self-interest. As Marjorie Nicolson thought (*Studies in Philology* 23 [1926] : 405–33), Milton may have reacted to Hobbes in what he wrote about the law of nature. There are, however, no references to Hobbes in the *CM* Index.

The remaining near-contemporary of importance was Bacon, to whose advocacy of an experimental approach to natural philosophy Milton responded as favorably as his binding commitment to scriptural truth allowed. His recommendation that the students of his ideal academy should have "the helpful experiences of Hunters, Fowlers, Fishermen, Shepherds, Gardeners, Apothecaries; and in the other sciences, Architects, Engineers, Mariners, Anatomists" (*Educ* 4 : 284) is unmistakably Baconian, and there are twenty-one entries under "Bacon, Sir Francis" in the *CM* Index. These include specific references to the *New Atlantis,* a "discours of church affairs," and *De Augmentis Scientiarum.* Bacon's advocacy of an inductive science is too well known to require elaboration here. Milton apparently accepted it, perhaps with unspoken qualifications, but his own program of studies detained him in other areas. No trace of experimentation can be found in Milton, whose physical speculations, such as they were, drew rather upon Aristotle, the Bible and its commentators, and a strong common sense. His *Brit,* which shows a healthy skepticism of legends, is perhaps his most Baconian work. Bacon had wished for less superstitiously credulous histories. Yet a general influence from Bacon may appear in Milton's readiness to question traditions and arrive at conclusions different from those most richly supported by authority.

Despite Milton's temperamental bias in favor of Plato and his perhaps qualified approval of Bacon, by far the most powerful influence on his philosophy was that of Aristotle, to whom some 154 references appear in the *Index* when duplications are eliminated. The reason is, of course, that when Milton was at Cambridge Aristotle dominated the curriculum to such an extent that a reference to the Philosopher (*ipse philosophus*) was immediately understood as indicating him. The impatience with scholasticism shown in *Prol* 3, 4, and 5 does not imply that Aristotle was usually wrong. Although Milton's *Logic* was based on Peter Ramus*, whose first lecture as a Master of Arts had been on the *sophisma* or startling paradox that "Whatever has been said by Aristotle is false," it includes no fewer than eighty-eight citations of Aristotle, of which only ten are in any way critical. Renaissance Neoplatonism, an intellectual force on the Continent for a century and a half, was to generate a variant in Cambridge Platonism but had not yet succeeded in infiltrating the English universities in an effective way. Whatever modifications Milton might introduce, it was next to inevitable that he should conceive of and discuss logic, ethics, physics, and metaphysics* in basically Aristotelian terms.

The extent of the Aristotelian dominance in the schools is described by William T. Costello in *The Scholastic Curriculum at Early Seventeenth-Century Cambridge* (1958) and by Harris Fletcher in *The Intellectual Development of John Milton,* vol. 2 (1961). The three chief academic exercises remained the *lecture,* the *disputation,* and the *declamation.* The lecture, which after the invention of printing tended gradually to disappear, had originated in the master's oral reading of Aristotelian texts which the students were unlikely to possess. In Milton's time not only the texts themselves but also manuals and digests of them were readily obtainable. The disputation was thoroughly medieval and required syllogistic reasoning based on "Questions" and "Responses." The declamation, which was belletristic and involved multiple references to the classic poets and often a half-playful handling of ancient myths, offered practice in rhetoric, a science of which Aristotle's *Rhetoric* was a distinguished source.

Aristotelianism had been most profoundly elaborated by Thomas Aquinas* (1225?–1274), but of course was subdivided into schools and sub-schools and anti-schools. Its impact on Milton, in its somewhat degenerate seventeenth-century form, is evident from the fact that only in his materialistic monism did he differ radically from any of its major tenets. The system's basis was the doctrines of Aristotle as these had been modified by, and then purified from, Arabian developments and adjusted to Christian doctrine.

Since logic or dialectic was at the core of the system, we may begin with Milton's *Logic*, a professedly Ramistic work. Peter Ramus or Pierre de la Ramée (1515–1572) had aimed at and been celebrated for the brevity of his treatment, and Milton's query, "why should we insist on brevity if clarity is to be sought elsewhere?" (11: 3) is an oddly backhanded tribute to his source. At this distance of time, the revolutionary character attributed to all of Ramus's work is difficult to appreciate. According to Walter J. Ong (*Ramus: Method, and the Decay of Dialogue* [1958], p. 9), the central trait of the logic was a tendency to think "in terms of spatial models apprehended by sight." The world is to be conceived "as an assemblage of the sort of things which vision apprehends—objects or surfaces" (ibid.). Because the *On Places* (*De Locis*) of Peter of Spain (13th century) had also encouraged the disputant to run his eye along a

mental diagram of *topoi* or "places" in choosing his next argument, the approach was not wholly innovative but may have received a novel stress. Milton's *Logic* is not, however, equipped with the familiar visual tables—simple at the left-hand edge of the page, exfoliating toward the right—and seems mainly to have attempted a reduction of the cumbersome apparatus derived from Peter's other work, the *Summulae Logicales*, by which Renaissance humanists were especially incensed. In doing so he moved back toward the principles of Aristotle's *Organon*: an inference supported by the multiplicity of Aristotelian citations mentioned earlier. A visual emphasis is hard to detect in a treatise so prevailingly conceptual. For the rest, *Logic* is notable for the number of illustrations drawn from poets and orators instead of from philosophers.

In ethics, the most detailed discussion of which appears in Book 2 of *CD*, chapters viii–xvii (17 : 192–421), Aristotle's influence is obscured, and to a considerable extent replaced, by the plan of "proving" assertions only by Scripture. Such duties as humility, zeal in hallowing God's name, and brotherly or Christian love have small Aristotelian warrant. Also, the conception of virtue as the mean between two extremes—as courage is a mean between timidity and rashness—is replaced by the specification of "opposites." Thus the opposites of temperance—one of the four cardinal virtues* of antiquity—are drunkenness and gluttony, those of contentment are anxiety, covetousness, and a murmuring against God's wisdom, and those of frugality and industry are, respectively, penuriousness and remissness (17 : 213–35). Fortitude, another of the cardinal virtues, is paired with patience as one of the "Virtues connected with the duty of man towards himself" (17 : 247–53). A total commitment to Christianity necessarily entailed a biblical foundation for the analysis not only of man's duties toward God but also of his duties toward himself and his neighbors. At other points an indebtedness to Aristotle, and particularly to his *Nicomachean Ethics*, is more apparent. Sometimes a Christian adaptation is explicit, as when Aristotle is mentioned in support of the view that sin is propagated from father to son (*CD* 15: 47–49). In connection with divorce, we are reminded that "no injury can be done to them who seeke it, as the *Ethics* of *Aristotle* sufficiently prove" (*Tetra* 4: 145). In general, it is probable that Milton respected Aristotle as perhaps the best of the pagan moralists but believed that revelation was the source of a higher law. *Tenure* alludes to "*Aristotle* . . . whom we commonly allow for one of the best interpreters of nature and morality" (5 : 12).

According to Harris Fletcher (*Intellectual Development*, 2 : 167), the physics to which Milton was exposed "was almost entirely a rehash of Aristotle's work with that title, *Physics*, or that branch of Greek systematic philosophy that was neither logic nor ethics." The distinction of physics from metaphysics lay in the fact that "physics deals with natural bodies, which have separate existences and can change . . . and metaphysics (theology) deals with pure forms that are unchanging and separately existing" (ibid., pp. 167–68). The Aristotelian texts—not only the *Physics*, but other related treatises—had been codified in handbooks and digests written by Magirus, Aegidius, Bartholinus, Burgersdijck, Keckermann, Pererius, Zabarella, and Stier, among others (ibid., p. 168); but where Milton's interest was engaged he may be assumed to have followed his usual practice of going to the primary source.

Milton's only writings devoted exclusively to physics are *Prol* 4 and 5, probably written on assignment and characterized by a resigned acceptance of academic duty. In the former Aristotle is cited as being "on our side" in holding that when an object is destroyed it is not resolved into primary matter (12 : 179). The same authority's testimony that "the sensible object does not abide during generation" cannot be offered in support of the opposing point of view (ibid., pp. 185–87). In *Prol* 5, on the subject "Partial forms do not occur in an animal

in addition to the whole," Aristotle is cited as plainly approving Milton's thesis (ibid., p. 197).

Other references to physics are comparatively few except in the detailed account of creation* in *CD* 1 : vii (15 : 2–53), where it is argued that God made the world not out of nothing but out of preexistent matter and that matter, being of God, cannot be destroyed. As elsewhere in *CD*, the authorities are not scholastic but biblical and patristic. In *Educ* we learn that the students of Milton's proposed academy were "to read any compendious method of natural Philosophy" and that, having once mastered Greek, they would find "all the Historical Physiology"—a subdivision of physics—"of *Aristotle* and *Theophrastus* . . . open before them" (4 : 283). In the *Marginalia* (18 : 499) we may unwarily imagine a hint of modern investigative procedures when we are told that Aristotle "notes well, that the nature of every thinge is best seen in his smallest portions," but the citation is of the *Politics*. The remaining allusions to physics appear in *Logic*. Matter is "commonly divided into primary and secondary; the secondary into proximate and remote" (11. 53). "*Generation, corruption, and the like*" are notions taken from physics (11 : 73). "Effects" are related rather to physics than to logic (11 : 75); and "the war over the substances" is said (11 : 135) to be the concern neither of logic nor of physics. (It was a theological issue.) Finally, we are given a capsule definition of physics when we are informed that "physics sets out from the definition of a natural body; then there is progress toward its causes or parts and general doings and then to the species" (11 : 479). Milton's interest in all this is evidently slight. Except in *CD*, where he tries to establish an unpopular opinion about creation, his remarks about physics are mostly limited to the kind of sorting out and pigeonholing that seems to modern readers to have constituted a major part of the scholastic philosophy.

At Cambridge metaphysics and theology were alternative subjects, the former being required for the B.A. in arts and the latter for the B.A. in theology (Fletcher, *Intellectual Development,* 2 : 182). The chief source of metaphysical doctrine was again Aristotle, especially the *Metaphysics*; but again compendia and digests were readily available. (For the names of authors see ibid., 2 : 184–94.) Once more we may suppose Milton to have preferred the primary sources to the handbooks; but his bent for metaphysics was far weaker than for theology, and his allusions to the subject are mostly disapproving. He speaks of voices cracked with "metaphysical gargarisms" or garglings (3 : 273), scorns "the pride of a *metaphysicall* fume" (3 : 347), wants "som wholsom bodie of divinitie . . . without schoole terms and metaphysical notions" (6 : 78), will not "premise a long metaphysical discussion" (14 : 197), lays aside "metaphysical trifling" (14 : 309), prefers "the simple truth of Scripture, unincumbered by metaphysical comments" (15 : 265). Metaphysics, he announces, is not knowledge "but infamous rocks, but a kind of Lernian swamp of sophisms, contrived for shipwreck and destruction" (12 : 277). It is "an old errour of Universities not yet well recover'd from the Scholastick grossness of barbarous ages" that "young unmatriculated Novices" are at once introduced to "the most intellective abstractions of Logick and Metaphysicks" (4 : 278).

Given this attitude, it is not surprising that such metaphysics as can be exhumed from *CD*—Milton's only extended treatise with metaphysical overtones—is not the school subject at all. Aristotle had conceived of metaphysics fundamentally as the science of the first cause or ultimate entity, who could only be God, and had often called the science "theology" (cf. Fletcher, *Intellectual Development,* 2 : 183). But Aristotle had not enjoyed the enviable Christian privilege of revelation, hence had been superseded by a more reliable authority. When he is mentioned, the purpose is not to close off further discussion. The word *beginning* in Revelation

3 : 14 ("the beginning of the creation of God") is wrongly interpreted "in an active sense, on the authority of Aristotle," although the Hebrew word admits no such meaning (15 : 9). Aristotle was, however, right in illustrating the principle that there is no time without motion (15 : 241) and is quoted against the idea that since there was no motion before the creation of the world there could have been no time (15 : 35). On the other side, again, Aristotle's description of God—which had become conventional—as "pure act" is improper (14 : 49). The first and last things, which might in the treatment of an intelligent man less resistant than Milton to academic fashion have emerged as school metaphysics, have been transmuted to scriptural interpretation.

In conclusion it may be suggested that, except in *Logic* and the undergraduate prolusions Milton's major philosophical effort was in ethics* (unless practical and theoretical politics is considered a philosophical discipline). Although he was capable of arguing on technical philosophical subjects and in technical terms, he did so with little *élan* and no apparent enjoyment. He had begun his academic career with a natural aptitude for scholarship and a passion for literature, and during his years at St. Paul's* he had been fortunate in sitting under the younger Alexander Gill* and in being tutored by Thomas Young*. His taste, however, was for the poets, the orators, and the historians; and the Cambridge routines, against which he rebelled in his first year, must have continued to seem almost unendurably focused on logic, physics, and metaphysics. As he matured he read widely in history and in and about the Bible : precisely the subjects on which he drew for his tracts against the bishops, in favor of divorce, and in support of the Parliamentary cause. In proving his points and refuting his adversaries no doubt he found his training in logic as well as in rhetoric useful, but the publication of his *Logic* implies a resentful memory of boring drills in that subject too. His reading of history, besides serving him in his controversies, led also to *Brit* and the more limited *Mosc*. When he was moved to work out an elaborate speculative synthesis, he chose to make it not philosophical but theological and to base virtually all his reasoning on the Bible and its commentators. The lack of attraction he felt in technical philosophy is suggested by *CB*, which included an *Index Oeconomicus,* and an *Index Politicus* (with references to an *Index Theologicus*), but no indexes of physics, metaphysics, or even logic. Evidently the long involvement with philosophy forced upon him at Cambridge had been somewhat traumatic. His tastes were more practical, so that of all the subdivisions of that vast subject only ethics and logic (again, unless political theory is a branch) engaged his best efforts. By stretching, we might include aesthetics, on which Ida Langdon has written a book (*Milton's Theory of Poetry and Fine Art* [1924]); but that subject, which was to attract the serious attention of philosophers only after the publication of Baumgarten's *Aesthetica* in the eighteenth century, is represented merely by scattered remarks on rhetoric and the surprisingly modern interpretation of Aristotle's *Poetics* in the preface to *SA*.

What has been said does not imply that Milton did not think hard on important topics. His intelligence was not only penetrating but also severe. No real service, perhaps, can be done him by torturing his remarks into pronouncements on matters that seemed to him humanly frivolous. [WS]

PICARD, JEREMY: *see* AMANUENSES.

PIEMONTESE MASSACRE: *see* WALDENSES.

PINDAR: *see* ODE, THE.

PITT, MOSES (or Pitts) was a printer and bookseller in London around 1667–1691; he died around 1697. His most important venture was *The English Atlas* (1680), but before and after this time he ran afoul of authorities, first through trying to publish Milton's state papers and later (1685) through indebtedness, for which he was imprisoned. In *The Cry of the Oppressed* (1691) he lamented the conditions of debtor prisons.

In an attestation of October 18, 1676, Daniel Skinner* testified that Pitt had told him about four or five months before that he had bought some of Milton's papers, that is, the state papers. He asked Skinner to procure an agreement between him and Daniel Elzevir in Amsterdam to bring out these papers, for Skinner had committed to Elzevir "long before" "the true perfect copy of the state papers to be printed." If such an agreement were not forthcoming, Skinner reports, Pitt would proceed on his own "and make the best advantage of them" (Public Record Office, SP Dom 29/386, p. 65). Skinner concludes that it was Pitt who had therefore brought about the publication of *Literae* in 1676, an "imperfect, surreptitious copy." The source of Pitt's copy may have been Edward Phillips or Milton's widow.

Aubrey* reports in a marginal note that Milton's reputed Latin dictionary was "in the hands of Moses Pitt," being perhaps some of the papers that he had told Skinner about. However, *Linguae Romanae Dictionarium* (1693), which advertises itself as being based in part on three volumes by Milton, has no known connection with Pitt. No such manuscript, in any case, is extant. (See also CANON.) [JTS]

PLATO (427–347 8.4.), clearly one of the writers whom Milton most admired and one whose ideas most frequently appear in his writings from *Mask* through the prose tracts to *PL* and *PR*. The fact that he is not cited in *CB* does not deny Plato's primacy, for in that work Milton was more concerned to record matters of history and theology than spiritual understanding or interpretation. It has been cogently argued, in fact, that, in earlier works such as *Mask,* Milton found in Plato, particularly in such dialogues as

Symposium, Phaedo, and *Phaedrus,* moral guidance and inspiration, and reflected the excitement of his discovery of Platonism in student days; but that later, notably in the prose writings, he sought specific support for political and religious concepts and activities. That he was not an uncritical devotee of Plato is indicated by his firm objections to the censorship of the arts, advocated by the *Republic.*

A number of specific ideas are central to the thought of both Plato and Milton, and the latter's acceptance of them strongly supports the conclusion that Milton consciously borrowed them : (1) virtue* is knowledge or reason*; (2) the soul* is divided into three parts : reason, to rule over passion and desire; (3) an analogy between the soul and the state; and (4) the doctrine of ideas—the imperfect sensory realization of actuality. Milton also cherished Plato's strong objection to an obsessive eagerness for change in child-training, dress, and behavior, as a menace to the state (*Laws* 7. 797–8), for he enlarged upon the idea by his inclusion of lapses in standards of language (Letter to Buonmattei*, *Epistol* 8).

Some minor but picturesque parallels in ideas between Plato and Milton deserve mention : the creation* of the world out of formless matter as set forth in *Timaeus*; a preference for the Dorian mode in music* because it has greater moral effect on man than the Phrygian or the Lydian mode; the existence of the music of the spheres*; and the comparison of the motion of the stars to a dance. *Prol* 2 and *Idea* are particularly relevant.

In brief, it may be said that in his relationship to Plato Milton found both poet and philosopher. He responded at once to Plato's sensitive apprehension of man's spirit and to his intellectual probing and ordering of human life on earth and its survival beyond death. True to Renaissance thought he was able to mingle the "greatest of the heathen" with Christ, for in his understanding Plato became a Christian humanist. The relationship has been fully explored in Herbert Agar, *Milton and Plato* (1928) and in Irene Samuel, *Plato and Milton* (1947). No summation, however, can be presented in brief compass; it can be found only in a close reading of all of Milton's writings. See also CAMBRIDGE PLATONISTS; METAPHYSICS; PHILOSOPHY. [DAR]

PLINY THE ELDER. Gaius P. Secundus (A.D. 23–79) is described as a man of indefatigable industry; during a busy life as state official he produced seven books. Of these, only the last, *Natural History,* remains, though materials from his other histories were used by Suetonius* and Tacitus*. Through succeeding centuries, the *Natural* History came to be one of the best-known works of classical literature. An exhaustive compendium of information on astronomy, geography, zoology, botany, mineralogy, and associated topics, Pliny's book represented one of the best sources of general knowledge. Pliny has been charged with credulity and other faults of judgment, but modern scholarship has come to respect his great scope and genuine scientific purpose; his very method of including as much information as he could find has preserved knowledge, particularly about ancient arts, that might otherwise have been lost. Like all Renaissance schoolboys, Milton knew Pliny's *Natural History* from an early age, and he lists it in *Educ* as one of the works to be read for the information it contains. Though he may speak ironically of "strange tales of Pliny" in *Prol* 6, Milton frequently bases his extended imagery on descriptions from the *Natural History,* perhaps even more frequently than the modern reader realizes. Of particular interest are several images in the major poems (other examples can be added) : the silent moon in *SA*; the Pygmean Race beyond the Indian Mount, the Gryfon through the Wilderness, and the Indian fig tree in *PL*. [PS]

PLINY THE YOUNGER. Gaius P. Caecilius (A.D. 62–110?), nephew and adopted son of the elder Pliny*, followed a similar career of public service under the emperors. From his *Letters,* "composed with some care," which he published himself, later ages have learned about social life, public events, and personalities of the Silver Age. Of particular interest are the letters describing the life and the death of his famous uncle during the eruption of Vesuvius, and the letter to Trajan concerning the new sect of "Christians." When Pliny was made consul in 100, he composed, as was the custom, a long oration in the grand style. Addressed to Trajan, it praised his character and actions, and expressed the hope that the new regime would be one of law : "a senatorial manifesto in favor of a constitutional monarchy." The *Panegyric,* although never so famous as some earlier classical orations, became known in the Renaissance as a description of the achievements of the worthiest of emperors, Trajan, a ruler bound by law. It is in this sense that Milton quotes from it at some length in *1Def.* For his purposes, the assertion of constitutional principles as against those of absolute rule, Pliny's *Panegyric* furnished nearly ideal support. [PS]

PLOTINUS. Born in Lykipolis, Upper Egypt, either a Greek or Hellenized Egyptian, Plotinus (205–270) is usually called the father of Neoplatonism*. He began the study of philosophy* in Alexandria when he was twenty-eight and was deeply affected by the teachings of Ammonius Saccas, about whom little is known except that among his other students were Origen* the Christian, Origen the Pagan, and Longinus*. After eleven years as Ammonius's pupil, Plotinus joined the expedition of Gordianus III against Persia, where he hoped to pursue his interests in Persian and Indian wisdom. After Gordianus was killed, Plotinus fled to Antioch and thence to Rome, where he taught philosophy and after ten years began to write. His student Porphyry collected his writings and rather arbitrarily arranged and edited them as six *Enneads,* so called because each of the six sections contained nine "treatises." The Greek text of the *Enneads* was first printed by P. Perna (Basle, 1580), together with Marsilio Ficino's Latin translation, which had already appeared in Florence (1492).

Whether Plotinus had any direct influence on Milton is a matter of conjecture. Milton does not mention him by name, and that fact alone should caution readers against making large claims for Plotinean influence. But other facts make it improbable that Milton could have been ignorant of Plotinus. St. Augustine*, whose works Milton knew well, cites Plotinus as a chief source of Platonic thought, and the Cambridge Platonists*, who flourished shortly after Milton left the University (Henry More chief among them), were keen exponents of Plotinus and other Neoplatonists. None of this means that Milton necessarily read Plotinus, but it would have been virtually impossible for Milton to escape the pervasive, if vague, influence of Neoplatonism, since it had thoroughly penetrated the Renaissance world views Milton shared, as Arthur O. Lovejoy's famous study, *The Great Chain of Being,* shows. If one wishes to study this aspect of Milton's intellectual milieu, he must perforce turn to one of its chief architects, cautious that he not make exaggerated claims for direct influence but confident that comparisons will prove illuminating.

Plotinus has most importance for the study of Milton's ontology, especially as it focuses on how a transcendent God is also immanent in his creation. For Plotinus, the philosophical question was how to account for the infinite multiplicity of the world in relation to the unity of the divine One. His answer, developed from Plato's *Parmenides* and *Theaetetus* and Aristotle's *De Caelo,* was a theory of emanation, in which all forms of being derived from the One in a deteriorating series of emanations, a scale of nature*. From the One, the first cause whose nature it is to emanate as is the candle's to give light, emanates Mind (*Nous*), which is the level of being that contains all the archetypal ideas. Then from Mind emanates Soul, the efficient cause of all things. Although rejected by St.

Augustine (*De Trinitate*), many writers in the Middle Ages regarded this Plotinean Triad as comparable to the Holy Trinity, overlooking the fact that in orthodox Christianity the Son creates rather than the Holy Spirit, which in an exact comparison with Plotinus the Spirit would have to do.

After the two hypostases of Mind and Soul, Plotinus's system becomes less clear, if one can say that there is any system at all. Up until this point, he is clearly a monist and so far as emanation continues downward through matter, his philosophy remains monist. The difficulty comes in that Plotinus seems at times to assert a duality between the One and the Universe, and would not therefore see the multitude of the sensible world as a level in his emanative scheme, but rather separable and distinct from it. There is, for example, the matter of this world, but since this world is an image of an Intelligible Realm beyond, there must be matter there also (*En.* 2. 4. 4). In any case, the difference between the One and the Universe is "indeterminate," as Dean Inge (*The Philosophy of Plotinus* [1948]) puts it: "The same thing may be Form in relation to that which is below it, and Matter in relation to that which is above it" (1 : 139). Such apparent fuzziness is made less so when one notes that matter for Plotinus means potentiality as it did for Aristotle*, a kind of primal flux from which things are made and therefore not material (*En.* 2. 4. 3).

These ideas bear directly on those lines in *PL* (7. 166–69) in which God says that by the Son He creates out of himself (*creatio ex Deo*) rather than from nothing (*creatio ex nihilo*):

. . . ride forth, and bid the Deep
Within appointed bounds be Heav'n and Earth,
Boundless the Deep, because I am who fill
Infinitude, nor vacuous the space.

Matter is an "efflux of the Deity" (*CD* 15 : 23) and as such is not evil. Nor does evil even exist for Plotinus—it is merely the absence of good. Space is not void,

and it is infinite because God is infinite. In a general way, Milton seems to be using a Neoplatonic concept of emanation that may be documented out of Plotinus, and the idea seems implicit also in Raphael's speech to Adam (*PL* 5. 469–90), who is told that "one Almighty is, from whom / All things proceed . . . one first matter all." So far as these lines reflect the idea of emanation, Plotinus is Milton's ultimate source, although Milton may have picked up the idea from any number of other writers who may knowingly or unknowingly have been indebted to Plotinus, from in fact nothing more esoteric than Magirus's standard school textbook of natural philosophy. Finally, for Plotinus the emanated beings return for reunion with the One. Milton likewise asserts that ultimately God "shall be All in All" (*PL* 3. 341; 6. 732; 11. 44), though his immediate authority is certainly 1 Corinthians 15 : 28.

Milton may also have been impressed by Plotinus's use of light to describe the effulgence of the One and by his theory that light diminishes in levels of being progressively removed from the One. Although the metaphoric scheme was commonplace, Milton uses it with exceptional skill to show Satan's original brightness diminishing as the fiend moves farther from God and thus toward Nonbeing.

The two basic ideas of emanation and of evil as the privation of good derive philosophically from Plotinus. How they could have been transmitted to Milton is not difficulty to follow, but whether Milton followed such a course is uncertain. [PEB]

PLUTARCH (A.D. 46?–120?), biographer and miscellaneous writer. Born in Chaeronea, he studied philosophy in Athens, lectured in Rome, and then traveled widely before returning to Chaeronea, where he directed a school and became a magistrate. Of his surviving works, the parallel *Lives* of noble Greeks and Romans are the best known, but the miscellaneous essays and dialogues called the *Moralia* have also been influential. Plutarch's method is always to illustrate ethical principles by examples drawn from active life. Distinguished by impressive learning and research, his writing is characteristically vivid, and he is one of the great narrators; his influence on such writers as Montaigne and Shakespeare can hardly be overestimated. Though he wrote as a biographer rather than a historian, Plutarch's descriptions of men and events form the foundation for what most men today know of classical history. Milton, needless to say, knew Plutarch thoroughly as one of his favorite Greek authors; he speaks of him several times as among the "gravest" of writers (no higher term of praise); and in *Educ* he lists his works among those to be read by his students. Citations from Plutarch's various works are numerous in Milton. Among those works drawn on more than once are "Isis and Osiris" from the *Moralia*, and the accounts of Lycurgus, Alexander, Pompey, and Solon from the *Lives*. [PS]

POETIC AMBITIONS: *see* DRAMATIC PLANS.

POETIC FORMS. Among major English poets Milton is notable in the variety of forms that he practiced. His writng is yet more unusual in that, having satisfied himself with a poem in a given form, he rarely attempted it again. It must also be emphasized that for every poetic form that he practiced there are literary antecedents, but before he turned away from each he almost always managed to make of it something quite original. A final point to remark is the fact that nearly all of the minor poetry is either written for occasions (most of which have been identified) or are purely literary exercises (like his various translations of the Psalms, *Time, Circum,* and *SolMus*). Only *L'Al* and *IlP,* and perhaps *May,* seem to be exceptions to this generality, though it is often difficult to evaluate just how far the occasion shaped the form. For *Mask* it was probably the dominant factor; for *Nat* Milton was surely a free agent.

The term *poetic form* includes both literary content and the manner in which that content is expressed in stanzas or otherwise. As for the former, Milton seems to have practiced every genre of which his age was aware except comedy (although some, like the epigrams and verse epistles, are found only among his Latin works; not all Latin forms, of course, are represented). One may recognize as examples the ode* (*Nat, FInf, Passion,* as well as the complicated Pindaric ode addressed in Latin to John Rouse), satire* (the University Carrier pieces), verse letters (*El* 1, 4, 6; *Salsillus*), lyric (*May,* songs in *Arc* and *Mask*), masque (the same), pastoral* (*Lyc, EpDam*), sonnet*, epitaphs (*EpWin* and various Latin poems), epyllion (*QNov*), epic* (*PL*), short epic (*PR*), and classical tragedy* (*SA*). In addition, there are several examples that are difficult to classify, at least in the English tradition: exercises or school pieces in Latin, *Time, Circum,* and *SolMus* (though these have Italian models), and especially *L'Al* and *IlP,* which seem to be unique to poetry. There can be no question that their immense variety proves Milton's concern for experiments in various forms. And it is worthy of remark that for many of them Milton's is the best illustration in English literature.

Just as varied is the prosody within which these contents are expressed (that is, in English). The Latin tends to the hexameter or the elegy, an alternation of hexameter and pentameter; exceptions are the Pindaric ode to Rouse and the school exercises on the deaths of the Vice Chancellor and the Bishop of Ely.

In one group are the poems written in octosyllabic couplets, a form very close to pure stress verse in that the number of stresses remains fixed at four while the unstressed initial syllable may be freely omitted or an extra one admitted terminally. The spacing of the stresses varies freely: "óver sóme wíde-water'd shóre" or "And sínging stártle the dúll níght." Such four-stress verse, ultimately related to the oral tradition and to Old English, had been adopted by Chaucer* (*Book of the Duchess,* an elegy), who made it a flexible narrative form in comparison with the wooden regularity of Gower's *Confessio Amantis,* which employs the same medium. Particularly to be noted is the narrative deftness of its use in the *House of Fame.* Jonson* returned it to elegiac verse with his "On My First Daughter" and other brief epitaphs that Herrick and others were to continue with great success. From this tradition comes *EpWin,* though Milton's piece is exceptionally long for the genre in the seventeenth century. Earlier he had used it to translate Psalm 136, including a regular refrain at the end of each couplet stanza, the only refrain in the entire corpus of his writing (one appears irregularly in *EpDam;* there are irregularly echoic lines elsewhere). The form appears briefly in *May* and in some of Comus's speeches. Perhaps with some suggestions from Chaucer's *House of Fame* Milton turns the form to a new subject and completely masters it in *L'Al* and *IlP*—and never used it again after 1634 except in *Mask* and Psalm 7 (and there the rhyme scheme is different).

The major part of his writing, however, is in syllabic-stress verse, almost always iambic pentameter, rhymed or unrhymed. The run-of-the-mill form of the earlier seventeenth century was the ten-syllable couplet, the vehicle for translations of poetry excerpted or complete (as in Sylvester's translation of DuBartas's* *Divine Weekes*) and for such extended independent poems as the satires and elegies of Jonson and Donne. Milton's earliest surviving poem, the version of *Ps 114,* is in this form. It surfaces again with much better control in *Vac,* the satires (*Carrier* 1 and 2), and *Shak,* when he abandons it (except for irregular appearances in later poems and as the vehicle for brief translations in *Ref* and *Brit*) until 1653 when he employs it for a single time in the translation of Psalm 1, though the unsual enjambment and caesuras hardly permit its recognition as the couplet of tradition. Nothing like this last use was to appear in English poetry for almost two centuries.

The unrimed ten-syllable line is treated elsewhere (*see* BLANK VERSE) but its first appearance may be remarked in *Mask* as Milton was turning from more traditional forms (nondramatic blank verse such as he came to write had almost no English antecedents, probably none at all so far as Milton himself was aware). It appears, of course, throughout his later career as the main vehicle for his major poetry. The only other unrhymed form in the corpus of his writing is the translation of Horace's Ode; the structure of this exercise was determined by the Latin original.

The first noncouplet stanza form that Milton employed in English is that of *FInf,* an ode rhyming ababbcc, the last line an alexandrine, which distinguishes it from the regular decasyllabics of the otherwise identical "rime royal" which traces back through Shakespeare's* *Rape of Lucrece* to Chaucer. The final alexandrine, of course, marks Spenser's* influence. Either Milton independently invented this Spenserian adaptation of rime royal, as is more probable, or he somehow had access to yet unpublished poems of Phineas Fletcher* that employ it. In any case, it appears again in the introductory stanzas to *Nat* and finally is part of the failure of *Passion.* Evidently he considered the form to be well suited to the ode. The Hymn of *Nat* is Milton's own successful if irregular invention, an eight-line stanza unique to English literature consisting of three-, four-, and five-foot lines with a concluding Spenserian alexandrine. Something of the same experimental nature appears in the opening ten lines each of *L'Al* and *IlP,* which alternate three- and five-foot lines in a unique rhyme scheme.

Mention must be made of the extension of such metrical and rhyming variations to the experimental *Time, Circum,* and *SolMus,* which in turn lead to the climactic and successful expression of *Lyc.* All four of these poems are constructed in what at first glance is verse with occasional, almost accidental rhymes, but on closer inspection turns out to be very carefully rhymed poems with lines of deliberately varied length—poems without any English model except possibly Spenser's *Epithalamium* but rather indebted to the Italian *canzone*. *Time* consists of two sustained sentences contained in irregularly rhyming three- and five-foot lines with a single four-foot line near the end and the last an alexandrine. *Circum* has the same fluid form, the lines now being two, three, or five feet but divided into two stanzas of fourteen lines each. *SolMus* sustains a single sentence through sixteen lines that rhyme regularly on three-, four-, and five-foot lines and then continues through eight more decasyllabic couplet lines. The experiment concludes with two more couplets, the last line being another alexandrine, Milton's last acknowledgment to Spenser of this particular influence. The same carefully contrived yet apparently accidental mode of varied length of line and rhyme dominates *Lyc,* which is considered elsewhere; and Milton finally used it in the choruses of *SA.*

Because the sonnets are considered elsewhere, they need only be mentioned as a mode that Milton handled with formal regularity. Their originality has been sufficiently remarked as to their contents and in the fact that no one earlier in English had ever handled the Italian model with anything even suggestive of Milton's freedom.

A final note must be made of Milton's later translations of the Psalms. Those which he did in April 1648 (Pss. 80–88) are unique in his poetry in that they show no sign whatever of experimentation in form. They are uniformly in the meter of the other popular psalters; Milton's sole interest seems to be the accuracy of his translation. But the translations—or rather paraphrases—of August 1653 (Pss. 1–8) are a unique group, as experimental as anything that he ever wrote. In this respect they should be seen as literally exercises, reflecting a tradition of translation stretching back through Wither to the Sidneys* rather than to Sternhold and Hopkins. Thus *Ps* 1 is in enjambed ten-syllable couplets, *Ps* 2 is in the terzetti best known from Dante, and *Ps* 3 is a kind of ode in four six-line stanzas unique to English literature. *Ps* 4 is in seven six-line stanzas, the first five of six syllables and the last of ten, rhyming abbacc. *Ps* 5 ostensibly consists of ten stanzas of the traditional common meter (four-line stanzas of eight and six syllables rhyming abab), but Milton shocks the conventionality that the first three lines establish by concluding each stanza with a decasyllable. *Ps* 6 is more traditional, iambic pentameter quatrains rhyming abba. *Ps* 7 consists of apparently unique four-stress lines (akin to the earlier octosyllabic couplets) rhyming ababba; and finally *Ps* 8 is the standard decasyllabic four-line stanza rhyming abab; its originality consists in the enjambing of the rhymes and the unusual elisions (a forerunner of some of the practices of *PL*). There are almost no models for any of these eight poems. For a forty-five year old polemicist in prose, they must have been in some ways his five-finger exercises, his scales, which he was practising in preparation for a return to the composition of poetry. [WBH]

POETICS, MILTON'S. Milton's thoughts about poetry—a topic obviously central to his concerns but one to which he devoted no separate treatise—must be inferred from his practice and collected from pages of criticism dispersed through his works. These pages bear witness to the persistent influence exerted on his own poetics by Aristotle's*. In the autobiographical introduction to the Second Book of *RCG,* making reference to projects he meditated in "the Epick form," he muses "whether the rules of *Aristotle* herein are strictly to be kept, or nature to be follow'd, which in them that know art, and use judgement is no transgression, but an inriching of art" (3 : 237). The word *nature* is equivalent to two phrases found in the immediate vicinity of the excerpt, "propensity of nature" and "instinct of nature," meaning the bent of one's native genius. Milton is allowing the individual talent to supplement but not to supplant the artistic "rules" of the philosopher. In planning the literary section of the curriculum of his ideal academy, in *Educ*, Milton considers the "sublime Art," which "teaches what the laws are of a true *Epic* Poem, what of a *Dramatic*, what of a *Lyric*, what Decorum is, which is the grand master-peece to observe," and points out where that art can be learned: "in *Aristotles Poetics*, in *Horace**" among the ancients and among the modern in "the *Italian* Commentaries of *Castelvetro**, *Tasso**, *Mazzoni**, and others" (4 : 286) —other sixteenth-century Italians, that is, who were also "commentators" on Aristotle, if only in the loose sense of reckoning with, and usually but not invariably accepting, his towering authority in the field of literary theory. That theory as it came to Milton, even if he got it directly from the original Greek, was highly colored by Cinquecento interpretations. The title page of the first edition of *SA* cites Aristotle's definition of tragedy epigraphically; and the epistolary "self-defence, or explanation" that serves as a preface, entitled "Of that sort of Dramatick Poem which is call'd Tragedy," is indebted to Aristotle both explicitly in the opening exposition of catharsis* and implicitly elsewhere. When Milton treats of poetry on these occasions, then, whether in general or in terms of epic or of tragic genres, whether as practitioner or educator, whether early in his career or late, he locates himself in the Aristotelian tradition of criticism. Since the *Poetics* deals primarily and the most fully with tragedy*, secondarily and briefly with the epic*, and very little with other genres, Milton's remarks on tragedy and composition of it must provide the basis of an inquiry into his way of understanding the treatise (see LITERARY CRITIC, MILTON AS).

In ascribing a didactic function to poetry, as he habitually does and perhaps more extensively and eloquently than anywhere else in *RCG* (3 : 238–241), Milton takes a stand with Plato* and Horace and the vast majority of Renaissance critics but not with Aristotle. Yet the first sentence of the epistle to *SA* reveals that the author is unaware of this deviation:

"Tragedy, as it was antiently compos'd, hath been ever held the gravest, moralest, and most profitable of all other Poems: therefore said by *Aristotle* to be of power by raising pity and fear, or terror, to purge the mind. . . ." No such causal connection as that which "therefore" posits between moral purpose and catharsis appears in the *Poetics*. Such modifications—sometimes conscious, sometimes not—are common in Aristotelian criticism of the Renaissance.

Aristotle considers the plot to be the "end" and "soul" and the highest among the six "parts" of the tragedy. He defines it as the arrangement of the incidents, which are to be synthesized on a causal principle, that of necessity or probability. Milton hardly confers so exalted a status on the plot when he defines it as "nothing indeed but such œconomy, or disposition of the fable, as may stand best with verisimilitude and decorum." The word *œconomy*, or organization, is nearly synonymous with *disposition*. *Verisimilitude* could refer to lifelikeness, credibility of representation, correspondence with universal truth, or else to the probability that should conjoin the incidents. The structure of the plot of *SA* would lead one to take the word in the former rather than in the latter sense. *Decorum* surely means here *decorum personae*, or "consistency of speech and action of the character," for that is Milton's ordinary usage of the word in English, as Thomas Kranidas has shown, though his many supporting instances do not include the one under consideration (*The Fierce Equation: A Study of Milton's Decorum* [1964], pp. 96–99). Such a conception of decorum can be traced, through the Cinquecento critics and Horace, back to chapters 15 and 17 of the *Poetics* and to Book 3, chapter 7, of the *Rhetoric*. Milton's criteria for ordering the fable vary from Aristotle's prescription for constructing plots.

The plot may be "intricate or explicit," Milton's terms for complex or simple, but the epistle does not specify the type to be found in the play. Aristotle favors the complex one, which exhibits peripety or "recognition" or both. *SA* has no "recognition," but a peripety does occur when the Philistines, who summon their captive for amusement, are unexpectedly destroyed by him, his intended humiliation veering to triumph (lines 1679–1691); and so the plot may be assumed to be "intricate."

This climactic reversal, which results from prior events only to the extent that they prepare Samson for his participation in it, could not have taken place without a late, sudden, and direct divine intrusion into the action. God prompted His Champion to the festival by means of "rouzing motions" (line 1382) and the Philistines to summon him in "a spirit of phrenzie" (line 1675). The five episodes, those in which the Chorus first, and then, in turn, Manoa, Dalila, Harapha, and the Officer confront the hero, are not interconnected by means of "probability or necessity." None of these confrontations renders another inevitable, and neither do they collectively make the peripety so. They appear, instead, transposable and random, to be a *post hoc* rather than a *propter hoc* sequence. That appearance turns out, though, to be deceptive. The plotted incidents gain, once the Messenger has reported the catastrophe, a new coherence as elements of a formerly hidden and now revealed design, that which the Chorus at last apprehends as "th' unsearchable dispose / Of highest wisdom" (lines 1746–47). The choral word *dispose* can recall *disposition,* a word applied to the fable in the prefatory definition of plot. The Deity and the tragedian in their diverse ways dispose events, the one omnipotently and the other mimetically, arranging them toward "the best found in the close" (line 1748) —the close of a life and that of the play. An "uncontroulable intent" (line 1754) operating from on high shapes the action, so that the visitors had entered and exited in unwitting execution of this "intent" to test the hero and thereby to purify him and enable him to make an adequate response when the divine intervention arrives. As Martin E. Muller

observes, "a teleological nexus replaces the causal nexus of probability and necessity" conceived of by Aristotle as the organizing principle of the plot (*ELH: A Journal of English Literary History* 31 [1964] : 159). In this conception, if letters stand for "incidents," A causes B causes C causes D. The series has a beginning, middle, and end, but differs from the arrangement of *SA,* in which A and B and B and C do not cause one another but are determined by a final cause, D. The latter arrangement does "want a middle," and Dr. Johnson* reached this conclusion from rigorously examining Milton's tragedy according to "the indispensible laws of Aristotelian criticism" (*Rambler* 139).

Aristotle not only distinguishes six constituent elements of tragedy—and four of the epic—but he fixes their relative priorities. Next after the plot (*mythos*) he places character (*ethos*), by which he means the ethical qualities of the agents of the action, and then thought (*dianoia*), by which he means their intellectual qualities. Milton nowhere regards these elements as a set or hierarchy and he does not always keep them distinct, but he does, in the epistle and elsewhere, have something to say about each separate one. The two highest constituents are blended when the notion of *decorum personae* is brought into his definition of plot. This notion governs Milton's dicta on dramatic characters : in a play "different persons are introduced, sometimes good, sometimes bad, sometimes wise men, sometimes fools, and they speak not always the poet's own opinion, but what is most fitting to each character" (*1Def* 7 : 307); and "the main consistence of a true poem" is "the choys of such persons as they [poets] ought to introduce, and what is morall and decent [= decorous] to each one." The "persons" are elevated above the plot here, where the context stresses the ethical value of poetry, a value that often arises from exemplary characters, as in poetry's "Teaching over the whole book of sanctity and vertu through all the instances of example" (*RCG* 3 : 239). Didacticism effects a subtle revision of the Aristotelian priorities. Whether the "trivial and vulgar persons" disapproved for tragedy are deficient in moral or mental qualities is difficult to determine, and so the distinction fades between the elements of character and thought. Language (*lexis*) comes fourth on the descending scale; the *Poetics* makes references to meter but may or may not include versification along with diction* and metaphor in this constituent of the poem. Milton's opinion quoted above, that dramatic speech should reflect the moral and intellectual traits of the characters, touches on a stylistic aspect of decorum. But the author of *PL* seeks a style that rather reflects, or is "answerable" to, his "more Heroic" argument, and by seeking it from his "Celestial Patroness" (9. 13–23), he attributes it to her inspiration. In *PR* the Son remarks the "majestic unaffected stile" of the prophets (4. 359) —as in a partially similar vein the author had earlier commended "the sober, plain, unaffected stile of the Scriptures" (*Ref* 3 : 34). In *SA,* according to the epistle, the style derives not from inspiration but from imitation, and imitation not of the Bible but of the three Greek dramatists set up as the artistic "rule" for making and judging tragedy. Milton's two most consequential pronouncements on versification* concern specific innovative features of his own practice. The note on "The Verse" of *PL* makes a case against rhyme in defending the introduction of blank verse* into the English heroic poem. The "measure" of the choral verse of *SA* is "of all sorts, call'd by the Greeks Monostrophic, or rather *Apolelymenon,*" that is, "freed" from stanzaic regularity; or if "divided into Stanza's and Pauses" the choruses "may be call'd *Allaeostropha,*" that is, with strophes of diverse lengths. The tripartite pattern of "*Strophe, Antistrophe,* or *Epod,* which were a kind of Stanza's fram'd only for Music, then us'd with the Chorus that sung," is "not material" to this poem, never intended for theatrical performance. Music (*melopoiia*) and spectacle (*opsis*), the least important of the elements, inessential to tragedy, whose emotional effect can be got

through reading, and not germane to the epic, have been eliminated by Milton's repudiation of the stage, and were utilized by him only in the masques.

The citation in Greek and Latin of the definition of tragedy from chapter 6 to the *Poetics* does more on the title page of *SA* than pledge poem and poet to the literary canons of Aristotle; that epigram also introduces, in the Latin, the pervasive and seminal concept of catharsis : "*per misericordian et metum perficiens talium affectuum lustrationem.*" A religious term, *lustratio,* taken from Goulston's translation (1623), signifies a ritual purification, originally by sacrifice, or an expiation, *expiatio,* the word in Hensius' translation (1610), being a synonym (Ingram Bywater, *Journal of Philology* 27 [1894]: 268). Milton nowhere uses the term *catharsis* itself, only this Latin rendering of ceremonial denotation, but the concept is elucidated both at the outset of the epistle and in the concluding speech of the play.

Milton writes at the outset that tragedy "is said by *Aristotle* to be of power of raising pity and fear, or terror, to purge the mind of those and such like passions. . . ." The verb *purge* would seem to bear the senses of voiding or purifying until it is given the unusual senses of tempering and attenuation : "that is to temper and reduce them to just measure with a kind of delight, stirr'd up by reading or seeing those passions well imitated." The "passions" that here consist of pity, fear, and other akin but unnamed, are called, in an earlier account of catharsis (1642), "perturbations of the mind," which poetry can "allay" to "set the affections in right tune" (*RCG* 3 : 238), and *affectus* is the Latin in the epigraph for these emotions. Once they are aroused in the reader or viewer they will be moderated by the pleasure he derives from the skillfully executed work of art. These passions will also be represented in the work, so that tragedy, while before recognized as an "*imitatio actionis seriae,*" is taken as well as an imitation of passions, and this assumption underlies the ensuing medicinal analogy : "Nor is Nature wanting in her own effects to make good his [Aristotle's] assertion : for so in Physic things of melancholic hue and quality are us'd against melancholy, sowr against sowr, salt to remove salt humours." Such a homeopathic interpretation of tragic catharsis had never before been advanced in English, although similar if not identical explanations, undoubtedly known to Milton, had been offered by the Italian critics Minturno* and Guarini (*Literary Criticism: Plato to Dryden*, ed. A. H. Gilbert [1940], pp. 290, 517). As like against like in "physic," so do the passions imitated *remove* the passions excited, the verb implying that the reader's emotions will after all be voided rather than merely tempered. This implication gains support at the end of the play with the final phrase "all passion spent." The epistolary explanation, then, gives catharsis a therapeutic meaning at variance with the religious one of the epigraph and leaves the issue unresolved of whether the passions are reduced or removed.

Most of the means recommended by Aristotle for achieving the emotional effect proper to tragedy have been ignored by Milton. That effect succeeds best when the calamity occurs within a family and will hardly succeed when enemy injures enemy, but Samson destroys his foes. That effect is better attained by a miserable than a fortunate end for the protagonist, but Samson goes from wretchedness to conquest, and for him the peripety at the Temple proves felicitous. The hero most likely to produce that effect is neither perfect nor villainous but displays *hamartia*, which has sometimes been thought a moral defect but more usually and properly a human error. Samson's "Shameful garrulity" in disclosing his "capital secret" (line 491, 394) partakes of both conceptions, though with the greater weight on moral weakness; but this fault was committed in his "past," its consequences are dramatized, and it eventuates in his triumph. That triumph depends on divine intervention but also, in part, on an *actio seria* enacted at the human level in the

form of a succession of choices : Samson's refusals to go home, to his paternal home or matrimonial one, with Manoa or Dalila, the acceptance of Harapha's challenge, and the refusal and then the inspired willingness to do the Officer's bidding. The middle episodes are not plotted on a causal but patterned on another basis as each engages Samson in an agon, each requires him to make and intellectually articulate a decision. A distinction between *mythos* and *praxis*, plot and action, is implicit in the *Poetics* (John Jones, *On Aristotle and Greek Tragedy* [1962], pp. 24–25). The decisions are right in each instance, they are the means and signs of the protagonist's growth in stature, and they elicit admiration, which may support and intensify but is distinguishable from the pitying and fearful reactions. An aspect of the plot that can produce these reactions is designated "suffering" by Aristotle and defined as "an action of a destructive or painful nature, such as murders on the stage, tortures, woundings, and the like" (Bywater translation). Samson's killing of himself and of the Philistines, "offstage," is a destructive action, but one that produces, when reported "on stage," not pain but rejoicing. He must undergo, physically, blindness and slavery, from inimical decrees enacted before the opening scene, and, mentally, "restless thoughts," but this suffering does not constitute an *action*.

This condition of blindness, bondage, and agony of a figure who proves himself increasingly admirable as the fable unfolds serves as the chief means of generating fear and pity, both in other characters, notably Manoa and the Chorus, and in the audience. The Chorus has an intermediary role in being dramatis personae in dialogic communication with the hero, while in being spectators and listeners —and only listeners when the Messenger reports—they can exhibit and enunciate the responses of an ideal audience. Aristotelian "pity is occasioned by undeserved misfortune," and for them Samson's misfortune, if not wholly undeserved, is not either commensurate with his just deserts but excessive (lines 667ff.). Aristotelian "fear" is occasioned by the misfortune of one "like ourselves." The choral "friends and neighbours not unknown" are, like Samson and unlike the reader, Hebraic and of the Tribe of Dan. They share with him *and* the reader a common humanity, and though they recognize Samson's superiority as to strength and heavenly appointment, they can look through his misfortune into the "mirror of our fickle state" (lines 164ff., 667ff.). Compassion and apprehension are attitudes common to Chorus and reader; as choral they are "imitated" in the drama itself, and the reader takes "a kind of delight" in the imitation. For him aesthetic enjoyment "tempers and reduces" these feelings, and so it is that part of the cathartic program announced in the epistle is carried out. Then once the Messenger has narrated Samson's feats at the Philistine "Theatre," pity and fear, now inappropriate, cease. The "passions" then are "spent" in the two sense of *used up* and of *paid out*. The Chorus's final speech contains a submerged metaphor of commercial transaction. The expenditure of passion brings a "new acquist / Of true experience," with "acquist," meaning *acquisition,* also a legal term referring to the gaining of property by a mode other than inheritance. The "true experience" so purchased is an experience of the truth, in this case the religious truth that a God who is rational ("highest wisdom") and almighty (of "uncontroulable intent") though he may proceed incomprehensibly (with "unsearchable dispose") turns out to govern human affairs justly and benevolently (ever toward the "best found in the close"). This illumination of "Eternal Providence" yields "calm of mind" to the "fit audience" as well as the Chorus, and allows both types of "servants" to be dismissed "With peace and consolation." The passions excited by the suffering protagonist, and tempered in the case of the reader by his aesthetic delight, are finally evacuated from the mind to leave it in a healthy state, serene, comforted,

and passion-free. From another perspective the reader has assisted at a tragic ritual, one conducted according to a rubric, the "rules" formulated in the *Poetics* and inferrable from the art of the Greek tragedians, a ritual that engages his passions and transcends them in the culminating epiphany attendant upon the sacrificial death of the hero. The catharsis is simultaneously a homeopathic process and a *lustratio,* and raises the reader's passions successively to moderate and to eradicate them, so that aspects of the term that had initially seemed to conflict become reconciled in the play.

Milton left no formal poetics nor definition of tragedy. A definition, however, might be pieced together from his scattered remarks, and such a composite definition, if juxtaposed with that of Aristotle in chapter 6 and abbreviated on the title page of *SA,* will show the similarities and differences in their conceptions of the genre. Tragedy for Milton is (1) disposition of the fable according to norms of verisimilitude and decorum; (2) with a subject ideally biblical but at the very least exhibiting religious and historical truth; (3) sad and grave in tone and (4) morally profitable in effect; (5) in metrical language, with the choral verse possibly varying in design from the rest but not necessarily fashioned for musical accompaniment; (6) in a dramatic form, though the narrative will also do (*PL* 9. 5–6), (7) with incidents raising pity, fear, and such like passions in characters and in the audience—in the audience these passions being tempered with aesthetic delight to the end of voiding the passions from the mind and leaving it calm and peaceful, illumined with a consoling insight into the operations of Divine Providence*.

Milton was probably not conscious in the first particular above but conscious in the second of his departure from Aristotle; the third is hardly a departure and the fourth a departure Milton was not aware of; the fifth and sixth are conscious modifications; and the seventh is a conscious elaboration and adaptation.

Many of these variations from Aristotle can be found, and had been by Milton, in one or another of the Cinquecento critics, as John M. Steadman among others has demonstrated (*Calm of Mind,* ed. J. A. Wittreich, Jr. [1971], pp. 175–207). But the overall conception, just this combination of particulars, had not been anticipated, and neither had the precise Miltonic formula for excelling in tragedy by integrating Hebraic fable with Hellenic artistry. Prior examples can be adduced of biblical story set to this form (John Arthos, *Milton and the Italian Cities* [1968], pp. 134–54), but Milton ignores them. He will admit only Aeschylus, Sophocles, and Euripides into his restricted circle of superior tragedians. They are superior on artistic and ethical grounds both, on the one by virtue of their "un-equall'd" command of mimetic technique, of such elements as style and plot, and on the other by virtue of their producing "the gravest, moralest, and most profit-able" of the genres. They are "unequall'd yet by any," and while they have not been matched, the word "yet" indicates that they can be. Their primacy is acknowledged—and challenged. If the "very critical art of composition" super-latively exercised by them and expounded by Aristotle, along with his Italian "com-mentators" and Horace, could be mastered and then used with the advantage "over and above of being a Christian," used to inculcate true instead of their false religion, to present a "divine argument" from Scripture instead of their pagan ones (*RCG* 4 : 236–38), the resulting tragedy would be incomparable, aesthet-ically on a level with those "antiently composed" and, with its catharic expe-rience terminating in tranquility and solace from a reaffirmation of faith, surpassing them doctrinally. The type of poem whose supremacy once rested on didacticism would now undergo a didactic reforma-tion. If Milton can prove himself artistic-ally qualified to enter the circle of the "three Tragic Poets" of Athens, he will be the fourth and only nonpagan mem-ber. He aspired to so lofty and singular an achievement with his "Dramatic Poem" (see DRAMATISTS, GREEK).

Aristotle was the master of those who know about literary theory; but this was the Aristotle of the Renaissance (see Bernard Weinberg, *Comparative Lit-erature* 5 [1953] : 97–104). Besides, Milton never hesitated to revise received opinions, in choosing to adapt, or as a poet to follow the "instinct of nature" and the Light that shines inward along with such authorities as Aristotle, the Greek poets whom he commented on, and the neo-classical critics who commented on him. [JP]

POLITICS, MILTON'S. Milton's part in the revolutionary affairs of his time was in an obvious sense a long interruption in his career as a poet. But the diversion of his energies from epic conceptions was actually their release on behalf of a heroic political image of Britannic fulfillment that was the analogue of his early ambitions to create an Arthuriad*. England was to be transformed by the perfecting force of religion, or sanctification by grace* was to make of national life—Nature* in its social form—the recoverable domain of Christ's Kingdom. This essentially poetic and religious inspiration underlying Mil-ton's politics is the source of its visionary strength and its ultimate weakness. He talked a common language, albeit with extraordinary effectiveness, when he spoke about the religious ends of power, and he had an uncommonly shrewd sense of how tactically to exploit in his prose im-mediate situations and issues. Yet he never seemed able to reconcile in a larger view the contradictions and inconsistencies to which his religious and libertarian con-victions brought him.

In his art opposing elements often sustain by their dynamic tension the whole structure of expression. But in politics there is no static arrest of ideas and in the end it became painfully apparent that the liberty* Milton championed for the few in the name of grace, or at least in the name of superior virtue, was the denial of the secular liberty desired by the many.

The next great revolution of political philosophy in the English-speaking world justified as natural the rights to life, liberty, and the pursuit of happiness. For Milton and the many others of his time who fought and worked for the "Good Old Cause," the ends of civil life were liberty and godliness, for where the latter flourished, Milton wrote, "other things follow as the shadow does the substance" (*Ref.* 3 : 37). So the conventional wisdom with which he began was that the church, a reformed church, effectively spoke for the religious ends of life through an intimate alliance with the civil power. His later view was that religion best defined the ends of a just state when it was totally divorced from civil power, except for one important condition : that power should be reserved for those so concerned for godliness as to keep the state from interfering—through the tyranny of a state church—with the exercise of pure spirituality. It was because no such guarantee could be expected of the majority that Milton, on religious grounds, found it necessary to jutify denying liberty to his fellow countrymen.

As the shift indicates, the relationship of church and state as a political issue underwent significant changes in the course of the Puritan Revolution. (*See* ECCLESIOLOGY.) The seeds of the problem were sown in the first reformation of the English church under Henry VIII and already began to bear fruit in the reign of his son Edward VI with the emergence of an active faction in the church agitating for further reform in the direction of Genevan Calvinism*. In the reign of Elizabeth the Puritans, as they came to be called, acquired the crusading zeal of a sectarian opposition even though on the main their wish was not to separate from the church but to win it over. Yet after almost one hundred years of agitating the Puritans had not only met with no success but were being harried from the land. When, therefore, the events of 1637–1641 (from the beginnings of the religious rebellion in Scotland to the constitutional crisis posed by the struggle between Charles I* and Parliament) shook to its foundations the political structure of England, most Puritans began pressing for the disestablishment of the English episcopal church in order to set up in its place a reformed national church. But as the shape of that program emerged and seemed within reach of realization, there were already other, more radical Puritan voices calling for complete disestablishment, with no national church set up that might constrain the religious liberties of an even smaller minority among themselves. Hence reformation came soon to mean a contradictory set of religious imperatives directed at those who held or sought political power, and few Puritans showed much taste for compromise.

The politics of religion was further complicated by the nature of the spiritual authority each Puritan grouping tended to invoke in self-justification, since each entrained a somewhat different posture toward shifting events and those successively who seemed to be directing them. Of the original Puritan coalition of 1640–1643 the Presbyterians*, who advocated a Genevan style state-established church, held the right wing, with a center or moderate position emerging among Congregationalists or Independents* who wished for some or complete autonomy for their local congregations within a Presbyterian national system. Later a distinct left wing appeared with the growth of Baptist* and other sectarian influences in Cromwell's army, in the city of London, and in certain regions of the country. The main differences over spiritual authority, however, emerged between Presbyterians and most of those to the left of them. By and large the former invoked for their program the authority of Scripture, whereas the latter tended to favor the authority of Scripture more freely and subjectively interpreted in the light of the special understanding given to the saints by the Holy Spirit, especially in the expectation of the latter days before the Second Coming of Christ. Politically the Presbyterians tended to be conservative, wishing not so much to disturb the established order as to coopt it in a new partnership with themselves. But so long as they had to contend with the hostility of the Crown, they leaned toward the Calvinist tactic of favoring a secondary order of legitimate political authority, which is why in the reign of Elizabeth and of the first two Stuarts their predecessors tended to make their alliances with Parliament or its members. And for the same reason they were zealous supporters of the Parliamentary side at the outset of the Puritan Revolution. But when Parliament itself came to be overshadowed by the Independents within it and the Army, most Presbyterians turned Royalist, finding they would rather trust the King or his heirs with their religious hopes than their erstwhile Puritan allies.

By contrast the Independents and other emerging sectarian groupings did not have so cohesive an ecclesiastical program. Instead, as individuals they tended to approach both religion and politics in less dogmatic terms, being on principle inclined to a pragmatic, empirical approach based in their great faith in the work of the Holy Spirit, which in political terms appeared to be an instinctive opportunism. Some Independent ministers called this opportunism their "principle of mutability," believing that if they went on in the quest for truth without binding themselves rigidly and narrowly, God would progressively give them further light—as He tended to do in the form of favorable political opportunities no less than through an emerging revelation. In the troubled times of a revolution such a disposition was a source of concealed strength to those who were least bound to accept previous arrangements as immutable and who were readiest to seize whatever opportunities arose as the dispensation and providence of God.

Only by assuming that Milton shared in this spiritually opportunistic disposition can we make sense of the mutability of his successive political loyalties which, in review, with all their opportune changes, might suggest the character of what the times called a "trimmer." As a young man he seems to have supported unquestioningly a strong centralized monarchy. But from the outset of the Puritan Revolution he espoused in turn the constitutional monarchy Parliament first contended for, the sovereign Parliamentary power directing the war against the King, the Parliamentary power purged by the Army and the Army leadership directing the war with Scotland in 1648, the more completely purged Rump Parliament which, with the Army, managed the regicide and the setting up of a republican commonwealth, the Army alone after its leaders had dismissed even the Rump, the Army decision to convene an appointed or Nominated Parliament, and the succeeding quasi-kingly Protectorate of Oliver Cromwell* and its Parliaments based on the Instrument of Government of 1653. As far as we know, Milton supported at least formally the succession to power in 1658 of Oliver's son Richard Cromwell* (whatever reservation he may have had about it), and then with the latter's downfall in 1659 he tried in several publications to suggest the best courses open to the various factions that stood some chance of stabilizing Puritan power during its rapid disintegration between 1659 and 1660. Seen *seriatim*, his shifts might suggest lack of principle, but in fact they were based on a clear element of continuity. Every shift is traceable to the object of influencing or supporting the current political authority—in the process of which he altered or abandoned previous positions—ultimately to one main end; to safeguard, by whatever political means the providence* of God made available, church reformation and Christian liberty—those essential religious interests to which he was successively dedicated.

The Presbyterians, to be sure, were also prone to invoke for their program the providential guidance and enlightenment of the Holy Spirit, but not as a species of emergent revelation by which Scripture was to be continually reassessed. And their laymen especially tended to find more security within the sheltering forms of traditional authority. Yet methods and forms aside, the religious imperative for all Puritans was constant and dominant. The theme of possibly thousands of political sermons was summed up by Milton in *CD*, with his recommendation to "those who have the direction of political affairs" that "they should . . . read again and again" Deuteronomy 28, where God warned the Jews that as they obeyed him they would prosper and that as they did not they would be given over into servitude. The Puritan understanding of this covenantal relation to God was entirely in keeping with its original biblical equation of the nation with the individual, of Israel with Jacob, so that they expected by the grace of God as thorough a transformation of the nation's outlook as the transformation of the individual's outlook once he had seen the light. The wholly personal ideals of conversion were taken by Milton and the Puritans as the standard of national achievement, and church and state were to be visibly penetrated by the supernatural influence of the Holy Spirit, as Israel and the primitive church once had been. Their polemical zeal, therefore, was analogous to the urgency of the minister preaching salvation to the hearts of his congregation, and herein lies much of its political significance.

As with most Puritan polemic, Milton's engagement should be seen not only in terms of what it directly accomplished, the minds he may have changed or the events he could have influenced, but also as part of the larger process by which in pulpit, press, and interminable oral debate Puritanism helped forge a revolutionary rhetoric*. Being religious men who put religion first, they enlarged the scope of political thought in momentous ways by their habit of invoking for immediate issues first and last principles, God's will and God's laws, in the evidence of events and in the extraordinary dispensations of His enlightenment, so as to diminish significantly the scruples about legitimacy and precedent that men in political life naturally might have in revolutionary situations. The enlargement was gradual, not dramatic, sustained by analogous

appeals to other first principles, such as natural law* and the social compact, and the religious appeals tended pragmatically to be accommodated to conventional prudence and the nominal upholding of the very institutions that in fact were being subverted. The significance of the distinctive Puritan contribution to debate was the inexorability by which the religious appeal to God's law was taken up in turn by every faction in opposition and defense, in the process of which the intellectual basis of political thought was extended and made more supple. But for the same reason it was eventually discredited, as Milton himself realized just before the Restoration, for only divisiveness could thrive where "every faction hath the plea of God's cause" (*Way* 6 : 36).

Ironically, it was the argument of divine right, that of kings, that helped bring to birth the English revolution. The Stuarts brought with them to England a lively faith in divine right, and when Charles I tried to govern on its basis he set the stage for the events that followed. For eleven years he called no Parliament, thereby alienating a large part of the country's traditional ruling class, who found themselves denied the role in national affairs to which they felt entitled. To govern alone, the King with his ministers and advisers administratively extended the royal prerogative, raising revenues by questionable means and using the courts to justify the royal exactions and suppress opposition. In those policies the Church of England not only concurred but played a leading part, with its resources, with its support from the pulpit, and by the censorship it enforced through the power of its ecclesiastical courts. And it was the Church that brought the whole effort down by overreaching. At Archbishop Laud's* suggestion, Charles was persuaded to strengthen his authority over Scotland by replacing the Scottish Presbyterian Kirk with an episcopal church of Scotland that would stand in the same direct relation to the Crown as did the Church of England.

The effort provoked rebellion and in two short wars the Scots carried the offensive into England, destroying the King's forces and setting conditions for the convening in 1640 first of a "Short" then of the "Long" Parliament which, to guarantee itself the right to that name, exacted certain basic constitutional concessions from Charles, not the least of which was to forbid their dissolution except by their own will.

The Scots sought indemnification and security against further interference in their church, which they felt could only be assured them when the English themselves had reformed their church. Here these wishes met with those of the Presbyterian leadership in England, which saw in the Parliament's mood to take some kind of punitive action against the bishops the ripened occasion to press for the abolition of episcopacy and the setting in its place of a Presbyterian national church system. At this point Puritan polemic indirectly began to bear on the constitutional and political issues uppermost for the members of Parliament, namely, the restoration to it of its traditional powers.

But that interest was complicated by the fundamental mistrust of Charles, shared by many of the members, especially in the House of Commons. The question was whether the King was genuinely prepared to accept even constitutional restoration, to say nothing of further reforms, or would deny what he had allowed when it was in his power to do so. Was Parliament safe in merely checking the King without rendering him harmless? And could it render him harmless without acting illegally or dividing the country? There was a point up to which Parliament could say it was restoring the constitutional balance. To restrict the King's powers beyond that would arguably be a violation by Parliament itself of its traditional limitations, the beginning of a Parliamentary revolution instead of a legitimate check to the abuses of the royal prerogative.

Such a view brought together on one side men like Edward Hyde* (later the Earl of Clarendon) and Lucius Cary*, Viscount Falkland, who with a sizable Parliamentary party took the position that redress was turning into revolution and who, after hostilities began, withdrew from Westminster to join the King. But the majority in the House of Commons, with a significant residue of the House of Lords, were driven by their mistrust and encouraged from the pulpit and press to claim for Parliament what amounted to a practical sovereignty that left little of the King's real powers. And there were in the meantime continually exacerbating events, not least of which was the Catholic rebellion in Ireland in the fall of 1641 that in some quarters induced near-hysteria and brought to a head the deepening constitutional crisis. To suppress the rebellion an army would have to be raised in England, an army lawfully the King's to command, but with which he could also quell his rebellious subjects in Parliament. The upshot of such fears was Parliament's passage of a Militia Ordinance in March of 1642, placing command of the Army in its own hands, an action probably necessary but certainly unconstitutional and one that made civil war inevitable.

This drift in Parliament toward necessary but unconstitutional action gave Puritan polemic its most advantageous social opportunities, for it was easier to argue on the religious side of matters, in relation to the role of the Church of England in the state, the incontestable preeminence of the laws of God revealed biblically and in nature over common law and the English constitution. But once the point was made that God's law had precedence, the road was broadened not only for the appeals already being made to the laws of nature in political matters but also for the appeals to Providence, to revelation, and to God's law as political forces. As moderates in Parliament wavered, the Puritan cry went forth strong and stronger that not human laws, not the constitution, not politics, nor legality were the real issues, but the "interest of Christ in the Nation," and that, as with the kings and prophets of Israel, the political reformation of the Commonwealth (the need for which seemed self-evident) had to begin with rebuilding the Temple of the Lord, that is, reforming the church.

The intransigence of the demand and its political implications were quickly and rightly interpreted by the defenders of prelacy as pointing toward civil war, something all parties thought they wanted to avoid. This then is the background to Milton's first entry into the debate, with *Ref,* in May of 1641, when it was becoming more and more difficult objectively to suppose that a root-and-branch reformation could be accomplished without a thorough alteration of England's whole political nature, and it partially accounts for Milton's tactical offensive, mounting as it did in his work to an apocalyptic climax at its end, that civil war would be averted and England embarked almost miraculously on a peaceful millennial age of perfected godliness. (*See* MILLENNIUM; APOCALYPSE.)

What persuaded Milton was the fact that Parliament, a legitimate authority, seemed favorably disposed to a thorough reformation, and his hopes so enlarged this support that he imagined all of England to be responding to an outpouring of God's grace. But almost certainly his mood was also charged by the undercurrent of revolutionary excitement that, if it presaged violence, suggested the apocalyptic transfiguration of England. That same month, May 1641, the impeachment and trial of the Earl of Strafford* came to its bloody climax with his public beheading (for advising the King to use force against Parliament) in an atmosphere tense with civil tumult and fears of plots. John Pym, the Parliamentary leader, declared his belief that there existed a Popish conspiracy to destroy English Protestantism and overthrow the constitution. Hence, to consolidate their religious support and respond to the stream of petitions flowing in to Parliament, a "Protestation" was itself circulated and signed in both Houses, to be tendered

for signatures throughout the Kingdom. Like most broad political appeals, the Protestation was ambiguous, a pledge to defend "the true Reformed Protestant Religion, expressed in the Doctrine of the church of *England,* against all *Popery* and *Popish* innovations," as well as to support "the powers and privileges of Parliament." But while one part of Parliament would have preferred not to spell out which ecclesiastical system they were pledged to defend, another part took it as meaning that episcopacy should be abolished root and branch, and yet another was certain that such an abolition would lead to civil war.

Milton's response was to gather under an apocalyptic fervency all talk of civil war and concentrate on his faith in England's election by grace, which meant not only that the nation could avoid war but was the more rather inclined freely to accept a Parliamentary legislated reformation that would liberate the spiritual potentialities of his countrymen. Crucial here was his faith in the regenerate man's *magnanimity,* an attribute that in *PL* belongs to Adam by virtue of his likeness to God and which as the dignity of man gives him power to "Govern the rest" of natural creation. In the middle political tracts magnanimity reappears as the peculiar franchise of the regenerate minority justifying their right to govern as by a law of nature. For the moment no such claim was pressed, there being it seemed a sufficient share of magnanimity in a Parliament duly elected and legally empowered, so that no conflict seemed to him possible between reformation and England's laws.

But for those who argued that the common law and the Church of England were too involved with one another to be safely separated, he brushed aside the common law, and the civil, which, he wrote, were not the foundations of the state. Rather, "piety and justice . . . are our foundresses" (3 : 69). To appeal to human law then was only a whit better than to appeal to politics, a word itself in disrepute. In a nautical metaphor that joins two separated passages in *Ref* Milton contrasted the aims of "a mere politician" with that of a reformer, the first being concerned only "how to stop a leak, how to keep up the floating carcas of a crazie and diseased Monarchy or State, . . . still upon her own dead lees" (3 : 38), whereas the second would have such holiness and virtue prevail that "the Civill Magistrate may with farre lesse toyle and difficulty, and far more ease and delight steare the tall and goodly *Vessell* of the Commonwealth through all the gusts and tides of the Worlds mutability" (3 : 65).

Milton's suggestion here and elsewhere that government could be so stabilized in a near perfect form as to ride out the vicissitudes of time has repeatedly induced critics to characterize his whole political stance from beginning to end as utopian. But the term is less than useful in that it suggests a tendency in his work that is not there, namely, a secular disposition to derive from human reason a doctrinaire model of political perfection. This is not the basis of Milton's hope for civil perfectibility through religious reformation. In its Presbyterian form the idea of subordinating society to the ends of religion was a survival of the medieval conception of a society dominated by the law of God manifested in some visible spiritual authority. But even at the outset Milton's religious idealism, while outwardly Presbyterian, depended less on the visible church than on his sense of the guidance of the invisible Spirit of God; less on ecclesiastical discipline than on the perfectibility that worked outward from those spiritually more nearly perfect than others. England, he wrote, in *Animad* (July 1641), was now "a Kingdome of free spirits" (3 : 112).

In this respect he was not so much a visionary as an incipient sectarian believing the Spirit of God to be at work enlarging human capacities. His optimism about the work of the Spirit, far from being utopian, opposed such premises as utopianism implies. Utopian perfectibility derives from social planning and is the product of a constitution or system so

balanced as to meet every need and contingency of human nature and experience, and hence so durable as to weather all time. It is a secular ideal. But the practice of devising constitutions, which makes the English revolution so interesting to political historians, was peculiar to the Levellers and to the circle associated with the Rota, a club influenced by John Harrington* and his political model for England of Oceania, published in 1656. Early and late such tendencies met with considerable sectarian opposition, particularly from the millenarians, who preferred "waiting upon God" to see what He and not men would bring forth. Though not a millenarian in a consistent political sense, Milton was similarly disposed. Waiting upon God meant for him the empirical quest for emergent truths with the revelatory help of the Holy Spirit. It was this disposition that in politics no less than in poetry inclined him to take old, honored forms and transpose them into the terms of new forms that heightened the expression of spiritual possibilities.

Politically, this sometimes inclined him to represent ideals as actualities when he wished to suggest that the spiritual potential implicit in what he praised was already at work. Thus, still in *Ref*, he minimized the actual tensions within the fractured regime to suggest that its turning onto the path of reformation was inherently the fruit of its ideal balance of power, with a "free, and untutor'd *Monarch*," who with "the noblest, worthiest, and most prudent men" and "with full approbation, and suffrage of the People," had together "in their power the supreame, and finall determination of highest Affaires" (3 : 63). This studied idealization of England's government Milton set in the context of a comparison to the account by Polybius of the admirably balanced constitutions of Sparta and Rome, the first conceived on an ideal or utopian model, while the second evolved naturally or pragmatically as a historical process. By inference the superior English balance, "more divinely and harmoniously tun'd," was a consummation beyond both the utopian blueprint or the evolutionary possibility open to states having only the wisdom of nature to guide them. England's constitution, inherently sound, was perfecting itself by means peculiar to the realm of grace, namely, the outpouring of the Spirit of God upon its leaders so that already the shape of a political masterpiece was becoming evident.

By April of 1642, however, when Milton published *Apol,* the King had abandoned London, with the royalist members of Parliament leaving that spring to join him; the Militia Ordinance had passed on the sole sovereignty of Parliament; and England no longer possessed a balanced constitution. Accordingly, a minor but significant quibble in Milton's tract (otherwise not politically oriented) signaled his endorsement of the new state of affairs. Replying to an unknown opponent who, writing under the old dispensation, had been so unwise as to praise the government as the noblest *"convocation . . . of King, Peers, and Commons"* (3 : 332), Milton seized upon the phrase as a derogation of the dignity of "the high *and sovran* Court of Parliament" (italics added). This thrust in the direction of revolutionary progress was supported by the caustic tenor of the work, which he justified at its outset as a zeal for the church, a too general absence of which had brought them all to the troubles the realm was enduring. But the time was fast approaching when Milton had to realize that his zeal had been misplaced. He had imagined England being providentially led to full reformation, its leaders sustained by God, Englishmen responding to the outpourings of the Spirit and all shortly to be embraced within a church of free spirits, none involuntarily constrained in religion by a civil power. Yet now the country was divided, and, most damagingly, the ministerial leadership on whose behalf Milton had entered the polemical battlefield did not seem to understand or value the significance of that voluntarism, that Christian liberty, so dear to Milton himself.

There were two immediate causes for Milton's break with the Presbyterians, the first the hostile clerical reaction to his divorce tracts of 1643 and 1644, the second their attempt to suppress those works and censure him for their publication. What surprised him about the first was the fact that his arguments for divorce* were, as he thought, developed on scriptural principles he believed he shared with them and in part along the lines of the Parliamentary justification for political resistance, which Presbyterians had espoused and in some cases had taken the lead in developing. But their attempts to suppress or discredit his views led him to identify himself in *Areop* with a freedom to publish unpopular religious views and associated him openly with the more radical Puritans who after 1643 emerged as the determined opponents of the Presbyterians. The political aspect of the divorce tracts is in itself only incidental —Milton at this point did not join those elaborating a theory of resistance to the King—but summarily it reflected the kind of thinking forced upon Parliamentary apologists who were involved with justifying rebellion as a dissolution of the social contract. For Milton his marriage* had become in some senses a microcosm of the civil war dividing England. Certainly he no longer found it easy to imagine England uniformly and harmoniously progressing toward a grand reformation.

In arguing that divorce was sanctioned by God's law, Milton had at one level to contend that the marriage contract was essentially a civil contract tending like the social contract toward an ultimate spiritual as well as to an immediate social good, and that, like other civil and social contracts, it might be dissolved. "He who marries, intends as little to conspire his own ruine, as he that swears Allegiance : and as a whole people is in proportion to an ill Government, so is one man to an ill mariage. If they against authority, Covnant, or Statute, may by the soveraign edict of charity, save not only their lives, but honest liberties from unworthy bondage, as well may he against any private Covnant . . . redeem himself from unsupportable disturbances" (*DDD* 3:374). What Milton called the sovereign edict of charity, in Parliamentary apologetics was called the people's good, *salus populi,* which was *suprema lex,* the highest law. Moreover, the positive object of the Parliament's concern was "*the constitution and reformation of a commonwealth,*" which Milton now found properly began with "the foundation thereof . . . mariage and the family" (*Bucer* 4:8). Confronted by the problem of divorce, he evidently redirected his thinking about the end of reformation, discarding as un-Christian and unreasonable the idea that a condition was imminently attainable that made unnecessary considerable allowances for human imperfection.

The way through the divorce tracts to *Areop* is indicative of the new phase of political partisanship and Parliamentary realignments that took shape between 1643 and 1645. The overriding consideration during this whole period was to bring to a successful conclusion an indecisively fought civil war. Throughout the early stages of the conflict, and particularly after the deaths of its leaders, John Pym and John Hampden, the Parliamentary side first showed signs of dividing politically into Presbyterian and Independent positions. The clearest distinctions first became evident within the Westminster Assembly* of Divines, convened in July of 1643 to advise Parliament on the settlement of religion. The body was made up of a Presbyterian majority (including a number of Scottish ministers), of Erastian* members of Parliament (those believing the state itself should on political grounds be the final authority in the choice of a religious establishment), and of a small number of Dissenting Brethren, or ministers who did not want to have a fully centralized Presbyterian church established. The last group were Independents because, though essentially Presbyterian in most respects, they preferred independence or autonomy for their congregations within a looser national system.

But within Parliament and the Army the alignment of those called Independents began to shape up on a somewhat different basis. In Parliament the members identifiably more radical in their views of religion were also those most keen on prosecuting the war vigorously to a quick and successful conclusion. Hence the Parliamentary Independents were almost surprisingly active in urging the Scottish alliance that would bring a Scottish Presbyterian Army into the field, and it was a Commission of mostly Parliamentary Independents who agreed in Edinburgh on the wording of the Solemn League and Covenant that would bind the two nations together in the quest for victory, peace, and a speedy reformation of the church. Within the Army Independency gathered head quite separately, largely through Oliver Cromwell's initiative in raising special troops democratically officered by men of sectarian principles. The Army Independents were also unabashedly anxious for a swift and complete victory and had not the inhibitions of such a Presbyterian commander as the Earl of Manchester who, in conducting his campaign against the King, was hampered by his sense of him as, notwithstanding their armed rebellion, the inviolable symbol of leadership in the state. Outside the Army Cromwell's officers drew upon the strong sectarian (Separating Congregationalist and Baptist) demands for Christian liberty and for the complete toleration of their separated churches, not simply for an accommodation within a decentralized Presbyterian national church. Politically, Cromwell himself may have been closer in views to the Westminster Assembly Independents and to those in Parliament who at first would not go so far as to advocate a complete toleration of separatism and all that it implied, but he was altogether without reserve in encouraging the rise of separatist officers in the Army.

In September of 1643 Parliament adopted the Solemn League and Covenant by which they sealed the new Scottish alliance. The Covenant itself, which had been worded ambiguously enough to satisfy all sides, pledged the defense of the privileges of Parliament, the safeguarding of the King's personal dignities, and the advancement of reformation according to the example of the best reformed churches and the word of God. (This last phrase especially was Sir Henry Vane's* significant stipulation when as a Parliamentary Commissioner, he helped to draft the document in Edinburgh, and it later enabled the Independents and sects to claim that they had never committed themselves to establishing a centralized Presbyterian church.) By the spring of the following year a combined Parliamentary Army was in the field under distinct Scottish, Presbyterian, and Independent commands, defeating an army under King Charles and Prince Rupert at Marston Moor in Yorkshire. But this victory was shortly to be offset in the west by the defeat of the Earl of Essex's Parliamentary Army, which Cromwell was somehow able to exploit as a Presbyterian humiliation in order to secure, in September of 1644, an Accommodation Order in Parliament on behalf of the Independents. Then in the following November two measures tending in opposite directions passed in Parliament—the first an approval for a Presbyterian initiative to send Charles peace propositions, the second a Self-Denying Ordinance meant to reorganize the Army by forcing the resignation of antagonist Presbyterian and Independent commanders. The upshot of the actual Army reorganization, however, was to eliminate only the peers and the Presbyterians from major commands, and to place the Army in the hands of the Independents and on a far more efficient war footing.

The evidence that Milton identified himself with the moderate Independents in the Assembly is principally to be found in the digressive commendation in *Areop* of a loosely organized national church, discountenancing separatism but also suggesting a generous accommodation for kindred Puritan ecclesiastical forms. His sympathy for the Army Independents and their urgent militancy is reflected more subtly in a choice of imagery depicting England as a sleeping warrior "rousing herself like a strong man after sleep, . . . shaking her invincible locks," and in describing London as "a City of refuge, the shop of warre." In the same vein he interpreted the proliferation of sectarian publications as squadrons of many different seekers after truth operating like "small divided" assault troops "cutting through at every angle" of the enemy's "ill united and unweildy brigade" (*Areop* 340ff.). His appeal to Independent as well as Erastian sentiment within Parliament is manifest in the anticlerical tone of his attacks upon the Licensing Ordinance of June 1643, particularly in his intimations that the censorship Ordinance was a vehicle for advancing an unholy ministerial quest for secular power. It was against the Parliamentary Licensing Ordinance that the work itself was principally conceived, but Milton's tactic was to suggest that its passage had been somehow an oversight that in wiser reconsideration Parliament would see actually worked against their hopes for reformation. Politically, he argued, freedom to express complaints, and when just to have them redressed, was "the utmost bound of civill liberty . . .that wise men look for." To imagine otherwise, that censorship was practicable, he insinuated, was unrealistic, a species of utopianism.

More important, he made use throughout the work of the argument for spiritual empiricism that had been sketched by the Dissenting Brethren of the Westminster Assembly in *An Apologeticall Narration,* the statement of their basic tenets. There, with the "principle of mutability," they renounced any dogmatic approach to the question of reformation, believing that dogmatism tended to consecrate human errors, whereas an uncommitted approach to the quest for spiritual truth was the most favorable frame of mind for the free and enlightening work of the Holy Spirit. Clearly this assumption was also the basis in *Areop* for Milton's defense of free inquiry and of the value of open-minded debate as the means to encourage the progressive revelation of emergent truths. The political implications of this position were those inherent in his views from his first public entry into polemical debate and which he spelled out later in *1Def* (1651) in justifying the pragmatic mobility, the opportunism of the more revolutionary members of Parliament. "Surely," he said, they "ought never to be otherwise than entirely free and uncommitted . . . nor so bound to their former opinions as to scruple to change . . . to wiser ones thereafter for their own or the nation's good" (7 : 525).

Through 1644 when *Areop* was published, Milton only peripherally concerned himself in his writings with politics, nor did anything else induce him to write on behalf of a major cause until the beginning of 1649, when Charles I was brought to trial and executed. At that time a climacteric in the revolution was reached, for not only was monarchy abandoned, but even the pretense of constitutional rule by the majority, although to most radical apologists the latter was regarded as only a temporary necessity. On the Parliamentary side Calvinist theory legitimatising resistance to anti-Christian tyranny on religious grounds had been hitherto vehement but auxiliary, supporting the shaky theoretical claims to Parliament's supremacy based upon traditional constitutional premises, the natural-law principles of the social contract, and the claim to be acting for the good of the people. The exclusion of the majority of the House of Commons by Prides's Purge in 1648, the regicide, and the abolition of the House of Lords and kingship that followed it in 1649, necessitated a restatement of the principles of resistance with a formula that had to take into account the altered picture, while still relating the justification of the Army's intervention and the regicide itself to well-established Puritan positions. Milton's *Tenure* (1649), which was undertaken before all these changes had been completed, was probably the ablest response to this necessity, and for his unsolicited efforts he was rewarded with the post of Secretary for Foreign Tongues* in the newly constituted Council of State*.

Milton subsequently wrote at official behest three other polemical works defending the regicide, two of which, *Eikon* and *1Def,* appeared under the purged or Rump Parliament. But while each modified in some way the position of *Tenure,* it was the first work that most coherently addressed itself to the major changes that had come about in the aftermath of the political stalemate that followed the King's defeat in 1646. What the Puritans had expected was that with defeat Charles would accept constitutional limitations upon his authority and either establish Presbyterianism in full vigor or, as the Independents and the sectaries wished, consent to support a church system allowing a form of accommodation or toleration of most Protestant forms, including probably a limited episcopacy. The King, however, would oblige neither party but intrigued with both, a course in which he was abetted by the mutual suspicions and fears of Parliament and the Army. In the interim, Parliamentary errors in attempting to disband the Army in 1647 welded the soldiers into a political instrument in which leaders representatively chosen from the lower ranks were set beside the officers in conciliar deliberation and policy-making. The Army, in short, was adjusting itself to becoming a political body of something like a Parliamentary consultative nature, and with certainly more than Parliament's power of direct action.

Within the Army an immediate community of interest and a characteristic sectarian religiosity united them all, but there were distinguishably three groups represented in their councils. The first was notably identified with the general officers of the high command—Cromwell, his son-in-law Henry Ireton, and Sir Thomas Fairfax*, all more or less affiliated with Independency outside of the Army, and who were, as compared to the others, the most instinctively conservative in their political views. Their policy as it emerged was to affect a settlement on the most moderate terms compatible with the safety of the Army and the preservation of a general liberty of conscience for Protestants. They would have preferred to see the King reestablished with limitations upon his authority and Parliamentary supremacy continuing to prevail, but subject to periodic elections based on the traditionally limited franchise, with fixed, not indefinite terms for sitting. The second group was in the main animated by the Leveller ideas first propounded outside the Army by John Lilburne*, William Walwyn*, and Richard Overton. Generally speaking, the primary objective of these men was to secure a political settlement on the basis of representation by an enlarged, more popular or democratic suffrage, and grounded on a written constitution that would effectively limit the abuse of either royal or Parliamentary powers. Although the Levellers used the language of the sects and desired toleration, their emphasis was largely secular.

The last group comprised the sectaries of the far left, principally Separating Congregationalists, Baptists, and those who were most strongly affected by the interdenominational currents of millenarianism and antinomianism. As a group they appear to have had less cohesiveness than the other two, perhaps because they had as yet no clearly definable interests other than a vague and greatly enlarged religious concern. Like the rest they wished to see social justice prevail, but their emphasis was on the privileges of the saints. They saw that, to secure religious liberty beyond any danger, an essentially theocratic settlement would have to be reached that would translate into reality their conviction that the interests of the saints were the real interests of the nation. It was this group that most insisted that the Army had by its victories a self-evident mandate to do the work of the Lord in England, meaning at least immediately to exact unrelenting justice for the crimes of their enemies. Beyond that they were suspicious of constitutional proposals and fixed agreements that took account of

men civilly only in their natural, not their regenerate capacities. For the most part, when faced with the dilemma of how to achieve a favorable settlement while forgoing careful constitutional planning, they had recourse to their faith in Providence. God would surely show His way to the destined heirs of His kingdom.

So brief an account necessarily oversimplifies the actual complexity of the process wherein these contrasting political ideas came into play and influenced the course of affairs. The lines between groups were by no means always clearly drawn, particularly the lines between the center and the Leveller and Millenarian wings on either side. For example, in the secularity of his thinking Henry Ireton was closer to the Levellers, and if he disagreed with them it was from a basically antidemocratic bias reflecting his prejudices as a landowner. Cromwell, on the other hand, for all his ingrained respect for English constitutional forms, had the makings of a religious enthusiast and was peculiarly responsive to the dictates of Providence, the will of God made known in the fortunes of men, rather than to legal or constitutional considerations. Hence, in the crisis that precipitated the King's trial and execution, Cromwell was willing enough to consider deeply the legal and constitutional reasons against subduing Parliament, but it was Providence, in effect, that convinced him that bringing the King to trial was a decision inspired by God and justifiable by God's law.

Milton's defense of the trial judiciously represented almost the whole range of political thought within the Army coalition that prevailed in the winter of 1648–49, but with a bias that might be said to be more central and Cromwellian than anything else. *Tenure* (5 : 4), in fact, began by undertaking to answer from a religious rather than legal point of view the damaging question Charles had raised before his judges, namely, by what authority other than force he was being tried. Practically at the outset Milton seemed to concede this strong point in Royalist and

Presbyterian polemic, that legality was on the side of the King, by referring the whole issue to a higher plane than constitutional legality, making a virtue out of the fact that the action was "above the form of Law or Custom." Those who tried Charles were warranted instead by God's law, which was the same thing as natural law, a point he strained to make again in *1Def* (7 : 67, 267), where he was led on by this postulate to equate the law of nature with scriptural examples of divine judgments upon tyrants and with the manner in which the Hebrews dealt with their Kings. He was on apparently sounder ground in taking up the position of earlier Parliamentary apologists by appealing to the people's safety (*salus populi*) and their sovereign power to resist tyranny, but here too his reasoning was flawed by the fact that the Army had clearly not acted in any ordinary sense on behalf of the people.

It is likely that he had in his mind the possibility that a settlement might shortly be reached in which this kind of Leveller argument for popular sovereignty would make sense, for the work obliquely reflects a certain stage of negotiations between the Army leaders and the Levellers. It was the latter particularly who wished to see some kind of constitutional basis set up for calling into existence a new popularly elected Parliament. In the event the negotiations were successful (they were not) it would then have been arguable that the Army leaders, a minority, had taken the initiative in the execution of justice only in order to clear the ground for such a political settlement as was intended to restore sovereignty to the majority, not in order to retain authority in their own hands. Otherwise, to justify the minority in and by themselves would have been very difficult in the light of the facts, unless on theocratic and millenarian grounds.

But even though Milton leaned toward secular justification where he could, there appeared in *Tenure* a marked theocratic bias in his vindication of the minority as having acted for the good of the people,

although strictly speaking not by their will. His disposition became more apparent in *Eikon,* when the extent of popular reaction against the King's execution began to be felt. A strengthening factor for the same tendency was the definite rupture of the negotiations between the Army leaders and the Levellers in March of 1649, which would have seemed to foreclose serious reconsideration of real popular sovereignty as the basis for justifying the Army and the Rump. At the same time the weakness in Milton's former argument, evident when simultaneously he invoked the people's welfare (against their will) and their rights under the social contract, could hardly now be patched over by saying that the minority in acting for their own safety had only acted for the people's good. Another, a theocratic line justifying the minority itself, simply had to be taken, although Milton seemed to hesitate over it.

To a certain extent the stress of contradictions could be alleviated by the fact that conventionally the will of a ruling minority had always been substituted for the will of the people, even in arguments based on the social contract, and that this substitution conformed to generally accepted political theory, which scarcely at that date favored the idea of democratic suffrage. But the critical question that remained was still, what qualified the minority if not their constitutional right or their traditional status in society? One answer was that the ruling minority in England were indeed legally constituted authorities in the Rump Parliament, if only as the beneficiaries of a progressive narrowing of delegated representative powers. Another was that in the persons of the Army's leaders they were entrusted by the still-constituted civil authority of that Parliament with an alternative and delegated power. Milton relied on both these answers. But increasingly he turned to the line of religious argument favored by the radical sects and that relieved him of the necessity to appeal to the constitution, or to a natural law that was tied to the will of the people.

He began instead with the universality of justice and its essential character as the keystone of divine law. "Justice and Religion are from the same God, and works of justice ofttimes more acceptable," Milton categorically affirmed in *Tenure*. While he distinguished between justice and religion, the universality of justice was actually one of his basic religious intuitions. Hence he explicitly advanced as a holy article of faith the proposition that "The Sword of Justice is above" every tyrant, and justifiably wielded by anyone "in whose hand soever is found sufficient power to avenge the effusion, and so great a deluge of innocent blood. For if all human power to execute, not accidently but intendedly, the wrath of God upon evil doers without exception, be of God; then that power, whether ordinary, or if that faile, extraordinary so executing that intent of God, is lawful, and not to be resisted." Who and what were the extraordinary instruments of the wrath of God needed little elaboration. The Army's and the Rump's leaders were God's chosen men, and by the same token they were not to be dissuaded from their divine commission by the ignorance of the popular will (5 : 277).

The sectarian note, with its explicit distrust of popular will and correspondingly its emphasis on the wrath of God and God's concern for his saints, Milton sounded more fully in *Eikon,* where he undertook to refute and discredit the extremely popular *Eikon Basilike**, attributed to King Charles. His preface spoke harshly of the people's degeneracy, their corruption by prelatical and Presbyterian preaching, and contrasted to them the small number of the faithful who retained the true English love of freedom. The latter were the spiritual as well as the political remnant, and the implication was that God, having providentially placed power in the hands of just and virtuous men, would not lightly remove it. Milton would not yet explicitly avow that he was defending a theocracy, but his vindication of the government increasingly moved in that direction, justified ultimately by the

same view of Christian liberty articulated some years before by the radical Independent Henry Burton. "We dare not," he wrote, "pin our faith upon the generality of men's opinions. . . . If the whole world might vote this day, the generality would be against Christ, as he is indeed the only annointed King, Priest and Prophet."

This sort of religious argument might dispense with the need to invoke popular sovereignty. The religious argument against monarchy moved along a parallel line, again setting as the prior consideration Christ's interest in the state. In traditional Calvinist theories of resistance, the translation of spiritual liberty into political action and rebellion was justifiable only when the Christian was unavoidably torn between his duty to Christ and his ruler, but in principle there was no incompatibility between religion and monarchy as such. But Milton now made the point that such opposition was inevitable, rooted in monarchy's fundamental incompatability with true religion. *"No man can serve two Masters,"* he wrote; "If God and earthly Kings be for the most part not several onely, but opposite Maisters, it will as oft happ'n, that they who will serve God must forsake their king" (*Eikon* 5 : 250). In that case not only was rebellion justified, it also followed that the subsequent settlement should be of some form of government other than monarchy and better suited to Christ's rule.

With both popular government and monarchy excluded, Milton turned to justifying minority rule in the only terms left to him, either as a theocracy or as an aristocracy. The providential aspect of the Army's rise to power through its God-given victories, and the religious unity it possessed, inclined him toward the first position, which had the virtue of support from the powerful millenarian element within the Army itself. The oligarchical aspect of the Rump Parliament, which was in principle the governing body of the republican commonwealth of England, inclined him toward the second position, which had or could win more general support on a wider basis. What he represented, therefore, as the character of the government in both *Eikon* and *1Def* partook of both theocratic and aristocratic elements. Indeed, just such a combination may have been his constant preference, for as early as *Ref* he had found occasion to praise in passing the polity of the ancient Hebrews during the period of the Judges, as "the mild Aristocracy of elective Dukes, and heads of Tribes joyn'd with them (3 : 40). By *elective* Milton evidently would have meant by now a selection as permanent and as irrevocable as the members of the Rump seemed to be making themselves, and which he recommended in the last political tracts as a specific way of choosing a governmental representative body. But his reliance on the Old Testament model is suggestive, for there God and men joined together in the choice of the nation's leaders, and such had been the evident election of the Long Parliament in those euphoric early days of the Revolution, when the greatest possibilities seemed open to England.

In *2Def* the millenarian tendencies in Milton's political justification for the rule of the minority were sharply checked and there reappeared in a modified form an argument for popular sovereignty. What dominates this work, at least in the part intended for home consumption, is neither a theocratic nor a popular theory of government, but rather a humanistically conceived vindication of the rule of just men. Now the benefits of an oligarchy of virtue were set foremost, with a particular representation of Cromwell and associated dignitaries as patriots and statesmen, godly men indeed, but also heroic lovers of liberty. Their idealization, as well as the political exhortation Milton addressed to his countrymen, is, of course, incidental to the primary purpose of the tract, which was addressed as a rebuttal to an attack from abroad upon the government and directly upon Milton himself. But the political interest of the work is entirely in its reflection of the course of internal events, especially those which had led Cromwell to dissolve both the Rump and

its successor, the Nominated Parliament, before finally assuming personal authority as Lord Protector of England.

In effect, England was beginning to show that it would remain ungovernable except by some reversion, whether or not disguised, to its traditional constitutional balance, discarding *ad hoc* arrangements alien to English institutions. When the Republic had been established, power was actually shared uneasily between the Rump Parliament and the Army's general officers, with a Parliamentary appointed Council of State, presided over by Oliver Cromwell, acting as the executive. In whatever direction this interim government was to evolve the first step had to be taken by the Rump Parliament itself, which alone possessed some vestige of constitutional legitimacy and could therefore impart such legitimacy to a new government it might call into being. But the Rump could not be brought to dissolve itself unless its members were assured that they might be reelected in a new Parliament and could reserve as well the right to exclude "malignants" who, if elected in sufficient numbers, might reverse the revolution and call them all—the Army and the Rump—to account for the past. Hence its program, as expressed finally in a proposed "Bill for a New Representative," was to sit perpetually, filling up its numbers as necessary with newly elected members. However, on various grounds, the Army's Council of Officers, where the real power lay, pressed very hard for the Rump's dissolution—voluntarily, if possible, forcibly if not. To many of the officers the Rump was odious as a mere continuation of the old order, unable and unwilling to complete a real revolution by legislating social justice, simplifying the laws, and placing the real leadership in the hands of godly men. The strongest pressure to move against them came from the millenarians behind General Thomas Harrison, who wished now to convene a Parliament of Saints. But there were other pressures too from some of the lawyers associated with the Council of State and from General John Lambert among the

Army leaders, who would have preferred even a few steps toward the restoration of traditional constitutional government.

When the Rump broke an agreement with Cromwell to dissolve itself and tried to pass instead its self-perpetuating Bill, Cromwell reacted in anger and with General Harrison and a file of soldiers dissolved it, dismissing with them the last elected representatives in England. But since none of the Army leaders could risk their lives and liberties in the probable royalist outcome of a free election, logic and hope prompted them to call a "godly representative." They thought of it as a temporary expedient, or, in the words of the Army's self-justifying Declaration, as a step to prepare for an eventual return to "the election of successive Parliaments." The Nominated Parliament that resulted was convened in July of 1653 and was, as Christopher Hill described it, a Party Congress with delegates sent up by the local party cells, that is, the well-affected Independent and Baptist churches. But their broad program of reforms quickly produced even among them a radical/conservative division so serious that, with Cromwell's connivance, they were led to dissolve themselves within months. As Milton tersely summed it up : "Cromwell, we are deserted; you alone remain" (8 : 223).

If the choice had to be between anarchy and limited dictatorship, Milton plainly thought the latter preferable. Yet the fact is that his support of Cromwell went beyond merely compromising with necessity and seemed genuinely based on a profound respect for the Protector. It seems that his endorsement of the new government was bound up with a real conviction that despite the shifts and changes that had reduced the Parliamentary cause to a temporary military dictatorship, the interests of liberty, as he saw that interest in indistinguishably religious and civil terms, had remained paramount throughout and were safe in the Protector's hands. Hence it was his special sense or understanding of liberty that Milton now drew upon to represent the new government as the real heir to the interest for which they had fought since the outset of the revolution, and this part of his argument in *2Def* seems to have been particularly directed to the adherents of the coalitions of 1648 through 1653, many of whom, after Cromwell's dismissal of Levellers, republicans, and Millenarians before assuming the power of the Protectorate, had turned against him.

In addressing unnamed former supporters—apparently Levellers and republicans of principle such as Algernon Sidney—he reminded them of what true liberty meant. It was not merely "freedom of suffrage" granted to corruptible electors who would probably return ignorant, low-born persons or self-seeking men. Nor did it means (in a thrust against "classical republicanism") the "foolish emulation of the ancients for the empty name of liberty." It meant very much liberty as the privilege of magnanimous men. Then, turning against the Fifth Monarchists or Millenarians who would equate such virtue purely with religious enthusiasm, he directed to them a warning, albeit veiled, against political claims narrowly based on religion but really rooted in ignorance and superstition. Against the claims of illusory liberties and ignorant fanaticism that would really enslave them, Milton opposed a political power based on what he called true liberty, which depended upon that inward rectitude he associated with an enlightened moral perception and the capacity for individual self-discipline, qualities grounded in magnanimity and a "discipline originating in religion."

These admonitions were directed at what Sir Henry Vane* (one of those now in opposition) had called the "Good Party"—those who had in varying degrees supported the regicide and one or another of its attendant revolutionary changes—to persuade them to support Cromwell's new government as the fulfillment of what they had most desired of the revolution and as an approximation to the form and nature of traditional English government.

For at the time Milton wrote, Cromwell, as the stand-in for the traditional sovereign, was calling his first Protectorate Parliament on the basis of the Instrument of Government that had been devised by General Lambert and the lawyers as a kind of constitutional definition of the regime. (Hence Milton's revival in a modified form of the principles of popular sovereignty.) And despite precautions aimed to secure a compliant, or at the least, a cooperative Parliament, there were still reasons for concern, particularly since the election would also test the viability of the Instrument upon which the prospects for anything other than martial law really depended. The encomia in Milton's address to the "Good Party" were therefore intended to balance the admonitions and suggest the implicit if not actual harmony among all those whose lives were in fact committed to the defense of the revolution of 1648–49. Cromwell himself was chiefly praised, and some were praised who had retired to a studied silence, but no man's name seems to have been included because he represented *opposition* to Cromwell, as has often been suggested. However unrealistic Milton might have been at times when enthusiastically inspired, he was scarcely inclined in cold blood to undermine the very ends for which he was addressing himself to fellow Puritans in this tract.

(Had Milton intended to urge a conciliation between Cromwell and his now hardened opposition in the Good Party, he would have included the names of Sir Henry Vane, and Major General Harrison, the leaders respectively of the Rump and of the Fifth Monarchists with whom he had broken after the dismissal of the Nominated Parliament. It seems that the key to the confusion about those he named is to be found in the unconsidered assumption of every commentator since Masson that the Sidney Milton was referring to in *2Def* for his glorious name was Algernon Sidney, the doctrinaire classical republican who, to be sure, qualifies as a hardened opponent of Cromwell. There is, however, every reason to believe that Milton was referring not to Algernon but to his brother, Philip Sidney —a name plainly more glorious in its associations—the 3rd Earl of Leicester, commonly known as Lord Lisle. Algernon Sidney is better known to posterity, but in the 1650s Philip Sidney was far more conspicuous as a high-born Cromwellian, who not only served and was to serve on the Protector's 1st, 2nd, 4th, and 5th Councils of State and had sat in the Nominated Parliament, but as Commissioner of the Great Seal had formally invested Oliver with his dignities in the ceremony creating the Protectorate. As one of the Protector's chief supporters, he strongly disapproved of his brother's opposition. It would seem almost certain that Milton, who must have known and worked with him, meant Philip Sidney instead of his brother, with whom there is no evidence to connect him and whose name does not really fit with the others praised.)

But the Protectorate received neither the electoral support it needed nor the cooperation of the disaffected members of the Good Party. In fact, the Parliament Cromwell called, and to lesser degrees subsequent ones as well, did just what Milton had feared they might do—they set out to question the legal validity of the authority that had called them. The results were, among other measures, Cromwell's prolonged consideration of the advisability of assuming the Kingship, and the military rule of England by Cromwell's Major Generals. If Milton was disappointed, it would have been more with the electors and their representatives than with Cromwell. Some time after Oliver's death he added to his *Brit* a comment on the inability of the English to follow the leadership of a worthy man God had placed over them, concluding with this significant generalization: "When God hath decreed servitude on a sinful Nation, fitted by their own vices for no condition but servile, all Estates of Government are alike unable to avoid it" (10 : 197–98).

In one crucial respect, however, Milton did find the policy of Oliver Cromwell wanting, and this emerges from his political writings of 1659 and 1660, wherein he addressed himself to the causes of the breakdown of the Cromwellian system, causes he thought resolvable by the proposals he recommended. Few of Milton's other political phases illustrate as clearly as this one the single-mindedness of his interest, for essentially his disappointment focused not on politics but on the continuance of official support for an established church, and by the late 1650s a safeguarded separation of church and state had come to seem to Milton the only and indispensable condition for the exercise of that Christian liberty which was the foundation of political stability.

Cromwell himself abhorred religious persecution on almost any grounds, but he had never seen it to be inevitable that a state-established church must be a threat to Christian liberty. On the contrary, he believed that his religious obligation as a political leader was, at the least, to see a preaching clergy properly maintained. One of his earliest recorded concerns had been his anxiety in 1636 to find means to support some of the Puritan clergy threatened by Archbishop Laud's suppression of the Feoffees of Impropriations, the financial system by which Puritan preaching lectureships had been maintained. Hence he took the lead as a Puritan layman to raise money in Huntingdonshire for a preacher who stood to lose his lectureship, reminding a reluctant contributor that "to withdraw the pay is to let fall the lecture; for who goeth to warfare at his own cost. I beseech you . . . let the good man have his pay." But this concern with pay, as an official policy, became for Milton and most of the radical sectarians who otherwise supported Cromwell to the end, a major offense and stumbling block. Other aspects of Cromwell's administration that Milton might have disliked, such as the persecuting zeal of the Protectorate Parliaments, and the offer of Kingship to the Protector, Cromwell himself had discountenanced and on those issues could

not have alienated Milton. But paying ministers was bound up with preserving an established church supported by tithes and having behind it the sword of the civil magistrate. Here Cromwell found himself bitterly resisted by the sects, and Milton's sympathy on this question clearly belonged with the sects.

It must have been a question over which he had long brooded in his retirement, for quite soon after Cromwell's death in September of 1658 Milton composed the first of two works planned as a sequence: *CivP*, which appeared in February 1659, addressed to Richard Cromwell's Protectorate Parliament; and then *Hire*, which appeared after the fall of the younger Cromwell's government. Both are essentially about Christian liberty and reveal the depth of Milton's concern for its survival in any system allowing the state to support the church and the church to invoke the power of the state against those whom it might choose to discipline on religious grounds. They are therefore devoid of political substance except in reaffirming the Christian condition for legitimating power. Religion and the state, Milton contended, would only flourish "when either they who govern discern between civil and religious, or they only who so discern shall be admitted" (*CivP* 6:2). Reduced to its essentials, his political position was now simply and clearly stated. A pledge to respect and preserve Christian liberty, in the form of separating the powers of church and state, should be made, he suggested, the primary condition for the right to hold office and presumably, therefore, for the right to vote. The only admissible and necessary function of the state in religion was to protect such Christian liberty, and to suppress atheism and popery as corrupting civil influences. And unless this separation were accepted and enforced, "I dare affirme," he wrote, "that no modell whatsoever of a commonwealth will prove succesful or undisturb'd" (*Hire* 6:44–45).

By the time *Hire* had been published, Richard Cromwell's government had been toppled by Army officers alarmed by his intention to bring the Army effectively under civilian control. Once rid of Richard Cromwell, the officers, almost at a loss for what to do, recalled the members of the Rump Parliament dissolved some six years earlier. When the Rump in turn attempted to control the Army, it too was dismissed by them, and England seemed to be drifting toward an anarchy of competing war lords.

The *Letter to a Friend* records Milton's shocked awakening to the gravity of the crisis and his instinct to put the best possible face upon the situation. First he condemned the Army's action, then accepted it as a *fait accompli* out of which a proper settlement might yet be achieved, namely, the formation of a government committed to safeguarding Christian liberty. He had apparently approved of the original recall of the Rump but had been disappointed that they too were not inclined to abolish tithes or disestablish the church system Cromwell's government had set up. Nonetheless, it was clear to him that the political survival of Puritanism stood a better chance with that battered relic of constitutionality, the Rump, than with a junta of ambitious Army officers. Barring the Rump's second restoration, he suggested in the Letter an expedient that, as Barbara Lewalski has shown, was actually adopted in the formation of a mixed Committee of Safety made up of both Army officers and former members of the Rump, while significantly he ignored a number of alternative millenarian suggestions advocating contrivances for some kind of "godly" council to keep in check any merely secular authority.

Milton's next work, *Proposals of Certaine Expedients for the Prevention of a Civill War now Fear'd* (unpublished during his lifetime) was advanced when it was clear that the Committee of Safety and the Army either would have to recall the Rump or face the prospect of waging civil war against General Monk's* Army, which had been occupying Scotland but was now marching toward London, its intentions undeclared. In effect, Milton's proposals (18 : 3–7) were that the Rump should be recalled on the condition that the members agree to guarantee full liberty of conscience, and to abjure both the rule of a single person and the reestablishment of a House of Lords. Instead, he suggested that the members should sit for life, recruiting replacements as vacancies arose, and electing from among themselves, as they had formerly, an executive Council of State. This scheme was most like the Bill for a New Representative, which the Rump had been just about to pass in order to perpetuate itself when it had been dissolved by Cromwell in 1653 and, pinning his hopes upon it, Milton introduced it again in the body of the first version of *Way,* which he wrote after the Rump had again been recalled. This last tract was designed above all to preserve the status quo in a situation rapidly moving toward the recall of the Stuarts.

Yet another set of proposals was set out, however, in the introduction to the work, apparently written after General Monk had completely altered the situation by forcing upon the Rump the readmission of the members excluded in 1648, thereby effectively restoring what was left of the original Long Parliament. This addition in the introduction was intended to suggest to the Long Parliament that it now perpetuate itself in exactly the same way Milton had earlier suggested the Rump should, by sitting for life and electing new members as vacancies arose. There can be no mistaking his main concern now, to persuade whoever might listen and with the power to prevent it, that under no circumstances should a new Parliament be called, for as anyone might forsee, it would almost surely bring about a Stuart restoration.

In general, this first edition of *Way* repeated again those essentially republican arguments based on natural law which Milton had advanced earlier in *Tenure,* again with the saving reservation that by the people was meant the better part who were to act on the people's behalf rather than as the expression of the will of the people. Here too he appealed to religion, as he had in *Eikon*, with the affirmation that nothing was more in conformity with the precept of Christ than republican government and nothing was more anti-Christian than monarchy. But after the vicissitudes of the revolutionary changes that had wearied them all, Milton was careful to avoid sounding like a millenarian advocate of the rule of the saints. The sum of what he urged was a permanent legislature that had been once elected and endowed by the people with an irrevocable sovereignty justifying it to sit for life and devise means for recruiting new members. Real power, he apparently thought, would lie in the class from which the members would be chosen, as he conceived it to be the case in the oligarchies of Holland and Venice, which he invoked as precedents, along with antique models as diverse as the Jewish Sanhedrin, the Athenian Areopagus, and the Roman Senate.

There is a hint in all this that Milton may have been responding, despite his previous dismissal of it, to the fashionable interest in the theory of classical republicanism. He was certainly responding to the popularity of John Harrington's *Oceana* among London intellectuals and to its model of a state based on a rotating governing council, though it was with express reluctance that he would admit a similar rotation in his perpetual council. The nub of his preference was, however, a governing body chosen carefully, but then so thoroughly insulated from the disturbances of the popular will as to be unconstrained to do what in fact the Long Parliament, responding to popular sentiment, was about to do in sending out writs for a "convention" Parliament—recall the Stuarts. By the time of the publicating of the second edition of *Way* these writs had gone out and the restoration of Charles II was a virtual certainty. There was bravery as well as bitterness in the clarity with which Milton regarded the end, knowing that his own tract might "be the last words of our expiring libertie."

But the generality of his countrymen evidently did not think as he did, that a freely elected Parliament, the first such election held in twenty years, was a loss rather than a gain in liberty.

The Restoration guaranteed a political amnesty to all but the worst offenders against the Stuarts, and Milton was one of those who narrowly escaped proscription. Thereafter he was prudently silent, except for an allusion to tyrants in *PL* that caused a small flutter, and for some observations on legitimate resistance to anti-Christian tyranny buried in the last chapter of his unpublished *CD*. But when the passage of years and the appearance of his major poems had restored something of his former stature among his countrymen, he was tempted by one last occasion to venture into a political controversy, though the true nature of his point was sufficiently veiled to suggest that he was merely addressing himself to a religious issue of general interest. The context was the Stuart dynasty's problems in acknowledging the extent of their interest in supporting an open toleration for Catholicism. In the spring of 1673 Charles II* had issued a Declaration of Indulgence wherein Roman Catholics were coupled with Protestant Nonconformists in such a way as to use official toleration of Puritan Dissenters as a cover for extending toleration to Roman Catholics. The issue was important to the Stuarts in that Charles himself, though he would not have declared himself so, was secretly a Catholic; his brother James, the heir apparent to the throne, was already a declared Catholic; and the French help Charles sought in an alliance against Holland was offered at the price of easing the conditions for all Catholics in England. While the full extent of the Court's commitment to Catholicism was not publicly known, the purpose behind the offer to extend toleration to Protestant Nonconformists was transparent.

Milton was one of those who rose to dissociate the Puritans from popery and to frustrate the Court's objectives. The full title of his work suggests how carefully he avoided any overt political note: *Of True Religion, Heresy, Schism, Toleration; And What Best Means May Be Used Against The Growth of Popery.* Its substance is an expression of basic views Milton had sketched in *Areop* and had elsewhere touched on, as in *Peace* (1649) and in *CivP*, namely, that the essentials of true Protestantism might be so minimally defined as to make it impossible to consider as schismatic or heretical almost any Puritan beliefs and practices. Now he admitted that all the contests between Puritans and Anglicans had also really been over things properly to be considered as doctrinally indifferent. Hence toleration should certainly be extended to all Protestants. Catholicism, on the other hand, was civilly dangerous and its toleration not in truth a question of religious freedom. With admirable affrontery Milton disingenuously reminded his readers how dangerous popery had proved "to kingdoms and states, and especially to this of England, [where it] thrones and unthrones kings, and absolves the people from their obedience to them" (*TR* 6: 172). He would not suggest that Catholics ought to be persecuted, only that the open practice of their religion should be suppressed. And in conclusion he urged Protestants to unite against the dangerous spread of popery throughout the land.

This tract, possibly the least sympathetic of all that Milton wrote, and one justly neglected, is an oddly fitting work with which to conclude a survey of Milton's politics. It lacked charity toward whatever was outside the range of its intense prepossessions—and in this respect it was characteristically Puritan, drawing its energies from that universally simplifying dichotomy whereby all things either contributed to the spiritual lives of the saints, or represented Antichrist's stratagems against them. It was also singularly opportunistic, as most of Milton's better political efforts were, but with only a limited insight into the wider issues that every political problem inevitably involves. Yet it betrayed a certain instinct that, in historical retrospect, seems both shrewd

and positive. Religion was not a simplifying element in Puritan politics, but ultimately, and almost despite itself, it helped broaden the range of civil concerns and extended the meaning of liberty. Throughout the seventeenth century the quest for religious liberty brought Puritans into opposition to the claims of Stuart absolutism and eventually that quest helped to establish the incontestable supremacy in England of Parliamentary government. From this point of view *TR* can be seen as Milton's intuitive response to yet another Stuart circumvention of Parliamentary government, and as a prophetic anticipation of 1688, when the issue would be at last settled against that dynasty. It is therefore just that the author of *TR* should have been remembered politically by a later generation as "that grand Whig, Milton." [MF]

POLYGAMY figures favorably in Milton's considerations of marriage, although there is no evidence that he himself ever desired to practice it. As early as *CB* there are entries supporting polygamy, one citing Ralegh's* *History* that "To forbid Polygamy to all hath more obstinat rigor in it then wisdom" (*CM* 18:158). From Caesar's *Commentaries* he observes in *Brit* (10:87) that "whereas other Nations us'd a liberty not unnatural for one man to have many Wives, the *Britans* altogether as licentious, but more absurd and preposterous in thir licence, had one or many Wives in common among ten or twelve Husbands." But his full argument on the subject is reserved for *CD* (15:123ff.), where in the section on marriage he wholeheartedly supports the practice. His argument there is entirely biblical, based upon the recorded practices of Old Testament patriarchs and refutation of the few individual texts that seem to imply a monogamous interpretation. As for the New Testament, he argues that Christ's statements on marriage are limited to issues of divorce. As he observes, even God himself "in an allegorical fiction, Ezek. 23:4 represents himself as having spoused two wives," implying that the practice cannot be "intrinsically dishonorable or shameful" (p. 145). On the other hand, Milton agrees that church officials are limited to one wife (in 1 Tim. 3 : 2 and Titus 1 : 6) so that they will have more time for church business. Amid the multitude of mid-seventeenth-century sects, some did approve of polygamy as the practice of Old Testament patriarchs seems to authorize, but it was strictly forbidden by the Presbyterians* and the Church of England. An extended study is Leo Miller's *John Milton among the Polygamophiles* (1974). [WBH]

POOLE, JOSHUA: *see* INFLUENCE ON SEVENTEENTH CENTURY LITERATURE.

POPE, ALEXANDER, was born May 21, 1688, into the Roman Catholic household of a modest linen tradesman. To be a Roman Catholic in England, especially after the expulsion of the Roman Catholic King James II in 1688, meant subjection to severe anti-Catholic laws, which prohibited Catholics from openly practising their religion, from earning degrees at public schools or universities, from entering several professions, and from sitting in Parliament or holding public office. Though the laws were often not strictly enforced, Catholics, during much of Pope's lifetime, were subject to double taxes, restricted from purchasing land, and forbidden residence within ten miles of London as well. Pope's preference for the Tory party may have come as the result of Whig affiliations with the radically intolerant anti-Catholic commercial classes.

Evidence of Pope's knowledge of Milton abounds in his poems, letters, prefaces, and footnotes, and in the record of his conversations. He mentioned Milton ten times in his poetry (see Edwin Abbott, *Concordance* [1875]). The letters Pope wrote to his friends and some written to him show that Pope revered Milton and could quote from him with ease. A letter to John Caryll mentions that Pope kept a picture of Milton hanging over his bed and another of Jacob Tonson* records Pope's avowal that Milton is "above" all

criticism, as Bentley* is "below." Jonathan Richardson, son of the Milton enthusiast, consulted Pope about *PL* and Pope sent to him a sonnet beginning "Fair mirror of foul times," which had allegedly been discovered at Chalfont and attributed to Milton. (The sonnet was a hoax, perhaps perpetrated by Pope himself.) In the *Grub Street Journal,* which was set up in Pope's interest and to which he was a "frequent contributor," appear pieces dealing with Milton. These are either reprinted or referred to in *Memoirs of the Society of Grub Street* (1737).

Raymond D. Havens (*The Influence of Milton on English Poetry* [1922]) demonstrates that Pope's borrowings from Milton are scattered throughout his work, not confined to a few pieces. Pope made as much use of Milton's early poems as of his epic. Lines and phrases appear from *L'Al, IlP, Mask* (nineteen), *Lyc, Nat, Arc, Vac,* and three of the sonnets. Forty-three borrowings from *PL* occur in the *Dunciad;* Havens lists fifty-six Miltonic expressions in Pope's *Iliad* and fifty-one in the *Odyssey.* In all, his borrowings amount to over two hundred.

At the age of twelve or thirteen Pope wrote a fragmentary epic of some four thousand lines on Alcander, Prince of Rhodes, which has not survived. Joseph Spence records that Pope claimed "there was Milton's style in one Part" of this poem, but because the other parts were modeled on Spenser, Cowley, Homer, and others, the work is supposed to have been influenced by *PL* only in "subject matter, diction, phrasing and possibly 'machinery' " (Joseph Spence, *Anecdotes . . . Collected from the Conversation of Mr. Pope,* ed. Samuel W. Singer [1820]; Owen Ruffhead, *Life of Pope* [1769]).

Pope's comment related in Spence's *Anecdotes* evaluating Milton's style* and decorum in *PL* reveals that he admired Milton for his control over and decorous use of sublime style : "Milton's style . . . is not natural; 'tis an exotic style. As his subject lies a good deal out of our world, it has a particular propriety for those parts of the poem: . . . wherever he is describing our parents in Paradise you see he uses a more easy and natural way of writing. Though his style may fit the higher parts of his own poem, it does very ill for others who write on natural and pastoral subjects" (*Anecdotes*). Pope elsewhere complains that imitations* of Milton "are not *copies* but *caricaturas* of their original," because they imitate the "exotic" (archaic) words Milton used to speak of Heaven, Hell, and Chaos, but err in applying them to natural subjects for which they are inappropriate (*Postscript to the Odyssey, The Twickenham Edition of the Poems of Alexander Pope*, vol. 10, ed. John Butt [1952]). In introducing Miltonic expressions into his own poetry, Pope scrupulously obeys the decorum Milton observed, and in *Peri Bathous* and the *Dunciad* he satirizes, among others, writers who, failing to understand Milton's decorum, use diction and figures too high for low subjects and thus fall into rant and fustian.

Pope's *Messiah: A Sacred Eclogue in Imitation of Virgil's Pollio* (1712) imitates both the *Pollio* and Isaiah's description of the coming of the Savior. In the "Advertisement" prefacing the poem Pope states his intention of showing "how far the images and descriptions of the Prophet are superior to those of the [pagan] poet," an intention related to Milton's in *PL* where he contrasts the lesser epic and heroism of pagan poetry, embodying them in Satan and the fallen hosts, with the Christian, divinely inspired poem. Like Milton, who, inspired by the "Heav'nly Muse" rises "Above th' *Aonian* mount" (*PL* 1. 15), that is, above the imaginations of the pagan poets, Pope addresses his muse "Ye Nymphs of Solyme . . . who touched Isaiah's hallowed lips with fire," saying that the theme of pagan poetry, "The dreams of Pindus and th' Aonian maid, / Delight no more" (lines 1–6).

Pope's *Messiah* parallels in subject Milton's *Nat,* a description of the effects of the coming incarnation upon the waiting earth, though in style and general treatment of subject little affinity shows.

Verbal echoes appear in Pope's line "He from thick films shall purge the visual ray" (line 39), which may have been suggested by Milton's description of Michael's removing "the Filme" from "the visual Nerve" of Adam (*PL* 11. 411–15), and in "He wipes the tears for ever from our eyes" (line 46, 1st ed.), which parallels Milton's "And wipe the tears for ever from his eyes" (*Lyc* line 181). Pope's description of the cessation of war, like Milton's, speaks of the silenced trumpets of war, but Milton's overall silencing of the fallen world's discordant and disordered sounds before the Incarnation* of the Word does not appear.

Windsor Forest (1713), Pope's long pastoral* poem celebrating the Peace of Utrecht wrought by Queen Anne to end the exhausting wars between France and England, the Wars of the Spanish Succession, makes of Windsor Forest a symbol of the cosmic principle of *concordia discors*. The various manifestations of this principle and its breakdown into chaos the poem treats directly or through a complex system of literary and historical analogy, allusion, myth, and symbol. The celebrated Peace of Utrecht, hunting within the forest preserve, world commerce, the balanced life of action and meditation, and art, specifically poetry, are all celebrated as various embodiments of the universal law of nature, a kind of finite "perfection," a "harmonious confusion," everywhere characterized by the balanced strife of active and passive, dynamic and static impulses. When excess upsets the tenuous balance of *concordia discors*, unguarded strife, war, tyranny, and destruction ensue. Pope uses war as a manifestation of and metaphor for chaotic discord within man and nature wrought at the Fall, as Milton does. To speak of such chaos Pope introduces into his poem allusions to Milton's depiction of Nimrod (*PL* 12. 25–62) as one who will dispossess "Concord and the law of Nature from the Earth; / Hunting (and Men not Beasts shall be his game) / With War and hostile snare such as refuse / Subjection to his Empire tyrannous." Pope's lines, "Proud Nimrod first the bloody chase began, / A mighty hunter, and his prey was man" (lines 61–62) compress and point the chaotic overthrow, not of perfect order as Milton's had, but of the finite, fallen order of *concordia discors*. Pope's lines also help to develop a historical, political analogy among Nimrod, William the Conqueror, and William III. They contrast with the more civilized "sylvan chase," the hunt, which helps to purge man's fallen, destructive impulses, making possible the "balanced strife" of the Peace of Utrecht.

The most pervasive use of allusion to *PL* comes in the poet's sustained comparison between Eden and Windsor Forest and between "song" and "description" of Eden, in which Eden "vanished now so long" (line 7), lives on, and his own song of Windsor Forest. This suggests that the Peace of Utrecht celebrates return to an ideal state, a Golden Age, but one that time may destroy as Edenic perfection was destroyed except as preserved in art. It also helps to build the poem's assertion that art perfects nature and that only art can eternalise perfection.

But Pope also uses allusion to Edenic perfection and the Fall to introduce strident ironies into the poem that seriously undercut the celebratory praise of Windsor Forest and the present age. In the description of the hunt (lines 93–164), a sustained depiction of *concordia discors*, Pope pictures pathetically the slaughter of innocent beasts and his lines "Beasts, urged by us, their fellow-beasts pursue, / And learn of man each other to undo" present the modern parallel to the discord that reigns in Eden immediately following the sin of Adam and Eve : "Beast now with Beast gan war, and Fowls with Fowls / And Fish with Fish; to graze the Herb all leaving, / Devour each other . . .' (*PL* 10. 710–12). Description of the beauteous partridge's "painted wings" (cf. *PL* 7. 434) and of the yellow carp covered "in scales bedropped with gold" (cf. *PL* 7. 406) suggest Milton's description of prelapsarian Eden, but their juxtaposition with scenes of violent, pathetic death creates irony

that reminds us that this is no real Eden. An ironic awareness that pastoral poetry depicting an Edenic or Golden Age must be carefully qualified to be a viable medium of expression for Augustan England pervades the poem. Through allusion to *PL* as well as to Ovid's* *Metamorphoses* and Virgil's* *Pollio,* which also picture a perfect state and an imperfect one, Pope constantly reminds his reader that Augustan metaphors of balance must not be confused with Christian ideals of real perfection.

Milton's influence on *The Rape of the Lock* appears chiefly in the "machinery" Pope introduced into the final version. The "light *militia* of the lower sky," his hierarchy of sylphs, as Geoffrey Tillotson has pointed out, "unite[s] the bodily fluidity of Milton's angels with the minuteness of Shakespeare's fairies" (Twick. ed., vol. 2). Pope avows (in the letter to Arabella Fermor preceding the poem) that he has fashioned the sylphs on "the *Rosicrucian* Doctrines of Spirits" and much of their treatment owes to a French treatise on the subject, *Le Compte de Gabalis* (1670), written by the Abbé de Montfaucon de Villars. But Pope's mock-epic form required an epic model against which to measure the delicate triviality and unnatural mission of the sylphs, who hover around Belinda night and day to protect her chastity and enter her dreams to warn her against the dire threat of man. Ariel, the "divine" messenger and leader of the army of spirits, at times presents an ironic parallel to Milton's Raphael, sent to warn man against the threat to his happiness and to instruct him in the terms of God's "rigid interdiction" (*PL* 5. 388–8. 651). In the long morning dream (*RL* 1. 27–114), Ariel instructs Belinda on the limits of her happiness and freedom and recounts to her, in ironic imitation of Raphael's narration to Adam and Eve of the nature of the angels*, the function and origins of the sylphs. At other times he suggests Satan pouring venom into the ear of Eve as she dreams and tempting her to think of herself as superior to man and her just station (*PL* 4. 800–809; 5. 38–93). Like Satan, who disguises himself as a "stripling Cherube" (*PL* 3. 634–44), Ariel enters Belinda's dream in disguise as a "Youth more glitt'ring than a *Birth-night Beau*" the better to attract the thoughts of the dreaming woman (*RL* 1. 23).

Through verbal echo Pope underpins the suggestive parallels. He describes the fluid bodies of the sylphs—"Dipt in the richest Tincture of the Skies" (*RL* 2. 65) —in words that echo Milton's description of Raphael as he lights upon the earth to convey his message : "And colours dipt in Heav'n . . . / Skie-tinctur'd grain . . ." (*PL* 5. 283–85). The parallel with Satan comes in the epic convention describing the leader as taller than his followers. Ariel is "Superior by the head" (*RL* 2. 70); Satan is "above the rest / In shape and gesture proudly eminent" (*PL* 1. 589–90).

At times Pope suggests Milton's angels, good and bad, in a more general way. The sylph who thrusts himself into the shears poised open to sever the lock is impotent against the decree of Fate* : "Fate urg'd the Sheers, and cut the Sylph in twain, / (But Airy Substance soon unites again)" (*RL* 3. 151–52). Pope's note to the lines points the imitation of Satan injured in his impotent attempt to thwart the will of God : ". . . but th' Ethereal substance clos'd / Not long divisible" (*PL* 6. 330–31). Like Milton's angels, Pope's mend their injuries. Also like Milton's angels, the sylphs, "Freed from mortal Laws, with ease / Assume what Sexes and what Shapes they please" (*RL* 1. 69–70; cf. *PL* 1. 423–25). Ariel's address to his troops—"Ye *Sylphs* and *Sylphids*, to your Chief give Ear, / *Fayes, Faries, Genii, Elves*, and *Daemons* hear !" (*RL* 2. 73–74)—echoes God's address to the angels : "Hear all ye Angels, Progenie of Light, / Thrones, Dominations, Princedoms, Vertues, Powers, / Hear my Decree . . ." (*PL* 5. 600–602). The placement of the sylphs around Belinda at the tea party—"Some, Orb in Orb, around the Nymph extend" (*RL* 2. 138) also echoes God's angelic host surrounding his throne : "Thus when in Orbes / Of circuit inex-pressible they stood, / Orb within Orb, the Father infinite . . ." (*PL* 5. 594–97).

In yet another way Pope imitates the angelic hierarchy. The activities of the sylphs are divided in the epic style : some bask in the pure air, some guide the course of the planets, some assist the forces of nature or guard the British throne, but the humble sylphs attend the maiden's dressing table (*RL* 2. 75–100). Pope accentuates the trivial nature of the least among the hierarchy and at the same time suggests a parallel with the fallen angels, who beguile their pains in divided activities : epic games, mock battles, geological expeditions, songs and discourse (*PL* 2. 528–628).

Belinda's unnatural role as proud goddess scornful of man, urged by the sylphs and forced upon her by her society's confused morals, Pope ironically points by twice comparing her to God through verbal echo. Belinda's God-like false pride shines through during the game of ombre, which imitates in mock-epic fashion the conventional epic battle. Belinda's war cry—"Let Spades be Trumps ! she said, and Trumps they were" (*RL* 3. 45)—ironically echoes God's fiat at the creation : "Let there be Light, said God, and forthwith Light . . ." (*PL* 7. 243). The second ironic comparison of Belinda with God comes in the lines, quoted above, which describe the sylphs surrounding her as God's angels surround Him in adoration.

The influence of *PL* upon *The Rape of the Lock* goes far beyond slavish imitation, for Pope incorporates Miltonic echoes and allusively calls the larger dramatic and moral context of Milton's epic into comparison with the confused moral and social values of Belinda and her friends. Belinda's affectation, unnatural emphasis upon appearance, and self-worship contradict God's plan for man and woman. Because she scorns her lover, playing inaccessible goddess, he must retaliate "by Force, or Slight" (*RL* 2. 105; cf. *PL* 1. 646). The Satanic echoes here and throughout the poem suggestively hint at the perverse evil underlying the varnished and fragile beauty of Belinda, her court of admirers, and the delicate sylphs.

Peri Bathous or "The Art of Sinking in Poetry" (1727) is Pope's mock rendition of Longinus's* ancient critical treatise, *Peri Hypsous* or "On the Sublime," which had become popularized in England during the latter part of the seventeenth century and the early eighteenth century through the modern translation of Boileau appearing in 1674. "On the sublime" praises a quality of writing above all characterized by great and noble thought expressed in language untrammeled by artificialities of style and calculated to present vividly the emotional impact of such thought. Pope knew and used Boileau's translation of Longinus as the model of *Peri Bathous.* Longinus was known as well to Milton, who recommended him in *Educ,* among others, as a teacher of "a graceful and ornate rhetoric," but did not indicate that he had any notion of Longinus as the father of sublimity, by nature an expression of ultimate values in art, particularly the epic, that reached far beyond mere rhetorical rules and theories of style. Irene Samuel believes that Longinus's poetics influenced Milton's, though no express evidence of this occurs in the poetry or in the prose (*Plato and Milton,* 1947). The extent of Longinus's influence upon Milton's poetry is yet to be assessed, but one can see that what Longinus praised in poetry corresponds with Milton's practice in *PL,* his "higher Argument" and "answerable style" (*PL* 9. 20–42).

In *Peri Bathous* Pope's satiric mouthpiece, the modern critic, naively praises all that is despicable in writing while he condemns all the aesthetic values of Longinian neoclassicism, particularly art as just imitation of nature. The mock treatise uses *Peri Hypsous* and the poetic values of great writing it fosters as an implied ideal against which Pope ironically measures the "greatness" of modern poetry.

In *Peri Hypsous* Longinus had clothed his praise of sublimity in a set of pervasive metaphors of spatial elevation, light, and vitality. Its opposite, the false sublime, which occurs when writers rising upon the wings of sublimity attempt to attain literary heights beyond their capabilities of mind and language, Longinus speaks of in metaphors of spatial descent or fall, darkness, unnaturalness, and solidification. Milton's metaphoric structure fraught with meanings moral and aesthetic alike bears significant parallels with the recurrent set of metaphors Longinus had employed to describe good and bad writing, sublimity and the false sublime. In *Peri Bathous* and, more extensively, in the *Dunciad,* Pope enriches and reinforces his satire of bad writing and misused language by allusion to and imitation of the landscape of Hell, the metaphors associated with moral and aesthetic decay and the inhabitants of Hell. He fuses the parallel metaphors of Longinus with those Milton uses to underscore both the moral and aesthetic evils of misused language and to suggest that such misuse continues Satan's destructive mission in the modern world.

The depiction of the Bathos shares similarities with Milton's cosmic moral stage. Pope stresses the downward track of the "profund" and invents a series of synonyms like "the bottom" and "the downhill way" to keep the idea of spatial descent ever before his reader's mind. He, in fact, invents an aesthetic landscape to illustrate and define the import of bad writing and aesthetic decay in much the same way that in *PL* Milton invents a moral landscape to illustrate and define moral degeneracy. Down the slopes of Parnassus flows the mythical stream Helicon, which inspires the poetry of Pope's "Highlanders," the good, sublime poets. The "Lowlanders," the bathetic poets, gain their inspiration from the muddy "common waters" that flow at the foot of the mountain (*The Art of Sinking in Poetry: A Critical Edition,* ed. Edna Leake Steeves, 1952). Into these waters dive and fall the fish, fowl, marine mammals, and amphibians who represent the modern poets. These creatures, who now and then lose their bathetic touch and stumble into sense unawares, leap and fall in fitful starts of wit or sublimity, but live generally in the bottom of confusion's muddy ditch. Their spatial movements become charged with aesthetic and moral meaning through Pope's imitation of the spatial metaphors of Longinus and Milton, though in the *Dunciad* the moral dimensions of poetic falling are more fully developed than in *Peri Bathous*.

Pope's use of animal comparisons for the bad poets suggests, as does Milton's pervasive depiction of the Fall in terms of passionate bestiality overtaking the reason, that the bad poets are less than fully human due to their loss of reason, their dullness. One of the chief uses of the bathetic diving machine is to assist man to "descend beneath himself" into the waters of profundity, which suggests that the bad poets have slipped down the chain of creation to become mere animals.

As well as a landscape, Pope hints at an aesthetic cosmos. The "Sublime of Nature" Pope describes as "the Sun, Moon, Stars, etc." These naturally elevated objects shine with a natural light Pope associates with the poetic elevation of true sublimity. The "Profound of Nature," the "Gold, Pearls, precious Stones and the Treasures of the Deep," lie at the bottom of the waters of the Bathos and are associated with unnatural, glittering light of false imitation in art fostered by low, dull writing. We are reminded that in *PL* Milton uses gold and glittering gems as metaphors for artifice and fraud in Satanic creations, which are thereby distinguished from the true creations of Heaven and the natural world. The Devils dig "Ribs of Gold" out of earth's womb, which they smelt and found "with wond'rous Art" to build Pandemonium*, a work that Milton says outdoes "*Babel* and the works of *Memphian* Kings" (*PL* 1. 690–707) in its artifice. The glistering artifice of the Pandemonium and the mount Satan builds in false imitation of the realms of Heaven (*PL* 5. 757–59) marks them as illusory phantasms.

Both Milton and Pope seem to have in mind the ancient idea of ornamentation in rhetoric*, which can be used to obscure truths rather than reveal them. Satan uses such skilled artifice in his rhetoric to promote his lies and frauds, and it is thus related to his moral confusion as it becomes translated into his speech. The bad poets also use such artificial ornamentation to promote poet lies—false imitations of natural truths.

In *PL* Milton repeatedly speaks of Hell, the Deep, and the burning lake of Hell as "profound," using it both as adjective and noun (*PL* 1. 251; 2. 438, 592, 585, and 980). This may have suggested to Pope the alternative name of the Bathos—the Profound; both writers use the word to mean "deep" or "depth." The waters of Milton's Hell are associated with the waters of confusion and chaos out of which creation rises at the Divine fiat, the waters of the Flood, which wreak destruction on the created world, and the "vast illimitable ocean" of Chaos. In *Ref*, as Isabel MacCaffrey points out, Milton had spoken of the opponents of truth lurking in a plumbless depth of muddy, obfuscating confusion that foreshadows the use of the abyss (*Paradise Lost as "Myth"* [1959]). The destructive waters of Chaos and Confusion dull the minds of the devils who fall into them in the same way that the muddy waters of the Bathos dull the minds of the poetic fish and birds who dive into them and quaff them for inspiration. In the *Dunciad,* to similar effect, the poets dive for laurels into the muddy Thames. The waters of the Bathos, thus, promote the main end and principal effect of the Bathos—"tranquility of Mind," the lack of intellectual vitality in dull writing responsible for the inert quality of the created artifact.

In chapter 11 of *Peri Bathous* Pope's satiric mouthpiece states that "A Genuine Writer of the Profound will take care never to magnify any object without clouding it at the same time : His thought will appear in a true mist and very unlike what is in nature." Pope imitates Dryden's* depiction of Flecknoe in *Mac*

Flecknoe (1678), his head enshrouded in fogs and mist, and also Dryden's parodies from *PL*—God seated upon his throne, His face enshrouded in clouds to ease His majesty (*PL* 3. 375–82). Elsewhere in *PL* clouds and mists similarly obscure realities and truths. Satan is himself associated with them through disguise by which he hides his identity and the truth he seeks to belie, and even in battle Satan comes seemingly enshrouded in clouds (*PL* 6. 539–40). Milton as poet prays to Holy Light to "shine inward" and purge and dismiss the mists from his inner eyes "that I may see and tell . . ." (*PL* 3. 52–54). The mists of the Profound, like the mists of *PL,* obscure the truth and hide and alter the forms of nature that the poet must imitate.

Throughout the mock treatise Pope everywhere depicts bathetic creativity as void of mind, unnatural, and materialistic, not inspirited by creative intelligence. In so doing he inverts Longinus's criteria for sublimity—poetry characterized by magnitude of mind and thought, poetry that captures in just language the vitality and truth of nature. Through allusion to *PL* Pope also associates bathetic writing with the impaired reason of Satan, his loss of the Divine Image, and the Satanic creations that falsely imitate in their sterile, hardened forms the vital radiance of Christ's creation.

The Dunciad, Pope's mock-epic satire, scourges misused language and dull minds in all areas of human discourse—poetry and drama, its patrons, purveyors, critics, and admirers; and education, religion, and government. Especially in the final four-book version published in 1743 the metaphors of darkness and light, rising and falling used to depict bad writing in *Peri Bathous* recur amplified through extended echo of and allusions to *PL.* Aubrey L. Williams points out that the majority of the Miltonic echoes come from Satanic contexts (*Pope's "Dunciad"* [1955]). Through imitation ranging from out-and-out allusion to mere hint Pope has managed to place the world of dullness squarely into the context of fraud-

ulent language caused by evil in the infernal regions. Satan, Sin, and Death, and the entire army of Satan's followers, are drawn into the action of the *Dunciad* and made to project an added dimension upon the characters and episodes of dullness.

At the opening of Book 2 Colley Cibber, King of the Dunces, appears as "the Antichrist of Wit," seated upon the Throne of Dulness surrounded by his cohorts :

High on a gorgeous seat, that far out-shone
Henley's gilt Tub, or Fleckno's Irish Throne,
. . .
Great Cibber sate: . . . All eyes direct their rays
On him, and crowds turn Coxcombs as they gaze.
His peers shine round him with reflected grace,
New edge their dulness, and new bronze their face.
So from the Sun's broad beam, in shallow urns
Heav'ns twinkling Sparks draw light, and point their horns.
(2. 1–12)

Pope notes as his source,

High on a Throne of Royal State, which far
Outshone the wealth of *Ormus* and of *Ind,*
Or where the gorgeous East with richest hand
Show'rs on her Kings *Barbaric* Pearl and Gold,
Satan exalted sat. . . .
(*PL* 2. 1–5)

And Gilbert Wakefield noted the parallel with,

Hither as to thir Fountain other Starrs
Repairing, in thir gold'n Urns draw Light
And hence the Morning Planet guilds her horns.
(*PL* 7. 364–66)

Though the allusion fixing Cibber as the Antichirst of Wit and comparing him with Satan, the original Antichrist, seems almost obscured by the comic surface where we see the dregs of malt and rotten eggs poured upon the heads of the dunces, underneath and insistently remains the suggestion of evil implicit in duncery and of the Satanic destructive mission continuing in the reign of the dunces. The above passage also parodies* God, the "Fountain of Light," seated on His throne surrounded by his angels and shedding "th' effulgence of his Glorie" upon the Son (*PL* 3. 388).

This explicit association of dullness and devilishness fairly well permeates the poem, though subtly. In Book 4 a master of public schools speaks and his description marks him both as a cruel child-beater and a modern-day Moloch: "His beaver'd brow a birchen garland wears, / Dropping with Infant's blood, and Mother's tears" (4. 139–42). The echo of Milton's Moloch, "horrid King besmear'd with blood / Of human sacrifice and parents tears . . ." (*PL* 1. 392–93) transfers a suggestion of human sacrifice to the activities of the public schools. Then Bentley appears as a modern Beelzebub: "Before them marched the awful Aristarch: / Plow'd was his front with many a deep Remark . . ." (4. 203–4). The parallel sources are two, Beelzebub, who in Pandemonium "rose, and in his rising seem'd / A Pillar of State; deep on his Front engraven / Deliberation sat and public care" (*PL* 2. 301–3), and Satan: "Above them all th' Arch Angel: but his face / Deep scars of Thunder had intrencht . . ." (*PL* 1. 599–601). Even the Goddess, Dulness, seems a modern counterpart of Satan in the line describing the adverse effect of light upon her: "Rowz'd by the light, old Dulness heav'd the head . . ." (1. 257). This recalls Satan, who never "had ris'n or heav'd his head" off the benumbing lake had God not intervened (*PL* 1. 209–1).

Like the Satanic angels, the dull dwell in the North. On one level this suggests that they are writers of the "Cold Stile" Longinus had identified as a species of false sublime; on another it identifies them with the traditional seat of evil and destructive powers—Satan's domain—and historically with the actual barbaric hordes who destroyed civilization. Pope's lines,

Soon as they down, from Hyperborean skies
Embody'd dark, what clouds of Vandals rise!

Lo! where Maeotis sleeps and hardly flows
The freezing Tanais thro' a waste of snows,
The North by miriads pours her mighty sons,
Great nurse of Goths, of Alans, and of Huns!
(3. 85–90)

were suggested by Milton's simile comparing the devils to "A Multitude, like which the populous North / Pour'd never from her frozen loyns, to pass / *Rhene* or *Danau,* when her barbarous Sons / Came like a Deluge on the South" (*PL* 1. 351–54). The unborn souls of the dunces, "Millions and millions on these banks he views, / Thick as the stars of night, or morning dews" (3. 31–32) Pope allusively compares with the army of Satan as it assembles for war against the most High: "*Satan* with his Powers / Far was advanc't on winged speed, an Host / innumerable as the Starrs of Night, / Or Starrs of Morning, Dew-drops" (*PL* 5. 743–47). And the encounter of the impressarios of the theater,

But lo! to dark encounter in mid air
New wizards rise: I see my Cibber there!
Booth in his cloudy tabernacle shrin'd,
On grinning dragons thou shalt mount the wind.
Dire is the conflict, dismal is the din,
Here shouts all Drury, there all Lincoln's-inn
  . . .
(3. 265–70)

reminds us of the encounter of Satan with the formless specter of the monstrous Death as "two black clouds": "Hov'ring a space, till Winds the signal blow / To joyn thir dark Encounter in mid air . . ." (*PL* 2. 716–18). The last two lines imitate these describing war in heaven: ". . . dire was the noise / Of conflict; over head the dismal hiss / Of fiery Darts in flaming volies flew, . . ." (*PL* 6. 211–13).

One notices a cluster of images commonly associated in *PL* with Satanic fraudulent rhetoric: obscuring clouds, wind, noise, shouts, and hissing. In fact, the whole idea of destruction so often associated with confusion in Milton's poem is inherent in the airy combat, vociferation, and applause of the theater. Cibber, "Reduc'd at last to hiss in my own dragon" (3. 286), on one level depicts the absurd antics of the popular stage where Cibber cavorted in a dragon's costume, but on another reminds us of the metamorphosis of Book 10 of *PL*, where Satan, reduced to a Serpent, "hears / On all sides, from innumerable tongues / A dismal universal hiss" (*PL* 10. 506–8). Here the similarity is not so much a verbal one as it is a parallel circumstance showing each reduced to brutishness.

Sin and Death are also suggested in the *Dunciad* when the dunces are drawn into what Maynard Mack (" 'Wit and Poetry and Pope' : Some Observations on his Imagery," *Pope and His Contemporaries,* ed. James L. Clifford and Louis A. Landa [1947]) calls "the gravitational field of Dulness"—"by sure Attraction led / And strong impulsive gravity of Head . . ." (4. 75–76). This imitates Sin's statement that, though traveling through the vast abyss, she cannot "miss the way, so strongly drawn / By this new felt attraction and instinct . . ." (*PL* 10. 262–63). Elsewhere Colley Cibber's statement of wonder and awe at the vision of the past, the present, and the future shown him by the ghost of Settle in Book 3 of the *Dunciad* recalls the amazement of Satan as he views the "monument" created by Sin and Death :

Joy fills his soul, joy innocent of thought:
"What pow'r, he cries, what pow'r these wonders wrought?"
"Son [Settle replies]: what thou seek'st is in thee."

                (3. 249–51)

"And are these wonders, Son to thee unknown?
Unknown to thee? These wonders are thy own."

                (3. 273–74)

Milton's passage describes Satan in much the same terms :

Great joy was at thir meeting, and at sight
Of that stupendous Bridge his joy encreas'd.
Long hee admiring stood, till Sin, his faire
Inchanting Daughter, thus the silence broke.
O Parent, these are thy magnific deeds,
Thy Trophies, which thou view'st as not thine own.

                (*PL* 10. 350–55)

The works of Dulness are truly the works of Colley Cibber, for as Prince of the Dunces he symbolizes the forces of evil manifest in the decaying of the word caused by mindlessness in writing and all other perversions of language and rhetoric. His comparison with Satan marks him as the heir of the Destroyer, who originally had commenced the process returning the world to the reign of Chaos and Night. The egocentricity of Cibber pointed out by Settle—"what thou seek'st is in thee"— echoes the self-reliance of Satan and his crew as they seek to found a world based upon self and denying the realities of nature and of God.

Though the verbal echo above suggests that Pope compares Cibber's vision with the meeting of Satan, Sin, and Death, a larger parallel is with Adam's vision in Books 11 and 12 of *PL* of the future works of sin in the world. The "Argument to Book Three" tells us that Settle leads Cibber "to a Mount of Vision, from whence he shews him the past triumphs of the Empire of Dulness, then the present, and lastly the future." Adam, led by Michael to "a Hill / Of Paradise the highest, from whose top / The Hemisphere of Earth in clearest Ken / Strecht out to the amplest reach of prospect lay" (*PL* 11. 376–80), speaks in joy and amazement, though Adam's joy alternates with sorrow as he sees what his actions have wrought upon the world of his children. Like Adam, whose eyes are instilled with drops that pierce "to the inmost seat of mental sight" (11. 418), Cibber is told that Dulness "unfolds to vision true / Thy mental eye" (3. 71–72). Though Adam's act finds mitigation through the grace of God, who brings good out of evil, his actions, prompted by the fraudulent temptations of Satan, bring evil to the world of history. In this sense Cibber is like both Satan and Adam. Pope merges the two scenes from *PL* with the scene in the *Dunciad* to underscore the ancient source of Cibber's evil. The second parallel, more situational than verbal, links Adam's Fall, which introduced decay into the world, with the activities of duncery.

At the beginning of Book 4 of

the *Dunciad* Pope suggests, though not through direct verbal imitation, Milton's invocation to Holy Light at the beginning of Book 3 of *PL*. But he inverts it to a prayer for "darkness visible"—all that can be hoped for at the final hour of creation before the world returns to chaos. The intent or mission common to devil and dunce is, as Williams notes, "the uncreating of creation, the disordering of order." Imagery of chaos occurs throughout the poem, but echoes of Milton's Chaos alert the reader to the chaos of modern thought and creativity. Satan's journey through confusion compares with Cibber's through his confused thought (cf. 1. 117–20, and *PL* 2. 927–34). Pope attaches this note to his depiction of chaotic thought : "The progress of a bad Poet in his thoughts being (like the progress of the Devil in *Milton*) thro' a Chaos, might probably suggest this imitation." Lintot in the race of the publishers imitates in his actions the turbulent expenditure of energy necessary to make headway when attempting to breach the wild tempestuousness of primeval anarchy (2. 63–67; cf. *PL* 2. 947–50).

Pope speaks of "the sable Throne . . . / Of *Night* Primaeval, and of *Chaos* old (4. 629–30). The lines recall these from Milton's poem : ". . . when strait behold the Throne / Of Chaos, and his dark Pavilion spread / Wide on the wasteful Deep; with him Enthron'd / Sat Sable-vested *Night,* eldest of things" (*PL* 2. 959–62). But probably the most important single passage from *PL* for understanding Milton's influence upon the poem is one that Pope does not directly imitate at any point. Satan's promise to the monarchs of Chaos that he will confound the Creator's works and return them to their original state of confusion (*PL* 2. 982–86) when compared with the *Dunciad* shows the common heroic mission of devils and dunces, whose misuse of words completes the "Restoration" of "her old Empire to Dulness," the "Daughter of Chaos and eternal Night." In Book 4 we see the final fulfillment of Satan's promise to Chaos and Night when the poet announces "Lo !

thy dread Empire, CHAOS ! is restored" (4. 635). The world's dissolution and return to chaos does not, of course, occur in the real world as Satan intended that it should. The poets carry on his work by making it happen to the world as it is pictured in their poems, thereby assuring that the destruction of civilization cannot be far behind. Pope amplifies the significance of artistic and linguistic decay by describing it in terms of its analogy with the real world.

Thomas R. Edwards has isolated the metaphors of light and darkness, rising and falling, as those that unify the four books of the *Dunciad* (*This Dark Estate: A Reading of Pope* [1963]). Joined with these are metaphors of waking and sleeping, organic growth and sterility or decay, sound and sense, creation and destruction—all images that occur in somewhat similar terms in *PL*. The blending of verbal echoes and imitation of Miltonic imagery in the *Dunciad* build Pope's "argument" in much the same way that Milton's imagery functions in his poem to embody thought in concrete images. A few examples of the major image clusters will show the similarity of the function of images, though it cannot fully suggest the scope of Pope's indebtedness to Milton's metaphoric structure.

Perhaps the most obvious strain of images in the *Dunciad* is that of light and darkness. Its ultimate significance becomes apparent in the ending of Book 4 : "Light dies before thy uncreating word : / Thy hand, great Anarch ! lets the curtain fall; / And universal Darkness buries All" (4. 654–56). In the 1728 version of the poem, Dulness's inversion of the divine fiat calls darkness down upon the face of creation. Through allusive comparison with Milton's Creator and the divine Word of Genesis upon which Milton bases his story, she emerges as the antithesis of the creative Force : "Let there be darkness ! (the dread pow'r shall say) / All shall be darkness as it ne'er were Day" (1. 337–54 [1728]). Darkness represents uncreation, nonbeing; light, as it did in *PL,* represents the informing spirit of creation. The Empire of Dulness, the daughter of Chaos and Night, dwells in darkness and even early in the poem Dulness's love of darkness is manifest: "O! ever gracious to perplex'd mankind, / Still spread a healing mist before the mind; / And lest we err by Wit's wild dancing light, / Secure us kindly in our native night" (1. 173–76). As in *Peri Bathous,* mist and fogs are obscuring barriers that keep out the light of creation from the mind. When Cibber sets afire the sacrifice of his unsuccessful writings, Dulness, "rowz'd by the light" of the blaze, reacts instinctively to extinguish the light so antipathetic to her nature.

The description of the "presence" of Dulness immediately following this incident shows her to be, like Milton's God, a being undefined in shape and form, surrounded by clouds and fogs (1. 261–62). King Colley is also surrounded by protective coverings of vapors as he sleeps in the lap of Dulness (3. 1–4). These obfuscating vapors promote the darkness of dullness and void of mind the poem "celebrates." (See also 4. 18–19; 3. 73–74; 3. 225–27.) In Book 4 the imagery of light and darkness, only a slight but insistent motif through the early books, reaches a crescendo. The spreading pall of darkness seen in Cibber's vision continues to engulf the precincts of Dulness's court. The dunces of the universities, the virtuosi, the collectors, and the critics bring darkness upon themselves and those associated with them until a vision of utter darkness ends the poem (4. 629–54). Light in this passage suggests the ordering vitality of the creating mind—God's and man's. The "uncreating word" destroys not only culture and civilization, but the created universe as well. Even God's light, the first and primary entity of created being, though last to go, expires, and with this ordering and informing source blotted out, all is returned to the primal state of Chaos from whence God had formed the creation through the agency of his divine creating word.

The imagery of darkness and obfuscation shutting out the light of nature relates as well to the games in Book 2 where, as in *PL,* we find images of sinking down into darkness. The love of the dunces for darkness and the intellectual and moral obscurity it represents explains their eagerness to cover themselves with mud and filth. The diving contests of the poets and "*profound, dark* and *dirty* Party-writers" merge the images of falling and darkness with other repeated motifs associated with dullness. The dunces dive into the Fleet-ditch, an outlet carrying the collected filth of the area into the Thames (2. 271–74). Pope calls the filthy waters further polluted by the mud-slinging of the divers "the black abyss" (288), "the deep" (300), "th' unconscious stream" (304) and "the flood" (307)—all terms Milton used to describe the waters of Hell into which Satan and his cohorts fell. In addition, we find that like the burning lake of *PL,* which is fed by the four infernal and mind-numbing rivers of classical mythology, "A branch of Styx here rises from the Shades, / That tinctur'd as it runs with Lethe's streams, / And wafting Vapours from the Land of dreams / . . . Pours into Thames . . ." (2. 338–44). Into this soporific flood the dunces plunge downward to darkness, imitating the diving fish and birds in *Peri Bathous.*

Metaphors of descent and falling can be found throughout the poem (cf. 1. 117–19, 181–85, 209–11; 3. 161–64, 403–8; 4. 81–84). The young men finished by the grand tour of dullness are degenerate creatures: "Now to thy gentle shadow all are shrunk, / All melted down, in Pension or in Punk!" (4. 509–10). The image of melting shows that the fall from hierarchy of being brings everyone to a state of chaotic sameness. The young are "dipped" into Euclid and petrified to stone, bringing "to one dead level ev'ry mind" (4. 263–70). Hierarchy collapses into sameness, the vitality of created being turns to stony sterility as all sinks into the shadow of dullness. We are reminded of the "petrific stone" of the monument to the devils, and detect in the dull the same stultifying, mindless rigidity of the once vital man that Milton attributed to those with "stony hearts" who, blind to God's grace will "hard be hard'nd, blind be blinded more" (*PL* 3. 200).

Clustering around the central images of rising and falling, darkness and light, are a number of related images and ideas. In *PL* noise characterizes the rhetoric and false language of the devils and relates their moral and linguistic discord to the concept of war and confusion. The passage in *PL* that best defines the meaning of noise in the epic as a whole is the description of chaos and its discordant mouths (*PL* 2. 891–954). In the *Dunciad* noise similarly represents the disordered language of the dunces. The second of the epic games during which Dulness teaches her sons "the wond'rous pow'r of Noise," shows the dunces trying to out-chatter monkeys, and the braying contest shows language reduced to subhuman mindlessness. Their voices echo through the precincts of dullness in much the same way as the trumpets, applause, and shouts of the devils resound through the hollow depths of hell to emphasize that both Milton and Pope depict the jarring noises of self-assertive *confusio* and its disordered language.

At the end of Book 1 the shouts of the dunces (1. 319–26) mark their joy at Dulness's announcement—"All hail! and hail again, / My son! the promis'd land expects thy reign"—of Cibber as "savior" of the land of dullness. The passage superimposes upon the scene from Book 2 of *PL* where the devils applaud Satan's announcement of his plan to found an empire through guile since he cannot by force, the scene from Book 3 where God announces his counter-plan to offer his Son as Savior of man. In Book 3 God, surrounded by the choirs of angels, hears them sing their wondrous approval of his plan. Pope pictures Dulness surrounded by her "Chosen" as she divulges her plan to found "the Imperial seat of Fools" (1. 272). The response to her announcement begins as a harmonious song by the Chapel-royal, but degenerates as it spreads out through her realm to the noisy croak "God save King Log!" (330).

Perhaps the image of dullness best remembered by readers is the image of sleep. From the very invocation of the muse where the author asks his muse to "say how the Goddess bade Britannia sleep, / And pour'd her Spirit o'er the land and deep" (1. 7–8) to the close where the muse, falling under the sway of encroaching dullness, succumbs to sleep (4. 626), the progress of dullness brings sleep to all the land. The images of sleep team with those of obfuscation to show that the dull, like Satan and his followers and the fallen Adam and Eve, do not share God's ability to see clearly. The "unsleeping eyes of God" and his angels, "his Eyes / That run through all the Heav'ns, or down to th'Earth" (*PL* 3. 650–51), stand as the absolute value against which Pope measures his yawning and insensible dunces. God's absolute reason and pure perception of truth are the positive values that the dull negate in their love for illusion and confusion and their inability to distinguish truth and represent it in their words.

In *PL* Satan's fraudulent language results from a split in the original unity between word and thing established at the Creation through Christ's divine Word. The fallen use language that fails to recognize this initial reality and create through words false imitations of nature. Or they falsely create new worlds, new definitions of reality based upon their self-sufficient use of language, their lies and sophistic substitution of terms. In the *Dunciad* Pope, too, expresses a concern that words not be wrenched from their primal meaning in relation to the things of nature. Through imitation of *PL*, Pope invests the current decayed abuse of language he deplores with moral significance.

The separation of word and thing occurs in *PL* quite pronouncedly in puns* and other forms of "wit"—especially in Satan's punning before God's angels when he presents the cannon during the war in Heaven* (*PL* 6. 558–70, 609–19). Satan and his angels and the fallen Adam fall into the habit of punning, a practice that treats words as if their meanings were various and ambivalent rather than fixed and innate. Scriblerus, referring to the puns of the fallen angels, suggests that Satan is the Father of Puns even as he is the Father of Lies (Note to 4. 247). Scriblerus's minute examination of the possible pun on "Canon" (4. 247) amusingly calls the reader's attention to the lines and establishes the association in his mind between Satan's puns and his artillery. Again Pope obliquely draws the parallel between Satanic language and duncery while suggesting that both—like Scriblerus—thrive on language wrenched away from its original purity and distinct meaning.

In the *Dunciad Pope* reveals the words of the dunces as void of common sense, void of reason, void of thought. The "master of public schools" ironically praises this decay of words to mere hollow sound : "Since Man from beast by Words is known, / Words are Man's province, Words we teach alone" (4. 149–50). The rhetorical exercises of the schools "confine the thought, to exercise the breath : / And keep them in the pale of Words till death" (4. 159–60). The empty sounds of dullness, the words empty of thought because wrenched away from realities, are nonsense. The pedant's ideal of education is to set boys to rhyming their first days at school and keep them ever reduced to wordy servitude. In the Royal Council boys grown to men remain confined to words forever (4. 175–80). Pope's note explains that the instructors of the young do their job well "but complain that when men come into the world they are apt to forget their Learning, and turn themselves to useful Knowledge." Dullness points out that the remedy for this situation is tyranny, whose interest lies in keeping men "from the study of things" and encouraging "the propagation of words and sounds."

The metaphysicians proudly disdaining knowledge based on "plain experience . . . / By common sense to common knowledge bred"—knowledge based on the proper relationship between words and verifiable realities—create a false God,

one reduced to humanity and human understanding, from the cobwebs of their soaring fancies : "Thrust some mechanic cause into his place : / Or bind in Matter, or diffuse in Space, / Or, at one bound o'erleaping all his laws, / Make God Man's Image, Man the final Cause" (4. 475–78). The attitude toward forbidden knowledge expressed in Raphael's lecture to Adam —"Be lowly wise"—and his demand that Adam confine his speculations to those that are relevant to man's proper place in the hierarchy of existence lie behind Pope's attitudes toward dullness. The dunces "see all in Self," "all relation scorn." Like Satan, who maintains he is self-created, the dunces are so far from seeing and describing God as the central reality of their existence and so completely lacking in self-knowledge that they commit the primal sin of pride. They self-sufficiently create God in their own image.

Many of the dunces find themselves enchained in the endless pursuit of words and useless abstruse reasoning totally separated from the realities—the things— of human experience. In this they are like the devils in Book 2 of *PL,* who pridefully sat upon a hill in Hell and reasoned "Of Providence, Foreknowledge, Will and Fate, / Fixt Fate, Free Will, Foreknowledge absolute, / And found no end, in wand'ring mazes lost" (2. 557–61). Others pursue "things" divorced from their proper significance in the ordered degree of creation. Eve elevated the Tree of Knowledge to a prominence in her thoughts (she substituted it for God as the subject of her prayer) that placed it above God. Like her, the collectors and virtuosi of Book 4 value indiscriminately whatever whim has mistakenly endowed with the reverence due their Maker.

The bug lover, accused of raping the carnation when he crushed it to seize his prey, defends himself by proclaiming his specialized, self-determined interest : "I meddle Goddess ! only in my sphere" (4. 432). He cares only about that corner of the universe whim has made dear to him and never stops to consider how it reveals the grandeur of the maker of all. The description of the butterfly-lover's chase invokes reminiscence of Milton's description of Eve self-enthralled as she gazes at her own reflection in the water: ". . . I started back, / It started back; but pleas'd I soon returnd / Pleas'd it returnd as soon . . ." (*PL* 4. 462–64). Pope in the notes compares these lines to his: "It fled, I follow'd; now in hope, now pain; / It stopt, I stopt; it mov'd, I mov'd again" (4. 427–28). Eve self-sufficiently endows the shadowy shape in the water with the adoration due Adam, and through Adam, God. Until God warns her and Adam calls, she basely misdirects the love due her superior. The virtuosi commit the same error. They misuse their rational powers by investing all their reverence in the "partial narrow shapes" of nature and allow the "Author of the Whole" to escape (4. 545–55). In each case through incomplete self-knowledge, which fails to acknowledge man's limited wisdom and significance in the chain of nature reaching up to God, the self-sufficient being redefines the meanings of things just as he redefines the meanings of words.

Pride, the natural result of being wrapped up in self, makes each dunce reverence his own "god." The gluttonous dunce worships "three essential Partridges in one" (562). Another may choose the "Hummingbird" or "Cockle-kind." Whether enslaved to words or to things matters not.

Dullness creates from muddle of mind a "new world" reflecting the chaos within, in parody of God's creation of an ordered universe reflecting the Reason that is the mind of God. Each comes about through the agency of words. The "uncreating word" of Dullness through her poets and playwrights destroys the order of God's world and miscreates in its stead an unnatural world (1. 71–75). Pope points up the parody of God's ordered creation by calling the creation of Dulness a "mazy dance." Though Dulness's "mazy dance" of creation is a mad one, it parodies Milton's dance of the stars and planets: "mazes intricate, / Eccentric, intervolv'd, yet regular / Then most, when most irregular they seem . . ." (*PL* 5. 622–24). The intricate and eccentric movements of Milton's heavens are the manifestations of order in a vital, breathing universe. In Pope's fallen world of dullness, that vitality becomes the mad jig of misbegotten monsters (1. 59–70; 3. 235–40, 243–48).

Out of topical references to contemporary staging devices and oddities, Pope builds a picture of the false world the playwrights make from their fraudulent language and illusory stage tricks. Pope depicts the machinations of the theater managers as they hang above the stage ordering the fake heavens and directing the course of the mock elements (3. 255–64). Through the antics of the dunces shines the "deep intent" of Satan to destroy the old world and create in false emulation of God a new context, a new world in which to view himself. When the moment of triumph comes for Satan and the forces of Dulness as modern comic fiends, the real world, not just the world of letters lies "uncreate."

The *Essay on Man* in four verse epistles claims as the thematic statement of the first epistle to "vindicate the ways of God to Man" (1. 16). This line, an obvious allusion to Milton's claim to "justifie the ways of God to men" (*PL* 1. 26), points to the generally common goal of the two poems, identifies Pope's conscious comparison of his poem with *PL,* and suggests by the changed verb in the allusion the way that the *Essay on Man* will differ from Milton's poem. Both poems attempt to show why evil exists. Milton seeks to assert the goodness of eternal Providence and defend God against the charge that human suffering shows the Deity to be cruel or unjust. To do this, Milton must claim to know and understand the working of God's plan, to explain the mind of God. Pope, however, in seeking to "vindicate" God attempts only to clear Him from censures a more limited goal, by examining the limited mind of the unbeliever who doubts the goodness of God's plan. While Milton's poem is essentially theological,

Pope's is essentially psychological, secular, and epistemological (David P. French, *Bucknell Review* 16 [1968]: 103–11).

The most obvious difference between the form and style of the poems is that Pope's is an "essay," a form described by Samuel Johnson's* dictionary as a "loose sally of the mind," an "irregular, undigested piece," "a trial or experiment," while Milton's is a religious, sublime epic. The epistle form, traditionally cast as conversational moral advice to a friend, is distinctly of the middle flight. The poem opens with a conversation between cultivated friends and a relaxed hunting metaphor—the game, folly, and pride. The *Essay* may be characterized as public, social, and classical befitting the eighteenth-century ideals of cosmopolitanism and sociality. The bond with a social audience is distinctive and determines the at times conversational, at times hortatory, style and tone. The contrast with Milton's epic magnificence inspired by a divine muse, his use of characters in dramatic action, ornate diction, and elaborate periodic structure points to the more humble, even more skeptical approach of a rational man who keeps ever before him the limits of rationality.

Milton finds the source of evil in the impulse to disobedience that led to the Fall of Man, but he insists that without free will and the necessity to make moral choices, man would be enslaved to goodness, incapable of any true virtue. Thus finite evil is actually divine benevolence, and even the Fall will eventually have happy results through man's future redemption. Pope proceeds by an approach that reveals his skepticism about man's ability to reason or to know the full truth about the terms of his existence. Man is too ignorant even to doubt God's wisdom: if he cannot comprehend God's universe, he cannot judge it. But like Milton, Pope sees finite evil as infinite goodness. Even man's limited reason is an important part of the beneficent plan of God.

Pope refutes the rationalist who would fly beyond sensory knowledge to claim a knowledge of the whole, which only God can know (1. 23–28). He argues that, could man attain such real knowledge, rational speculation would have no value. But man can no more expect to understand such matters than the horse can hope to comprehend the motives of the men who own him (1. 61–66). We have such knowledge as we need for daily life but no more; in fact, our ignorance is often our bliss. Our greatest error is false pride in our power of reason, for man was not meant to understand Heaven (1. 193–206). The moral is that man must "Submit" (1. 285), for we should "Presume not God to scan; / The proper study of Mankind is Man" (2. 1–2).

Pope's strictures against reasoning pride parallel Raphael's lectures to Adam during the astronomy lesson and his warning to Adam to "be lowlie wise: Think onely what concerns thee and thy being" *PL* 8. 173–74). The *Essay* closes with the admonition to religious humility that Pope argues for throughout: "And all our Knowledge is, OURSELVES TO KNOW" (4. 398). Adam's Fall comes from failure of self-knowledge, which includes the knowledge of his proper duties and place with respect to both Eve and God. Like Milton, Pope argues that only through knowledge of his limitations is man truly free to enjoy his blessings.

Maynard Mack argues that in the *Essay* Pope manages to show, as Milton had in *PL*, "the story of a conflict between religious humility and irreligious pride, . . . the story of universal order, the ways it can be violated, and the ways it can be restored" (*An Essay on Man* in Twick ed., 3 : xlvii–lxxx). Pope's world agrees with Milton's in its orderly hierarchy. Hierarchy is law in Pope's world—"Heaven's first law" (4. 49)—and the creatures who rebel and disobey the laws of hierarchy and union "invert the world, and counterwork its Cause" (1. 123ff.; 3. 241ff.). Hierarchy is the means to union, a fellowship sustained by love. God's love circulates up and down the "everlasting Chains" to bind the elements, planets, animals, men, and angels into one mutually dependent system. Love works through the mating of beasts, the formation of families, civil societies, and religions. Man's proper understanding of the order that contains him is to see it interdependent, a "union of the rising whole," where his duties lie in the love of God and of man. But Pope's vision of concord incorporates the Heraclitean *concordia discors,* wherein all opposites like self-love and social love, reason and passion, through balanced tensions make an overall order and bind into a concordant whole the various and seemingly discordant impulses of prideful individuals. The ruling passion, which drives individuals along various paths of excess, is really the God-inspired means of arriving at individual virtues and universal goodness: "Heav'n forming each on other to depend, / A master, or a servant or a friend, / Bids each on other for assistance call, / 'Till one Man's weakness grows the strength of all" (2. 249–52). Here Milton's conception of a past innocence of perfect virtue corrupted by the unleashing of sinful pride until a future time at which Christ's death through love will restore to man the possibility of re-created happiness, "a paradise within," Pope replaces by a vision of the present goodness of the whole inherent in the very sin and vice existent in all men. "One man's weakness" refers not to the original entrance of evil into the world through the act of Adam, but to the evil coexistent in all men, mitigated by reason's counsel, but necessary to the plan of overall goodness. Milton's emphasis upon the importance of man's rational volition and moral choice Pope replaces by a view of man as a creature whose reason is severely limited, only a "weak queen," and whose volition is for the most part subsumed within the working of God's plan. Pope removes the dimension of Christian chronology in which good is brought out of evil for a simultaneity in which good and evil paradoxically coexist and are one in the temporal realm as in the eyes of God. Life is both a "mighty maze" and a "plan" that incorporates the infinite variety of man's world within the unity of God.

But man is also seen as a potential violator of unity. In the first Epistle the subject is man's rebellion against his level in the chain of created being. When in his pride he aspires above himself or envies purely physical powers below him, he revolts against his human limitations and breaks the order of God's universe: "The least confusion but in one, not all / That system only, but the whole must fall" (1. 249–50). Pope images the clash of irreligious pride with religious resignation, but he does not dramatize it as Milton had done; because man's vision is limited he must be taught to submit to the dictum that "Whatever IS, is RIGHT" (1. 239–94). He must accept this on faith and such faith can come only when he gives up all pride in his ability to know.

The sequent epistles further elaborate the theme of pride and the necessity for self-knowledge, which for Pope, as it had also for Milton, means knowledge of man's nature, limitations, and place within the scheme of things. In the second Epistle, Pope repudiates all conduct that glorifies man as a creature of intellect alone and he underscores the duality of body and spirit with which man must come to terms. The third Epistle scorns all the ways by which man undertakes to set himself apart from the fellowship of created things: "short of Reason he must fall / Who thinks all made for one, not one for all" (3. 47–48). When man assumes that the lower creatures exist exclusively for him, he makes way for the tyrant, who insolently assumes that other men exist for him. Milton's God praises Adam for his instinctive knowledge that he cannot dwell in solitude, that he is incomplete in himself. Pope sees that man's societies originate, as those of the animals do, in such God-directed instinct, not in reason. When men violate this natural law they become tyrannous in the realm of nature, in civil life, and in religion. Pride seeks to abstract itself from the scheme of God and nature: religious and social humility realize that no such abstracted political or religious dogma can be better than natural rectitude. For Milton, such abstraction of the self from the whole breaks order and constitutes sin. Pope draws heavily upon Milton's thought and imagery to depict disorder in personal and social as well as theological terms.

Also in the third Epistle, Pope recounts a fable of civilization's progress through innocence and a "fall" to a regenerate concord. In the beginning is an ideal, natural state, "the reign of God" (2. 148), during which man lives without pride in natural innocence, singing hymns to God and guided by instinct. Pope's depiction of the state of nature seems a conscious answer to the Hobbesian view that man is naturally evil and possessive. If *PL,* as Marjorie Nicholson has suggested, is a seventeenth-century reply to Hobbes (*Studies in Philology* 23 [1926]: 405–33), Pope makes a reply in his own way that is characteristic of his century.

From this natural innocence civilisation fell to the reign of the fury-passions: man butchered the animals he had lived with in innocent harmony and turned savagely against his own kind. Tyranny replaced the patriarch honored by all and reason's steady light was broken by oblique wit. Superstition made gods and fiends and set man to sacrifice at "grim idols smear'd with human blood" (3. 266). This may be compared with Milton's account of the reign of Nimrod and of history before the coming of Christ in Books 11 and 12 of *PL.* But the same self-love that founded the tyrant brought government and laws to restrain him: "Self-love forsook the path it first pursu'd/ And found the private in the public good" (3. 280). In this regenerated state benevolent, generous-minded men restore the faith and morals that nature had originally given. Corcord reigns once again; "jarring int'rests of themselves create / Th' according music of a well-mixed State" (3. 293–94).

The three-part history is analogous to the three-part structure of the Christian story of human society, but in Pope's version both fall and regeneration come

from the same source—self-love—which can never be equated with sin because it paradoxically corrects the evil it introduces. The process takes place without any specific divine intervention or heroic martyrdom. Compared with Milton's reasoned argument backed by Christian dogma, Pope's has seemed to many philosophically unsatisfactory because it seems to raise more questions than it answers.

The fourth Epistle explores man's desire for happiness and finds that it rests in virtue alone. All attempts to find it elsewhere—in creature comforts, fame, or material possession—exhibit pride. The attitude of acceptance of man's lot stressed throughout the *Essay* coalesces into praise of Charity, which is the supreme felicity, and one that binds together the individual with the whole of which he is a part. All four epistles picture the disorder pride threatens, but end with a vision of the whole as seen from increasingly more human-oriented points of view. Maynard Mack describes this as an affirmation of "complex unity creatively achieved among dissimilars (the *Many* resolved in *Man*), which is akin to and indeed is the mirror image of the complex unity of existence sustained in the mind of God."

The *Essay on Man* illustrates a tendency in modern literature to internalize and translate toward abstraction matters that earlier ages cast in tale, romance, or myth. Even in *PL* the prohibition of the apple becomes a rationalized symbol of obedience, as it was not in Genesis. It is thus internalized and the consequences of eating it are at least partially internalized in the rebellion of the passions and the birth of lust. The epic narrative Milton used has been replaced in the *Essay* by the image of the chain of being, or scale of nature*, which had been implicit in Milton's cosmic stage. To this more traditional image attach suggestions of Newtonian mechanism, whirling planets and atoms, translating the image into a viable metaphor for Newtonian cosmology. But the order it represents exists internally as well as in the system of the planets. In the *Essay* the "paradise" to be regained is not as in Milton partly inward and partly objective in the Second Coming, but entirely internal. Pope tries to define poetically the nature of man and the justice of God outside the realm of religious allegory, heroic drama, and scriptural story. Lord Bolingbroke in a letter to Swift of August 2, 1731, describing the writing of the *Essay* then in progress, sums up its approach when he says it defends God's justice by "irrefragable reasons" and without resting proof of the point on revelation.

The *Epistle to Dr. Arbuthnot,* written in 1734 but unpublished until 1735, is an answer to the fears of his longtime friend, Dr. Arbuthnot, that Pope would put himself in danger by making examples of particular persons in his satires. The poem concerns both Pope's personal reasons for writing barbed satire and a defense of his ethos as a satirist. The first part of the poem tends to be of a literary nature and emphasizes the exasperation he has suffered at the hands of literary zealots, envious rivals and pedantic critics. The second part tends to be moral in subject and stresses the infamies to which he has been subjected by "moralizing his song" in service to virtue and the commonweal.

The portrait of Sporus is biographically about Lord Harvey, vice chamberlain to George II and confidant to Queen Caroline, who, with the assistance of Lady Mary Wortley Montague, had savagely attacked Pope's physical deformities, character, and works in *Verses Addressed to the Imitator of Horace* (1733). Poetically it is about evil, the evil of flattery, slander, betrayal, and lies that Milton had embodied in Satan. The picture of Sporus "at the ear of Eve, familiar toad" (319) recalls Milton's description of Satan, "Squat like a Toad, close at the ear of *Eve*" (*PL* 4.800). Pope underscores the parallel between Sporus and Satan while alluding to Harvey's moral and physical ambiguity, his homosexuality and effeminacy: "Eve's tempter thus the rabbins have expressed, / A cherub's face, a reptile all the rest; / Beauty that shocks

you, parts that none will trust, / Wit that can creep, and pride that licks the dust . . ." (330–33). Because the lines associate Sporus with evil in the most profound sense the poet utilizes this passage to accomplish the tonal transition from mere personal impatience with folly in the opening passages to the impersonal righteous tones of the public moralist so necessary to remove the apologia for his life from any charges of mere petty vindictiveness. [JB]

PORTRAITS. The history of Milton portraiture is complicated by the art form itself, which operates according to unsettled principles : there are those artists intent upon achieving an "unbiassed recreation of the physical phenomenon"; and there are those who are primarily interested in "feeling [their] way into the psychology of the model, so that, in effect, the actual appearance is subordinated to an 'idea' " (M. J. Friedländer, *Landscape, Portrait, Still Life* [1949], p. 247). By the end of the eighteenth century, the latter tradition modulated into an iconoclastic attempt to cast off all obligation and servitude to the artist's subject and thus became involved in a "struggle to avoid reportage by means of periphrasis or aphoristic exaggeration of characteristic features" (Friedländer, p. 262). Both these traditions impinge upon Milton portraiture, but the latter precipitates the emergence of a large number of fanciful depictions of the poet and encourages considerable variations even within those portraits founded upon authentic representations. The history of Milton portraiture is complicated still further by an array of spurious portraits and by many portraits mistakenly identified with Milton; and there are, besides, recorded references to portraits that may or may not be authentic. In his edition of Milton's prose works (1738), Thomas Birch* refers to a Milton portrait that depicts the poet as he was about the age of twenty-five or twenty-six (1 : lxii); in his *Memoirs of John Milton* (1740), Francis Peck* alludes to a self-portrait on the authority of information reported to him by Roger Comerbach (p. 104); and a portrait, now lost but signed W. Hassel and dating from about 1650, was exhibited at the beginning of this century at the Fogg Museum. Amid all of these difficulties, there is, however, one certainty: of first importance are the five portraits made between 1618 and 1670; they are actual representations, and they provide the models for the vast majority of later portraits.

The Pierpont Morgan Portrait (1618). The usual attribution of this portrait to Cornelius Johnson (Janssen), traceable to the *Memoirs of Thomas Hollis* (1780), p. 619, has been challenged by C. H. Collins Baker who, finding "no documentary or stylistic evidence" for such an attribution, associates the portrait instead with Marcus Gheerhaerts (*Lely and the Stuart Portrait Painters* [1912], 1 : 80). In the hands of Milton's third wife until her death in 1727, this portrait was purchased by Charles Stanhope and later came into the possession of Thomas Hollis. Subsequently the portrait was owned by Thomas Bland, Mr. Lane, Leigh Hunt, and J. Passmore Edwards. While still in the possession of Hollis, the portrait was twice engraved, first by I. B. Cipriani for Hollis's *Memoirs* and then by W. N. Gardner for William Hayley's* three-volume edition of Milton (1794–1797). In his biography, John Aubrey* explains that Milton "was ten yeares old, as by his picture : & was then a Poet. his schoolmaster was a puritan in Essex, who cutt his [Milton's] haire short"; and elsewhere in his biography Aubrey indicates that he is responsible for the name and date that were much later painted on the picture for purposes of identification. The portrait is finely described by David Masson in *The Life of John Milton* (1881): "[It] . . . convey[s] a far more life-like image of the little Milton, as he used to look in his neat lace frill, with his black braided dress fitting close round his little chest and arms, than any of the ideal portraits of the poetic child. The face is, indeed, that of as pretty a boy as one could wish to see. The head, from the peculiarity of having the hair cut close all round it,—and here the reader must supplement what hardly appears in the engraving, and imagine the hair a light auburn, and the complexion a delicate pink or clear white and red,— has a look of fine solidity, very different from the fantastic representations, all aerial and wind-blown, offered as the heads of embryo-poets. In fact, the portrait is that of a very grave and intelligent little Puritan boy with auburn hair. The prevailing expression in the face is a loveable *seriousness;* and in looking at it, one can well imagine that these lines from *Paradise Regained* . . . were really written by the poet with some reference to his own recollected childhood :—When I was yet a child, no childish play / To me was pleasing : all my mind was set / Serious to learn and know . . ." (1. 66–67).

The National Portrait Gallery Portrait (1629). John Aubrey reports that Milton's "widow has his picture drawn (very well and like) when a Cambridge scholar . . . which ought to be engraven; for the pictures before his books [according to Mrs. Milton] are not *at all* like him." Aubrey's story is corroborated by George Vertue who was told, upon visiting Milton's daughter Deborah Clarke, that Milton's wife "had two paintings . . . one when he was a lad and went to school, and another about twenty years old." The oil portrait of Milton as a student at Cambridge is presumably the second of the two portraits alluded to in this conversation. Like the first, it remained in the hands of Milton's wife until her death, at which time, says Vertue, it "was bought by a Gent. who brought it to london and sold it to the Hon^le Arthur Onslow, Speaker [of the House of Commons] from whence I engraved it." Many engravings were made from this portrait while it was still in Onslow's possession, the first by Vertue for the Bentley* edition of *PL* published in 1733 and others by Cipriani, Gardner, and Benjamin Van der Gucht, who also made two "perfect" copies of the portrait in oil about 1792, one of them still in the possession of the Harcourt family and the other at Milton's cottage in Chalfont St. Giles. Masson, in his *Life,* offers an appreciation and appraisal of the painting : "There could scarcely be a finer picture of pure and ingenuous English youth; and, if Milton had the portrait beside him when, in later life, he had to allude, in reply to his opponents, to the delicate subject of his personal appearance, there must have been a touch of slyness in his statement that 'so far as he knew he had never been thought ugly by any one who had seen him.' In short, the tradition of his great personal beauty in youth requires no abatement" (p. 308).

The William Marshall Portrait (1645). Commissioned by Humphrey Moseley and designed by William Marshall, this portrait is thought by Milton to be "totally without likeness." As the poet explains in *3Def,* he consented rather diffidently "at the instance and from the importunity of the bookseller, to employ an unskilful engraver, because at the period of war there was no other to be found in the city" (9 : 125). Through this remark and through the Greek epigraph printed with the frontispiece-portrait in the 1645 edition of Milton's poems, the poet himself has fostered the widespread opinion that Marshall as an artist is inept and graceless. Yet such conclusions do not make the portrait, for which no original exists, any less problematical. The portrait, depicting an aged, rather stern, man is discordant with the legend that surrounds it : Ioannis Miltoni Angli Effigies Anno Aetatis Vigess : Pri. The face in the portrait is clearly that of a man well beyond twenty-one years; yet the face itself resembles the depiction of Milton as a Cambridge scholar, as well as the representation of him years later by William Faithorne. Milton may not have liked the portrait *qua* portrait, but that should not obscure the fact that there is a resemblance between this representation of Milton and others. The important point about this portrait is made by George Williamson, who suggests that it "is . . . to a great extent imaginary and cannot be said to represent the poet at thirty-seven, being in fact much more of the nature of

a caricature, although evidently the same man as in the Faithorne portrait" (*The Portraits, Prints, and Writings of John Milton* [1908], p. 6). By way of contrast, William Riley Parker conjectures that the portrait is a "cruel joke" : "the face," he says, "is that of a sour old fellow with a double chin and pockets under his eyes, looking exceedingly silly and trying to hide what might be a withered arm" (*Milton,* 1 : 289). Not only is Parker's description of the portrait fanciful, but the judgment it implies is preposterous : the motives that Parker would attribute to Marshall simply are not justified when the frontispiece is considered whole.

A more reliable description of the frontispiece is provided by J. R. Martin in *The Portrait of John Milton at Princeton* (1961) : "Milton is pictured in fashionable attire. He wears a broad falling band edged with lace and matching cuffs; the sleeve of the doublet is paned so as to reveal the shirt sleeve; and a cloak is worn over the right shoulder and gathered under the arm. Behind him hangs a curtain, which is drawn aside to reveal a rustic scene, with shepherds dancing to the music of a piper. In the corners outside the oval, are four Muses. . . . It is tempting to imagine that the pastoral figures in the background might have been suggested by . . . lines in *L'Allegro*" (p. 5). Though Milton probably did not sit for this portrait, it is clear from the lines in *3Def* that Milton did at least meet with Marshall to arrange for the making of a portrait. This portrait, especially the legend surrounding it, suggests that Milton made available to the artist the National Gallery portrait and that Marshall, in turn, preserved the pose and features of it, adding lines to suggest age and changing the poet's costume. It would also appear from the details that surround the portrait that, as Parker suggests, Milton had a hand in its composition or, more likely, that Marshall had a knowledge of the poems for which his portrait was to provide a frontispiece. However poor the likeness of the portrait to Milton, the portrait is clearly a compliment to the poet and may best be viewed as belonging to an old but well-recognized tradition of portraiture in which physiognomy means very little.

It is worth recalling with Friedländer that "the more resolutely painters begin with ideas the more thoroughly they destroy the individual, stylizing or caricaturing it" (p. 155). The objective is to portray an idea of a person, not the person himself; and the technique is to obliterate physical likeness while at the same time conveying an idea of the person through the attributes assigned to him and through the details that surround him. Marshall's "idea" of Milton is conveyed not by the portrait *per se* but by what adorns it and by the context given to it; his portrait clearly says, "I am a picture, not reality." And the accompanying epigram underscores precisely this point. Viewed from this perspective, the pastoral scene is of real significance : its components are four birds in the sky and two shepherds dancing to a tune played by a third shepherd who sits beneath a tree with his pastoral reed. On the outer edge of each corner of the portrait is a muse* —Erato, Clio, Urania*, and Melpomene, each represented with different attributes and in a different attitude. Moving clockwise from the upper right corner of the portrait, one sees Erato, the muse of lyric poetry and especially of hymns, holding a book in her lap and extending a lyre at which she gazes; Clio, the muse of history, sitting with book and stylus; Urania, the muse of astronomy, pointing with a staff at a globe; and Melpomene, the muse of tragedy, holding a staff in one hand and a stylus in the other. The muses, traditionally connected with prophecy, identify the figure they surround as a poet-prophet; and, as Alexander Ross* observes, "an evil poet" is depicted without the muses, who are "the inseparable companion of learned mindes" and who fill such minds "with knowledge of heavenly things." The muses, moreover, insure the poet of comfort in "his own private and solitary life"; and themselves "perpetual Virgins," they testify to the chastity of the poet that is preserved against all assaults. Finally, the muses are a reminder that poetry "is a divine gift," with Urania symbolizing the heaven from which the poet's learning comes, Clio and Erato the glory and love of learning, and Melpomene the harmony produced from the learning that infuses the poet's mind (see *Mystagogus Poeticus* [1648], p. 297).

The ornaments surrounding the portrait, then, lend considerable rhetorical force to the frontispiece : besides identifying Milton with the chaste poet who through contemplation has achieved the prophetic strain, they summarize the literary achievements and interests of an inspired prophet who in his lyric poems, especially *Nat* and *Lyc,* assumes the prophetic stance and who in his orations explores the immediate problems of England within the context of Christian history. And though Parker questions the propriety of Melpomene, the muse of tragedy, it is clear that by this time Milton has at least contemplated a tragedy on the story of Samson and that he has begun one called *Adam Unparadised.* Moreover, the identification of Milton's poems with prophecy and of Milton with the long line of prophets is reinforced by the interior of the frontispiece. Clearly the figure depicted is beyond the twenty-one years suggested by the legend that encompasses the portrait, and indeed, the characteristics of old age are so prominent that they suggest a man much older than Milton's thirty-seven years at the time the portrait was engraved. The fact that the pastoral scene, visible through the window behind the poet, recalls the poet of *L'Al* and specifically the lines that tell of "many a youth and many a maid, dancing in the chequered shade," poses the possibility that the frontispiece is intended to invoke a contrast between the piper of innocence and the aged bard of experience who, *IlP* promises, will achieve the prophetic strain. The frontispiece to the 1645 edition of Milton's poems, then, involves an iconography of praise that Milton himself would have understood. There is no doubt that Milton saw this frontispiece before the publication of the volume, and there is no evidence at all that he saw Moseley's preface to his poems. It is very likely that Milton, who had already remarked upon the poor likeness of the portrait, chose to comment through the title-page quotation on the praise implied by the fron- tispiece. An epigraph from Virgil's *Seventh Eclogue* appears on the title page, ". . . wreathe my brow with foxglove, / Lest his evil tongue harm the bard that is to be"; and that epigraph, according to H. F. Fletcher, alludes to Moseley's preface and invokes the idea that extravagant praise may be "evil" in the sense that it excites the envy of the gods or in the sense that strong commendation of a poet may encourage him to relax his struggle to achieve perfection and thus may cause his poetry to "dwindle away into nothing" (see *Poetical Works* [1943], 1 : 154, and *Virgils Eclogues*, trans. W. L. Gent [1628], p. 132). Fletcher grasps the implications of the lines from Virgil, but he does not grasp that the praise bestowed by Marshall's frontispiece rather than by Moseley's preface is their likely referent.

The William Faithorne* Portrait (1670, line engraving). Perhaps com- missioned by James Allestry as a front- ispiece for Milton's *Brit,* this portrait (particularly rare in its first state, which bears the date "1607") has been much admired by all but Milton's wife, who told Aubrey, "The pictures before his books are not *at all* like him." The im- portance of this portrait, says J. R. Martin, "cannot be exaggerated" : as "a doc- umented likeness of Milton at the height of his powers, taken by a competent artist with the sitter's consent, and published during his lifetime, it has some claim to be regarded as the 'official image' of the poet" (p. 8). The first of many engravers who worked from the Faithorne portrait was William Dolle, who prepared the frontispiece for Milton's *Logic* (1672); Robert White engraved the portrait for the 1688 Tonson* edition of *PL,* but it should be noted that his engraving, which claims to be a portrait from life, is merely a copy of the portrait that Faithorne drew

from life. Of this portrait Masson says, "The face is such as has been given to no other human being; it was and is uniquely Milton's. Underneath the broad forehead and arched temples there are the great rings of eye-socket, with the blind un- blemished eyes in them, drawn straight upon you by your voice, and speculating who and what you are; there is severe composure in the beautiful oval of the whole countenance, disturbed only by the singular pouting round the mouth; and the entire expression is that of English intrepidity mixed with unutterable sor- row" (*Life,* 6 : 649). Because of the vast number of copies of this portrait, it is worth observing with J. R. Martin that the most distinctive feature of the portrait is the collar that adorns Milton's costume: "This consists of a broad, square-cut fall- ing band, the two sides of which meet edge to edge; beneath it may be seen the tasselled ends of the band-strings. Only two buttons of the waist-coat are visible, the rest being concealed by a cloak which is wrapped about the shoulders and made to cross the chest in a series of long, curv- ing folds" (p. 7).

The William Faithorne Portrait (crayon portrait). Before executing an engraving, Faithorne customarily prepared a detailed drawing, several of which have been pre- served for his other portraits. However, if there was a preliminary drawing for the Milton portrait, it "was destroyed or otherwise lost. There is certainly no justification for the theory . . . that Faithorne's original drawing still existed in the eighteenth century" (Martin, p.8). But there exists a color portrait, formerly known as the Baker or Bayfordbury por- trait, now in the Princeton University Library, with the collector's stamp of Jonathan Richardson* in the lower right corner. This drawing, says J. R. Martin, "is either by Faithorne himself . . . , or it is a copy after Faithorne's print" (p. 11). Acquired in 1749 by the Tonsons, this portrait later came into the possession of William Baker, Richard Tonson's nephew, in whose family it remained until 1953, when it was sold to William H. Scheide, who then gave the portrait to the Princeton Library.

Very subdued in color, this portrait is of special importance insofar as it provides "the archetype of a whole class of Milton portraits, and must therefore be regarded as one of the principal sources in the iconography of the poet" (Martin, p. 11). The first recorded reference to the depiction is made by Vertue in a notebook entry for August 10, 1721; and it is mentioned again by Jonathan Richardson, Sr., in 1734. Receiving authentication from Deborah Clarke (" 'tis my Father, 'tis my Dear Father! I see him! 'tis Him! . . . 'tis the very Man!"), this drawing was used as the preparatory design for the engraved portrait of Milton made by Vertue in 1725. It also provided the model for a drawing of Milton by Richardson, now in the British Museum, inscribed on the back : "From an Original in Crayons by Faithorne." This crayon drawing so closely resembles the engraving that it is particularly important to notice the differences in pose and dress : "the most revealing difference lies in the face, which, with its sightless eyes, is calm and impassive. It is the image of one who, though touched by suffering, is now beyond suffering. And this serenity, together with the arrangement of the hair, parted in the middle and falling in long waves to the shoulders, gives to the pastel portrait an almost Christlike quality that is wholly lacking in the engraving" (Martin, p. 11). Though there is no way of documenting the fact, the Princeton portrait is probably what tradition says it is—the work of Faithorne (see Martin, p. 27). As Martin conjectures, "the crayon picture of Milton may have come into Vertue's possession through his connection with John Bagford and the Earl of Oxford." Bagford (1650–1716) was a friend and the biographer of Faithorne, and librarian to Robert Harley, first Earl of Oxford (1661–1724). Whatever the source of its transmission to posterity, this portrait has the distinction, along with the Faithorne engraving, "of preserving . . . 'the Face of him who wrote *Paradise Lost*' " (Martin, p. [30]).

Besides these formal portraits, there are a number of anecdotal ones, which represent a phenomenon that became especially popular during the 1790s. This category of portraits, as Marcia Pointen explains, falls into three groups, "each symptomatic of one particular aspect of the Milton cult" (*Milton & English Art* [1970], p. 251). There are, first of all, a great number of pictures that show Milton dictating either *PL* or *SA;* the most famous of these is by George Romney. There are, secondly, a number of drawings with a particularly Romantic appeal, such as those which show Milton in association with other intellectual titans or in an attitude of triumph, having overcome one or another of his adversaries. Finally, there are those depictions in which the interest is unmistakably political and historical—depictions that result in "the crystallization of the concept of Milton . . . as a great revolutionary, nonconformist protagonist of liberty" (Pointen, p. xxvii). The greatest examples of these last two categories of painting are the illustrations that accompany the epic poem by Blake* to which Milton gives the title. Intent upon exhibiting the "spiritual form" of his favorite poet, upon mythologizing Milton, Blake departs from the usual iconography that shrouds the poet and instead depicts him, unclad, going through the fires of purgation (plate 1) as prologue to his transfiguration (plate 16); and in this same set of designs Blake shows Milton triumphing over his spectre Satan (plate 18) and later, nude and in one version with penis erect, in the moment of poetic inspiration, joining with his emanation Ololon (plate 42). There are also illustrations of Milton struggling through the cave of error (plate 46) and in the attitude of forgiveness (plate 45). These various anecdotal representations of Milton, however distant they may be from actual likenesses of the poet, testify to a new interest in and understanding of Milton, both the man and his poetry; and they participate in the apotheosis of the poet that occurs in the first part of the nineteenth century.

Of related interest are various busts,

medallions, and seals from which a number of Milton portraits were derived. Particularly important is a bust of Milton, now in the collection at Christ's College*, Cambridge, which was acquired by Vertue, later owned by Hollis, and allegedly "modelled from and big as life . . . executed soon after Milton had written his 'Defensio pro Populo Anglicano,' as some think, by one Pierce a sculptor of good reputation in those times, or by Abraham or Thomas Simon" (*Memoirs of Thomas Hollis,* p. 619). Vertue is responsible for the first attribution and Hollis for the second. Decorated with apple and serpent, this bust is reproduced in both the 1738 and 1753 editions of Milton's prose works by Thomas Birch*, and it is the prototype for the emblematic print of Milton triumphing over Salmasius* initially intended as a frontispiece for Hollis's projected edition of Milton's prose works but then included in his *Memoirs.* Another noteworthy Milton bust was done by Michael Rysbrack for the temple of British worthies at Stowe (1732). Rysbrack also cut the monument at Westminster Abbey, which includes a bust designed by H. Gravelot; Milton's name is inscribed on the pedestal of the bust, and its history is given below it. Also important are the various busts by Roubilliac. In May 1751, four busts (one of Milton) were sent to Madame du Bocage. All four of these busts are now at Stourhead, with two additional busts by Rysbrack, one depicting the young Milton and the other representing the poet in old age. Besides the Roubilliac bust at Stourhead, there is a terra-cotta bust by Roubilliac in the National Portrait Gallery in Scotland and yet another plaster bust, resembling the former two and dating from at least the mid-eighteenth century, in the private collection of G. William Stuart. The Roubilliac busts are of special importance because they provide the prototype for the Wedgewood bust, now in the Henry E. Huntington Art Gallery, that is associated with the artist Theodore Parker and that is, in turn, the prototype for most of the modern busts of Milton and for the

Wedgewood cameos, intaglios, and portrait medallions. There are besides an engraving by W. Ridley from a bust reproduced in Cooks's edition of *Select Poets,* and another designed by Richard Smirke and engraved by Abraham Raimbach that serves as frontispiece to *Cowper's Milton* (1810); there is, finally, a marble bust presented by Denis Saurat to the National Portrait Gallery in London, which has in addition a plaster cast of the Hollis bust made from the original in 1925. The Hollis bust has also been the source for a steel puncheon and a seal, and the Rysbrack bust has provided a medal engraved by John Sigismund Tanner. Of interest, too, is the Woodcock miniature, which, as Dr. Williamson explains, dates from the mid-seventeenth century and has an "unassailable" pedigree, "bear[ing] a very strong resemblance to Milton and having come from [the] family" of Milton's second wife (pp. 23–24).

Any student intent upon studying the history of Milton portraiture should be reminded that he "faces a bewildering task, because of the great number and variety of portraits said to represent the poet" (Martin, p. 1). What one should recognize is that artists, sculptors, and engravers of later times have been called upon to bestow "posthumous honor" by representing features that recall extant portraits without actually reproducing them; thus one should look "not so much for a literal rendering of the features of the original as for a work of art, in which those features are impressed with the artist's idea of what is characteristic of the man" and for his age's idea of what is especially noteworthy and praiseworthy about him (J. F. Marsh, "On the Engraved Portraits . . . of Milton," *Transactions of the Historic Society of Lancashire and Cheshire* 12 [1860]: 168).

The problems of Milton portraiture were first focused in *Memoirs of Thomas Hollis* (1780), which reproduces the Pierpont Morgan and National Gallery portraits, as well as the Faithorne crayon portrait, between pages 94–95, 506–7, and

528–29, and which reproduces besides a portrait that shows Milton triumphant over Salmasius, the "arms" of Milton, and the Hollis bust of Milton between pages 382–83, 528–29, and 532–33. Subsequently, various efforts have been made to catalogue both the engravings after the five authentic portraits and those from portraits that are either mistakenly identified with Milton or that are after portraits with no authority. The first major effort of this sort was made by John Fitchett Marsh (cited above) who catalogued 164 engravings; then George C. Williamson (cited above) presented a catalogue of some 180 likenesses a year before the Grolier Club issued its *Catalogue of an Exhibition . . . of John Milton . . . , Together with Three Hundred and Twenty-Seven Engraved Portraits* (1909). More recently, John Rupert Martin (cited above) has dealt specifically with the portraits engraved after the Faithorn crayon drawing, and more recently still he has presented a list of addenda in *Princeton University Library Chronicle* 24 (1963): 168–73. Both the New York Public Library and the Henry E. Huntington Art Gallery have large and impressive collections of Milton portraiture. [JAW]

POSTSCRIPT, A. Added to *An Answer to a Booke entituled, An Humble Remonstrance,* by Smectymnuus* (dated March 1641), is an unsigned ten-page recitation of precedents and events drawn from British history that argue for the abolition of episcopal hierarchy. "A Postscript," as it is called, appears on pages 85–94 (i.e., sigs. M4, N1) in the uncorrected state of pagination and signatures, and on pages 95–104 (i.e., sigs. N4, O1) of the corrected state. The volume was printed by Thomas Newcomb and published by John Rothwell. It was reprinted as *Smectymnuus Redivivus* in 1654 with a preface by Thomas Manton, with "A Postscript" on pages 71–78, and reissued in 1660 (twice), 1661, and 1669. Again the publisher was John Rothwell. A sixth edition appeared in Edinburgh in 1708 from the press of John Moncur; "A Postcript" is given on pages 69–75.

Milton's authorship has been suggested on the basis of parallels, the nature of the material cited, the similarities between the sources and source references and those in *CB,* the style, and the spelling, as well as Milton's relationship with Thomas Young*. All that has been advanced in disagreement with this attribution is a seeming discrepancy between statements concerning the reading of Martin Bucer* in "A Postscript" and in *Bucer.* Authorship is therefore considered unsettled. If it is Milton's, it is his first published prose. [JTS]

POWELL, MARY, Milton's first wife. She was baptized on January 24, 1625, in Forest Hill, Oxfordshire. No records of her early life or acquaintance with Milton have been preserved, but E. M. W. Tillyard suggests, with no substantiating evidence, that the poet, "had liked the look of Mary as a child, and had determined to marry her when she was of suitable age" (*Milton,* p. 139). On the other extreme, Masson suggests that Milton had never seen Mary or at least had no romantic interest in her before he visited her father in 1642 to collect a debt, only to have Mrs. Powell "heave" her eldest daughter at him (*Life,* 2 : 503). What is known is that sometime in late spring or early summer of 1642, Milton brought a young bride back to London with him after an excursion to the Oxford area.

Up to recent times, 1643 has been the date assigned to Milton's marriage to Mary Powell. However, this date has been challenged on the basis of the difficulty in reaching Oxford from London after the Civil War began late in 1642, the Powells' Royalist sympathies (since they might be reluctant to marry their daughter to a Parliamentarian supporter), and publication of *DDD* in August 1643 (which would require that Milton wrote the tract not long after the marriage and published it before Mary had deserted him). The currently accepted date, 1642, obviates the main difficulties noted for the 1643 date, but no evidence in the form of marriage records or clearly datable information is available.

In the late spring of 1642 (or 1643), about Whitsuntide (the middle of May), Milton "took a Journey into the Country; . . . after a Month's stay, home he return[ed] a Married-man, that went out a Batchelor" (Edward Phillips, in Helen Darbishire's *Early Lives,* p. 63). The Anonymous Biographer recalled that the poet "in a moneths time (according to his practice of not wasting that precious Talent) courted, marryed, and brought home" a young bride (*Early Lives,* p. 22). Within a month of the bride's taking up residence with her husband in Aldersgate Street, she returned to her parents in Forest Hill. The circumstances of her departure are variously reported. The Anonymous Biographer, noting that Mary was very young and accustomed to a life of pleasure and comfort, recalled that her friends urged her to leave her older, too-philosophical husband. In contrast, Phillips asserted that she left by her own desire, using her parents' wish to see her as an excuse. Mary herself is reported to have requested reconciliation on the grounds that "her Mother had bin the inciter of her to that frowardness" (*Early Lives,* pp. 22–23). On the other hand, in July 1651 Mrs. Powell asserted that Milton had "turned away his wife" (*Life Records,* 3 : 62), though the interpretation can be various.

Mary's visit to Forest Hill was apparently to be for only a few months, with return to her husband scheduled for the end of the summer. However, despite Milton's inquiries about her plans, she did not return to her home in Aldersgate Street. Confused about the sequence of dates, Edward Phillips asserts that his uncle "thought it would be dishonourable ever to receive her again, after such a repulse; so that he forthwith prepared to Fortify himself with Arguments for such a Resolution, and accordingly wrote two Treatises [*DDD* and *Tetra*], by which he undertook to maintain, That it was against Reason . . . for any Married Couple disagreeable in Humour and Temper, or having an aversion to each other, to be forc'd to live yok'd together all their Days" (*Early Lives,* p. 65). On the basis of this statement scholars have assumed a close relationship between Mary's desertion and the writing of the divorce* tracts. However, the short and apparently hastily written first version of *DDD* (August 1643) does not advocate divorce for desertion; nor does the very long period between Mary's nonreturn and the publication of the tract suggest a direct cause-and-effect relationship. Possibly his marriage choice crystallized his general ideas about divorce into a coherent view, but that Milton would have turned to the subject of divorce as part of his treatment of domestic liberties* even without the events of 1642 cannot be doubted.

Sometime in 1645, possibly learning of Milton's supposed interest in divorcing Mary and remarrying, her parents urged her to make a surprise appearance during Milton's visit at the house of a relative. Humbly begging forgiveness and placing blame on her mother, she implored her estranged husband to accept her back. Milton apparently felt no hesitation at receiving her, since despite her proximity for several years to the garrison at Oxford, he never suspected her of infidelity, according to Aubrey* : "As for . . . wronging his bed, I never heard the least suspicion : nor had he of that, any Jealousie" (*Early Lives,* p. 14). Aubrey did, however, wonder at Milton's complacent assumption of her chastity : "I have so much charity for her y^t she might not wrong his bed but what man (especially contemplative) w^d like to have a young wife environ'd & stormd by the sons of Mars and those of the enemi partie" (*Early Lives,* pp. 3–4).

Thus, late in 1645 Mary joined her husband in the house on the Barbican to which he had moved at the end of the summer, probably in September, after a short stay with his brother's mother-in-law Mrs. Webber*. It was here on July 29, 1646, that their first daughter, Anne, was born. On October 25, 1648, their second daughter, Mary, was born in the house in

High Holborn, near Lincoln's Inn, to which the family had moved in the autumn of 1647. And on March 16, 1651, at the house in Scotland Yard, Whitehall, to which they had moved in November 1649, Milton's only son, John, was born. Their last child, Deborah, was born on May 2, 1652, at the house in Petty France, to which they had moved in December 1651. About three days later, on May 5, 1652, Mary died, leaving the blind poet with three daughters and a son. When the boy died six weeks later, Milton's sense of loss might have crushed a lesser man.

Despite their early misunderstanding, there is no reason to doubt that Milton accepted Mary back with anything but love and continued to love her up to and beyond her death. In *3Def*, Milton recalled "mourning the . . . loss of two relatives" (9 : 15), identified by Masson as Mary and John (*Life*, 4 : 468). The subject of *Sonn* 23, "Methought I Saw," traditionally assumed to be Katherine Woodcock, Milton's second wife, has in recent years been suggested as Mary Powell (William Riley Parker, *Review of English Studies* 21 [1945] : 235–38). If this view is correct, then she was not, as John S. Diekhoff has suggested (*Milton on Himself*, p. 24), his "fell adversary, his hate or shame" (*PL* 10. 906), any more than she was the model for Dalila.

Such enduring devotion is perhaps surprising when one recalls the provision in Milton's nuncupative will* that his daughters receive "the porcōn due . . . from mʳ Powell, [his] former wives father, . . . [of which he had received] noe part" (*Life Records*, 5 : 91). Of Mary's dowry, which was probably to have been £1,000, Milton never saw a shilling. [AA]

POWELL FAMILY. Little is known of the early life of Milton's first father-in-law, Richard Powell. His date of birth is not recorded. In 1621 Powell leased the manor and estate at Forest Hill*, near Shotover, Oxfordshire, for 20 years at an annual payment of £5. In the same year he achieved some local prominence by

being appointed tax collector. Two years later, Powell secured a second lease on Forest Hill, this one extending to 1672. Despite these leases, his possession of the estate was frequently challenged in the following years, placing him in a state of insecurity commensurate with all his financial dealings.

As early as 1626, Powell was involved in business transactions that were to lead eventually to debt and financial ruin. His first verifiable contact with the Miltons came in 1627, when, on June 11, he borrowed £300 from John Milton, Senior. The loan, secured by a statute staple bond of £500, was to be repaid at a rate of 8% annually (£24 paid semiannually in June and December).

Perhaps concerned that Powell would be unable to meet the June 12 payment, Milton, Jr., went to see him in Forest Hill in late May 1642. Or it is possible that Powell had already missed the June 12 payment. If so, Milton's journey to his estate would probably be about the middle of June. In any event, Milton paid a call on Powell, and during the visit he may have met Mary Powell for the first time. In the event of their marriage, which shortly took place, her father promised a dowry of £1,000.

The payments on the 1627 loan were faithfully made through December 12, 1643, about one-and-a-half years after Mary had left her husband of a few months to return to her parents at Forest Hill. Either his conviction that the broken family ties in some way excused continued payments, his belief that the Royalist cause would succeed and the debt to a Parliamentarian advocate would be canceled, or his own poverty may have led to Powell's failure to keep his bond on June 12, 1644. As Justice of the Peace for the county of Oxford, Powell was a man of some importance, but his financial chicaneries, documented and analyzed in detail in Stevens, *Milton Papers* (1927), French, *Milton in Chancery* (1939), and the *Life Records*, kept him in constant pecuniary straits.

When Mary returned to her husband

in 1645, her family remained in Forest Hill, close to the Royalist forces. In 1646 the Powells left their estate for Oxford to have the advantages of safety in the King's garrison. On June 16 of that year the estate was appraised and put up for sale. Powell's fortunes sank with Charles's, and when Oxford surrendered on June 24, 1646, he was ruined and homeless. After receiving permission to leave Oxford, he apparently headed immediately for his son-in-law's spacious home on the Barbican, London. The Powells were probably in London by July 29, when Mary delivered her first child, Anne. With the Powells were probably at least their five youngest children.

During the following months, despite the unaccustomed security of his new home, Powell's physical condition weakened rapidly. In his will dictated on December 13, not long before he died (before January 1, 1647), he did not forget his promise of a dowry for his eldest daughter: "And my desire is that my daughter Milton be had a reguarde to in the satisfieing of her portion and adding thereto in Case my estate will beare it" (*Life Records,* 2 : 166). Unfortunately for his daughter and her long-expectant husband, the estate did not bear even the minimum dowry, nor did it provide for paying off the debt of 1627. For many years following, Milton was to be involved in settling the financial muddle left behind by Richard Powell. The unpaid dowry was not forgotten, however, and Milton left it in his nuncupative will* to Mary's three daughters as a reminder of their grandfather's perfidy.

Milton's first mother-in-law, Anne Moulton Powell, was born about 1601. She probably married Richard Powell around 1620, shortly before he leased Forest Hill. Between 1621 and 1639 she bore him eleven children.

John Milton probably met Anne Powell for the first time in May or June 1642, on his fateful visit to Forest Hill. Her statement on June 4, 1656, that she had known him "for about fourteene yeares" could be taken very literally if Milton visited the Powells to inquire about the approaching or already existing non-delivery of the June 12 semiannual payment on the 1627 debt.

Milton's troubles with his mother-in-law apparently began as soon as he brought his young bride to London. According to the "earliest" biographer, within only a few days Mary left him "and went back into the Country with her Mother" (Darbishire, *Early Lives,* p. 22). Aubrey also writes that Mary "went from him to her Mother" (Darbishire, p. 2). Edward Phillips allows for a longer honeymoon, but he too notes that "Her Friends" begged her to return to Forest Hill for the summer (Darbishire, p. 63). Mary herself was to blame her mother as "the inciter of her to that frowardness" ("earliest" biographer, Darbishire, pp. 22–23) when she returned to plead her case in 1645. But in 1651 Mrs. Powell was to cast blame for the separation on Milton.

In the summer of 1646, Mrs. Powell, bringing along their younger children, accompanied her husband to their son-in-law's house in London. Perhaps in a spirit of reconciliation, or perhaps merely because she was present, the Miltons named their firstborn after her grandmother. After Powell's death at the end of December 1646, she and her family stayed with Milton long enough for him to complain in a letter to Carlo Dati* (April 20, 1647) of the wearisome company "closely conjoined . . . by the tie of law" which "all but plague[d him] to death" (12 : 47). Shortly thereafter, Mrs. Powell and her brood apparently moved to some property they still held at Wheatley, Oxfordshire.

Like her son-in-law, Mrs. Powell was to be engaged for many years after her husband's death in attempting to unravel his financial entanglements. However, Milton acquired in November 1647 what was left of Powell's property at Wheatley (in satisfaction of the 1627 bond), and his payment to his mother-in-law of one-third of the income from the estate may have led to further acrimony when in March 1651 he was ordered to receive all income from the property, thereby denying Mrs. Powell her portion. In the following two years she petitioned repeatedly for redress. On April 16, 1651, she claimed "her thirds . . . due by lawe for the maintenance of herself & eight children" (*Life Records,* 3 : 21), the youngest of whom was only twelve years old but four of whom were over twenty. The petition was denied three days later. On July 11 she again petitioned for her thirds "to preserue her & her children from starving" (*Life Records,* 3 : 61). To her petition she appended a personal appeal, noting that her abject poverty prevented a law suit and her fear of antagonizing her unsympathetic son-in-law, who had sent his young bride away shortly after their marriage : "By ye law she might recouer her thirds without doubt, but she is so extreame poore, she hath not wherewithall to prosecute, & besides Mr Milton is a harsh & Chollericke man, & married M^rs. Powells daughter, who would be vndone, if any such course were taken ag^t him by M^rs. Powell, he having turned away his wife heretofore for a long space upon some other occasion" (*Life Records,* 3 : 61–62). Parker sees in this accusation evidence of Mrs. Powell's deep hatred for her son-in-law, stemming from their early brushes and his connection with the Parliamentarians, whose victory inflicted upon her and her family such a disastrous blow. However, it is possible that their relations were not so strained as Parker suggests, since Milton supported his mother-in-law in this petition despite her caustic words. Further possibilities for their basic amity might be seen in his receiving Mary in 1645, his taking in the Powells in 1646, his naming the firstborn *Anne,* his allowing Mrs. Powell and her family to remain with him some months after her husband's death, his paying one-third of the income from the Wheatley property with no legal requirement to do so, and his continued support of her petitions for redress. Perhaps the accusations against Milton were designed, with his consent, to win sympathy from the commissioners. This petition was again denied.

But the persistent Mrs. Powell was not to be deterred. Faced by "utter ruine" (*Life Records,* 3 : 119), she petitioned again in early 1652, and again in the fall of 1652, and again at the end of 1652. Each petition was reviewed by the commissioners, always calling for examination of witnesses; hearings were set and postponed. Finally, on July 15, 1653, Anne Powell triumphed, and in October of that year the Wheatley property was removed from sequestration. They had additional good luck in 1657, when Milton's claim against them was declared settled and he was ordered to return their property at Wheatley; however, he continued to manage it until November 29, 1659, when the statute staple bond was canceled. In April 1673, their long-time support of the Royalist cause was finally rewarded in their regaining of Forest Hill. The family enjoyed prosperity, but the £1,000 dowry for Mary, now long dead, remained unpaid. On October 24, 1678, Anne Powell made her will, leaving bequests to Mary Milton and Deborah Milton Clarke, perhaps restoring to them part of what they did not gain through their father's will. Mrs. Powell died in 1682. Forest Hill manor was bought by Lincoln College, Oxford, in 1808; it was torn down in 1854.

The Powells had eleven children : Richard (1621–1696?); James (1623–before 1678), who studied at Christ Church, Oxford, 1640–1644; Mary (1625–1652), John Milton's first wife; Anne (1626–after 1693), the executrix of her mother's will and wife of Thomas Kinaston (or Kingston); Sara (1627–after 1693), who married Richard Peirson and had a son, Richard; John (1629–before 1678); William (1631–December 1652), who reached the rank of captain and was killed in Scotland while serving with General Monk*; Archdale (1633–before 1678); Elizabeth (1635–after 1693); George (1637–before 1678); and another named Elizabeth (1639–after 1693). One daughter named Elizabeth married Thomas Howell; the other married Christmas Holloway. The eldest child, Richard, studied at

Oxford and the Inner Temple. His father bequeathed him the house and lands at Forest Hill (no longer his to leave), the woods and timber at Forest Hill (confiscated by Act of Parliament in 1646), and the household goods at Forest Hill (already seized and sold). He refused to act as executor of his father's will, thereby losing ownership of Wheatley to his mother. It is not clear whether he accompanied his mother to London in 1646, but he went abroad in March 1647 instead of returning with her to Wheatley. He was called to the bar in 1653 and belonged to the Inner Temple in 1663, as did Christopher Milton. In 1674, he was in a financial position to make good on Mary's dowry when Milton died, but no evidence exists that he aided his nieces. He married Anne Brokesby (?) and had a son, Richard. [AA]

POWER, THOMAS: *see* TRANSLATIONS OF MILTON'S WORKS.

CONTRIBUTORS TO VOLUME 6

AA   Arthur M. Axelrad. California State University, Long Beach, Calif. 90840.

ACL   Albert C. Labriola. Duquesne University, Pittsburgh, Pa. 15219.

AG   Ann Gossman. Texas Christian University, Fort Worth, Texas 76129.

BKL   Barbara K. Lewalski. Brown University, Providence, R.I. 02912.

DAR   Donald A. Roberts. Box 1077, Vineyard Haven, Mass. 02568.

DB   Douglas Bush. Harvard University, Cambridge, Mass. 02138.

EBS   Elaine B. Safer. University of Delaware, Newark, Delaware 19711.

ERG   E. Richard Gregory. University of Toledo, Toledo, Ohio 43606.

FLH   Frank L. Huntley. University of Michigan, Ann Arbor, Mich. 48104.

HFR   Harry F. Robins. University of Arizona, Tucson, Ariz. 85721.

JAD   James A. Devereux, S.J. University of North Carolina, Chapel Hill, N.C. 27514.

JAR   James A. Riddell. California State College, Dominguez Hilla, Calif. 90747.

JAW   Joseph A. Wittreich, Jr. University of Maryland, College Park, Md. 20742

JB   June M. Bostich. 6410 Percival Drive, Riverside, Calif. 92506.

JGT   James G. Taafe. Case Western Reserve University, Cleveland, Ohio 44106.

JLG   John L. Gribben. Kent State University, Kent, Ohio 44242.

JMS   John M. Steadman. Huntington Library and Art Gallery, San Marino, Calif. 91108.

JP   Joseph Pequigney. State University of New York at Stony Brook, Stony Brook, N.Y. 11794.

JRK   John R. Knott, Jr. University of Michigan, Ann Arbor, Mich. 48104.

JTS   John T. Shawcross. City University of New York, N.Y. 10031.

KW   Kathleen Williams. Late of University of California, Riverside, Calif. 92502.

LN   Leonard Nathanson. Vanderbilt University, Nashville, Tenn. 37235.

MF   Michael Fixler. Tufts University, Boston, Mass. 02155.

ML   Michael Lieb. University of Illinois at Chicago Circle, Chicago, Illinois 60680.

MT	Mason Tung. University of Idaho, Moscow, Idaho 833843.
NH	Nathaniel Henry. 200 East Horne Avenue, Farmville, N.C. 27828.
PEB	Purvis E. Boyette. Tulane University, New Orleans, La. 70118.
PMZ	Paul M. Zall. California State University, Los Angeles, Calif. 90032.
PS	Philip Sheridan. Carleton College, Northfield, Minn. 55057.
REH	Ralph E. Hone. University of Redlands, Redlands, Calif. 92373.
RF	Robert Fox. St. Francis College, Brooklyn, N.Y. 11201.
RHS	Roger H. Sundell. University of Wisconsin—Milwaukee, Milwaukee, Wisc. 53201.
RRC	Robert R. Cawley. Late of Princeton University, Princeton, N.J. 08540.
TK	Thomas Kranidas. State University of New York at Stony Brook, Stony Brook, N.Y. 11794.
VRM	Virginia R. Mollenkott. William Paterson College, Wayne, N.J. 07470.
WBH	William B. Hunter, Jr. University of Houston, Houston, Texas 77004.
WM	Willis Monie. P.O. Box 105, Hartwick, N.Y. 13348.
WS	Wayne Shumaker. University of California, Berkeley, Calif. 94720.